THE SCHUMAN PLAN AND THE BRITISH ABDICATION OF LEADERSHIP IN EUROPE

THE SCHUMAN PLAN

and the British Abdication of Leadership in Europe

Edmund Dell

OXFORD UNIVERSITY PRESS
1995

Oxford University Press, Walton Street, Oxford OX2 6DP

Oxford New York
Athens Auckland Bangkok Bombay
Calcutta Cape Town Dar es Salaam Delhi
Florence Hong Kong Istanbul Karachi
Kuala Lumpur Madras Madrid Melbourne
Mexico City Nairobi Paris Singapore
Taipei Tokyo Toronto
and associated companies in
Berlin Ibadan

Oxford is a trade mark of Oxford University Press

Published in the United States
by Oxford University Press Inc., New York

British Library Cataloguing in Publication Data
Data available

Library of Congress Cataloging in Publication Data
Dell, Edmund.
The Schuman plan and the British abdication of leadership in
Europe / Edmund Dell.
p. cm.
Includes bibliographical references
1. Great Britain—Foreign economic relations—Europe. 2. Europe—
Foreign economic relations—Great Britain. 3. Great Britain—
Economic policy—1945– 4. Schuman Plan. 5. Europe—Economic
integration. 6. European federation. I. Title.
HF1534.5.E9D45 1995   94–44523
337.4104—dc20
ISBN 0–19–828967–7

1 3 5 7 9 10 8 6 4 2

Typeset by Graphicraft Typesetters Ltd., Hong Kong
Printed in Great Britain
on acid-free paper by
Bookcraft (Bath) Ltd., Midsomer Norton, Avon

For Susi

Preface

On 28 October 1971, I voted with sixty-eight of my Parliamentary Labour Party colleagues against a three-line whip in favour of Britain joining the European Economic Community on the terms negotiated by Edward Heath. As a minister in the Wilson and Callaghan governments of the 1970s, I was a frequent participant in the proceedings of the Council of Finance Ministers and of the General, or Foreign Affairs, Council. In December 1978 I was invited by the European Council to be one of three 'wise men' whose function it was to review the operation of the institutions of the Community. My colleagues were Barend Biesheuvel, former Prime Minister of the Netherlands, and Robert Marjolin, who had been the first Secretary-General of the Organization for European Economic Co-operation and subsequently Vice-President of the European Commission.[1] I was not, therefore, unacquainted with European issues, and with the subsequent history of Britain's relations with the European Community, when my researches brought me to a consideration of the Attlee government's refusal to join the Schuman Plan in 1950.

Lord Franks was Provost of The Queen's College, Oxford, when I was a history don there. During his time as Provost, 1946/8, he was also Chairman of the Committee for European Economic Co-operation. He told me of his regrets that Britain seemed so unwilling to play a leading role in European integration. Robert Marjolin was one of the wisest men I have known. I was totally in sympathy with his unideological attitude to European issues. He told me that Britain could have held the leadership in Europe, in the years immediately following the Second World War, if it had had the will to do so. These two distinguished Europeans were much in my mind as I studied the British reaction to the Schuman Plan.

[1] Our *Report on European Institutions* was delivered to the European Council in Oct. 1979 and published in 1980 by the Council of the European Communities, Brussels. See my article 'The Report of the Three Wise Men', in *Contemporary European History*, 2/1 (Mar. 1993). To complete the story, I should add that, in 1978, I opposed British membership of the Exchange Rate Mechanism of the European Monetary System. See my article 'Britain and the Origins of the European Monetary System', in *Contemporary European History*, 3/1 (Mar. 1994).

I was led to write the book because I had arrived at conclusions which conflicted with accepted wisdom. The Schuman Plan was not a bolt from the blue. Domestic political circumstances did not make it impossible for Britain to join. Membership of the European Coal and Steel Community would have been compatible with Britain's assessment of its global and Commonwealth role. Moreover, I was left feeling that the handling of the issue by the Attlee government and, in particular, by Bevin and the Foreign Office, was governed too much by resentment at lack of consultation by France and too little by attention to the national interest.

I owe a very special debt to Professor Geoffrey Warner. Discovering a joint interest in the subject, he encouraged me to persevere with the writing of this book, discussed with me many of the issues it raises, read successive drafts, and pointed me in the direction of sources both primary and secondary that I might otherwise have missed. I am grateful to Dr Anne Deighton and Professor J. W. Young for their stimulating and encouraging reactions to an earlier draft from which my book has greatly benefited. The responsibility remains mine.

Edmund Dell

9 July 1994

Acknowledgements

Crown copyright material from the Public Record Office listed among the references, in Cmd. 7970, and in *Documents on British Policy Overseas*, series ii, vol. i, is reproduced with the permission of the Controller of Her Majesty's Stationery Office. Material from House of Commons debates is subject to parliamentary copyright. I am grateful for the following permissions to quote copyright material from private collections: to Lady Younger for the Kenneth Younger diaries; to the Master and Fellows of University College Oxford for the papers of Lord Attlee held in deposit from University College in the Bodleian Library catalogued as MS Attlee; to the British Library of Political and Economic Science for the Ernest Davies and Hugh Dalton Papers. I am grateful to *The Economist* for permission to quote copyright material from its issues of May and June 1950.

Contents

Abbreviations

BISF	The British Iron and Steel Federation
BLPES	British Library of Political and Economic Science, London
CEEC	Committee for European Economic Cooperation
CEPS	Central Economic Planning Staff
CGA	Confédération Générale de l'Agriculture
DBPO	*Documents on British Policy Overseas*, series ii, vol. i
ECA	European Co-operation Administration
ECSC	European Coal and Steel Community
EDC	European Defence Community
EEC	European Economic Community
ELEC	European League for Economic Co-operation
EPB	Economic Planning Board
EPC	European Political Community
EPU	European Payments Union
ERP	European Recovery Program
FG Committee	Committee on Proposed Franco-German Coal and Steel Authority
FG (WP)	FG Committee Working Party
GATT	General Agreement on Tariffs and Trade
HC Debs.	House of Commons Debates
IAR	International Authority for the Ruhr
MRP	Mouvement Républicain Populaire
NATO	North Atlantic Treaty Organization
NCB	National Coal Board

NEC	National Executive Committee
NUM	National Union of Mineworkers
OEEC	Organization for European Economic Co-operation.
PLP	Parliamentary Labour Party
QRs	Quantitative Restrictions
SPD	Social Democratic Party (German)
TUC	Trades Union Congress
UN	United Nations

1
A Time for Heroes

Even in the politics of democratic countries, there is a time for heroes. It was such a time during the Second World War. It was such a time in the years immediately following. Among the dominating questions in the aftermath of victory in 1945 were relations between the West and the Soviet Union, the recovery of Europe, and the future of Germany and Japan. It was, therefore, a time for big decisions and hence for heroes. What other description would be appropriate for those statesmen fortunate enough to be, in the words of Dean Acheson, American Secretary of State from 1949, 'present at the creation'?[1] Out of the deliberations of the heroes would come determination to resist Soviet expansion, Marshall Aid, the North Atlantic Treaty Organization (NATO), the division of Germany, the Schuman Plan, and the beginnings of the construction of a new Europe.

Was there a name that Britain, still claiming to be a global power, could add to the gallery of heroes present at the creation? The Foreign Secretary in the new Labour government was Ernest Bevin, lucky enough to be plucked at the last moment from the impossible responsibilities of Chancellor of the Exchequer. Bevin was a big man, liked, even idolized, by Foreign Office officials.[2] Critics and admirers have referred to his dominating personality. It was a personality reinforced by an experience unique among ministers. He had been the creator of a major trade union, the largest in the world. He had been its leader for many years. He was the outstanding British trade-unionist of his generation and probably of the century. He had fought, and won and lost, battles without number on behalf of his own members and of the trade union movement generally. During the war he had been Minister of Labour, responsible for the mobilization of the nation's manpower resources. He had an acquired authority, and an understanding of political conflict and of negotiation, which few could equal.

[1] *Present at the Creation* is the title of Dean Acheson's memoirs.
[2] For an example of his officials' admiration see Sir Frank K. Roberts, 'Ernest Bevin as Foreign Secretary', in Ovendale.

There are those who write as though Bevin, by the sheer force of his personality, alone made Britain a fit partner at the high table of international negotiation.[3] There is no doubt that Bevin was a man out of the ordinary. But at the time, and perhaps even more in retrospect, something has been added to his reputation due to the fact that it was a time when a British Foreign Secretary was still permitted to sit and negotiate with the mighty on terms of apparent equality. The equality was not real. It was the twilight of empire. Britain no longer had the resources for the global role Bevin wished it to fill.

Yet there were still cards for a British Foreign Secretary to play. In the first few years after the war, the UK was the only major Western European country with a stable government. Germany was under four-power occupation. French governments came and went. They were always uncertain of their command over the French electorate, over French public opinion and of majorities in the National Assembly. On the right they were threatened by the Gaullists. On the left they were confronted repeatedly by disruption organized by a powerful Communist Party. They were obsessed by fear of a reviving Germany.[4] This obsession was the more compelling in that the problem of Germany had been taken out of their hands by the USA. French governments found that they were not permitted to impose their own solutions for the German problem and that, although they had their own zone of occupation, they lacked the means successfully to obstruct American solutions. To their dismay, American policy-makers, after some confusion and hesitation, took a view diametrically opposed to that of France. They decided that Germany must be persuaded to co-operate in the economic recovery of Europe, and in defence against the Soviet Union. The time for treating it as an enemy must be brought to a close. French attempts to frustrate the policies of their most powerful ally proved counter-productive and the failure of these attempts was itself a further source of political instability.

Britain therefore had an exceptional opportunity to influence events both as the most reliable interlocutor of the USA, which had emerged as the Western superpower, and as a spokesman for Europe. But just as it was an exceptional opportunity, it was an exceptional moment. It

---

[3] See e.g. Bullock 94 quoting George Brown 243 and 244. See also Bullock himself: 'If Bevin had not possessed such qualities, if he had not been able to convince the Americans and the Europeans that he was a man to whom they could look for leadership and on whom they could rely, he would never have been able to play the part he did as one of the principal architects of the Western alliance': Bullock 90.

[4] Except where the context makes it clear otherwise, references to Germany are to West Germany which, in 1949, became the Federal Republic of Germany.

would never recur. As the states of Western Europe regained their self-confidence and their economic independence, the relative role of the UK was bound to diminish to one appropriate to its resources and its economic performance. The real test of Bevin as Foreign Secretary is how far he appreciated the exceptional nature of the moment and of the opportunity, how far he exploited it for the benefit of his own country. As he sometimes saw, this implied a closer relationship with Western Europe. Unfortunately it was too easy for a British Foreign Secretary to be diverted from that vision by pretensions that were no longer sustainable.

Bevin is given credit for his prompt and positive reaction to General Marshall's speech at Harvard and for the creation of NATO. But it cannot seriously be argued that he could have reacted in any other way to these offers of American support for Europe, one for its economy and the other for its security. The French were only marginally behind Bevin in their appreciation of the significance of Marshall's speech. Where the UK government had a real choice was in identifying an appropriate relationship with Europe. The ultimate defining moment came with the Schuman Plan because Britain had not pre-empted it with its own ideas for reconciliation with Germany and European economic integration. At this moment of real choice, Bevin's reaction, and that of the Attlee government under his guidance, was myopic. The invitation from France to participate in the negotiations leading to the Treaty of Paris and the creation of the European Coal and Steel Community (ECSC) was refused. A typical excuse for Bevin's failure offered by friendly historians and memorialists is that no other decision was conceivable in the political circumstances of the time and that it did not really matter, that Britain's crucial error came five years later after Messina.

An extreme expression of the view that error occurred only at, or after, Messina is to be found in reflections by Sir Frank Roberts, at one time Bevin's Private Secretary. 'I . . . reject the view that Bevin missed the European bus. On the contrary, he prepared the way for Britain's eventual membership of the European Community. The bus was missed later, to be precise at Messina in 1955, or five years after his death.'[5] Sir Frank's loyalty is admirable but beyond reason. The key error in the

[5] Roberts 35. In the course of a highly distinguished career, Sir Frank Roberts was to be Ambassador to Yugoslavia, NATO, the USSR, and the Federal Republic of Germany. The meeting of the Six at Messina established the Spaak Committee which Britain was invited to join. The work of the Spaak Committee was a step on the road to the Treaty of Rome.

British reaction to the Schuman Plan was the failure to perceive that participation in it was consistent with Britain's view of itself. It could be a global power, and at the centre of the Commonwealth and sterling area, and still participate in the Schuman Plan. It could persist with its intergovernmental model of European co-operation and still participate in the Schuman Plan. There were too many illusions about Britain's place in the world. Wiser leaders would have abandoned them sooner. But even if they were not abandoned, Britain could still have found its place in the ECSC. This is the argument of this book.

Certainly the rejection of France's invitation did matter. It was a turning-point. It decided the course of post-war European history. Britain thereby proved itself superfluous to Franco-German reconciliation. It had thereby done its best to prove itself superfluous to the construction of a new Europe. Britain was now on the periphery of Europe, politically as well as geographically, excluded from the intimacy which developed between the Six. A sufficient number of observers understood at the time what was happening to deny defenders of Bevin's failure the response that critics are employing hindsight. Acheson saw that Britain's deliberate absence from the Schuman Plan was a major error of policy.[6] *The Economist* flayed the British government in successive issues.[7] There were doubts even in the junior ranks of the government. On the evidence of the Schuman Plan, and the preceding story of the UK's post-war relations with continental Europe, the predominant impression is of a Foreign Secretary who failed at the most difficult choices, and was poorly served.

On the other hand, the history of the British reaction to the Schuman Plan should not be left to the European federalists.[8] Their grief at a British failure is assuaged by the thought of their idea triumphant, at least for the moment. For them, the Schuman Plan is the beginning of the history of post-war European federalism. In fact the Schuman Plan, centred on a sovereign High Authority, provided the wrong model for European integration and it was discarded in the construction of the European Economic Community (EEC). Jean Monnet, who proposed this false model, and persuaded Robert Schuman, the French Foreign Minister, to adopt it, is the federalist hero. Like other heroes he too was capable of myopia. His own federalist convictions were of questionable

---

[6] Acheson 385.   [7] See Ch. 12 below.

[8] The federalists in question are not just Europeans. For an example of American historiography see Gillingham. His book, referred to several times in these pages, is a faithful, indeed enthusiastic, reflection of American ideas for Europe.

depth and were technocratic rather than democratic. He helped to deceive the US Administration into believing that there was a market in Europe for their advocacy of federalism. But he also had his insights. He saw that it was vital that France take an initiative towards Franco-German reconciliation. In developing policy based on that insight, he could well have taken the view that it was better to establish his Community on his own terms in the absence of the incorrigible British. Ernest Bevin appears to have believed that that was precisely the view Monnet did take and that he did not want the UK at the negotiating conference called by France following Schuman's announcement of his Plan. Yet, despite the UK's well-known opposition to European federalism of which Monnet had much, to him frustrating, evidence, he made persistent efforts to secure British participation. He annoyed the Foreign Office with his persistence. It was irregular. It confused channels.

Many in France remained anxious about the future of a France linked to Germany without the balancing weight of the UK. Monnet's actions suggest that either he was among them or, at the very least, he saw a need to prove that he had made every reasonable effort. On the other hand he wanted British participation on French terms. This was not unreasonable. It was a French initiative and in fact the French terms for British participation were a great deal less burdensome than the Attlee government pretended to itself and to France. If Monnet *had* manœuvred to exclude the UK for the sake of a federalist idea whose time had not in fact come, that would be serious criticism. By speaking the language of federalism, he did make it easier for a British government, already resentful at having lost the initiative, to claim that it was being required to enter into unacceptable and premature commitments. But examination of the evidence places the responsibility for Britain's exclusion squarely on the shoulders of the Attlee government.

The excuse that the British were not wanted, and that therefore Bevin cannot be blamed, is argued, among others, by Sir Frank. 'He [Bevin] felt, with some justification, that the [Schuman] plan had been designed to exclude Britain and resented the fact that we had been deliberately kept in the dark during its preparation.'[9] Although British politicians, officials, and historians have allowed themselves to be persuaded by such excuses, perhaps for want of anything better, the probability is that the British *were* wanted, as will be shown in the following pages. Even if the charge against Monnet was true, Foreign Secretaries who shrink

---

[9] Roberts 35.

from negotiations simply because they are not wanted must be a rarity in the annals of international diplomacy. Bevin was no shrinking violet. His life had been largely spent making himself felt in places where his opponents would have preferred not to find him. Even if he had wished to exclude the British, Monnet could not have succeeded without the collaboration of a British Foreign Secretary and a British Diplomatic Service lacking in imagination and understanding, not to mention elementary diplomatic skills.

2
France Bids for the Leadership of Europe

FRENCH IMAGINATION, BRITISH COMPLACENCY

No German soldier under arms had set foot on the mainland of Britain in either of the world wars. Britain was protected by a barrier more effective than any Maginot line. It had its moat. France, in a period of seventy years, had thrice suffered the humiliation of German occupation, on this last occasion for four long years. It was France that had to forget the passive collaboration of most of its people with the German invader. France had suffered immense damage as the Western allies fought their way back to the German frontier. It was from France therefore that was to be expected the fiercest opposition to any policies of reconciliation with Germany or which gave priority to German recovery. Yet it was France rather than Britain, Schuman rather than Bevin, who demonstrated the imagination to seek *rapprochement* with Germany.

For France, the long-standing problem of German aggressiveness remained paramount. To resolve it was France's priority whatever alternative priorities its Anglo-Saxon allies might press upon it. Given the experience of defeat and occupation, it was hardly surprising that, in the immediate aftermath of the war, French policy was directed to ensuring that Germany could never rise again. But the French government failed to persuade its allies to split Germany up as a guarantee of French security, or at the very least to detach the Ruhr, that great centre of German military and industrial power. The Attlee government did not believe in the dismemberment of Germany. As Bevin put it: 'His Majesty's Government have always considered that dismemberment would inevitably start an irredentist movement causing a resurgence not of a peaceful Germany, but of a spirit of war.'[1] Germany, contrary to

---

[1] HC Debs. 22 Jan. 1948, col. 386.

the initial plans of the US Administration, was not transformed into an agricultural society.[2] Instead, the Truman Administration began to develop a key role for a strong and prosperous Germany in the confrontation of the two superpowers. In American eyes, Germany was perceived as an ally in the cold war that had just started rather than as the enemy of the previous war. The best that a weakened and diminished France could obtain by way of guarantee for its security was a continuing American involvement in Europe. This was, in fact, a most valuable prize but only as long as the commitment lasted. Such was France's experience of Germany that security guaranteed by others, however welcome, could not afford the peace of mind to which France, emerging from occupation, felt entitled.

Politically, therefore, a major question after 1945 was by what stages, under what pressure, and after what debate, would French governments accept that any desire for revenge on Germany must take second place to the insistence both of the US Administration and of the American military that there was now a problem more important than the balance of power between France and Germany. Conflict between the Soviet Union and its wartime allies had become irreconcilable. The conjuncture was a test for French policy-makers. They would need to observe and understand how the world had changed, what forces were framing American policy, and how little part was being played in its formulation by gratitude to wartime allies, whether France or Britain. After all, Britain and France had not rescued the USA. Rather the USA had rescued Britain and France.

In France, and in French exiled circles, even in the midst of war, there were those who, however deep the emotions, rejected a policy of revenge on Germany. Many of the brighter spirits realized that the Versailles approach to German aggression had been a misfortune and had simply led to a second war. They saw that the road to peace in Europe, and prosperity for France, lay through the reconstruction of a prosperous Germany within an economically integrated Europe. One milestone along that road would be a Franco-German *rapprochement* upon which reliance could be placed. That would constitute a buttress for French security. Prominent among such visionaries were Jean Monnet

---

[2] Henry Morgenthau, then US Treasury Secretary, had in 1944 advocated a plan for the dismemberment and deindustrialization of Germany. It was discussed at the second Quebec Conference in Sept. 1994. For the UK it was to have the advantage that it would enable it to take over German export markets. Churchill agreed, reluctantly, to consider the plan, but was clearly sceptical.

and Robert Marjolin from the *Commissariat Générale du Plan*. Others were to be found in the Quai d'Orsay. Most of the French advocates of reconciliation with Germany would have welcomed it if Britain had taken the lead in procuring and guaranteeing such a *rapprochement*. They learnt not to expect any such lead. But Britain's failure to act could not deny them the right to their own initiative when the opportunity occurred. American pressure could help to create the opportunity. September 1949 saw the emergence of a Federal German government. It was still, however, under the control of the Occupation Statute.[3] France was now confronted with its last opportunity to establish a special relationship with its ancient enemy while the power of Germany remained under some restraint. Some French initiative was likely if France was not to lose this last chance. The problem for France was to find the right way to Franco-German *rapprochement* and the support for it of French public opinion. That would require an idea.

WASHINGTON'S PERCEPTION—EUROPE WITHOUT BRITAIN

Washington insisted on European integration. In its view, European security and European prosperity both required it. George Kennan, Head of the State Department Planning Staff, feared in 1948 that a West German government would 'become the spokesman of a resentful and defiant nationalism' and that it would be 'almost compelled to negotiate with the Russians behind our backs for the return of the Eastern provinces'.[4] Washington was, therefore, anxious to avoid the re-emergence of a German problem by absorbing a democratic Germany within a European community.[5] A further insight was that this could only be achieved if France felt secure. France's concerns about Germany were striking a chord in the State Department. Kennan wrote of 'old German nationalism'.[6] For the Americans, the Atlantic alliance was not simply a deterrent against Soviet aggression. It was as much concerned with creating the basis for European stability through German integration in a European community.[7]

---

[3] The Occupation Statute limited the freedom of the Federal government on defence, foreign affairs, the cost of the occupation, matters relating to the Federal and Land constitutions, reparations, foreign trade, exchange controls, international borrowing, decartelization, matters relating to the ownership of the Ruhr industries. Powers to allocate coal between domestic and foreign markets was retained by the International Authority for the Ruhr (IAR).

[4] Leffler 279–80.   [5] Ibid. 280.   [6] Ibid. 319.   [7] Ibid. 282.

Washington's initial preference was for Britain to lead its neighbours along the path to European integration. There was, indeed, doubt among American policy-makers whether European integration could be achieved without British leadership, or at least participation. Britain alone had a stable government. With British leadership Washington could feel greater confidence that Europe would not move in a neutralist direction. The US Administration had some concern that, under the only alternative, French leadership, precisely that might happen. It proved easier to talk of British leadership in the cause of European integration than to extract it from the Attlee government. The reasons for British reluctance had been explained to Washington *ad nauseam* over the years since the war. They will be set out in Chapters 4 and 5. It was not surprising that Kennan had become convinced that the unity of Europe should be established under the leadership of France, not of Britain. In his memoirs, Kennan writes how, after extensive consultation, he put his views to Secretary of State Acheson in July 1949:

I found both serious and compelling, in their totality, the reasons that caused the British to hesitate in associating themselves with any move towards a continental union—so serious and compelling that if any such movement had to include the British, then, I thought, it could not go very far. It could be taken as axiomatic, I wrote, that no framework of association which included the United Kingdom but excluded the United States and Canada would be permitted to advance to a stage resembling a real merging of sovereignty. British reservations and hesitations would thus inevitably constitute the ceiling beyond which unification would not be able to advance. . . . The conclusion I drew from these reflections was that what we should aim for was a continental union, sufficiently detached from Britain to have some chance of absorbing the Germans into something larger than themselves . . .[8]

Kennan discussed this thesis with Foreign Office officials in London in the summer of 1949. According to his own account, there was little reaction. His colleagues in the West European Department of the State Department still disagreed with the emphasis he gave to French leadership. Nevertheless, while it might not be the first best option, nothing else seemed available.

Sir Oliver Harvey, British Ambassador to Paris, himself believed at the time that only a Britain active in Europe could sponsor Franco-German reconciliation and hence end the bitterest of intra-European conflicts.[9] This view was encouraged by indications elsewhere in

[8] Kennan (1968) 453–4.   [9] Young (1984) 141.

Europe. Much opinion in France was to the effect that European construction was possible only if it included Britain.[10] Count Sforza, the Italian Foreign Minister, believed that Germany could only be prevented from again becoming a danger to Europe if Britain, France, and Italy kept as close as possible together.[11] This widespread conviction that Franco-German reconciliation and European integration were impossible without Britain no doubt encouraged complacency in the British Foreign Office. It was a comforting thought that anything the UK did not sponsor must necessarily fail. Complacency was encouraged by the problems of economic co-ordination within Europe. Economic coordination could impose unwelcome sacrifices on participant countries. Greater competition could lead to higher unemployment. The failures thus far, for example in the attempt to establish a form of Franco-Italian customs union, did not encourage optimism that other initiatives without Britain would succeed. The neutralism that inspired much French political activity would be of concern to the USA and even to some potential European partners. European integration without Britain would be discouraged by its internal contradictions.

If European integration without British leadership was impossible but Britain would not lead, Washington had a problem. Any illusions Secretary of State Acheson might have retained about the prospects for British leadership in Europe had been dissipated by his conversations with Bevin and Sir Stafford Cripps, British Chancellor of the Exchequer, in Washington in September 1949, just before the sterling devaluation. He was now persuaded that nothing could be expected from Britain. He had to find an alternative. In any case, as Kennan had argued in July, a deeper European integration would be possible only if Britain was not involved. It was thus more desirable as well as more feasible if France, rather than Britain, took the lead.[12] In the same month, in New York, and in the presence of Bevin and with his apparent assent, Acheson told Robert Schuman, the French Foreign Minister, that Britain and America were looking to France to define an Allied policy on Germany.[13]

---

[10] See e.g. the views of Paul Ramadier reported in Massigli 224.
[11] Dispatch from Sir V. Mallet, British Ambassador in Rome, 1 June 1950: *DBPO* 74.
[12] Leffler 316.
[13] Monnet recounts in his memoirs how he told Bernard Clappier, Schuman's *Directeur de Cabinet*, about his ideas. Clappier referred to the meeting of the Big Three in New York in Sept. 1949. Clappier said: 'I was there when Acheson said, with Bevin's agreement: "We fully concur in entrusting our French colleague with formulating our common policy on Germany"': Monnet 299. Massigli discusses the significance of this story in

Acheson then found that a new problem had been created in Franco-American relations by the British devaluation which had taken place without consultation with France. The French resented what they saw as American favouritism to Britain. Henri Queuille, the French Prime Minister, was vexed that the Americans seemed to be showering special privileges on the British by dealing with them separately, and by consenting to a devaluation that went much further than the French considered appropriate.[14] Acheson felt it necessary to reassure Schuman. He emphasized to Schuman that the future of Europe depended on Franco-German co-operation. Only France had the capacity to seize the initiative and bring about a new Europe. The United States would not exert pressure but would leave it to France to set the pace.[15]

Despite everything that had happened, the conviction that European integration required British leadership was still shared by American diplomats in Europe. The US Ambassador to France, David Bruce, reflected the views of other senior US diplomats, when he wrote on 20 October 1949 that

no integration of Western Europe ... is conceivable without the full participation of the UK. This is fully realized by the Continentals themselves. No Frenchman, however much of an Anglophobe he may be or however embittered he may now find himself as a result of the events of the last few months, can conceive of the construction of a viable Western world from which the UK would be absent.

The State Department, Bruce concluded, is 'unrealistic in urging that France alone take [the] lead in bringing about the reintegration of Germany into Western Europe, [for] France ... cannot take the lead without the full backing of the US and UK'.[16]

Unrealistic it might be but, on 30 October 1949 Acheson wrote to Schuman:

I believe we would be wise to give an 'advance' of good will to the Germans in view of the strength of the safeguards which we have erected and our ability to call upon the powers we have reserved. Although we have those powers we cannot reasonably hope to recreate a German will to co-operate if we once permit it to die for lack of nourishment.

Massigli 190. Alexandre Parodi, Secretary-General of the Quai d'Orsay, told Sir Oliver Harvey that Clappier was the originator of the Schuman Plan, that he had then convinced Monnet, and that together they had placed it before Schuman: *DBPO* 44 n. Clappier was later Governor of the *Banque de France* when the European Monetary System was inaugurated.

[14] Leffler 318.   [15] Ibid. 318.   [16] Gillingham 168.

I believe that our policy in Germany, and the development of a German Government which can take its place in Western Europe, depends on the assumption by your country of leadership in Europe on these problems.[17]

Acheson's letter to Schuman was copied to Bevin.[18] This gave the Foreign Office one further opportunity to consider the implications for Britain of this evidence that Washington, despairing of British leadership in Europe, and increasingly sceptical of the value of British leadership even if there was evidence of it, had turned to the only possible alternative, France. Neither Acheson's statement to Schuman in New York, nor his letter of 30 October, implied that he was encouraging Schuman to act without further consultation with his allies. Nor did Schuman invoke them as an explanation of his unilateral action when, without previous consultation, he announced the Schuman Plan.[19] But the statement and the letter were clear signals that, in the light of British recalcitrance, the US Administration was now looking to France for leadership on European integration.

THE SCHUMAN PLAN

On 3 May 1950 Schuman raised his Plan in the French Cabinet in general terms.[20] On 9 May there was a vigorous discussion at Cabinet which focused on the supranational aspects of the Plan. Georges Bidault, the Prime Minister, was reluctant to relinquish any part of national sovereignty. René Mayer and René Pleven gave strong support to Schuman.[21] That afternoon, with Cabinet agreement, Schuman announced his Plan for the control of the French and German coal and steel industries by a supranational High Authority with sovereign powers. Almost exactly five years after the end of the war in Europe, France, through its Foreign Minister, was making the grand gesture of reconciliation

---

[17] Milward (1984) 391–2.   [18] Bullock 737.
[19] Massigli 191.   [20] Poidevin, *Schuman* (1986) 259.
[21] Ibid. 260. There is a conflict between Poidevin and Monnet on how much the French Cabinet understood what they had agreed to when they endorsed the Schuman Plan. According to Monnet, Schuman's remarks (at the Cabinet) were 'even more elliptical and less audible than usual'. Most members of the Cabinet 'learned its precise terms only from the next day's press': Monnet 303. It is unclear whether the Cabinet appreciated that they were being asked to approve the establishment of a High Authority with sovereign powers. Mayer was Minister of Justice. Pleven was Minister of Defence. Both Mayer and Pleven were, later, Prime Minister and Mayer succeeded Monnet as President of the High Authority.

with Germany. It was, he said at his press conference, 'a leap into the unknown'.[22] It is highly doubtful whether, without the encouragement provided by Washington, any French government would have dared to propose the Schuman Plan or would have found the necessary political support within France. René Massigli, French Ambassador in London at the time of the Schuman Plan, and for many years before and after, comments: 'On the American origin of the ideas which were the basis of the Plan, there exists in my mind no doubt.'[23]

Only France and Germany were mentioned by name in Schuman's announcement.[24] All other European countries were invited to participate by bringing their own coal and steel industries under the same supranational control. But Germany was the target of French policy and France made clear that only the refusal of Germany would be allowed to kill the Plan. Alone among European leaders, Federal Chancellor Adenauer had been privileged to be allowed a few hours' advance notice of the Plan.[25] That was all he had needed to indicate his support. Schuman therefore knew, when he made his announcement, that Adenauer had already given his agreement. According to Monnet, Schuman did not raise his Plan at the French Cabinet on 9 May until he had received a message from his emissary to Bonn that he would have Adenauer's support.[26]

The Schuman communiqué declared:

The gathering together of the nations of Europe requires the elimination of the age old opposition of France and Germany. The first concern in any action undertaken must be these two countries. With this aim in view, the French Government proposes to take action immediately on one limited but decisive point; the French Government proposes to place Franco-German production of coal and steel as a whole under a common high authority, within the framework of an organisation open to the participation of the other countries of

[22] Poidevin, *Schuman* (1986) 263.   [23] Massigli 195.

[24] When, on 9 May 1950, René Massigli passed the text of the Schuman communiqué to Ernest Bevin he commented: 'If in the presentation of it [the communiqué] to the press particular stress is laid on the Franco-German aspect of the scheme this is in order to give to the grand idea which is the inspiration of the scheme, as striking a form as possible, particularly with regard to German opinion': Cmd. 7970/2. See also Massigli 189.

[25] Adenauer was informed, during a meeting of the German Cabinet, in a letter handed to him by Schuman's emissary on the morning of 9 May: Monnet 303. Sahm 14 suggests that the emissary was Schuman's *Chef de Cabinet* but Monnet tells a different story. According to his memoirs, Adenauer knew nothing of the Schuman Plan until a few hours before it was publicly unveiled. For Adenauer's account of his reception of the news of the Plan, see Adenauer 257.

[26] Monnet 303.

Europe. . . . The common high authority entrusted with the management of the scheme will be composed of independent personalities appointed by Governments on an equal basis. A chairman will be chosen by common agreement between Governments . . .[27]

Raymond Poidevin tells us that this language was the product of nine drafts extruded between 16 April and 6 May.[28] That there were nine drafts is confirmed by Monnet.[29]

The fundamental thought behind the Schuman Plan was that, by uniting the coal and steel industries of the Ruhr and Lorraine under supranational control, German economic independence would be curtailed, and a strong bond would be forged between France and Germany which would make war between them an impossibility. 'The solidarity in production thus established will make it plain that any war between France and Germany becomes, not merely unthinkable, but materially impossible.'[30] The principle behind this statement was clear. As Adenauer himself explained in a speech to the Bundestag on 13 June: 'There was no better way of dispelling French doubts about the German people's love of peace than to bring together the two countries' coal, iron and steel, which were always the mainstay of rearmament, so that each partner in this pact would know everything that was happening in this important sphere.'[31] But while the principle was clear, the language was obscure. What did it mean to place Franco-German production of coal and steel under a common High Authority? What did the term 'solidarity in production' signify? The statement referred to the management of the 'scheme', not of the industries. How was it to make war between France and Germany 'materially impossible'? One could place a maximalist or a minimalist interpretation on these words.

The Schuman Plan was also to have a series of other exciting purposes:

Europe, with new means at her disposal, will be able to pursue the realisation of one of her essential tasks, the development of the African continent. . . . [T]he task with which this common high authority will be charged will be that of securing in the shortest possible time the modernisation of production and the improvement of its quality; the supply of coal and steel on identical terms to the French and to the German markets as well as to the markets of other member countries; the development in common of export to other countries;

[27] French communiqué translated in Cmd. 7970/2. The original French is given in *DBPO* 2. Cmd. 7970 refers to a common *Higher* Authority. The translation used here is common *High* Authority.
[28] Poidevin, *Schuman* (1986) 258.   [29] Monnet 297.
[30] Cmd. 7970/2.   [31] Adenauer 265.

and the equalization as well as improvement of living conditions of workers in these industries . . .[32]

A FEDERAL EUROPE?

The Schuman Plan was promoted as a first small step towards a federal Europe. 'By pooling basic production and by instituting a new high authority, whose decisions will bind France, Germany and other member countries, these proposals will build the first concrete foundation of the European federation which is indispensable to the preservation of peace.'[33]

After a war which had caused immense destruction and misery, it was natural that the minds of those whose countries had been invaded and devastated should turn to constitutional devices to prevent it ever happening again. This was something that British people, isolated behind their moat, did not sufficiently understand. But a European federation was not indispensable for the preservation of peace. Nor was it what the French, at that time, really had in mind. The idea of federation suggests trust between the member states. Bevin, not without justice, frequently alleged that France's apparent willingness to sacrifice its sovereignty to a federal Europe arose from the fact that, given the political and economic chaos in France, it lacked any sovereignty to sacrifice. But while the French might be prepared to sacrifice some sovereignty, they were not yet prepared to trust Germany.

Dirk Stikker, at the time Netherlands Foreign Minster, comments:

The French Government sought on the one hand to contain Germany and keep it under control. On the other hand the French wanted to bring Germany into a European federation—although not as an equal partner. The execution of such a policy was bound to stumble over its inherent contradictions, not the least being the deep-rooted anti-German popular sentiment, with its pressure for the containment theory.[34]

Though Germany hoped to be regarded as an equal partner in the Schuman Plan, France did not yet intend to offer Germany full equality. At his press conference, Schuman said that Germany was in the position of a minor who had to ask permission of its guardians before it could sign an agreement. This meant that the three occupying powers

---

[32] Cmd. 7970/2.   [33] Ibid.   [34] Stikker 299.

were all in a position to protect their interests if they thought his proposal ran contrary to them.[35] With some reason, the assumption was generally made that it was implicit in the Schuman Plan that Germany would be released from the restrictions on its steel output and capacity, and its right to install finishing equipment deemed dangerous from a security point of view. Thus the *Manchester Guardian*'s own correspondent in Bonn quoted the *Düsseldorfer Nachrichten* as saying that the Plan 'will lead to the elimination of those Allied controls which keep us back in so many ways'.[36] Schuman evidently found any such assumption embarrassing. At his press conference he said that the controls would remain.[37] He may have felt that such a statement was politically necessary if French opinion was to be carried in support of his Plan.

This attitude was hardly compatible with the concept of Germany as an 'equal' partner. There was a meeting in London of the Foreign Ministers of Britain, USA, and France on 13 and 14 May. It produced a declaration which included the following words:

The allies are resolved to pursue their aim . . . that Germany shall re-enter progressively the community of free peoples of Europe. When that situation has been fully reached, she would be liberated from controls to which she is still subject, and accorded her sovereignty to the maximum extent compatible with the basis of the occupation regime. . . . Progress will depend on the degree of confident and frank co-operation displayed by the Government and people of the Federal Republic.[38]

The declaration of the three Foreign Ministers contained no mention of the Schuman Plan. The Federal government professed itself satisfied with what it did say. Adenauer issued a statement: 'The communiqué on Germany is satisfactory in every respect.'[39] But the declaration was criticized by Kurt Schumacher, leader of the Social Democratic opposition, because of the absence of precise proposals. Clearly Germany was still on probation. The *Düsseldorfer Nachrichten* blamed Bevin for the fact that the declaration included words rather than deeds and called it 'a document which illustrates the caution with which Britain approaches the German problem'.[40] No doubt the declaration represented progress but what it augured was far from equality. Schuman

---

[35] *Manchester Guardian*, 10 May 1950.   [36] Ibid., 11 May 1950.
[37] *DBPO* 23.   [38] *The Times*, 15 May 1950.
[39] Adenauer 260, reported *Manchester Guardian*, 15 May 1950.
[40] *Manchester Guardian*, 16 May 1950.

was still repeating his own cautionary message as late as the conference of his party, the Mouvement Républicain Populaire (MRP), on Sunday, 18 June: 'As far as Germany is concerned, all the control measures and restrictions imposed—for example on steel products—will be maintained. The high authority must not have power to weaken them.'[41]

More important, France remained deeply opposed to German rearmament which the US Administration was beginning to canvas.[42] The leading French socialist Jules Moch argued that the continuation of safeguards against German rearmament should be a condition of socialist support for the Schuman Plan.[43] France wanted her friends, and notably Britain, to stand with her on that issue. In September 1950, three months after the outbreak of the Korean War, Schuman still had to tell Acheson in Washington that if he were asked to accept the need for German military units, even in principle, the French Assembly would repudiate him.[44] As Monnet puts it, French policy was once more in danger of 'heading into the cul-de-sac of a categorical refusal'.[45] The way out of the cul-de-sac was to be the Pleven Plan. On 24 October 1950 René Pleven, then French Prime Minister, announced his Plan for a European Army, based on thinking similar to that which had inspired the Schuman Plan though its institutions were to be very different. This time there would be no High Authority. There would be a European Defence Minister but he would be responsible to a Council of Ministers. France and Germany would not enter the European Army as equals. Alone among the participating nations, Germany would not have an army of its own. German units would be under quite rigid control. This was not equality and it was not trust. Four years later, after the ECSC had been up and running for two years, the European Defence Community (EDC) was voted down in the French Assembly. It was a vote not so much against German rearmament, now a foregone conclusion, but against a link with Germany that threatened French independence. The vote displayed that the trust necessary for federation was not yet present.

---

[41] *Manchester Guardian*, 19 June 1950.

[42] The US Joint Chiefs of Staff pronounced in favour of German rearmament at the end of Apr. 1950. In this they had the support of the UK Chiefs of Staff. Formal proposals to that effect were made by the USA in Sept. 1950.

[43] *The Times*, 29 May 1950. See also Poidevin, *Schuman* (1986) 266.

[44] During the ratification debate on the North Atlantic Treaty in 1949, Schuman had told the National Assembly: 'Germany is unarmed and will remain unarmed. . . . It is unthinkable that she should be allowed to join the Atlantic Pact as a nation empowered to defend or help defend other nations': quoted Monnet 337.

[45] Monnet 343.

'A NEW HIGH AUTHORITY WHOSE DECISIONS WILL BIND'

No one could suppose that the Schuman Plan would itself create a European federation. At best or worst, that was for the future. More immediately threatening to British opinion than the words 'European federation' was the suggestion that the decisions of the new unelected High Authority would 'bind' France, Germany, and other member countries. The Schuman Plan had its origin in the French fear of German revival and the uses to which a revived Germany could put the resources of the Ruhr. The idea that the High Authority could make binding decisions was attractive to the French. They did not want the Germans to have the power to override its decisions in the interests of a possibly aggressive German policy. If the Germans were not to have that power, the French would have to make the equivalent sacrifice. Some years later, Schuman explained why 'this new-fangled supranational institution' was necessary. It was 'to enable Germany to accept restrictions on her own sovereignty. . . . We want to accord Germany equality in rights and treatment, and we cannot do otherwise. But equal treatment means that we cannot retain for ourselves more power in the sector concerned than Germany will have.'[46] As Sir Oliver Harvey put it, the High Authority 'seems to [the French] the only chance of preventing exclusive German control of the Ruhr, which to their minds still represents the greatest potential danger to French security'.[47] Indeed, in a secret internal memorandum, the Foreign Office recognized the value of a strong High Authority with the power to bind:

Putting the case in its extreme form, it might be more in our political interest to see established a strong Authority which effectively harnessed Germany to the West, but with which we could not fully associate ourselves, than a weak Authority which we could join but which would not effectively provide the Franco-German link so necessary for political reasons.[48]

The French were determined that the Germans, once they had entered the Plan, must have no escape. What Monnet had in mind for the Germans was clearly expressed in the statement to the Press issued after the first sessions of the Schuman negotiations. According to his own account, Monnet insisted on including the following stipulation:

[46] Schuman 21.
[47] *DBPO* 103, message from Sir O. Harvey to Kenneth Younger, 16 June 1950.
[48] *DBPO* 104, 'Constitutional Problems involved in a Supra-national Authority as Envisaged by M. Schuman', 16 June 1950.

The withdrawal of a State which has committed itself to the Community should be possible only if all the others agree to such withdrawal and to the conditions in which it takes place. This rule in itself sums up the fundamental transformation which the French proposal seeks to achieve. Over and above coal and steel, it is laying the foundations of a European federation. In a federation, no State can secede by its own unilateral decision. Similarly, there can be no Community except among nations which commit themselves to it with no limit in time and no looking back.[49]

Germany was voluntarily to imprison itself for all time in a Community designed by France. Nor was it, for the French, purely a matter of military security. Commercial considerations also entered. The logical purity of this French idea was impeccable. How much force there would be behind the idea was, as yet, unclear. Germany was moving towards complete freedom. It was not likely to be delayed indefinitely. While the implications of the verb 'to bind' could not be ignored, it rapidly became apparent that Germany, and other member states, would have concerns about the power to bind vested in the High Authority. They would therefore negotiate to ensure that the power would not be used against their interests.

France may have deceived itself in believing that the vesting of sovereign powers in the High Authority would make war between France and Germany materially impossible. But that was the intention. Britain's perspective was different. It had nationalized coal. It had legislated, much more controversially, to nationalize steel. At the time it produced one-half of the coal and one-third of the steel of the seven countries that might participate in the Schuman proposal. Coal and steel were believed to be the commanding heights of the economy. Was public power over them to be surrendered to a supranational authority whose decisions would be binding and which would itself be but a staging post to a European federation?[50] It was not public ownership that was questioned by the Schuman Plan. What appeared to be brought into question was public power over coal and steel enterprises however owned and hence the UK government's power to plan for economic development.

[49] Monnet 326. In fact there was a time limit. The Treaty of Paris had a duration of 50 years and therefore expires in 2002.
[50] The word 'supranational' did not actually appear in the Schuman announcement, a point made much of by the Conservative Opposition in the House of Commons debates of 26 and 27 June 1950. According to Monnet it did appear in the fourth draft of the Schuman announcement. But 'I disliked the word, and always have': Monnet 297.

Schuman's announcement had asserted the limited nature of his proposal as seen by the French government: 'the French Government proposes to take action immediately on one limited but decisive point . . .'[51] But for a government that was bringing the nation's basic industries into public ownership for the purpose of planning their future, the Schuman Plan did not emerge as a limited proposal. It appeared to go to the very roots of national economic sovereignty. France might gain from reconciliation with Germany and from equal access to the Ruhr resources. Germany might gain from recognition of its restored status in Europe. But what could Britain gain to justify participation in a scheme that apparently went to the roots of national economic sovereignty by establishing an authority that could bind governments? It was natural and right that a British government should ask itself such questions. All prospective participants were bound to ask themselves comparable questions. It was only if the answers revealed that the threat to national economic sovereignty was being grossly exaggerated by the presentation of the Plan that British participation was at all likely.

The immediate danger was that the British government would think less constructively about the Plan because it had not been consulted. Massigli, who had also not been consulted, and therefore had his own reasons for annoyance, was concerned that Bevin should have been left in ignorance of the Plan until the last minute. When first informed of the Plan the day before its announcement, he had foreseen that Bevin 'with his weaknesses, his poor health and his vanity' would not be pleased. After all, Germany was a question for the allies, not just for France, and the Ruhr was in the British sector. Massigli hoped that Bevin's anger might be assuaged by emphasizing the European context of the proposal.[52] It was not enough. Bevin was very angry. Massigli had considerable sympathy with Bevin's anger. How, he wondered, could Schuman have exposed his plan to Adenauer without first clearing it with Acheson and Bevin? How could he make it public without first discussing it with these colleagues? How could his advisers allow him to act in this way?[53]

Massigli refers to the official French reaction when, in March 1950, only two months before the Schuman announcement, Adenauer had told an American journalist that he envisioned a complete Franco-German union, with common citizenship, joint political institutions,

---

[51] Cmd. 7970/2.   [52] Massigli 186–7.   [53] Ibid. 190.

and a single economic policy.[54] The French government had not been amused. It issued a statement saying that Europe was now to be organized not on the basis of a Franco-German tête-à-tête but around the Organization for European Economic Co-operation (OEEC) and the Council of Europe. How was it, Massigli asks, that only two months later a plan could be announced without the least mention of the Council of Europe?[55] The reason, as Massigli saw it, was that Schuman was putty in the hands of Monnet and that the Quai d'Orsay had lost control of foreign policy.

Massigli believed that a good ambassador should not limit himself to making known and defending the views of his government. He regarded it as an important part of his duty to make the Quai d'Orsay understand the views of the British government. Here the danger was that, precisely because of Massigli's sympathy with Bevin's anger, he would fail to convey Schuman's firmness of purpose. When an ambassador is too sympathetic to the views of the government to which he is accredited, there is always a danger that the result will be to mislead.

GENERAL DE GAULLE

General de Gaulle who, even in exile at Colombey-les-Deux-Églises, was not entirely without influence on French public opinion, did not approve the Schuman Plan. In his view, it put the cart before the horse. The priority should have been a political settlement not this technical plan. Moreover, like many others, he feared a Franco-German tête-à-tête which left French industry without adequate protection and added to the danger of German industry supplanting French industry.[56] Nevertheless, he appeared to take a less jaundiced view of Adenauer's interview:

If one were not constrained to look at matters coolly, one would be dazzled by the proposals of what could be achieved by a combination of German and French strength, the latter embracing also Africa. . . . Altogether, it would mean giving modern economic, social, strategic and cultural shape to the work of the Emperor Charlemagne.[57]

[54] Mr Kingsbury Smith, chief European correspondent of the American International News Service: *DBPO* 27 n.
[55] Massigli 191–2.   [56] Poidevin, *Schuman* (1986) 266.
[57] Adenauer 244–7. Quoted by Monnet 287.

The General could already see the benefits to France of reconciliation with Germany. The General was the last person to prejudice French sovereignty. As Raymond Aron commented: 'General de Gaulle a few months ago gave a favourable reply to an interview given by Herr Adenauer on the subject of a Franco-German union. The uncrowned king of French nationalism had thus become the advocate of the diplomatic revolution . . .'[58] De Gaulle's reaction could have been one more warning to the British that there were *ententes* available to the French other than the *entente cordiale*.

THE LEADERSHIP OF EUROPE

Monnet, in advocating the Schuman Plan, spoke of breaching the 'ramparts of national sovereignty'.[59] Indeed his expectations from the Plan far exceeded what was, in the end, realized. Meanwhile his hyperbole increased the probability of an adverse British reaction. He should not have been surprised. He knew the British too well. Ministers and officials were too ready to take what he said at face value. They allowed themselves to be bemused by words. A limited proposal packaged politically for a European and American ideological market was interpreted as a real threat to British national sovereignty. Monnet had not in fact yet won the battle for federalism either in France or elsewhere. The ramparts of national sovereignty were not to be so easily breached. What Schuman and he *had* achieved was rather different. They had, for the time being, won for France the leadership of Europe. Their satisfaction would not have been diminished by the enthusiastic reception from so many Americans. Ambassador David Bruce considered the Schuman Plan the most constructive French action since liberation. Averell Harriman deemed it the most important development in Europe since the Marshall Plan.[60] John Foster Dulles considered it 'a brilliantly creative idea'.[61] President Truman capped it all. He issued a statement calling the Schuman Plan 'an act of constructive statesmanship' and a 'demonstration of French leadership in the solution of the problems of Europe . . . in the great French tradition'.[62]

[58] *Manchester Guardian*, 30 May 1950. See also Adenauer 248.

[59] An earlier draft of the Schuman announcement included the sentence: 'This proposal has an essential political objective: to make a breach in the ramparts of national sovereignty which will be narrow enough to secure consent, but deep enough to open the way towards the unity that is essential to peace': Monnet 296.

[60] Harriman was the ECA's special representative in Europe.

[61] Leffler 348–9.   [62] Acheson 386. *The Times*, 19 May 1950.

3
A Bolt from the Blue?

Robert Schuman was born in Luxembourg in 1886. He became a German citizen and lawyer in Alsace. He fought in the German Army in the First World War. He became a French citizen in 1919 when Alsace became part of France. In 1948 he became Foreign Minister. It rapidly became clear that he wished to establish a new relationship between France and Germany. To that end he would strive, within the limits of the politically possible, to end French obstruction to a German settlement. In March 1949, under instructions from Schuman, André François-Poncet, the French High Commissioner in Germany, told George Kennan in Frankfurt that 'The differences which had arisen among the Allies over the handling of the German problem were absurd, tragic and unnecessary . . . We should seize the occasion to place the whole German question on a new and higher plane.'[1] The specific question that gave rise to these sentiments was the drafting of the Occupation Statute. In its then form, Schuman considered it over-complicated, impractical, and deadening. Schuman himself conveyed the same message to the American Military Governor, General Lucius Clay, in Paris on 20 March 1949 in what Clay described as the most satisfactory exchange he had ever had with any French official.[2] The Americans had been looking for a more co-operative attitude from France on the German question. Evidently they were beginning to get it. At their meeting in Washington on 31 March and 1 April 1949, Bevin and Acheson found that Schuman was expressing a point of view on Germany different from that to which they had become accustomed from France, and was trying to bury past enmities.[3] Schuman's switch in policy led to speedy agreement on many aspects of the German problem at this tripartite meeting.

Roger Bullen makes a strategic point: 'With Germany politically, economically and perhaps militarily integrated into the western alliance

---

[1] Bullock 665. André François-Poncet had been Ambassador to Germany in Hitler's time.

[2] Ibid. 665, 668.   [3] Ibid. 667–9.

France could finally abandon the need to keep open the traditional option of a Franco-Russian rapprochement to contain a powerful and independent Germany.'[4] But surely the problem for France was the other way around. As the Russian alliance was no longer available, France itself had to find the way to settle with Germany. That was France's realistic option. Finding the way was being eased by the fact that, at last, the USA was taking French concerns about Germany seriously. The only question was whether any French government could carry French opinion in favour of a settlement with Germany on a basis of reasonable equality. By 1950, this was the only basis upon which Germany was at all likely to accept it for any length of time. A settlement with Germany, at France's initiative, could have, from France's point of view, another merit perceptively argued by Bullen: 'France and Germany would negotiate as equals, whereas the French believed that on many issues the British and American High Commissioners protected German at the expense of French interests.'[5]

If Schuman was to succeed in burying the ancient enmity with Germany, he needed to find the right idea, the instinct to seize on it if it was offered to him, and the political strength to carry it through. It turned out that the right idea was a very old idea, the idea of supranational control of Franco-German heavy industry on a non-discriminatory basis. In an article in the *Manchester Guardian*, Raymond Aron proposed the pertinent question. 'One may ask how it is that an idea as banal as this should now be accepted as something vital and new...'[6] The answer was that this old idea had become the instrument of France's new policy of reconciliation with Germany.

IN THE WIND

The Schuman Plan was developed in great secrecy. There had been no consultation with the coal and steel industries in France.[7] The Quai d'Orsay, at official level, had played no part. Alexandre Parodi, the Secretary-General of the Quai d'Orsay, was only informed on 7 May.[8] At a meeting of British ministers on 10 May in London, with Prime Minister Attlee in the chair, the French were accused of 'springing this proposal on the world'.[9] The British government had been taken aback

---

[4] Bullen, in Bullen *et al*. 197.   [5] Ibid.
[6] *Manchester Guardian,* 30 May 1950.   [7] Poidevin, *Schuman* (1986) 259.
[8] Ibid.   [9] *DBPO* 3.

by the lack of consultation. Nevertheless, the announcement was much more of a surprise than it should have been, given proper attention to the options then open to the French government and to the switch in French policy on Germany.

In the usual way, those whose business it was to be 'in the know' claimed, after the event, to have known that something was in the wind. Massigli had been kept in the dark by his own government but asserts that, by the spring of 1950, what was to become the Schuman Plan was 'in the air'.[10] W. G. Hayter, British minister in Paris, wrote: 'The idea of associating the French and German metallurgical industries has after all been bandied about for some time.'[11] Sir Edmund Hall-Patch, the leader of the UK delegation to the OEEC, first learnt of the Schuman announcement when shown the text by Dr Dirk Stikker, Foreign Minister of the Netherlands. In an immediate reaction he said that 'this was a crystallisation of ideas which the French had been airing for some years, but they now appeared in an extreme form'. Stikker himself commented that 'The French he knew had been fiddling with this idea for years and it was really most unfortunate that they should produce it at this particular moment in so uncompromising a form.'[12] Whatever these gentlemen did or did not know, the message clearly had not reached London. Hence the rapid series of meetings, both ministerial and official, to help the government prepare its response.

Whatever could have been known in advance about the detail of the Schuman Plan and its timing, the Attlee government should have been ready for an announcement of this kind. Indeed it should have been pre-empted. Something was in the air and had been for many months. The only aspect of the Schuman Plan itself at which the British government was entitled to be surprised was the idea of a High Authority consisting of independent personalities and equipped with sovereign powers. There was also the lack of consultation which left a bad taste. But even in default of consultation, the Attlee government should not have been so surprised. There was enough evidence that the French, faced by the collapse of their plans for the control of Germany and anxious to find some alternative, were beginning to think in terms of an entirely new relationship with Germany. If there was to be a French initiative on relations with Germany, not a great deal of imagination would be required to anticipate that the impact would be increased if France appeared to

---

[10] Massigli 194.   [11] *DBPO* 20, Hayter to Bevin, 15 May 1950.
[12] *DBPO* 6, Hall-Patch to Bevin, 10 May 1950.

be solely responsible for it. This chapter attempts to illuminate two questions. The first is whether the relationship that had developed between France and Britain by 1950 was one that encouraged France to consult. The second enquires how much justification for surprise there was that the French should propose the pooling of European coal and steel under a supranational authority.

THE RELATIONSHIP

If Bevin expected to be consulted by Paris before any major French initiative, he had underestimated the drift towards mutual exasperation in Britain's post-war relations with France. Tension has never been absent, even at the best of times, from the relationship between the two great historic nation states of Western Europe, France and Britain. Massigli comments on the problems of developing mutual comprehension between these two neighbours, so near and yet so far, each with its distinct philosophy of action, and each with its own, but different, world view. Misunderstandings, according to Massigli, were the rule.[13]

Britain had fought for the liberation of France. During the war it had supported de Gaulle against American criticism. At the end of the war it had striven to secure for France a more prominent place in the post-war world than the Americans and Russians would have conceded without British pressure.[14] In the years after the war the UK, often condescendingly, only too overtly conscious of the blow to French pride inflicted by the war, continued the policy of encouraging a French role in European recovery and security.

Perhaps because, after the war, it felt weak, Britain attempted to extract gratitude from its allies. Gratitude for its services in the war was demanded from the USA and was to be expressed in the form of a large grant-in-aid. It was not forthcoming. Gratitude was to require that France, however much its perception of its own interests might be ignored by Britain, must look to it for leadership, not try to exercise leadership itself, and certainly not without consultation. The annoyance that the French did not show sufficient gratitude was to spread across parties.

[13] Massigli 190.

[14] 'I should like to say here that it is especially due to the friendship of Great Britain that, in the course of the year 1945, France was able so rapidly to regain her position among the Allies': Schuman. Schuman also attributed the establishment of the French zone in Germany to 'the friendship of Great Britain': see p. 7.

The Tories might excuse it when a Labour government was the victim. But they, in their turn, would learn that gratitude is an insecure basis for friendship among nations. Harold Macmillan, whose application for membership of the EEC had been vetoed by President de Gaulle, later reflected in retirement on this unfortunate characteristic of sovereign states: 'If it has now happily been possible for the French to forget the injuries which they have suffered at Germany's hands, for the benefits which they have received from Britain it seems impossible for them to extend any sincere forgiveness.'[15]

While the large figure of General de Gaulle was inflicting his resentments on his allies, there could be no other expectation than of friction. The restoration of French independence necessarily implied the continuation of disagreements on colonial policy between the UK and France, for example in the Middle East. There had been many such disagreements during the course of the war itself. They had cooled relations between Churchill and de Gaulle. Shortly after the surrender of Germany, British troops intervened to stop the shelling of Damascus by a French force. De Gaulle told the British Ambassador: 'We are not, I recognize, in a state to wage war on you now. But you have outraged France and betrayed the West. That can never be forgotten.'[16] There is no reason to think that he ever did forget.

Even after de Gaulle's resignation in January 1946, relations were often difficult. The Attlee government was at first hostile to the idea of German rearmament and gave France reason to think that it would stand with it against American pressure for a German military contribution to the defence of Western Europe. Then, on 28 March 1950, in a debate in the House of Commons on Foreign Affairs, Kenneth Younger, Minister of State at the Foreign Office, said: 'We and, even more, our friends in Europe are entitled to adequate guarantees against the revival of the German war potential, and until we can be satisfied that Germany is able and willing to take her place as a part of the Western community, we do not intend to be stampeded into ill-considered action.'[17] Statements of this kind can have many meanings. No government will confess a readiness to be stampeded. But it would not require great subtlety to interpret it as opening the door to British acceptance of German rearmament. The change in the Attlee government's posture on German rearmament may have been justified. Yet, as an ally of France, Britain appeared a broken reed. Regularly it renounced its own policies

---

[15] Macmillan 483.   [16] Bullock 44.
[17] HC Debs. 28 Mar. 1950, col. 216.

when it met disagreement from Washington until British policy was regarded in France as simply a pale echo of American policy, a voice that could not be relied on even on those occasions when it did find itself diverging from that of its transatlantic benefactor.

The French wanted strong economic partners. They wanted help in preventing the resurrection of German economic dominance in post-war Europe. From the earliest days after the war, the French saw Anglo-French economic co-ordination as one way of providing security against Germany. In August 1946 Bidault as Prime Minister wrote to Attlee proposing the co-ordination of the British and French economies. The French were elaborating the Plan for the modernization and re-equipment of the French economy, the so-called Monnet Plan. The two countries could plan their economies together. In the view of at least one influential British minister, the British also needed a plan. Already, in August 1945, just weeks after his appointment in the new Attlee government, Sir Stafford Cripps, President of the Board of Trade, had been pressing for a five-year plan.[18] Bevin's response to the French approach was discouraging. It was not so much a rejection of planning, to which the Attlee government was also committed even if it never achieved it, as a rejection of economic collaboration with France.

In December 1946 Leon Blum became interim Prime Minister and Foreign Minister. The Monnet Plan had, by this time, been prepared though it was still awaiting Cabinet approval. As one socialist Prime Minister to another, Blum suggested the integration of the British and French recovery plans. The British feared that the French proposals were an attempt to make the UK pay for the Monnet Plan. Many of the proposed French exports were of luxury goods which the British government was unwilling to import at a time of austerity. The French wanted to return to the pre-war pattern of trade by which they earned convertible sterling from their exports to Britain. They therefore expected to find agricultural markets in Britain. The British saw no reason to give France advantages in their foodstuffs market. Britain wanted to build on its success in developing its own agriculture during the war. In any case, Britain had no governmental machinery capable of under-taking the lead role in such discussions until well into 1947.

Other attempts at economic collaboration failed. The French believed that the Germans were discriminating against them in the pricing of coking coal. They felt that the revival of the German steel industry was being assisted by unequal conditions of competition and that this

---

[18] Clarke 77.

threatened French security because of what it portended for German power in Europe. They were interested in benefiting from supplies of British coal, no doubt at a favourable price. Leon Blum's approach to Attlee in the winter of 1946/7 included the question of coal supplies. Nothing came of it.

The thinking that led to Britain's neglect of economic collaboration with France and Europe is explained in Chapters 4 and 5. Here it is enough to emphasize that Britain's relationship with France was not free of the arrogance with which a victor may regard the vanquished. Another source of this arrogance was the appearance, deceptive as it turned out, that British economic recovery was progressing more satisfactorily than that of its continental neighbours. Even Monnet was at first deceived. He was obsessed with federations and at first sought a role for Britain in his European federalist fantasies. In April 1948, dissatisfied with the extent of European economic co-operation, he wrote to Schuman and Bidault declaring that a Western European federation led by Britain and France was the only way to economic salvation. In June 1948 he suggested an Anglo-French federation. He had recently returned from a visit to Britain where he had been impressed by British national discipline and relative economic success. He believed that an Anglo-French economic union would help both countries. Britain would obtain larger markets. French recovery would be promoted.[19] The ideas were left for another day.

French policy was directed towards the creation in Western Europe of a customs union. One project was for a Franco-Italian customs union. A Treaty for a Franco-Italian customs union was signed on 26 March 1949. It was not ratified.[20] Another project, known as Finebel or Fritalux, would have incorporated the Benelux countries as well as Italy. On each occasion when the French had investigated the possibilities of a European customs union excluding Germany, they had been confronted by a demand from Benelux for the participation of Germany. The insistence on the inclusion of Germany was compelling France to think about its relations with Germany from an economic as well a political point of view.[21] Germany was regarded justly, particularly in

[19] Young (1984) 120.

[20] The 1949 Treaty was superseded on 23 June 1950 by a Franco-Italian Customs Union Convention which was also not ratified.

[21] 'When the West German government took office the international bonds which restrained the Promethean strength of Germany's steel industry were already being tested and broken. Some new policy was needed if a Franco-German settlement was to become a reality and reconstruction to be achieved': Milward (1984) 371.

Benelux, as the key to European economic prosperity. Including Germany would create a better balanced customs union. Its large market would make it easier for European industry to accept the increased competition that such a customs union would unleash. France had never before been ready to include Germany. The political difficulties seemed too great. It was still only five years from the end of the German occupation. There was also the problem of how France was to prevent German competitiveness from destroying French industry.

Britain's refusal to become involved was unwelcome to France. British participation in a customs union could have brought forward the time when France was ready to incorporate Germany in an economically integrated Europe. Britain's refusal, explained in Chapter 5, made Franco-German *rapprochement* politically much more difficult. But political difficulties can sometimes respond to imagination and leadership. Though there was deep scepticism in the Foreign Office about the quality of French leadership, it was not beyond the bounds of possibility that France would find both imagination and leadership.

Sir Edwin Plowden, Chief Economic Planner and Head of the Central Economic Planning Staff (CEPS), accompanied by Robert Hall and Alan Hitchman, held conversations with Monnet at his home at the end of April 1949. The talks were another attempt to discover whether co-operation between France and Britain could be made mutually beneficial. Monnet remembers: 'They did . . . admit that the growth of their foreign trade was due in large measure to Germany's temporary eclipse as a supplier of capital equipment.'[22] Plowden reports the conclusion of these discussions:

At the end of the discussions we drew up a list of limited proposals to take back to our governments, including an idea to ameliorate the shortages of food and coal in the United Kingdom and France by a system of mutual exchange. When on our return . . . we put these proposals to Bevin via Cripps, they were immediately rejected as Bevin felt that even these would go too far in the direction of a surrender of British sovereignty.[23]

The British liked exploiting their power in the market for coal. They were not so rich that they could abandon positions of economic strength. The UK's policy on trade in coal was a source of friction with the USA as well as a disappointment for France. Just as the Germans were

---

[22] Monnet 279. Hitchman was Plowden's deputy at the CEPS. During the war he had been Bevin's Private Secretary.
[23] Plowden 75.

suspected of operating dual pricing in coal, lower prices in the home market than for export, so was the UK. The Americans accused Britain of holding up economic recovery in Europe by subsidizing home consumption of coal, thereby inflating home purchases and reducing the amount of coal which could be exported at lower prices to assist recovery in the rest of Europe. As will be seen in Chapter 5, in the British view this was a case of the American pot calling the British kettle black. Robert Marjolin, Secretary-General of the OEEC, proposed that West Germany and the UK should end dual pricing for coal. In December 1949 the Attlee Cabinet flatly refused to do any such thing despite continued American pressure. The Germans, also subject to American pressure, did reduce the differential.[24] But they too refused to end dual pricing. The British Ministry of Defence was particularly angry with the pressure coming from the USA on this topic. The Americans did not appear to understand that what they were trying to do would damage the UK's defensive capability. '[I]t might go a long way to break the defensive wall which they are trying to build up in Europe.'[25] Another area of possible Franco-British collaboration had been closed. Monnet was repeatedly coming forward with ideas for Franco-British collaboration in the economic field. The British government was repeatedly turning them down. Nor did it have any ideas of its own with which to respond to the obvious French anxiety for collaboration with Britain.

Nothing could excuse in French eyes the lack of consultation before the sterling devaluation of September 1949. It was a move that was bound seriously to affect continental Europe. Bevin and Sir Stafford Cripps, Chancellor of the Exchequer, were in Washington in early September 1949. They briefed the US Administration on their intentions. Indeed, Washington had for months pressed devaluation upon them. Robert Schuman and Maurice Petsche, the French Minister of Finance, were in Washington at the same time but were not informed. The incident aroused bitter criticism in French political circles and in the French media even though France had behaved quite as badly with its own devaluation the previous year. London's distrust of French security in handling sensitive information, though intelligible, was not an argument easy to advance in mitigation of a sin that Cripps himself

[24] Milward (1984) 387. From DM 8.00 a tonne to DM 5.46.

[25] *DBPO* 16. The expectation was that if the UK had entered any kind of European coal and steel organization, it would have to abandon dual pricing but that dual pricing could not in any case survive much longer. See e.g. *DBPO* 128, Report of Ministerial Committee, 1 July 1950 and *DBPO* 132, minutes of Cabinet meeting, 4 July 1950.

came to recognize. Robert Hall, Director of the Economic Section of the Cabinet Office from September 1947, and an official highly influential in the early post-war years, reports a meeting that he and Edmund Hall-Patch had with Jean Monnet two months after the devaluation.

[Monnet] expatiated at length on the harm done to our relations by the manner of the devaluation. Hall-Patch told him that S[tafford] C[ripps] had warned Petsche two months before that *if* we had to do it, we could only give two days' notice. And these two days were given. But Monnet said that whatever the truth was (he did not dissent or agree on this) there had been a deplorable lack of imagination on both sides. Surely the last two days could have been used as 'a cloak of consultation'. As it was no one in France would believe that we cared a damn for consultation.[26]

In mid-January 1950 Oliver Harvey warned the Foreign Office that, although French leaders preferred Britain to share leadership in Western Europe, they had shown themselves willing to pursue Finebel without Britain. When Bevin was in Paris early in February 1950, on his way back from the Commonwealth Conference in Colombo, he expressed the hope that France would not find it necessary to make a decision about Finebel. Apparently he thought that Britain's refusal to participate should act as a veto on French initiatives. The French warned Bevin that they did not want to proceed without British agreement but added that they were under strong pressure to draw up plans for Europe.[27] Poidevin reports that in the spring of 1950, Schuman and Monnet began to think in terms not of a general economic union, which had proved difficult politically to bring to fruition, but of a union limited to two products, coal and steel.[28] Despite the French warning to Bevin, the British remained complacent in the confidence that nothing could be done without them. So far as the British were concerned, nothing important could happen in Europe without British involvement and therefore all that was necessary in relation to any French proposal of any kind was to say no and the French would simply go away and sulk. It was not a relationship that encouraged the French to undertake prior consultation with Britain about policy departures. Repeatedly French representatives told British representatives that if the UK wanted friendly relations with France, it should show more evidence of it.

[26] Hall, 16 Nov. 1949. Attlee claimed that the French *had* been given 48 hours' notice of the devaluation: HC Debs. 27 June 1950, col. 2162.
[27] Bullock 753. Finebel, otherwise Fritalux, eventually came to nothing.
[28] Poidevin, *Schuman* (1986) 245.

The sterling devaluation on 18 September 1949 was a warning that all might not be as well with the British economy as it seemed, but it was successful in rebuilding the UK's reserves and transforming the current account of the balance of payments. This solved the immediate crisis and held out hope of further progress for the UK economy. Economic crisis is soon forgotten when the upturn comes, even when the upturn is due mainly to the depreciation of the currency. One politician who saw more deeply was R. W. G. (Kim) Mackay, Labour MP for Reading North and a strong supporter of British participation in the Schuman Plan. He insisted that there was no room for complacency in Britain about its economic performance. During the debate in the House of Commons on the Schuman Plan on 27 June 1950, he pointed to the fact that 'With a world boom for the last five years, with no competitors such as Germany and Japan . . . with customers whose pockets are filled with sterling to buy our goods, we are not exporting more today than we exported in 1913'.[29]

Hugh Dalton, formerly Chancellor of the Exchequer, still a leading member of the Cabinet, and a strong opponent of any European entanglement, was more optimistic. In a speech made in July 1950 he proclaimed the success of British economic policy:

We British have steadily built up our strength since the war. We have made new records in capital development, in production and in exports. We have gone further than any other country in West Europe towards closing the dollar gap. We have maintained full employment through five years of Peace—an achievement unprecedented in our history.[30]

Something must be allowed to party propaganda. But it was not just party propaganda. Something also must be allowed to the conviction that government policy and planning had been an important contributor to this success. There is no mistaking the pride in what the British had done relative to their continental neighbours and the note of confidence in the successes of British economic policy.

It was premature. Too little account was being taken in Labour circles of the special factors that made the UK performance appear better than it was. First was Marshall Aid in the distribution of which the UK acquired a differentially favourable status despite its opposition to American pressure for European federation. Secondly, the trading relationship between Britain and the Commonwealth provided the UK with

---

[29] HC Debs. 27 June 1950, col. 2123.
[30] Speech at Middleton-in-Teesdale, 22 July 1950.

markets and with sources of supply for raw materials outside the dollar area at prices which the UK was frequently in a position to dictate.[31] Non-dollar sources of food and raw materials which could, to some extent, replace dollar sources were particularly valuable in a world in which dollars were in short supply. Thirdly, there was the protection which British exports enjoyed and which helped them to flourish. They were protected in the first instance by the dollar shortage. If the UK could supply, a sterling source was likely to be preferred to a dollar source. Then they enjoyed the protection provided by the initial absence of German competition. But by 1950 Germany was catching up fast and the predominance of the British among European economies was disappearing.[32] This was not a factor of which officials were ignorant.[33] If from no other source, officials would have been aware of the concerns in British industry.

Complacency was combined with blindness. The Attlee government was incapable of seeing itself as others saw it. This failure related particularly to France. How would a French government, which Britain sometimes seemed to go out of its way to estrange, regard its neighbour on the other side of the English Channel? The UK might consider that with the USA it had a special relationship. Certainly, with the possible exception of Jean Monnet, British representatives appeared to have better access to the US Administration than French. This was partly because, despite its frequent economic crises, it did have a stable government, a Foreign Minister who was co-operative on all security issues, and an Ambassador, Sir Oliver Franks, who was on the closest personal terms with Acheson. But Washington was under no illusions as to Britain's real strength. What appeared to the UK as a special relationship was, in Washington, regarded simply as a tool to secure from the UK help towards achieving American objectives in Europe. In any event, was a special relationship with Washington to be the prime measure of status in the post-war world? To France, the UK's position

---

[31] See Ch. 5 below.

[32] Over the period 1948–50, before the arrival of the demand stimulated by the Korean War, British exports stood still, at least in current prices, while the exports of the Europe of the Six to the rest of Western Europe increased by a half, and by more than a third to the rest of the world: Milward (1984) 352.

[33] A relevant example. 'In 1949 German steel exports made their re-entry into European markets and in that year they were about one quarter the value of British exports. In 1951 they were to exceed them.' In Mar. 1950 Adenauer had asked for an increase in the limits to German steel output and in the same month production exceeded 1m. tonnes: Milward (1984) 368, 372.

appeared as subservience rather than independence and this harsh judgement was justified by the experience that, again and again, Britain, in the end, submitted to American pressure. Though the UK's point of view might be legitimate, it carried less weight than it should have done because it was not seen as independent and certainly not as European.

At a time when Washington had come to understand the importance of reassuring France, the British failed to take sufficiently seriously the continued French preoccupation with the resurgence of Germany from a security as well as an economic point of view. In February 1950 Monnet warned Plowden of the continued French preoccupation with Germany and of the need for France and the UK to act jointly to cope with the consequences. He went so far as to suggest that the British government had not thought the matter through.[34] He was right. London had become bored with French schemes. It knew that they came to nothing.

Britain, which considered itself the leading power in Europe, seemed incapable of finding the right gesture of support for its ally France. There was neither generosity of spirit, nor, what might have been rather less expensive, any scintilla of imaginative understanding. Instead there was this unhappy history of unrequited approaches from Paris to London and the unexpectedly large sterling devaluation which France had been denied the opportunity to influence. France was left disenchanted by the repeated rejection of its proposals for Anglo-French economic co-operation, and disillusioned by the continuously negative attitude being displayed by the UK in any matter relating to the economic integration of Europe. The UK made no serious attempt to find any reconciliation between its interests as the centre of the Commonwealth and sterling area and the economic opportunities which involvement in European economic integration might open up.

The result was to make it rather less likely that a French government would wish to consult Britain in advance of a strategic development in its German policy, particularly as it felt it now had the support of the USA. Consultation might be owed to the British as it was to the Americans. But the relationship with Britain had become too uncomfortable for such duties to be regarded in Paris as compulsive, especially when there appeared to be something to be gained from ignoring them. This delinquency, to describe it as Bevin might have been tempted to do, was quite consistent with a continuing hope in Paris that, despite

[34] *DBPO* 20 n.

Britain's record since the war, it would join France in acting as a counterweight against a revival of German dominance in Europe. Massigli criticizes Schuman for not perceiving that his route to Franco-German reconciliation could damage Franco-British relations.[35] The extent of any such damage was, however, a matter for Britain and not just for France. Schuman was holding the door open for Britain. It was up to Britain to decide whether to enter.

The French could be annoying. It was annoying that France so often seemed to see no better way of persuading its allies than by being obstructive in allied councils. It was annoying that France which was so weak, and had been so humiliated by defeat, wanted to be treated as though it was strong and should have influence. It was annoying that France, though it made little effort to rearm, and was dissipating such military strength as it had on a fruitless war in the Far East, continued to emphasize the dangers of German aggression even when it had become quite clear that the potential aggressor was no longer Germany and when Germany, indeed, had to be persuaded to stand in the battle line against the real potential aggressor. The persistence in France of neutralism, of the wish to constitute a third force committed neither to the USA nor to the USSR, was worrying. Such sentiments persisted even after the creation of NATO and the Marshall Plan, and were not limited to the left but were to be found among people, in all parts of the political spectrum, who questioned whether French security had yet been adequately safeguarded. It was annoying that the French took initiatives without considering British views and without even thinking their proposals through. The Schuman Plan was by no means the first example. In August 1948 Robert Schuman summoned a conference to launch a European Parliament. Bevin told the British Ambassador in Paris that 'on this issue the French Government are playing politics, that they have not given any serious study to the matter and that he declines to be bustled into folly simply to suit the temporary convenience of the French Government'.[36] Bevin was opposed to any genuine European Parliament and was determined that the Assembly of the Council of Europe, when it came into existence, should be purely advisory and limited in the subjects it could discuss to matters of little importance. Above all, perhaps, it was annoying that the French changed their governments so frequently, though it might have been held in mitigation of this offence that they changed their Foreign Ministers

---

[35] Massigli 184. [36] FO 371/73097: quoted Warner 68.

rather less often. Yet all these annoyances that made such frequent appearance in Foreign Office studies, and distracted ministers from serious thought, were the merest persiflage of European diplomacy.

The Foreign Office, under Bevin and its Permanent Secretary, Sir William Strang, was far more interested in writing one more paper proving to its own satisfaction the inadequacies of French government and society than in visualizing what some of the bright souls who had emerged in French government service during and since the war might be contemplating. In March 1950 the Foreign Office began an analysis of French deficiencies in answer to the question 'In building on France are we not building on sand?' It was completed on 13 June after the announcement of the Schuman Plan. On the paper Bevin commented: 'Almost too optimistic, but even then a sad story.'[37]

THE RUHR AND EUROPEAN HEAVY INDUSTRY

At the centre of French anxieties about Germany was the Ruhr. These anxieties arose both from the French perception of the Ruhr as the motor of German aggression and from fear of German competition exacerbated by the suspicion that the French steel industry was suffering from price discrimination in the supply of Ruhr coking coal and consequently was at risk. France was dependent on German coking coal from the Ruhr and demanded prices which did not discriminate against its steel industry and in favour of German steel producers.[38] The Ruhr had long been a source of anxiety not just for France but also for the UK. From this arose the British proposals for nationalizing the Ruhr industries which were then abandoned because the US Administration did not agree.

French anxieties had been enhanced by discontent with the way their arguments were dismissed or ignored by their American and British allies. The International Authority for the Ruhr (IAR) had been established as a gesture intended to quieten French anxieties. Its functions and powers were left ill-defined. The outcome of the negotiations on the IAR was summarized in a Foreign Office memo of 28 May 1948, to Edmund Hall-Patch: 'You will be quick to observe that the Ruhr

[37] *DBPO* 136 and 136 n.
[38] Milward says: 'During the Schuman Plan negotiations much evidence emerged that the freight rates charged by the railways through the Palatinate were highly discriminatory': Milward (1984) 379.

document is full of sound and fury but signifying practically nothing . . . one of the principal problems has been to find relatively harmless things for the "Authority" to do.'[39] There seems to have been no appreciation of the implications for France, and therefore for French policy, of such an attitude to the establishment of the IAR. The policy was supported by the UK in subservience to Washington. It ensured that the IAR could not satisfy French ambitions for control of the Ruhr resources.

A specific factor provoking the Schuman Plan was Law 75 which had been promulgated in November 1948 by the commanders of the Anglo-American Bizone in Germany despite French opposition.[40] Once more French anxieties had counted for nothing as against American imperatives. De Gaulle called it 'the gravest decision yet taken in the twentieth century'.[41] By Law 75, the decision as to the future ownership, and therefore structure, of the Ruhr industries was left to the Germans. The significance of the Law was greatly enhanced by the emergence of the German state in September 1949. It could well be followed by an increase in the present ceiling of 11.1 million tons on German steel production. The French justifiably saw it as releasing, yet further, Allied control over the Ruhr industries. There were those in France whose nightmares were even more frightening. The Ruhr industries might be nationalized under the control of the new German state and thereby would be established what *The Times*'s diplomatic correspondent called 'an excessive economic power in the hands of the German government'.[42] The Schuman Plan was the answer. Schuman's hope was that French anxiety about Law 75 could be overcome if, under the Schuman Plan, the Ruhr industries were under the control of, and could be bound by, a High Authority. Ownership would seem less important, especially if there was an effective competition policy.

The control of Ruhr coal and steel had been the subject of debate for decades. As long before as 1924 Adenauer had thought that prospects for European peace might be improved by joint management of the coal, iron, and steel industries of the Rhineland, eastern France and

---

[39] Milward (1984) 157.   [40] Law 75 was later reissued as Law 27.
[41] Milward (1984) 153.
[42] *The Times*, 11 May 1950. Although Dr Adenauer was unlikely to wish to nationalize the Ruhr industries, there were political circumstances, involving the need for coalition between the Christian Democrats and Social Democrats in North Rhine-Westphalia, which could require, as a compromise, some nationalization. This possibility was examined in an article entitled 'The Ruhr on the Eve of the Schuman Plan' in *The Economist*, 20 May 1950.

Lorraine.[43] During the debate on the Schuman Plan in the House of Commons, Robert Boothby referred to a visit he made to the Ruhr in 1928:

These industrialists, including Fritz Thyssen, expounded to me a plan for a European coal, iron and steel consortium, under British leadership. They said that in the modern world this would have to be under political control and that the problem would, therefore, have to be approached at the political level. They also said that it was the only hope of avoiding a Second World War.[44]

As Boothby himself made clear, this would have been an agreement on markets and prices. But the very fact that there had been pre-war cartels should have focused attention on the possibility that coal and steel might be the subject of some continental initiative and that, unlike other sectors of industrial activity, the interests of the countries of continental Europe might coincide sufficiently to make some kind of agreement possible.

After the war there was a proliferation of ideas for various forms of international control of the Ruhr. The European Congress at The Hague in May 1948 recommended an international authority for the Ruhr. It was perfectly true, as Stikker had remarked to Hall-Patch, that the French had been 'fiddling' for years with the ideas behind the Schuman Plan. A Quai d'Orsay memorandum of 30 November 1948 proposed a European pool, incorporating French and German steel production. The memorandum emphasized that the arrangements would include equality between France and Germany and that the offer should be made while France was the stronger partner.[45]

The German interest was that international control of the Ruhr should not be discriminatory. If the Ruhr industries were to be controlled so should the rest of European heavy industry. In February 1948 discussions took place between Massigli and Lewis Douglas, US Ambassador in London. Out of them emerged the idea of an international regime which, without discrimination against Germany, would place the resources of the Ruhr at the disposal of Europe. Massigli describes this as a 'sketch' of the Schuman Plan though with the difference that the Authority would have been international not supranational. He also points out how ideas of this kind were being canvassed on all sides.[46] On 1 January 1949 Dr Karl Arnold, the Minister President of North Rhine-Westphalia and a member of Dr Adenauer's party, advocated the

---

[43] Milward (1992) 330.   [44] HC Debs. 27 June 1950, col. 2114.
[45] Poidevin, *Schuman* (1986) 224.   [46] Massigli 192–3.

industrial reorganization of Western Europe on the basis of a 'common economic pool' to which France (especially Lorraine), the Saar, Belgium, and Luxembourg could all contribute. This was as an alternative to the IAR which, even if powerless, German opinion resented as being one-sided. John McCloy, the American High Commissioner in Germany, and a friend of Jean Monnet, endorsed the idea and suggested the inclusion of British heavy industry within its scope though in this he was expressing a personal view, not a statement of United States policy.[47] *The Times* and the *Manchester Guardian* each, in their initial reactions to the announcement of the Schuman Plan, reminded their readers editorially of Arnold's proposal.[48] In April 1949 Adenauer proposed a European coal and steel organization.[49] Massigli records that these ideas were judged in Paris to be acceptable in principle but premature.[50]

In December 1949 the Economic Committee of the Council of Europe, under the influence of the French socialist André Philip, called for a public authority for the European steel industry, to advise on investment, prices, and production as the first step to similar sectoral planning in coal, electricity, and transport.[51] Harold Macmillan recalls how, months before the Schuman announcement, he had advocated a form of control of German heavy industry that was not invidious, in other words it would apply equally to the coal, iron, and steel industries of Belgium, Holland, Luxembourg, France, Italy, and Britain.[52] In March 1950 the problems of international control of the heavy industry of all Western Europe were discussed by a study group convened by the International Socialist Conference at Witten in the Ruhr. Wilfred Fienburgh, a leading back-bench Labour MP and a supporter of steel nationalization, was a participant in the Witten conference.[53] He concluded from its deliberations that, although it would not be as effective as international control operating in a socialist Western Europe, 'international control of basic industries is possible . . . between socialist and capitalist countries'

---

[47] Massigli 195. *Manchester Guardian*, 11 May 1950. See also Poidevin (1986) 251.

[48] *The Times* and *Manchester Guardian*, 11 May 1950. North Rhine-Westphalia included the Ruhr. According to Sir Frank Roberts, Karl Arnold was one of Bevin's 'favourites': Roberts 35.

[49] Young (1984) 145–6.

[50] Massigli 193.

[51] Milward (1984) 394–5. Philip had already presented his ideas to a group of French and German parliamentarians in Bernkastel on 26 and 27 Nov. 1949: see Gillingham 223.

[52] Macmillan 186. Massigli refers to Macmillan's ideas at this time: Massigli 194.

[53] Fienburgh argued the case for steel nationalization in W. Fienburgh and R. Everly, *Steel is Power: The Case for Nationalization* (London, 1948).

provided 'first, that each country should run its economy with the object of maintaining full employment, and second, that each country should have control over its own basic industries even though they may be in private hands'.[54] Poidevin recalls that between March 1948 and May 1950 the idea of European co-operation in the field of coal and steel made frequent appearances in the columns of the French Press.[55]

In political circles in Europe there was a widespread fear that, left to themselves, the heavy industries of Europe would revive the pre-war cartels. These suspicions were not unreasonable. The indications were that there had been over-investment in steel in Western Europe. At the beginning of 1950 there was already a surplus of steel in the market, a situation which should have alerted the British government to the possibility that some proposal for rationalization of the steel industry might come forward and that it was likely to come forward from France.[56] France had invested a great deal in the steel industry since the war. According to *The Economist*, France had since the war pressed expansion 'to some extent irrespective of costs'.[57] The French Cabinet's rapid acceptance of Schuman's proposal confirms that it corresponded to ideas that were in the air at the time and had achieved a high level of acceptance.

If the British government had to protest that a French initiative on coal and steel had been sprung upon it, it was only because it had not been listening.

ECONOMIC INTEGRATION AND REGULATED MARKETS

There is no better illustration of British ignorance of continental thinking than the conviction that whereas the British Labour government believed in planning for full employment, the continentals believed in *laissez-faire*. This view found expression in *European Unity*, a Labour

---

[54] Wilfred Fienburgh, *International Control of Basic Industries* (Labour Party: London, Apr. 1950), 7, 6.

[55] Poidevin, *Schuman* (1986) 251.

[56] Milward says: 'When the Western European countries had to present national recovery programmes to CEEC they all incorporated into those plans proposals for a substantial increase in steel output. . . . The American Administration was sternly critical of the programmes, seeing them as mercantilist and nationalistic, inasmuch as each Western European country was interested in maximizing its own output of steel irrespective of the optimum distribution of the industry in Western Europe as a whole': Milward (1984) 362–3.

[57] *The Economist*, 20 May 1950.

Party pamphlet which caused uproar in Europe and America and which will be discussed in Chapter 10. In fact the British government had no monopoly of concern about prospects for employment. European governments had been alerted by the American recession of 1949 to the possibility that liberalization could endanger employment. Although the Continent had emerged relatively unscathed from the American recession, it had caused governments to think about what they could do to avoid becoming victims of another American recession. In March 1950 Robert Marjolin was warning of a serious American recession within the next eighteen months, possibly much sooner.[58] The German government remained committed to liberalization. But some other European governments and politicians, and a variety of vested interests, were looking for preferable alternatives to unregulated integration and trade liberalization. While, in 1949 and 1950, ideas for European economic integration were bubbling up all over Europe, there was increasing insistence that the process could not be left to market forces alone, that integration needed to be regulated and that there were dangers, especially to employment, in the unregulated trade liberalization then in vogue under American inspiration.

France's proposal, in November 1949, of an association with Italy and Benelux was intended to harmonize major industrial sectors in the five economies. The French were looking for sectoral integration rather than trade liberalization. Quotas and quantity controls on trade were to be removed but not tariffs. A European Investment Bank was to be created and capital transactions were gradually to be freed. There was to be a common agricultural policy. Despite the political and industrial difficulties it would cause, the inclusion of West Germany was contemplated but without commitment to it.[59] Both France and Germany were highly protectionist in their attitude to their agricultural industries. In November 1949 the French *Confédération Générale de l'Agriculture* (*CGA*) expressed its opposition to the liberalization of trade in agricultural products and to any customs union, such as that negotiated with Italy, which did not offer French agriculture improved export opportunities in return for greater access to French markets. As the UK was hostile to the idea of opening its markets freely to French agricultural products, the *CGA* concluded that there was 'only one solution: the opening up to France of another regulated market which imported foodstuffs, namely Germany'.[60]

---

[58] Gaitskell 181.   [59] Milward (1984) 308–9.   [60] Milward (1984) 443.

Dutch foreign economic policy had changed from what Milward describes as the 'firm liberal stance taken after 1945'.[61] The Dutch too were concerned about the implications for employment of uncontrolled trade liberalization. They agreed the sectoral basis proposed by the French but, foreshadowing the Stikker Plan of June 1950, they wanted more in the industrial area; trade liberalization in *European* agriculture; faster removal of quotas and tariffs; protection for Dutch infant industries; and a last attempt to persuade the UK. The Dutch also insisted that Germany must be included. As with the French, a common agricultural policy was becoming a prime Netherlands objective. The Italians and Belgians had their own distinct ideas for European arrangements beneficial to their economies. The Belgian government would fight hard for the protection of Belgian coal when it came to negotiate participation in the Schuman Plan. But, at this stage, the Belgian and Italian governments opposed the sectoral approach and the investment bank.[62]

Thus, even before the Schuman Plan, the idea of sectoral arrangements, including in agriculture, was in debate in France as well as elsewhere in Western Europe.[63] It was beginning to be accepted that if such ideas were to go ahead it might have to be without the UK. This was not the object of continental governments. But they were coming to accept that if nothing could be done with the UK, it might be necessary to act without the UK.

ON BEING TAKEN BY SURPRISE

Given all the indications, the Foreign Office might have done better than to be taken so totally by surprise by the Schuman announcement of 9 May 1950. Having observed the existence of the problem facing France and the centrality in it of the Ruhr industries, the Foreign Office might even have generated ideas of its own in the friendly spirit appropriate to its relations with so close an ally. Yet, to be taken by surprise should not frustrate policy-making. There are many tests of the quality of a policy-making machine. One might be how often it is taken by

---

[61] Ibid. 446.   [62] Ibid. 311–12.

[63] In June 1950 the International Federation of Agricultural Producers met at Saltsjöbaden in Sweden. The French and German delegations agreed on proposals for a Franco-German common market in agriculture, resembling Schuman's proposals for coal and steel: Milward (1984) 444.

surprise. Another would be how it reacts when it is taken by surprise. That is the story that must now unfold. Into the decisions made in London would be incorporated both emotion and reason. The emotion would expose essentially the annoyance, if not more, at being taken by surprise. The reasoning would reflect the great debate that had been in progress in Whitehall since well before the end of the war about the implications of Britain's inevitably reduced status in the world after the war.

4

The Big Questions

The cohesion of this [sterling area] system is a vital element in the maintenance and restoration of economic health to a free world. The United Kingdom is the banker of the sterling area system and has a special responsibility for its health and vigour . . .[1]

As the war drew to an end, there were, for Britain, what R. W. B. Clarke called 'the big questions'. Clarke, a Treasury official of great brilliance and energy, known as Otto because he was tall and looked like a German, had been a *Financial News* journalist. The war had brought him to the Treasury and to the problems of overseas finance. He sparkled ideas, not all of them good or practicable or consistent with what he had argued the previous month or year. But the flood of ideas, as exemplified in his minutes and memoranda, was formidable. His dominance in the Overseas Finance area of the Treasury was such that it was known as the Ottoman empire. Plowden says of him, 'he certainly made the Treasury a brighter and more interesting place'.[2] For Clarke the big questions were economic. But, in the eyes of the government, the first big question was relations with the United States. It was a relationship that was vital for Britain's security as well as for its economy.

A DEFERENTIAL RELATIONSHIP

Britain's post-war overseas policies began with a bleat. President Truman cancelled Lend-Lease. His action was attributed in Britain to inexperience or ill will. Roosevelt, had he lived, would, it was thought, have

---

[1] Sir Roger Makins to Ernest Bevin, 17 June 1950—Notes for debate on Schuman Plan: MS Attlee dep. 102. Makins was Deputy Under-Secretary of State; later Ambassador to Washington, Joint Permanent Secretary to the Treasury, and ennobled as Lord Sherfield.
[2] Plowden 30.

been more understanding. The reality was that American opposition to the continuation of Lend-Lease had built up in Congress. Two days before Roosevelt's death, a measure to kill its use for post-war reconstruction was defeated in the Senate only on the casting vote of Vice-President Truman. Truman was advised that, under the law, he had no option but to do what he did in cancelling Lend-Lease. Lend-Lease had been granted under an Act entitled 'An Act for the defence of the United States'. The war was over. The law had been drawn in the interests primarily of the USA not of the UK, and Truman could not dispense with the law. This incident should have taught all the necessary lessons. There was as much sense complaining about American policy as about the weather. But if the lesson of Lend-Lease was not enough, there was an ever expanding curriculum of educative incidents. Whatever the British people may have thought they deserved, they had acquired no special credit in Washington simply because they had fought from the first to the last day of the war and had made huge and debilitating sacrifices. When Lord Keynes was sent to Washington by the Attlee government to negotiate a grant-in-aid of $6 billion or, at least, an interest-free loan of that amount, he found, contrary to his expectations, that the USA had not become a charitable institution. The intensely difficult negotiations ended with a loan of $3.75 billion at 2 per cent interest repayable over fifty years from 31 December 1951 but also with the concession by the UK of premature commitments to sterling convertibility and to non-discrimination in trade on both of which it was forced to default. British and French views on reparations were treated with disdain by the US Administration and dismissed without benefit of courtesy.[3] The Attlee government would have wished to take a far tougher line with Germany than emerged from the American rethink after the abandonment of the Morgenthau Plan.[4] It would have wanted to ensure that the Ruhr industries, whose private owners were held largely responsible for Germany's policies of aggression, were taken into public ownership so that they could no longer exercise such malign influence over German policy. Although the Ruhr was part of the British zone, the idea of public ownership was abandoned under American pressure. Atomic collaboration with Britain was unilaterally suspended by the American government.

---

[3] See Bullock 663–4.
[4] The Morgenthau Plan was put forward in 1944 by the then US Treasury Secretary, Henry Morgenthau. It proposed the deindustrialization of Germany.

On the other side of the balance sheet was the substantial fact of Marshall Aid. Even there, Britain had its grievances. The Attlee government felt humiliated in being lumped together with continental Europe in the planning of the European Recovery Programme (ERP). The US Administration brushed aside both the UK's wish to be considered a partner in the ERP and its insistence that it was not 'just another European country'.[5] It was stupid to invite the rebuff. The forecasts made by the Treasury of the social consequences if the UK was denied, or denied itself, Marshall Aid horrified the British Cabinet into acceptance. It did summon the courage to resist a series of conditions in the original draft of the bilateral treaty with Washington which required, among other matters, that Britain should stabilize its currency, balance its budget, consult with the US Administration about exchange rate policy, give twelve months' notice of termination of the agreement, and extend most favoured nation treatment to trade with Japan. If, as was claimed, these conditions were an outrage against British sovereignty, so had been the conditions under which the American loan had been accepted two years before. This time, the Attlee government decided to resist. The hope clearly was that the USA and the UK were condemned to agree for political reasons and that therefore a little resistance would not provoke a major breakdown. Robert Hall reflected: 'I sometimes wish that Ministers *would* refuse the aid—it would be very popular and do the country a great deal of good, and people might actually work if they had the prospect of independence in front of them.'[6] There was no serious intention of a breakdown. Strong representations secured wording more consistent with UK pride.[7] But, for a supposedly global power, the dependency was demeaning. American ruthlessness may not have been pretty but the lesson was clear enough and the Attlee government would have done better to learn from it than to recriminate about it.

Marshall Aid had a purpose beyond the economic recovery of the separate nation states of Western Europe, beyond even the protection of democracy against Communism. The Americans knew the answer to Europe's problems. It lay in federation or, at the very least, the closest obtainable economic integration of Western Europe. To achieve that purpose, they would give aid but they would also twist arms. For Britain, European federalism was a sticking point. On this, Britain's policy did not deviate, whatever the pressure. Yet this was the element in American policy that began to have attractions for some in France.

⁵ Bullock 413–14.   ⁶ Hall, 17 June 1948.   ⁷ Plowden 41–3.

Germany, contrary to earlier French hopes, was being allowed to establish a powerful central government. It was likely that, in due course, it
would be allowed to rearm. France was being compelled to abandon its
rougher alternatives for the control of Germany and to find some way
of living with it on a basis of equality. European federation could be the
answer. By the end of 1949, those in France attracted to this idea could
expect the support of the Federal German Republic. Contemporary with
the announcement of the Schuman Plan, the Federal German government had decided to accept the invitation to join the Council of Europe.
It was drawing up a bill through which to secure the agreement of the
Bundestag. Adenauer was saying that he had concluded that 'The co-
operation of Europe on a federalistic basis is necessary in the interests
of all European countries, especially the Federal Republic. The Council
of Europe is the beginning of such a co-operation.'[8]

Out of Marshall Aid grew the OEEC which the Americans wished to
endow with executive powers under a Director-General so that it could
become the primary instrument of European economic integration. The
British government, fearing the federalistic implications of American
ideas, wished the OEEC to be a purely intergovernmental organization,
subject in other words to national vetoes, and to deny it executive
powers. On that, at least, much to American disappointment, the UK
won the argument.

The Attlee government tied itself to the USA but, in the circumstances, without enthusiasm. Despite disagreements, it was a deferential
relationship. For British deference to American leadership, there were
three obvious reasons. First, British security was dependent on a continuing American presence in Europe. Secondly, British recovery owed
much to American aid. A third reason was the cost of managing the
British zone in Germany, which included the Ruhr. This made one
more massive demand on the UK's scarce resources at a time when
they were sufficiently strained by the problems it faced in achieving its
own economic recovery. The drain led the British to accept the American invitation issued in the summer of 1946 to unite its zone with that
of the USA. The hope was that this would diminish the cost. Attlee told
the British Cabinet in October 1947 that the drain of dollars to the
Bizone had become a major influence on UK policy.[9] On 17 December
1947 the United States relieved Britain of its bizonal dollar obligations
for the final two months of 1947 and the whole of 1948, at the same

[8] *The Times*, 13 May 1950; Adenauer 258.   [9] Milward (1984) 151.

time reducing those in sterling from one-half to one-quarter of the total.[10] The creation of the Bizone made Britain hostage to American policies for Germany. It implied the abandonment of the intention to take the major Ruhr industries into public ownership. This was a policy to which Bevin had been wedded. It was advocated in the UK even by non-socialist sources.[11] But it was opposed by the Americans and that was enough.[12] By the end of 1947, in face of Soviet intransigence, American policy had hardened in favour of rebuilding a West German state, with a market economy, and the UK was following on behind.

On these three substantial grounds the deference was understandable. It was reinforced when British ministers and officials visited Washington and sensed there the power that the British government knew it no longer possessed. Power attracts, it wins converts, but it also repels. In the recesses of Whitehall, officials and even ministers murmured against their subservient role. Envy of the superpower on which the UK found itself so dependent was combined with irritation at the naïvety of so much American policy, for example its fetish for a European federation for which there was little evident European demand, and its pressure for non-discrimination in trade when the post-war dollar shortage made it impossible. The envy and the irritation felt in London were allowed to become an obstacle to constructive thought about the European future. The US Administration saw post-war Britain as it really was, diminished in power, and consequently in influence. Britain's role, it believed, was now in Europe. In Europe, it believed, Britain could still exercise influence. For that, it still had the means and the reputation. In the early post-war years it pressed for UK leadership in Europe as a guarantee against the dilution of the Atlantic relationship by neutralist or third force ideas popular with some European politicians. It was disappointed at Britain's refusal of its allocated role. Whenever the USA is disappointed, it is inclined to reach for its box of threats. The private thoughts and communications of US officials, which demonstrated intense impatience and irritation with their wartime ally, were

---

[10] Gillingham 128–9.

[11] Gillingham says: 'The nationalization of heavy industry, though official policy, amounted to little more than an attempt to head off domestic critics; never, certainly, would the British seriously encourage German efforts to socialize production:' Gillingham 127. But it was widely supported in the UK outside government circles. See Bevin, HC Debs. 2 Feb. and 22 Oct. 1946; *The Economist* of 6 Apr. 1946; the *Observer* of 14 Apr. 1946. See also Bullock 343, 372, and 435–6.

[12] Law 75, by placing the decision in the hands of the German authorities, in theory revived the possibility of nationalization. There was certainly still some fear of it in government circles in France.

not always translated into impatient and irritable action. The US Administration did consider what threats could be used to bring the UK into line.[13] It wisely decided that their use might be counter-productive.

But though Washington, in the end, took a relaxed attitude towards British recalcitrance, there was a price to pay. While the US Administration was looking to the UK for leadership in Europe, London had a bargaining position. When, in default of Britain, France emerged as the USA's favoured partner in the reconstruction of Europe, the UK inevitably lost bargaining strength. France, at least equally dependent for its security on the American presence, and, in the early post-war years, at least equally dependent on Marshall Aid, has never accepted deference to American policy as the necessary consequence. But then France, with mounting self-confidence as economic recovery came, has exploited its key role in the construction of Europe. It was an opportunity that Britain denied itself.

THE BIG QUESTIONS FACING THE ECONOMY

Though it had not been invaded, the war had left Britain economically impoverished. Its overseas assets had been devastated. Before the war it had relied on the income from these to cover a sizeable proportion of its imports.[14] Invisible income had suffered also from the loss of shipping during the submarine war in the Atlantic. Exports had been allowed to decline in order that manpower could be moved to war production and the services. The USA had also insisted that Lend-Lease must not be used in aid of British exports. By 1945 they were making only a fraction of their pre-war contribution. Large debts had been accumulated in the form of sterling balances.[15] Britain, supposedly

---

[13] In the summer of 1948, influenced by Averell Harriman and Paul Hoffman to find ways of bringing pressure on the UK, the State Department cabled Lewis Douglas in London for advice. 'We consider the solution may well involve steps on our part affecting the whole range of US–UK relations beyond those arising directly from ERP': Milward (1984) 184–5.

[14] Sales of investments abroad exceeded £1,000m.: Cairncross 49.

[15] At the end of the war the UK's short-term liabilities to foreign banks and official holders was nearly £3,500m. against gold and dollar reserves of just over £600m: Cairncross 47. See also Harrod 587. In a sense, Dalton claimed, Lend-Lease had made the situation worse. 'And this distortion was deliberately worsened by Lend-Lease itself. We deliberately forced down our exports to the bare minimum. Why? To make munitions . . . to man the Navy, the Army and the Air Force': HC Debs. 12 Dec. 1945, col. 423. Lend-Lease had been granted on condition that Britain neglect exports and transfer yet more men into the services and into war production. See Alan P. Dobson, 'The Export White Paper, 10 September 1941', *Economic History Review*, 2nd ser., 39/1 (Feb. 1986).

victorious in war, had become the world's largest debtor. British industry was run down due to lack of investment. At best, recovery would
be a long and difficult process. Yet, at the same time, the British Labour government insisted not merely on creating the Welfare State
promised at the 1945 general election but on retaining a global role
deploying large military forces not just in Europe but throughout the
world. The policy was costly not only in foreign exchange but in diverting Britain's resources of labour from its principal economic priority,
building up its exports.

In the economic field, the first big question defined by Otto Clarke
in 1945 was how to survive in a world in which there would be a severe
dollar shortage. The second was whether Britain should adhere to the
Bretton Woods system elaborated in 1944 by Harry Dexter White of
the US Treasury together with Britain's John Maynard Keynes. Membership of Bretton Woods implied commitments to a fixed rate of exchange against the dollar, and to sterling–dollar current account
convertibility.

For his part, Keynes dismissed the idea of a dollar shortage. 'I do not
think there is any serious risk of an overall shortage of gold and dollars
in the first three years.'[16] He felt able to recommend acceptance by the
British government of the American loan, which he had negotiated, on
the three principal conditions upon which Washington insisted. The
first was that Britain should join the Bretton Woods system at once as
a founder member. The second was that sterling should become convertible into dollars by July 1947, one year after Congress had approved the loan agreement. The third was that Britain should commit
itself not to discriminate in its trade against the dollar. Clarke had been
more sceptical. He thought that there would be a dollar shortage which
would have serious implications for Britain's economy. He thought,
contrary to Keynes, that before Britain committed itself to Bretton
Woods, the sterling exchange rate should be devalued from $4.03 to
about $3.50. He wished to delay negotiations with the Americans for a
major loan until 1947 and therefore to avoid, for the time being, any
British commitment on these big questions. By 1947, he thought, the
nature of the post-war world would be clearer.

Clarke lost the argument. It was Keynes, not Clarke, who won
the ear of the new Labour government with results that Clarke later

[16] Minute from Keynes to Sir Wilfrid Eady, 9 July 1945: Clarke 58, 134. Eady was
Clarke's boss but Clarke did the thinking.

described, with total accuracy, as 'a terrible fiasco'.[17] Britain had accepted all the American conditions. Sterling convertibility had been
introduced, as planned, in July 1947. The American loan, though massive, was then found not to be massive enough to absorb the world's
greed for dollars. The resulting haemorrhage of dollars from the reserves led to the suspension of convertibility under duress six weeks
later. In September 1949 sterling was devalued against the dollar. Britain was still unable to conduct its economic relationships on a non-
discriminatory basis. Non-discrimination was a commitment which sat
uneasily with the practical requirements of the British economy which
were to discriminate wherever possible against dollar supplies.[18] Non-
discrimination proved, as had indeed been forecast, not just impracticable but an absurdity. Otto Clarke wrote on 16 June 1947, in a paper
entitled 'The World Dollar Crisis', 'our commitments under the Anglo-
American Financial Agreement make the whole position worse . . . we
must obviously cut down our imports from the American continent to
the bone. But under non-discrimination, we have to cut down our imports from other sources likewise. This in turn forces them to cut down
their imports from us . . .'[19]

The Americans increasingly accepted discrimination against American supplies as a fact of life especially when they came to perceive the
need for allies against the Soviet threat. They accepted, indeed encouraged, the discrimination against them implied by liberalization of
trade within the OEEC member states.[20] Their acceptance of the realities did not prevent their displaying their grievances officially at every

[17] Clarke 62.

[18] The practical significance of the non-discrimination clause is discussed by Gardner
331 ff. The Agreement did permit discrimination in certain cases. Britain was permitted
to discriminate in favour of its colonies, and to assist countries whose economies had
been disrupted by war—this, presumably, included Western Europe. Non-discrimination
did not apply to British government purchases which represented a major share of Britain's import trade. Some people argued that the Anglo-American Financial Agreement
would compel the UK to cut down on tobacco imports from Rhodesia if it was forced
by dollar shortage to cut imports of Virginia tobacco from the USA. This was probably
not true but the British government did take the step, in Apr. 1947, of notifying Washington that it proposed to authorize such discrimination. It was certainly not discriminatory to buy more cheaply than was possible in the USA if goods of appropriate quality
were available from non-dollar sources.

[19] Clarke, Document 20, 16 June 1947.

[20] The liberalization covered the OEEC countries and their dependent territories. There
was objection from both the USA and Canada when there was a proposal from Australia
and New Zealand that they should be allowed the benefits of liberalization within the
OEEC. The proposal embarrassed the British government which was asked to press it
within the OEEC. See FO 371/87141.

opportunity. Their attitude reinforced the feeling in government circles in London, official as well as ministerial, that Washington did not understand, and was constantly pressing on Britain policies that were not merely self-interested but impracticable given Britain's problems. But, so far as non-discrimination was concerned, the Americans were only pressing a policy that the UK had accepted in 1945.

Another big question was how to ensure full employment. After the miseries of the 1930s, and the assurances given by both the major political parties at two general elections, the maintenance of full employment was a priority. The Labour Party hoped that Keynes had found the secret of full employment. That hope had turned many of them, such as John Strachey, away from Marxism.[21] The Labour Party and government did not want the maintenance of full employment in the UK to be put in peril by arrangements with other countries which were less committed to full employment. There was continuing concern after 1945 whether full employment could really be guaranteed. Robert Hall wrote in 1963: 'before 1951, it was a matter of constant concern to the Labour Government whether they could maintain full employment at all: and it was not generally recognized for several years after the Conservative Government came to power, that they would and could follow their predecessors in this respect . . .'[22] The anxiety whether full employment could be sustained increased after experience of the American recession of 1948–9 which forced Britain into devaluation. Britain put itself on guard lest foreign entanglements imperilled one of the Labour government's supposed achievements, full employment.

THE DOLLAR SHORTAGE

The problem of dollar shortage had been partly relieved by the 1946 American loan and, subsequently, by Marshall Aid. But there was still a dollar shortage because of the continuing difficulty experienced by the non-dollar world in earning dollars. The USA was a source of essential supplies. Apart from raw materials, there was not much it needed to import. There was disagreement between the USA and the UK as to the source of the dollar shortage. The Americans attributed it to the failure of Europe to produce. European economic integration

---

[21] Strachey, 'Tasks and Achievements of British Labour', in Crossman 182.
[22] Robert Hall, Foreword in Dow, p. xv.

was, for them, a major part of the solution. The British attributed the shortage to the collapse, as a result of the war, of the old triangular pattern of international settlements. Because the war had reduced the dollar-earning capacity of the Far East, neither Britain nor continental Europe were able to offset their dollar deficits with surpluses earned in the Far East. Until this situation was rectified there would be no end to dollar shortage and British policy would have to be operated within that context whether the Americans liked it or not. European economic integration would not help.[23]

One of the problems for Britain was that Washington, and American business, wished to destroy the sterling area. The sterling area actually operated convertibility but it was based on sterling which was not freely convertible into dollars. It was protected by a system of imperial preferences. This combination of imperial preference with a currency not freely convertible into dollars was attacked in Washington as an obstacle to American trade. The official leading for the State Department in the negotiations over the American loan had been William L. Clayton, Under-Secretary of State. As the historian of Marshall Aid puts it, 'Clayton had an aversion that bordered on mania when it came to the sterling area and the system of imperial preferences.'[24] In defending, in December 1945, that part of the American loan agreement which imposed a policy of non-discrimination, Sir Stafford Cripps, President of the Board of Trade, had told the House of Commons:

We have ... in the course of arriving at the terms of this document, done our utmost to see that our particular interests as a country are not prejudiced unduly, that our special relationships within the Commonwealth and Empire are not affected seriously, and that our own domestic decisions as regards national planning of our agriculture and industry are not made too difficult; but we have had also to meet the quite different views and requirements of the United States of America arising out of their own political theories and their own industrial necessities.[25]

Hugh Dalton, Chancellor of the Exchequer 1945–7, put it more bluntly, in his memoirs: 'We fancied that they wished, in effect, to take over the sterling area themselves, and make it a commercial dependency, or colony, of the United States ...'[26]

Both the sterling area and imperial preference had become major targets of American policy. British weakness, after a war in which

[23] Newton (July 1985).   [24] Hogan 50.
[25] HC Debs. 12 Dec. 1945, col. 482.   [26] Dalton (1962) 82.

Britain had made major sacrifices including of overseas assets, was perceived across the Atlantic as providing American business with an unparalleled opportunity to undermine the sterling area and the system of imperial preference and any other position of commercial advantage that the UK had secured over the years and had managed to retain despite the war. It was all to be done on the great principle of free multilateral trade. Britain might resent the pressure. The key question was how long it could resist it and how long, indeed, Commonwealth countries would find it in their interest to help Britain to resist it.

The dollar shortage was a factor in virtually every policy decision the Labour government had to make. In the Treasury a variety of schemes were formulated for freeing Britain from its consequences. One idea was that Britain should federate with the USA. That would certainly solve the dollar problem. Otto Clarke advised Sir Edward Bridges, Permanent Secretary to the Treasury, that 'The Americans would get great advantage out of it, for we should be a profound stabilising influence, and we would give them just what they need to carry out their responsibilities as world leader'.[27] Evidently the British were to be wise and subtle Greeks advising those crude Romans in Washington.[28] Another idea was to form a multilateral non-dollar world by recruiting all the other European colonial empires to the sterling area.[29] From this world, the USA would, of course, be excluded. It would be a form of multilateralism, almost certainly impracticable, but one for which the USA was, in any case, unlikely to be enthusiastic.

THE UK AND MULTILATERALISM

British governments have always, at least in words, been advocates of multilateralism and hence of non-discrimination. They have repudiated discrimination as they have repudiated sin. In its advocacy of multilateralism, as in so much else, the UK echoed the USA. Because of its advocacy of multilateralism, the UK was the more willing to accept the American condition of non-discrimination at the time of the American loan. But the discrepancy between British words and British deeds led to criticism from the USA. Britain wished to preserve the sterling area and imperial preference because, in the 1940s and for most

---

[27] Clarke, Document 26, memorandum from Clarke to Bridges, 27 Sept. 1948.

[28] Harold Macmillan later postulated a 'Greek' role for Britain.

[29] See e.g., Clarke, Document 7, circulated by Clarke in June 1945.

of the 1950s, it believed that a world divided by the inconvertibility of sterling and by trade preferences was, for it, a more practical world than a world moving too rapidly towards multilateralism. There could be long arguments between Washington and London about the sources of the dollar shortage. The immediate practical requirement as seen in London was to maintain discrimination against American supplies. There might, one day, be a 'one world' economic system. For the time being there had to be at least two worlds, the dollar world and the sterling world. Sterling was at the time the currency in which about 50 per cent of the world's visible and invisible trade was being conducted. Scott Newton writes: 'By running the sterling area as a discriminatory bloc, the British were . . . able to sustain multilateralism throughout the Commonwealth and Empire and insulate themselves against the deflationary pressures of the dollar shortage.'[30] By 1950 it was perfectly clear that anything that could be described as multilateralism or non-discrimination was decades off. As a first step, multilateralism would require the end of the dollar shortage, and convertibility not just of sterling but of the other principal currencies. Ideally, it would require the abolition of exchange control. Even four decades later, multilateralism would still be subject to numerous significant distortions. In 1950 it might be a lodestar. It was not a practical policy.

In the Labour government there were three young economists, Hugh Gaitskell, Douglas Jay, and Harold Wilson. Although Wilson was in the Cabinet and Gaitskell was not, the most influential of the three by the spring of 1950 was already Gaitskell.[31] This was attributable to the leading role that he had played in the summer of 1949 in persuading the Chancellor of the Exchequer, Sir Stafford Cripps, and the other leading members of the government of the necessity of a sterling devaluation. In February 1950 Gaitskell was appointed Minister of State for Economic Affairs to assist Cripps who was unwell. He was allocated within the Treasury responsibility for overseas financial policy. Even as a lodestar, Hugh Gaitskell had his doubts about multilateralism, doubts shared by his two economist colleagues. Four months after the Schuman Plan announcement, Gaitskell would be Chancellor of the Exchequer.

Robert Hall wrote a 'think-piece' entitled 'Note on Integration', the final version of which is dated 5 January 1950. Hall, not a permanent civil servant, had been one of the earliest in Whitehall to see the

---

[30] Newton (May 1985) 172.
[31] Wilson was President of the Board of Trade, Douglas Jay was Economic, then Financial, Secretary to the Treasury.

necessity of devaluation. He had considerable influence on policy. He wrote:

There is, of course, a long-standing illogicality in American views. . . . For historical reasons they have a certain innate hostility to the Empire; they very much disliked the Ottawa Agreements for Imperial preference: and they wrote into the Loan Agreement a prohibition against 'discrimination arising from the so-called sterling area dollar pool'. On the other hand, there is some evidence that they want a united Europe, partly to relieve them of some of the calls now made upon them, and that they think this can only be a success with the participation of the U.K. Thus they sometimes seem to urge us into courses in Europe to which they object strongly when we adopt them elsewhere, although by and large, we are more complementary and therefore *prima facie* more suitable for integration, with Commonwealth countries than with most European countries.[32]

The inconsistency to which Robert Hall referred lay between the American advocacy of multilateralism on the one hand and their acceptance, on the other, that European economic integration, for which they were pressing, might result in discrimination against them. But a comparable inconsistency existed in British policy with its advocacy of multilateralism on the one hand and its attachment to the sterling area, sterling inconvertibility, and imperial preference, on the other.[33] Hall went on to suggest: 'A debating point which we might make would be to extend all these arguments to the world as a whole and to say that we did not want to reach any agreements with Europe which would in any way prejudice the reaching of the "one world" which the US want.' However, he quickly added: 'While the US would be sensitive to this argument it is doubtful whether we would in reality attach much importance to it.'[34]

It was in fact an argument to which the USA was likely to attach no greater importance than would the UK. Unlike Hall, the Americans did not seem to find their attitude at all illogical. They pushed for European integration for political as well as economic reasons. They wanted a united Europe as an ally in the cold war and as an answer to the German problem. In so far as they saw economic reasons for European

---

[32] FO 371/87136. The purpose of the paper was to assist the British Embassy in Washington in countering American criticism of UK policy.

[33] Geoffrey Warner draws attention to Bevin's fear in Jan. 1947 that *gradual* deepening of Anglo-European economic co-operation might be held to be inconsistent with the undertaking not to engage in discrimination against US supplies: Warner 64.

[34] FO 371/87136.

integration it was because they believed, on the model of the USA itself, that it would help European economic recovery even if there was discrimination against the USA. The fact that the US Administration was prepared to accept discrimination against American supplies in order to achieve a great political objective like European unity in no way implied that it would as willingly tolerate the discrimination implicit in imperial preference for the greater advantage of a Britain standing apart from Europe.

The hope that American pressure on the sterling area and imperial preference could be resisted was encouraged by illusions among officials in Whitehall. In his 'think-piece', Robert Hall added that though 'temperamentally' against the Commonwealth, 'It is probable that the more responsible officials in Washington, and a certain section of public opinion in the U.S., fully accept the need for a strong British Commonwealth and indeed believe that if the world is ever to get back to a single trading currency it will have to be sterling'.[35] Nor, in their comments, did other officials dissent from this gross overestimate of the support that was to be expected from Washington for the role of sterling on economic grounds. If, in the end, the U.S.A. was ready to leave the sterling area to disintegrate under its own centrifugal pressures, it was only because of the imperatives of the cold war and because American officials came to realize that there were policy priorities higher than destroying the sterling area.

It would be difficult be to improve on Robert Hall's summary of Britain's position on multilateralism. It clearly demonstrated the practical limits on British enthusiasm:

Our primary objective is to find a system which will give a high and stable level of trade ('high' meaning as high as is compatible with mutual advantage) but which will not expose us to the risk of losing gold or dollars. Unfortunately our position is somewhat vulnerable owing (a) to the large amount of sterling outstanding in the world as a whole; (b) to the fact that sterling can in fact be converted into dollars, either directly if it can find its way into an account with a ceiling, or indirectly through a variety of 'cheap sterling' transactions.

Thus there are dangers both that other countries will be able to lay their hands on sterling, which we would like to see immobilised, and that they will try to increase their sterling balances by direct trade with us in the hope of turning them into dollars. We have already gone far towards liberalisation and could not contemplate going any further unless other countries will in fact pursue the same policies. We do not try to earn gold or dollars from any OEEC

[35] FO 371/87136.

country and we are not willing that they should be able to do this from us. We think that we are able and willing to carry out our undertakings and we want to be confident that other countries will do the same. Thus we do not want to go too far until we can see what our surroundings will be like.

This led to Hall's conclusion: 'we are most reluctant to be committed to any rigid set of undertakings going into the distant future, as we cannot yet see the shape of that future.'[36] In other words, at that stage, Hall did not want a multilateral system at all or even commitments about the distant future.

In his 'think-piece', Robert Hall drew a distinction between the American and European attitudes to freedom of trade:

Most countries put obstacles in the way of the free movement of goods, capital and labour because they fear that if they do not do so, they will have to make painful adjustments of a general or particular kind to their economic system. This conflict should always be borne in mind. In the U.S.A. thought on the whole has laid more stress on freedom of movement than on stability. Though they have always been ready in practice to protect or subsidise their own industries when these have been threatened by external competition, they consistently press other countries towards freedom of external trade. But at any rate since 1914, most other countries have moved increasingly towards stability as an objective, at the expense of freedom of trade (though it cannot be said that they secured much stability before the war, and the position today is very precarious).[37]

E. A. Radice of the Foreign Office commented on 2 February 1950 on Hall's paper:

I might start by taking up the remark in . . . Mr Hall's note that in the U.S.A. more stress is laid on freedom of movement than on stability. Now this may be true in the broad sense but it is arguable that from the point of view of foreign countries the internal economic measures taken by the U.S. are extremely nationalistic, and have done great injury to other countries. Here I refer not to the tariffs but to the vast programme of agricultural price support which, though no doubt necessary in the interests of internal American stability, have probably done foreign countries and this country in particular more harm than anything which the high tariffs of the Hoover period ever did. The calculations on this subject are difficult but I wonder what the dollar balance of the OEEC countries in 1950/51 would look like if there was no price support programme in the U.S. My point is that for foreign consumption the Americans pretend they are Liberals, whereas in fact they are just as anxious to secure stability at

[36] FO 371/87136.   [37] Ibid.

home as any of the European countries. The peculiarity of the American position is that their policy on ensuring the welfare state for the Middle Western and Southern supporters of the present Democratic regime forces foreign countries to pay excessively high prices for American products because the U.S. is in a monopoly position or nearly so as regards so many crops. In this country, on the other hand, except in the case of coal the policies of the welfare state and full employment tend to turn the terms of trade against us.[38]

There was a dinner in Paris on 25 March 1950, at which Hugh Gaitskell was the host and at which the guests included Averell Harriman and Milton Katz from the USA, Robert Marjolin, Secretary-General of the OEEC, and Dirk Stikker, Foreign Minister of the Netherlands.[39] According to Gaitskell's diary, Edmund Hall-Patch

weigh[ed] in with a reminder of the violent issue of dollar viability. . . . If the Americans had the right to tell us not to discriminate, we must have the right to remind them of their responsibilities in the matter of imports policy. A position in which we were suppliants and they tried to bully, or bribe us into doing things which we did not believe to be sound, or even practicable, was wrong.[40]

If Radice had referred to tariffs, he might have said something like the *Financial Times* was to say editorially on 30 May 1950:

The American tariff—both its size and its method of administration—remains a serious obstacle to European exporters, in spite of the reductions that have been made in individual duties in recent years. And it is, as the Economic Commission for Europe pointed out in its annual report last week, precisely in those items where the European competitive position is naturally strongest that the tariffs have their maximum effect.

A CONTEST OF DEBATING POINTS

Eric Berthoud, Assistant Under-Secretary of State in the Foreign Office, reported to Sir Roger Makins on an official meeting on the Stikker Plan, one of the plans emerging on the Continent for a regulated rather than an unregulated liberalization of European trade: 'The one important

---

[38] FO 371/87136. As indicated in Ch. 3 above, it was perfectly true that the British, in practising dual pricing, were doing with coal exactly what Mr Radice was accusing the Americans of doing with agricultural products.

[39] Katz was General Counsel at the Economic Co-operation Administration (ECA) in Paris.

[40] Gaitskell 180–1.

point which was made by Mr Robert Hall and others was that if we brandish our keenness on the multilateral world wide approach too much as a reason for opposing closer European co-operation, there is a risk that we may be forced too quickly towards convertibility etc.'[41]

There was thus always a danger that Britain would be hoist by its own hypocritical petard. It would be the UK that would be caught out in a contest of debating points, advocating multilateralism, denouncing European integration as inconsistent with multilateralism, while itself practising discrimination. It did not actually do much good to trap the Americans in a comparable hypocrisy. They too said one thing and practised another. But the USA was too powerful to be troubled by academic debating points. It was easy to point the contrast between American words and American deeds but it did not resolve any British problems.

The UK was not wrong at that time in its practical preference for a divided world. It had severe problems with the balance of payments and overseas holdings of sterling. In 1950 the balance of payments was improving following devaluation and the resulting surplus led to the formal end of Marshall Aid to the UK on 1 January 1951. Whether there had been a permanent transformation in the UK's balance of payments position was less certain. In that there was little confidence at the beginning of 1950. While it was not wrong to prefer a divided world for the time being, what was wrong was that the UK appeared to want its cake and yet to eat it, to advocate global solutions and yet to live in a divided world. It preferred to talk as an exponent of one world. It thereby hoped to deny Washington the moral superiority which belongs to champions of multilateralism. But it was well aware of the realities of its economic situation. The British insistence on preaching multilateralism while practising discrimination, together with resentment in Whitehall at American pressure and American hypocrisy, would, in due course, play their part in deflecting the British government from sober appraisal of the Schuman Plan.

[41] FO 371/87161, memorandum of 30 June 1950. The Stikker Plan is discussed in Ch. 13 below.

5

The Big Questions and Europe

It was already clear ... that the Brussels Treaty and the OEEC
were not enough. Western Europe, with the United Kingdom, was
not strong enough to stand alone. ... Hence the negotiation of
the Atlantic Pact and the conception of an Atlantic Community
of Brotherhood. Where, in this chain of endeavour, which His
Majesty's Government did more than any other country in Europe
to forge, is the isolation and lack of interest in Europe with which
we are charged?[1]

THE BIG CHOICES

The big questions dictated the priorities among Britain's various overseas relationships. There were three inescapable relationships. First,
there was the Commonwealth and Empire, of which the UK could
claim to be the centre. Then there was the USA to which Britain felt
bound by alliance in war, shared language, and democratic ethos, as
well as by a supposedly special relationship. Last, and certainly least,
was Europe, the continent of which, geographically, Britain was part.
The casualty of the early post-war years was the wartime alliance with
the Soviet Union. In evaluating the three continuing relationships, there
were two criteria. The first was security. The second was economic
recovery. It fell to the Attlee government to make this evaluation. The
outcome was hard-headed on questions of security, assiduous in exploiting relationships with the USA and the Commonwealth, but ambivalent on Europe. For reasons of security, there was no escaping
involvement with Europe. The economic arguments, on the other hand,
pointed persuasively in a different direction, towards priority for Britain's links with the Commonwealth and the USA.

All countries have global interests in the sense that these days all

---

[1] Sir Roger Makins to Ernest Bevin, 17 June 1950—Notes for debate on Schuman
Plan: MS Attlee dep. 102.

countries may be seriously affected by events far away. The UK's claim not just to have global interests but to be a global power was based on its links with both the self-governing and not yet self-governing countries of the Commonwealth. Many of them had rallied to the support of the UK during the most difficult years of the war. How far, once the war was over, this was still a source of strength was less clear. The white dominions would find their own path in the world. Though there were still benefits to be derived from the sterling area, Australia and New Zealand knew that their own security had been guaranteed far more by American entry into the war after Pearl Harbor than by anything a remote Britain could do to help. Independence had been achieved by India, Pakistan, Burma, and Ceylon as early as 1947. Others, not yet independent, could not be denied it indefinitely though this was not yet clearly perceived in London where dreams of empire continued to influence policy. Despite its mountain of diplomatic exchanges and the survival of the sterling area, there was a danger that the Commonwealth would become a source of illusions rather than of power.

The Conservative Party's sense of priority did not differ from that of the government. Even that most 'European' of British statesmen, Harold Macmillan, who, as Prime Minister a decade later, would commence Britain's fight back for a role in Europe, knew in 1950 that for Britain the Empire must come first. 'The Empire must always have first preference for us: Europe must come second in a specially favoured position.'[2] Everyone who made such statements had at the back of their minds the further thought that, owing to the demands of security and economic recovery, the Empire must share first place with the USA which had emerged from the war unquestionably the greatest power on earth, militarily and economically. As for the continent of Europe, Britain's relations with it would be a favour conferred rather than received.

The ambivalence towards Europe displayed by the British government was certainly shared by the British people. They had had their fill of Europe. Twice in a lifetime the protection of British independence and European liberty had imposed a heavy price in lives and treasure. The temptation, having survived the war with the essential help of the USA and the USSR, was to retreat behind the moat. That temptation was particularly strong among returning servicemen. It was certainly shared by this author.[3] In his Reith Lectures of 1954, Sir Oliver Franks

---

[2] In an article in the *Manchester Dispatch*, 11 Oct. 1950, quoted in Horne 329.

[3] Lieutenant Edmund Dell, RA (Antitank) received early demobilization in Nov. 1945 in order to return to complete his degree at Oxford University.

said of 'what has been happening in Europe' that 'there is no subject of absolutely first class importance to Britain on which the great majority of the British people have thought less and cared less'.[4] Servicemen had voted overwhelmingly for a Labour government. The programme on which the new Labour government had been elected was domestic. Certainly there was the aftermath of war to settle. There were penalties to be extracted from the aggressors. There were peace treaties to negotiate and sign. As the years passed, new external menaces would develop. But the priority was recovery and prosperity at home. It was by that criterion that the new government would be judged, not by its thoughts on Europe.[5]

As Peter Hennessy has perceptively observed, another barrier between Britain and the continent of Europe was a suspicion of the Catholicism shared by so many of the continental advocates of European integration.[6] Stikker recalls: 'Adenauer of Germany, Schuman of France, Alcide de Gasperi of Italy, [Paul] van Zeeland of Belgium, and [Joseph] Bech of Luxemburg were in charge of foreign policy when as six we started the European Coal and Steel Community and the European Defence Community. I was the only Protestant in this group.'[7] Catholicism was regarded by many in the Labour Party as the epitome of reaction. It entered into the assessment of personalities. The diary of Kenneth Younger, serving at the time as Minister of State and deputy to Ernest Bevin at the Foreign Office, is of interest on this point as on many others. He says of Robert Schuman that 'he is a very attractive person, and politically good in many ways. I would not however pin too much faith to him as he is an odd personality with too much of the mystic for my liking. A bachelor and a very devout catholic who is said to be very much under the influence of the priests.'[8] Such an appraisal did not encourage a warm reception in the Labour Party of any plan carrying Schuman's name.

In the early years after the war Bevin believed that any steps leading to Western European integration, and therefore to the division of Europe into two opposing camps, would inevitably increase Soviet suspicions of Western intentions.[9] He did not want to do anything that

[4] Franks 38.
[5] One returning serviceman who did not switch Europe off was a certain Edward Heath who, in his maiden speech in the House of Commons in 1950, on the Schuman Plan, showed a strong commitment to European unity.
[6] Hennessy 396.   [7] Stikker 177.
[8] Younger's diary, 14 May 1950. For Harold Macmillan, 'Robert Schuman was a man of remarkable moral and intellectual power': Macmillan 186.
[9] Warner 62.

would exacerbate an increasingly difficult relationship. But by 1948 the division of Europe was an established fact and Bevin was the last person to ignore that reality. That reality did not, however, appear to turn him towards Europe except where he had no choice, in matters of security. Although he dallied with a variety of ideas for European economic integration, his priorities were defensive alliances with the UK's immediate neighbours and an American commitment to the defence of Europe.

A *rapprochement* with Germany did not figure. The survival of Britain as an independent nation had, in the course of thirty years, twice been threatened by Germany. Yet an Anglo-German *rapprochement* did not have the priority that it had begun to have for the more creative French politicians and civil servants. Britain had escaped invasion. The British government, nevertheless, had similar fears to those of France— that what the Germans had tried before, they would try again. That they might try again was a frequent theme of Bevin's speeches even when it had become perfectly clear that, if there was a threat, it came from the Soviet Union. As late as January 1948, when he was talking about the prospects of consolidating Western Europe, he nevertheless found it necessary to say: 'We have been in favour of a centralised German Government but not an over-centralised German Government which in our view could be a danger to peace.'[10] Opposition to German rearmament persisted even longer. Yet a British *rapprochement* with the Germans could have constituted a corner-stone in the structure of European security. British neglect of this objective was partly because the UK, not being under the same pressure as the French to find a solution, felt itself freer to nurse its memories of German aggression, partly because the continued presence of American troops in Europe provided a guarantee, partly because it was considered that it was not primarily to Europe that the UK must look for its future politically and economically.

SECURITY

For generations the policy of the Foreign Office had been to ensure that there was no dominating power on the continent of Europe that could threaten the security of the UK. Thus it had long been the policy of the

[10] HC Debs. 22 Jan. 1948, col. 404.

UK to prevent European unity, not to establish it.[11] While a divided Germany fought its civil wars, Britain could safely play balance of power politics in Europe while dissipating its own strength on empire. No question arose that its security as a European island might thereby be imperilled. Europe had lived its history throughout the ages blithely unmindful of the sleeping giant within its limits. The problem emerged, and the awakening came, after Germany's enormous economic and military potential was liberated by the creation of the first Reich in 1871. The unification of Germany by Bismarck was effected by the military defeats inflicted consecutively on Denmark, Austria, and France. Though it was not at once perceived, Britain no longer itself had the weight to balance the scales in Europe once Bismarck had unified Germany.

Germany's own defeat in two world wars was accomplished only after the intervention of the USA. Nothing underlines its military and economic prowess more than the ability of Germany, during the Second World War, without effective European allies, to withstand for so long the military might of the USA and Britain combined as it was with the massive and unexpectedly effective military power of the Soviet Union. Hitler overreached himself but no other European state could even have conceived of undertaking such a programme of conquest. It was Britain that, at its moment of maximum peril in 1940–1, looked across the Atlantic to the majesty and might of an America that had also been its saviour in a previous German war a quarter of a century before. More desperately than in an earlier diplomatic stroke, Britain called once more to the New World to redress the balance of the Old. The New World intervened, with Lend-Lease as well as with military forces. But its intervention was only just in time.

The experience of two wars had demonstrated that Britain and France alone were not an adequate counterweight militarily to Germany. By 1950 it was unquestionable that France and Britain, even together with Germany, now once more divided, would lack the military weight to withstand the Soviet Union. The inescapable conclusion was that there was a need to encompass American forces in the security of Europe far into the future, beyond the limits of human foresight. An American armed presence in Europe would provide a dual guarantee, first against the revival of German nationalism, and secondly against the threat of

---

[11] Sahm quotes an internal Foreign Office memorandum of 30 May 1930 commenting on the Briand Plan of 17 May 1930 for a federal Europe. The language greatly resembles that in which the Schuman Plan was considered: Sahm 18–19.

a Stalinist takeover. While the time might have come, for presentational reasons, to use the language of European unity, the real problem, in the British view, was to persuade the US Administration to undertake this commitment, unprecedented in time of peace, to the security of Western Europe.[12] As a first step Bevin negotiated the Brussels Treaty in alliance with four other European powers.[13] The Treaty, signed 17 March 1948, provided evidence of the collective will of the signatory powers to collaborate in their own defence. In the view of the British government, it was in fact questionable whether, despite the Treaty, the will to defend themselves was present among its continental allies. The resources certainly were not. As an instrument of European security, the Treaty could only be of value as a stepping-stone to the creation of a North Atlantic Treaty Organization (NATO) involving the Americans. The Atlantic Pact establishing NATO was signed on 4 April 1949. For Britain, as for Western Europe, it was a moment of intense relief from many anxieties, anxieties in respect of Germany and not just about the Soviet Union.

The alliance for European security did not inspire in British minds any wish further to deepen the relationship with the Continent. So defeatist was political sentiment in Western Europe that no serious resistance could be expected from continental armies. Soviet forces, it was feared, could roll to the English Channel virtually unhindered. British policy towards Europe was laid down at an informal meeting of senior officials from the Treasury, the Foreign Office, the Dominions Office, and the Board of Trade on 5 January 1949. It was one of a number of such meetings and the assembly was known as the Bridges Committee because it took place under the chairmanship of Sir Edward Bridges, Permanent Secretary to the Treasury. Among those present were two men who were to play key roles in the controversy over the Schuman Plan, Sir Roger Makins and Sir Edwin Plowden. The policy they laid down was subsequently endorsed by the Cabinet. According to the minutes of the meeting, they resolved, 'We hope to secure a special relationship with USA and Canada within [the Atlantic Pact] for in the last resort we cannot rely upon the European countries . . .'[14] If

---

[12] Attlee reports his conversation with Massigli, 7 June 1950: 'I assured him that we were in broad agreement with the conception of building up European unity': *DBPO* 94.

[13] The Brussels Treaty setting up Western European Union bound its five signatories to come to the aid of any of their number if attacked. The five were the UK, France, and Benelux: Bullock 529. The Brussels Treaty did not have only defensive objectives. Its full name was 'Treaty of economic, social and cultural collaboration and collective defence'.

[14] Clarke, Document 27, 5 Jan. 1949.

European countries were not to be relied upon, the UK must be as capable of standing alone against an occupied European continent as it had been when the enemy was Hitler not Stalin. If the UK was too deeply embedded in European political structures, or in the European economy, that ability to stand alone might be prejudiced. The British government hoped that this was an argument with which the US Administration would feel some sympathy. It was a hope that would be disappointed. American military forces had already twice been summoned from the New World to redress the military imbalances in the Old. American policy had various objectives, among which Britain's ability to stand alone figured less prominently than the British government desired. American objectives were, to secure from Europe a significant contribution to its own defence, to deter the Soviet Union, and to control German nationalism. These objectives required the creation of a united and strong Europe, including Britain if possible, without it if necessary.

ECONOMIC RECOVERY

Britain's concentration, in its relations with Europe, on questions of security left an empty space in its European policy. There was a profound reluctance to contemplate European economic integration. The empty space was filled only by Bevin's haphazard meanderings among ideas of Anglo-French union, a European customs union, a European monetary union, and anything else that emerged from time to time in his conversations with European leaders. In the early years after the war, the Foreign Office was speculating about a number of such possibilities. It had not yet been outgunned by the economic departments and it was willing to think the unthinkable. All these ideas were, however, offered with the caution that they needed further study, none was advanced with conviction, some were stillborn at birth, and the remainder died in the economic departments in London.[15]

---

[15] Early in 1947 Bevin proposed a study of a customs union, or other form of closer economic co-operation, with France or with Western Europe including the western zone of Germany. Later that year he proposed a study of a customs union incorporating the Commonwealth and Empire and how it might be related to a European customs union. In Sept. 1947, in a meeting with Ramadier, he volunteered an examination of a closer understanding and even union between the UK and France. None of this came to anything. The Treasury and Board of Trade were opposed and Bevin was himself never sufficiently persuaded to persist: Bullock 358, 462, 487–8.

When these ideas were studied, economic recovery was not found to provide persuasive arguments for deepening relations with Europe. On the contrary, economic integration with Europe was seen as an obstacle to Britain's economic recovery, not a help. Economic policy towards Europe had been defined by the Bridges Committee at the same meeting on 5 January 1949:

5. . . . On merits, there is no attraction for us in long-term economic co-operation with Europe. At best it will be a drain on our resources. At worst, it can seriously damage our economy. . . .

10. Our policy should be to assist Europe to recover as far as we can, we should be prepared to assist the Europeans to earn sterling, we should be prepared to let them have supplies. But the concept must be one of limited liability . . . we should not be prepared to provide them with dollars (except where this suited us in our own interests). Nor can we embark upon measures of 'co-operation' which surrender our sovereignty and which lead us down paths along which there is no return.[16]

A EUROPEAN CUSTOMS UNION

The idea of a European customs union had been canvassed in London in the years after 1945. The arguments against had, however, been found overwhelming. Only a quarter of Britain's trade was with Europe. This fact was taken as a datum rather than as a challenge. The dominating question was how a European customs union, or indeed any form of European economic integration, would help with Britain's dollar problem. It was not Britain alone that suffered a dollar shortage. It was a problem shared by the rest of Europe. But the sharing of the problem did not mean necessarily that there was, for Britain, a European solution. The economic departments considered that almost any form of European economic integration would cost Britain dollars, not help to earn them. There were two principal reasons for this conclusion. The first was that European economic integration might divert British exporters from the markets that should be their priority. They should be exporting to markets that earned Britain dollars, and not be diverted to markets that would pay in currencies not convertible into dollars. That made Europe a market of low priority. Clarke's view on European economic integration in February 1948 was clear enough: 'By this

[16] Clarke, Document 27, 5 Jan. 1949.

token it is arguable that we should not seek to increase *general* intra-European trade at all for it is more likely to hinder than to help the process of readjustment.'[17] As we shall see, there were, in his view, exceptions to this general ban, and one was steel. But here he was stating the general position as he saw it.

The second reason why the dollar problem was, for Britain, a bar to a customs union was that within the union there would be balances to be cleared.[18] The gyrations in the sterling–franc exchange rate demonstrated the fundamental disequilibrium in European trade. It would be expected that the balances would be cleared, after some allowance for reasonable credit, in gold or dollars. If Britain ran a deficit with Europe, or with individual European countries, it could cost gold and dollars. Imbalances in trade within Europe implied that a European customs union would need dollar support if the imbalances were to be cleared in dollars. Britain would prefer to have a share of any dollars available for the purpose to spend directly in North America. In 1948 it appeared unlikely that the USA would be prepared to fund imbalances unless at the sacrifice of imperial preference. In the same minute, Clarke wrote: 'It is . . . necessary that we should develop a European payments system in which settlements are made without gold or dollars passing between European countries. . . . Europe has to find a means . . . of conducting its affairs without the use of gold and dollars.' The impact of such arguments is explicable only because of the magnitude of Britain's dollar problem after the war and the anxiety it had caused two successive Chancellors of the Exchequer, Dalton and Cripps. These arguments turn up again and again in the discussions of British ministers with their American counterparts and, in its way even more significant, in the Labour Party's statement *European Unity*, discussed in Chapter 10, which was published just in time to embarrass the Labour government at the height of the controversy over the Schuman Plan.

Even given the dollar shortage, these arguments against European economic entanglements do not sound totally persuasive. Nor should they have been. They take a somewhat static view of economic management. Larger markets are not normally regarded as a disincentive to investment and economic growth. Trade with Europe should have been given a much higher status than this advice permitted.

---

[17] Clarke, Document 24, minute from Clarke to Sir Wilfrid Eady, 27 Feb. 1948.

[18] In the world as a whole, by definition, exports = imports though the statistics did not show this, there always being a balancing item. What was true of the world, was not true of Europe.

In September 1949 sterling was devalued. The success of the devaluation, and its implications for British policy, were not yet apparent by the time ministers met at the OEEC at the end of October. There was a confrontation between Paul Hoffman, Administrator of the Economic Co-operation Administration, and Stafford Cripps. For the USA, the creation of a single, integrated, European market was the least that could be expected as repayment for American efforts through the ERP to assist economic recovery in Europe. They would have preferred Europe to federate but if that was not, for the moment, a realistic option, then a large open European market became the objective. This is what Hoffman demanded in a speech to the OEEC on 31 October 1949. In his speech he used the word 'integration' thirty-one times. Fiscal, monetary, and investment policies must be anti-inflationary and harmonized. By early 1950 the OEEC should come forward with a plan to achieve these goals and a programme that would take it 'well along the road to economic integration'. He would have liked to say more but he had modified his argument under political pressure from Bevin mediated through Acheson who feared that the original ideas for his speech would have seemed to imply the surrender of national sovereignty by European countries in return for aid.[19] Acheson, though he was a strong supporter of European integration, brought to its problems a more sophisticated mind than was characteristic of the enthusiastic businessmen and economists in the ECA.[20] According to Massigli, the Quai d'Orsay saw Hoffman's speech as an encouragement to France to act independently of Britain.[21]

Acheson, in his personal exchanges with Bevin, provided as his definition of integration, 'the freest possible movement of goods and persons in Europe involving the removal of quantitative restrictions, free movement of funds, and the use of tariffs as a cushion and not as a form of quantitative restriction'.[22] This was somewhat less threatening than a European customs union. Some level of liberalization could be accepted as the British alternative to integration. Britain had proposed a programme for the removal of quantitative restrictions on European trade in May 1949.[23] But there remained questions of degree and speed of liberalization. In October 1949 Bevin and Cripps took the question of economic relations with Europe to Cabinet. As a result, it was reaffirmed that the UK would not involve itself in any European

---

[19] Milward (1984) 297–8, 303.   [20] Leffler 316.
[21] Massigli 177.   [22] Milward (1984) 304.   [23] Ibid. 300.

association beyond the point at which it could withdraw. Bevin and Cripps argued that devaluation had proved Britain's need to rely on countries outside Europe. America and the Commonwealth must 'take priority over our relations with Europe'. They insisted that the UK must not surrender its sole responsibility for its own budgetary policy and its own reserves; that nothing must be undertaken that would hinder attainment of equilibrium between the dollar area and the sterling area. 'We cannot sacrifice opportunities for dollar-earning (or dollar-saving) in order to make it easier for other European countries to earn or save dollars.' Britain could not engage in any form of joint European planning which might imply the reduction in size of any dollar-earning industry. On this basis, even the liberalization of trade with Europe could not have a high priority. The paper still talked of doing everything possible to help European economic co-operation but a message was sent to Acheson to make clear the limits of Britain's European commitment.[24]

Thus it was with the support of this recent Cabinet authority that Cripps, in his official reply to Hoffman at the OEEC on 1 November 1949, restated the Attlee government's policy of not integrating the British economy into Western Europe in any way that would prejudice British responsibilities elsewhere in the world. His only concession was a declaration that Britain would encourage 'regional' schemes.[25] The speech was bitterly criticized in France although it said nothing new and British reluctance had been demonstrated on many previous occasions. Hall-Patch told Sir James Helmore of the Board of Trade that there were, in France, reflected in the French Press, doubts about Britain's liberalization policy. Cripps's speech to the OEEC had been interpreted as 'in effect a rejection of European unification'. Hall-Patch added that 'we run a considerable risk that the OEEC in general and ourselves in particular may be thought to be doing nothing in particular'. He attached to his message an article by Raymond Aron in *Le Figaro* which discussed Cripps's speech and concluded: 'The only new fact is the recognition of the bankruptcy of the OEEC in its function of unifier.'[26]

Gaitskell and Jay were determined to control trade with Europe.[27]

---

[24] Young (1984) 127; Milward (1984) 310.   [25] Milward (1984) 303–4.

[26] T 232/183, 11 Nov. 1949, Sir Edmund Hall-Patch to Sir James Helmore of the Board of Trade. Raymond Aron in *Le Figaro* of 5–6 Nov. 1949: 'Le seul fait nouveau, c'est la reconnaissance de la faillite de l'OEEC dans sa function unificatrice.'

[27] Gaitskell was not in the Treasury until after the Feb. 1950 election, but he was a member of the Economic Policy Committee.

They would resist further liberalization. They resisted deflation as a means of bringing the country's payments into balance. They were critical of what they regarded as the deflationary policies of other European countries because of their effect on Britain. They criticized Belgium for its deflationary policies which they saw as responsible for the Belgian payments surplus with Britain. It was sucking gold and dollars out of the UK.[28] Gaitskell and Jay made a distinction between essential imports, much of which came from the Commonwealth, and inessential imports, much of which came from Europe. On 17 November 1949 Jay minuted Cripps, arguing that trade liberalization on inessentials was socially regressive. Jay accepted, reluctantly, that it might be politically necessary to make proposals for liberalization of trade with Europe but it was not economically or socially right and would lead to lack of control. On the other hand, liberalization of essentials, food and vegetables for example, was wholly desirable.[29] Gaitskell and Jay probably briefed Denis Healey, Labour's International Secretary, on their views. In a pamphlet which he wrote at this time, *Western Europe—The Challenge of Unity*, Healey made the same point: 'Britain's imports from the Commonwealth are mainly indispensable raw materials, whereas her imports from Europe are less essential.'[30]

On 9 December 1949 Jay minuted Cripps again. There was, he said, already too much sterling in the hands of foreigners. Relaxation on imports would add to the sterling in their hands. 'The whole position of our reserves and dollar prospects is, in my view, far too precarious to take risks of this kind.' He added: 'All the evidence is that the strain on our balance of payments is going to extend to non-dollar countries as well as dollar countries in 1950.' On 12 December Jay minuted Cripps once more, pleading that 'ice cream spoons etc. etc.' should not be included in the UK's programme of liberalization when others were doing less. 'We have already gone so far unilaterally with "liberalization".' Cripps had accepted some advance in the liberalization of private trade as the British alternative to the integration desired by the US Administration. He was probably not too pleased with Jay's advice.

---

[28] Newton (May 1985) 172. There was some protection. In Mar. 1948 the UK and Belgium agreed that Belgium would have to accumulate a surplus of £12m. before transferability into hard currency became possible.

[29] T 232/183, 17 Nov. 1949.

[30] Published under his own name in Jan. 1950 by the Canadian Institute of International Affairs.

He did not feel he needed instruction on the permissible limits of liberalization. On Jay's minute of 12 December he scribbled: 'I don't think that ice cream spoons would make a great deal of difference.'[31]

The attitude of officials to trade with Europe was changing due to experience following devaluation. Following the devaluation, the reserves were rising month by month. While discrimination against the dollar was still necessary, the attraction of trade with non-dollar areas including Europe was becoming greater even if it cost dollars.[32] Officials were now prepared to combat the Jay view on the need for restrictions on trade with Europe. Robert Hall wrote of Jay's 'rather mystical view of the distinction between essentials and inessentials'.[33] The distinction was strongly criticized in a memorandum by Christopher Dow of the Treasury.[34] The effect of Jay's policy would be to divide Western Europe into a dozen high-cost markets but was unlikely to restrain total expenditure on inessentials. By March 1950 Hall and Clarke were in alliance on the issue despite the latter's previous insistence on protecting the balance of payments by managing imports. Hall and Clarke had been forced into unusual agreement by their combined effort to persuade Gaitskell.[35] The fact that devaluation had changed the mind of officials in the Treasury and economists in the Economic Section of the Cabinet Office did not mean that the mind of ministers had yet changed. Whereas officials were now ready to see the advantages of trade with Europe, this in no way implied that they, any more than Gaitskell, would support a European customs union. The devaluation of September 1949 had, in their view, confirmed Britain's interest in an eventual one-world economic system. Meanwhile, the success of devaluation depended far more on trade relations with the USA and the Commonwealth than with Europe.[36]

Officials, having instructed ministers on policy, often find it time-consuming to persuade them that circumstances have changed and that, therefore, policy should change. This was particularly the case with ministers such as Gaitskell and Jay who had minds of their own, were wedded to planning and to import controls as weapons of policy, and were deeply suspicious of any liberal inclinations in their advisers. As the statement *European Unity* was to show, it was the Gaitskell–Jay

---

[31] T 232/183.   [32] Hall, 28 Mar. 1950.   [33] Hall, 5 Jan. 1950.
[34] T 232/183, 23 Nov. 1949.   [35] Hall, 17 Apr. 1950.
[36] Cairncross (1992) 83.

view that held support in the National Executive Committee of the Labour Party at the time the Schuman Plan was announced.[37]

The structure of a future European Payments Union (EPU) was discussed at Gaitskell's meeting in Paris with Averell Harriman and Milton Katz on 25 March 1950. Gaitskell questioned the use of gold payments within the proposed system. He was aware that this was intended as a means of exercising discipline on debtor countries. He accepted that it was the duty of a debtor to get his balance of payments right. He insisted, however, that this could be done by devaluation or import controls, not only by deflation. He could not accept any obligation to deflate. Robert Marjolin, who was at the meeting, complained that British discrimination against continental suppliers caused bitter feelings. Gaitskell replied that the UK only discriminated to avoid the loss of gold and dollars and insisted on the right to do so.

There were circumstances in which, in Gaitskell's view, co-operation with Europe could be an aid in handling the dollar shortage. At the same meeting he was warned by Marjolin that a more serious American recession was to be expected in the next eighteen months, possibly much sooner, and that it might break up European co-operation. Gaitskell's account of the conversation with Marjolin is worth quoting:

I said I did not think this was necessarily so. We would certainly wish to maintain a high level of income and employment in the UK, so that the problem would present itself as another dollar crisis. In these circumstances we should wish to replace dollar supplies wherever we could, and we should be ready to rely more not less on Europe in this respect. But, I said, we cannot do that if Europe is tied to the dollar. He said that he was quite clear that when the US recession came Europe would have to abandon the dollar entirely. I said it seemed to me far better to do this in advance.[38]

In fact what came was not another American recession but the war in Korea. But Gaitskell's conversation with Marjolin confirms that, as the minister responsible for overseas finance in the British government, he would have been prepared to contemplate closer association with Europe provided it did not cost Britain its scarce dollars. At a time when his advisers had begun to contemplate the possibility, still perhaps distant, of one world in trade, Gaitskell saw no other possibility than two worlds. For Gaitskell, the dollar problem was still, despite devaluation,

---

[37] The statement was published in June 1950 but drafting was well advanced by Apr. and the thinking that went into the drafting long predated the beginning of the drafting.
[38] Gaitskell 181.

and despite the advice of his officials, an obstacle to developing trade with Europe.[39]

The efforts of officials to persuade Gaitskell continued. In July 1950 the character of a British report to the OEEC was under consideration in Whitehall. On 1 July Clarke wrote to D. B. Pitblado, his colleague in the Treasury dealing, among other matters, with the Schuman Plan: 'We do not want to show that we cannot "afford" free imports from the non-dollar world.'[40] Robert Hall agreed. He wrote to Clarke: 'I should myself be opposed to an exercise which assumed that we would be insufficiently competitive and can only maintain full employment at home by import restrictions. This seems to me to be quite the wrong spirit in which to approach the exercise at all, though it was justified before devaluation.'[41] The implications of devaluation for British policy was summed up by Pitblado in a submission to Gaitskell:

[T]he main argument in favour of being ready to let other countries obtain dollars from us if they can earn them is that by this means we encourage competition in production and an increasing level of world trade flowing as freely as possible through multilateral channels. Our prosperity as a trading nation and our general standard of living is so bound up with the expansion of world trade, that it is in our own interests to foster this even at the expense of direct dollar purchases.[42]

The message was in conflict with everything that Gaitskell had brought with him into politics and thought he had learned since entering Parliament in 1945.

The dollar problem was not the only reason why Gaitskell would not have been prepared to contemplate a European customs union. In his view, deflationary economic policy on the Continent would not merely suck dollars out of the British economy. It would also imperil full employment in Britain. This attitude is illustrated in a passage in Gaitskell's diary written when he was negotiating UK participation in the EPU, a negotiation which for much of the time ran parallel with those on the Schuman Plan:

In contrast to the Anglo-American economists, with whom we might associate the Scandinavians, we had the Belgian, French and to some extent Swiss banker

---

[39] Britain did join the EPU in the summer of 1950. Scott Newton explains: 'Britain was able to participate in the European Payments Union, established in September 1950, in the knowledge that it would be compensated by the ECA for losses of gold and dollars incurred in the multilateral use of sterling balances within Marshall Europe': Newton (May 1985) 176.
[40] T 229/291.   [41] Ibid.   [42] Ibid.

outlook, who invariably took the side of the creditor and wanted a much tighter system of credit. . . . No doubt this is partly due to the extent of inflation that there has been in these countries vying with a dislike of control. We are much more frightened of deflation and unemployment and are quite prepared to impose controls to prevent inflation. They are much more frightened of inflation than they are of deflation and unemployment and are unwilling or unable to impose controls. Hence their insistence on keeping the volume of credit down.[43]

A factor that Gaitskell ignored was that it may not have been Belgium's economic policy that was out of step but Britain's with its simultaneous commitment to full employment, the creation of a Welfare State, and a vast overseas deployment of military force.

Thus there was a fear that continental governments were insufficiently Keynesian. It was not confined to British socialists. France also was following a high employment policy and was as concerned about the dangers of unemployment as the UK. The major continental countries in which unemployment remained high were Germany and Italy. One factor holding up French ratification of Finebel was the fear, in France, of tying itself to countries with high unemployment and which were conducting deflationary policies. This consideration did not prevent the Benelux countries from demanding German participation in any customs union but then Belgium was regarded in London as itself a prime European example of deflationary economic policies. In the event, German unemployment proved a temporary phenomenon. The world economic boom was burning up unemployment as effectively as the sun burns up a mist. Later, the confidence displayed by British Keynesian economists that they had found an insular answer to British unemployment would be revealed for what it was, hubris.

Whatever the future might hold, differences in economic philosophy were, at the time, an obstacle to British membership of a European customs union. The dollar problem was seen as one major obstacle. The maintenance of full employment was seen as another. These were not the only obstacles. The list of problems identified in Whitehall memoranda constituted a deterrent force that ministers would ignore at their peril. A customs union, it was argued, would lead inevitably to political union which would be inconsistent with the UK's international links. Opposition was reinforced by the expectation that a European customs union would be inconsistent with imperial preference. The objection to anything that would prejudice imperial preference was bipartisan. It is

[43] Gaitskell 191.

to be found in the first of two articles by Sir Arthur Salter in *The Times* in May 1950. Salter was later Minister of State for Economic Affairs in the Churchill government.[44] He argued that

a Customs Union, the complete form of economic unity, is incompatible with imperial preference. If Britain has to choose between western Europe and the Commonwealth, she will choose the latter. If a Customs Union, which would mean the abandonment of Imperial preference, is an integral part of European union she will stand out, and without her it cannot succeed.[45]

The idea that nothing in Europe could succeed without British participation was integral to British complacency about Europe. Salter, however, was in favour of European integration. A few days later, he was a signatory of a letter to *The Times* stating that the UK should 'take a full share in working out the Schuman Plan'.[46] Other signatories included Julian Amery and Harold Macmillan. They wrote as members of the European League for Economic Co-operation (ELEC). Salter's solution to the conundrum posed by the inconsistency of a European customs union with imperial preference was to propose a limit on tariffs within Europe of, say, 20 per cent. This would permit a margin of imperial preference while enabling European economic integration. Salter's idea could not be more than a temporary solution to the problem. If European economic integration was to progress, such a ceiling would inevitably be lowered with the passage of time and hence would erode imperial preference.

A SHORTAGE OF RAW MATERIALS?

Western European countries understood that imperial preference could be a bar to British participation in a customs union. There were indications that some might be prepared to consider concessions to the UK point of view.[47] Probably what they had in mind was something of the kind that Salter was proposing. There was justification for this co-operative spirit. Industrial production was expanding far faster than the supply of raw materials. The USA was stockpiling strategic materials.

---

[44] Salter was also a close friend of Jean Monnet. In 1933 he wrote a book entitled *The United States of Europe*. He had been Director of the Economic and Finance Section of the League of Nations.

[45] *The Times*, 16 May 1950.   [46] Ibid., 22 May 1950.

[47] See Ch. 13 below regarding the Stikker Plan for the Dutch readiness to find a solution to the problem of imperial preference.

A shortage was expected. There was, as a result, speculative demand for raw materials engendered by the expectation of rising prices and shortages.[48] Economists identified a long-term problem for the industrial world. As Edwin Plowden puts it:

Economists in Whitehall believed at the time, wrongly as it turned out, that primary products were, for the foreseeable future, in general likely to remain much scarcer than they had been in the 1930s. This led them to advise close ties with the Commonwealth, which had ample resources and which could both supply us and earn dollars for the Sterling Area.... The concomitant of this was that any future links with Western Europe must not weaken Commonwealth links.[49]

Given the analysis, the UK's privilege of preferential access to non-dollar sources of raw materials from the Commonwealth was understandably regarded as a major benefit not just for the present but indefinitely. Among the commodities flowing to Britain from sterling area sources were wool, meat, and butter from Australia and New Zealand, textiles from India, rubber from Malaya, and raw cotton, copper, oil seeds, and cocoa from the African dependencies. Moreover this was a privilege that Britain had, and which the continental countries did not have or had to a much lesser extent. As Kenneth Morgan puts it, 'Labour's colonial thinking . . . concentrated on imperial partnership and development rather than on decolonization.'[50] The privilege of independence conceded to the countries of South-East Asia was not to be extended, for a long time, to the remaining dependent territories of the Empire. Other European governments shared the belief that shortage was endemic and that Europe needed privileged access to raw materials. This was something that the Commonwealth, and the other overseas territories of Western European countries, could provide. The illusion, fed by what proved to be temporary shortages, that Europe was dependent on privileged access to raw materials from its overseas territories was highly influential. The illusion could have two, directly contradictory, effects. It could make continental Europe more willing to entice Britain into Europe by finding a way to accommodate imperial

[48] The *Economic Survey of Europe in 1950* estimated that there had been no increase in the production of the twelve major raw materials: Dow 55, 55 n. 2.

[49] Plowden 33. In their resignation speeches in 1951, both Aneurin Bevan and Harold Wilson gave it as an explanation for their resignations that the extent of the proposed rearmament, in the USA and the UK, would make unacceptable demands on the world's scarce raw materials and was in fact unrealizable for that reason: Dow 60 n. 6.

[50] Morgan (1990) 25.

preference. On the other hand, it could persuade British policy-makers to seek to hoard their apparent advantage by denying any share in it to competitors in continental Europe.

At a time when Bevin's mind was playing more constructively upon European affairs than in 1950, it appeared that he was prepared to contemplate the economic integration of Western Europe together with all its overseas territories including the British. On 22 January 1948 he told the House of Commons:

The organisation of Western Europe must be economically supported. That involves the closest possible collaboration with the Commonwealth and with overseas territories, not only British but French, Dutch, Belgian and Portuguese. The overseas territories are large primary producers and their standard of life is evolving rapidly and is capable of great development. They have raw materials, food and resources, which can be turned to very great common advantage, both to the people of the territories themselves, to Europe, and to the world as a whole. . . . There is no conflict between the social and economic development of the overseas territories to the advantage of their people, and their development as a source of supplies for Western Europe, as a contributor . . . so essential to the balance of payments.[51]

Even when he made the speech, the economic departments in London had already won the argument against so generous a view of Britain's obligations to Europe. Thereafter, while British spokesmen emphasized the problems of reconciling imperial preference with European economic integration, continental spokesmen seemed to be seeking an opportunity to address those problems together with their British colleagues. At a meeting with Acheson and Schuman on 10 November 1949 Bevin said: 'I must warn my colleagues that the United Kingdom—because of its overseas connections—could never become an entirely European country . . .' To this Schuman responded that 'Europe was inconceivable without Great Britain and the British people must not feel that they had to choose between the Commonwealth and Europe.'[52] The leading European federalist, Paul-Henri Spaak, was prepared to go so far as to say:

In Europe . . . no one would ever think to put one day Great Britain before a choice between the Commonwealth and Europe. First of all because we know that in that case Great Britain would choose, and rightly, the Commonwealth, and then because we want our United Europe to keep with the Anglo-Saxon

[51] HC Debs. 22 Jan. 1948, cols, 398–9.   [52] Warner 71.

world, the Commonwealth and the United States the closest relationship, and Great Britain is our most natural link for it.[53]

So, in the view of this leading European federalist, Britain, if compelled to make the choice, would rightly choose the Commonwealth. But such a choice could be avoided to mutual benefit.

Within Britain, those who wanted British participation in European integration insisted that Britain's relations with the Commonwealth were not an obstacle but an advantage. Robert Boothby, a leading figure in the European Movement, said in the debate on the Schuman Plan in the House of Commons:

As for the Commonwealth, there was no responsible European statesman at [the Council of Europe Assembly at] Strasbourg who did not believe and declare that the Commonwealth must be closely associated with European union at every stage. They know perfectly well that without the Commonwealth and without their own overseas associated territories, Western Europe can never hope to be viable either politically or economically.[54]

Europe, apparently, could not live without its overseas territories. Quintin Hogg, speaking in support of British participation in the Schuman Plan negotiations at the urging of Winston Churchill himself, was making the same point when, earlier in the same debate, he said: 'Nor will Europe ever be prosperous and safe unless the Commonwealth is united behind the United Kingdom.'[55]

Among officials there was a difference of view between those who wanted British participation in European economic integration and those who did not. Oliver Franks was one who wanted to find the way. He would have liked to find the way to incorporating not just Britain's dependent territories but the sterling area as a whole in some kind of European integration.[56] In a memorandum of 7 August 1947 Edmund Hall-Patch warned Bevin against the 'well-established prejudice in Whitehall', and especially in the Board of Trade, against British participation in a European customs union. The Board of Trade, he said, was

---

[53] In a speech in Philadelphia, 14 Jan. 1950. Spaak made several speeches on this theme at the time. Spaak was the American candidate for supremo in an OEEC with executive powers, had it ever occurred. See also Massigli 181.

[54] HC Debs. 27 June 1950, col. 2120.   [55] HC Debs. 26 June 1950, col. 2051.

[56] FO 371/87141. See Franks, Washington, to Foreign Office, 4 Mar. 1950 regarding New Zealand proposals that OEEC liberalization should be extended to it. The problem for the time being, as Franks saw it, was American objection to the extension of the area of OEEC discrimination against American trade. See also Milward (1984) 239–40; Danchev 73–4.

'overstating the case against it'. 'If some such integration does *not* take place, Europe will gradually decline in the face of pressure from the United States on the one hand and the USSR on the other.'[57] Despite such powerful advocacy, the weight of opinion in the UK economic departments continued against it. Where Britain had an advantage, it would be foolish to dilute it by opening it to Europe let alone the world. Enthusiasm for the global economy went only so far. Scott Newton writes of the Board of Trade's 'unimaginative and blatantly protectionist campaign against British membership of a European customs union'.[58] If there had been a will, there would have been a way. The fear of raw material shortage encouraged it. But the economic departments were opposed and neither Europe's willingness to compromise on imperial preference nor the possibility of finding the way round any other problems was tested.

In coming to the conclusions that they did, the economic departments deceived themselves on two counts. They believed that relations between Britain and the Commonwealth were benign and a source of mutual advantage. Bevin believed it too, as his speech in the House of Commons on 22 January 1948, quoted above, proves. This view was certainly too optimistic or, alternatively, too careless of the interests of the overseas territories. The dependent countries of the sterling area fed the dollar pool. The independent members drained it. Scott Newton writes: 'It is hard to deny that Asian and African peasants laboured to support . . . living standards throughout the white Commonwealth. . . . The determination of ministers such as Bevin, Strachey and Shinwell to preserve Britain's prosperity and independence by developing the material resources of Africa would have been applauded by Joseph Chamberlain.'[59] Through the machinery of the sterling area, through its control of commodity prices at levels below world prices, and through the regulation of colonial trade, Britain was able to exploit its colonies. The British government, if it noticed at all what it was doing, may have felt that during the war Britain had suffered on behalf of all and that now it was entitled to ensure that any further sacrifices were shared.

Such benefits as Britain gained would be in peril as the colonies moved towards independence. If they could earn a dollar surplus, there was no reason why they should subscribe it for the benefit of people in Britain, or elsewhere in the independent Commonwealth, much better

---

[57] FO 371/62552: quoted Hennessy 363.
[58] Newton (May 1985) 171.   [59] Ibid. 177–8.

off than themselves. On the other hand, the enthusiasm of the independent members of the Commonwealth for the sterling area was a function of its capacity to help solve their own dollar problems by drawing on the sterling area dollar pool.[60] Similarly in peril would be any benefits gained by the other imperial states of Western Europe from their overseas territories. In due course Europe would have to survive from its own skills and resources. It would not always be possible to conscript overseas territories for the benefit of European current accounts and standards of living.[61]

In any case, the fundamental premiss of the policy was mistaken. The long-term shortage of raw materials did not occur. Trade with other industrialized countries flourished more strongly than with raw material producers. The incentive to improvement provided by direct competition with other industrialized countries was a greater spur than could be provided by protected trade within the sterling area. At the time, policy was understandably dominated by the immediate reality of the dollar gap. That made the Commonwealth appear a more suitable trading partner than Europe. In the slightly longer term, contrary to the views of Robert Hall[62] and of the Board of Trade, the converse was the case. The supply of raw materials would respond to market demand. It would not for ever be possible to impose prices below world levels. In anything but the shortest term, it was better, therefore, to be linked to competitive economies than to those supposed to be complementary. It was better, in other words, to be linked to Europe rather than to the Commonwealth. This is hindsight. But even to those to whom this insight was denied at the time, it should have seemed unlikely that, in any long term, such a vast area of the globe would accept a special, and unfavourable, economic relationship with one single industrial power not of great size or potential, the more especially as discrimination in international trade was being challenged by the USA. In so far therefore as the link to the Commonwealth was of economic benefit, it was a benefit not to be relied upon in building the UK's future. The path indicated by Franks and Hall-Patch along which the British government was so reluctant to travel had greater potential.

---

[60] Cairncross (1992) 56.

[61] The exploitation of Britain's overseas territories is examined by Fieldhouse 95–8. He says that the UK controlled prices for colonial commodities below world price levels for the benefit of UK consumers. He calculates that 'one way or another, the colonies were lent or given some £40 million by Britain but were forced to lend or tie up in London about £250 million'. See also Morgan (1984) 202.

[62] In his 'think-piece'.

COMPETITIVE AND COMPLEMENTARY ECONOMIES

Inconsistency with imperial preference and prejudice to Britain's dollar account did not end the list of objections to British participation in a European customs union. An intriguing argument regularly employed by the economic departments in Whitehall was that the European economy was competitive with that of the UK whereas the Commonwealth was complementary. So far as Britain was concerned, a complementary economy was one which supplied raw materials not available domestically. Other European economies were competitive because they produced goods, whether industrial or agricultural, which competed with Britain's in world markets. It was not in Britain alone that the concept of complementary and competitive economies held sway. Monnet explained the failure of the Franco-Italian customs union as being due to the fact that 'the two economies, both exporters of agricultural produce, were competitive rather than complementary'.[63] In Britain, the argument emanated, among other sources, from the supposedly *laissez-faire* Board of Trade. The argument was inconsistent with Britain's multilateral professions, redolent of the most primitive mercantilism. It reflected the economics of empire against which Adam Smith had loosed his shafts nearly two centuries before. The Board of Trade might have had the excuse that in 1950 it was virtually without the advice of economists employed as such.[64] But the leading economist in the government made the same mercantilist distinction. Robert Hall, in his 'think-piece' on integration, observed that 'we do not expect any early or large advantages to accrue to O.E.E.C. countries from liberalisation, as we don't think the countries are very complementary to one another in the economic sense. But this is in itself not a reason against moving this way.'[65]

The substance behind this preference for complementary as against competitive economies was the spectre of revived German competition which one day would return in full force. The spectre was haunting Europe. It was haunting French industry as well as British industry. Poidevin writes of concern in the Quai d'Orsay about the speed of German recovery.[66] Fear of German competition made it appear to British governments even more desirable to avoid irrevocable commitments to Europe and instead to maintain a sterling area within which

---

[63] Monnet 281.   [64] Brittan 38.   [65] FO 371/87136.
[66] Poidevin (1986) 254.

Britain had a competitive advantage. Scott Newton suggests that there were different forms of customs unions on offer which could have provided protection against Germany. 'While the Belgians and Italians, with American support, favoured a union based on old-fashioned liberalism, the French desired a planned and regulated customs union precisely because they shared Britain's anxiety about the consequences of German recovery.'[67] It is difficult, however, to see how a European customs union could have been created without increasing the exposure to German competition.

In the years after the war, fear of German competition inspired a number of attempts by British industrialists to hobble German industry.[68] Unfortunately for such schemes, German economic recovery was important to the UK both for reasons of security and to help lighten the burden on the British economy of the British zone in Germany. In any case, the US Administration would not have permitted it. The British government was brought under strong pressure from the US Administration to bring reparations to an end and they were virtually abandoned after the Petersburg agreements of November 1949. British industry was left with no choice but to face the prospect of a revival of German competition. Inevitably that competition would first be faced in Europe. That thought confirmed the priority given to dollar markets which, under government pressure, British industry could not ignore. It underlined the attractiveness of the markets of the Commonwealth where British competitiveness would, at least to some extent, be underpinned by imperial preference.

A EUROPEAN CUSTOMS UNION REJECTED

By 1947 opinion within Whitehall was moving strongly against British participation in a European customs union. An official Committee concluded that 'it is not in our interest to encourage the idea of a European Customs Union of which the United Kingdom would be a member, and that in any case a general Western European Customs Union is out of the question as a matter of practical politics.'[69]

---

[67] Newton (May 1985) 171.

[68] For example, Lord McGowan, Chairman of ICI, tried to have dyestuffs manufacture in Germany prohibited. For this and other examples, see Milward (1992) 402 ff.

[69] T 236/808, London Committee, Sub-Committee on Integration of Europe, 23 July 1947, quoted Milward (1984) 239.

The absence of warm political support for the idea even on the continent of Europe was a final and conclusive argument against a European customs union. There was no value in the UK peddling an idea if its prospective partners would shoot it down. This final argument, that it was politically impractical, should have been sufficient. But the fear remained that perhaps, despite all Britain's scepticism, it might just be practical. Indeed, the judgement of Robert Marjolin was that, with British participation, it might have been practical:

This more modest idea of European integration in the form of a customs union might have become a reality as early as the beginning of the fifties, had the British not rejected it out of hand. It would take nearly ten years before the scheme was reborn among the Six and nearly twenty-five years before Britain found her place in it. . . . In fact a project for a Franco-Italian customs union had already seen the light of day and negotiations had begun between the two countries to extend it to Benelux. The enterprise foundered because of Britain's refusal to join. The French were opposed to Germany's being a part of it, but were to reverse their attitude in 1950.[70]

By 1949 the Board of Trade was scared even of any mention of a European customs union by British representatives. Sir Oliver Harvey, UK Ambassador to Paris, referred to the idea in a speech to the Paris diplomatic Press on 14 December 1949. He pointed out that it would not be possible for Britain to become part of a European customs union without making reservations in respect of its interests in the Commonwealth. He added that this did not necessarily mean that the Commonwealth and a European customs union were irreconcilable. His remarks immediately set the alarm bells ringing in the Board of Trade. There was nothing new in them. Harvey was, indeed, following closely what Cripps had said to the OEEC on 1 November. But his comments elicited a personal and confidential letter dated 13 January 1950 from Berthoud:

As you know, the Board of Trade are highly sensitive on the whole subject of Customs Unions with the result that any allusion to it in public fills them with concern . . . although (as they themselves admit) you went no further than what the Chancellor himself has publicly said in one context or another. What the Board of Trade are, of course, afraid of is that any fresh mention of the subject, however innocuous in itself, might, unless made in reply to a direct question, give the impression that we were beginning to think in the direction of joining

[70] Marjolin (1989) 213.

such a Union, whereas in fact the present view of Ministers is that we must remain completely uncommitted.[71]

Britain, which was refusing to involve itself in any plans for European federation, was also rejecting economic integration with the rest of Europe. All that was left was trade liberalization conditional on its being of a kind that did not cost Britain dollars, rob the Commonwealth of its preferences in the British market, or Britain of its preferences in Commonwealth markets. Gradual liberalization of European trade, on these conditions, was preferable to a customs union. The defensiveness that made the UK afraid of economic integration with the rest of Europe, afraid even of mentioning the idea of a European customs union, was hardly conducive of any substitute British initiative which would encourage the Continent to believe that Britain valued its role in Europe. The discovery of a substitute would require the imagination that was being focused on the European problem in Paris. Britain's reluctance became a spur to France. If Britain would not lead, it might encourage France to shoulder the burden of leadership.

A TALE OF LOST OPPORTUNITIES

This was the background to the UK failure to provide persuasive leadership in Europe. Even if it was accepted that the arguments against a European customs union were, at the time, overwhelming, that did not necessarily imply that Britain could not, if it could find the will and the imagination, generate other proposals for specific forms of economic integration that might, perhaps, have a political rather than an economic motivation. There was, in British policy towards Europe, too much of a philosophy of 'watch and wait' caused by suspicion of continental motives, by the need to husband dollars, by fear of a revival of German competition, and by the primacy given to imperial preference and relations with the Commonwealth. Where the issue was the security of Europe, the UK had ideas and a role. Even there it fell short in allotting insufficient importance to Franco-German reconciliation and to the contribution that Britain might make to that end. Where the issue was the economic integration of Europe, Britain was bankrupt of ideas. Creativity was left to others, to the Americans as in the Marshall Plan, to France as in the Schuman Plan, and then to any other European

[71] FO 371/87136.

government that had a problem that it thought could be eased by European economic integration. Only to the French did it occur that a limited exercise in economic integration could be linked to reconciliation with Germany. If one were to specify a single error in UK policy towards Europe, it would lie in the UK's apparent belief that it could exercise leadership in Europe without imaginative effort.

Before the disillusionment caused by British policy and by the 1949 devaluation, the other European powers were, after the war, prepared to regard Britain as different, as more capable of leadership, as the essential key to the reconstruction of a prosperous Europe. It was a view of the UK hardly justified by the facts but as it *was* held, it gave the UK opportunities that it wasted. Marjolin has commented that Britain's

prestige was immense. Had she not in 1940–41 taken on single-handed and with iron determination an enemy who was infinitely more powerful? Had she not been the base from which the Allied armies set out to reconquer Europe? Her economic power in those dark days of 1945–6 appeared immeasurably greater than that of the devastated countries of continental Europe. Was she not the centre of an immense Empire, of which no one could know that it would disintegrate so rapidly? Was the sterling area not the biggest currency area in the world? It was not until 1946–7 that we were able to realize that behind that imposing façade, which conveyed the impression of enormous strength and potential, was an economy sapped by six years of war, total mobilization and progressive liquidation of foreign assets, six years in which there had been no renewal of the nation's capital stock. Gradually the world had to face the fact that, far from being able to help with the reconstruction of Europe, Britain herself would need a large amount of external aid in order to get back to normal.[72]

Britain would also need to exert its powers of leadership. But they were as scarce as the dollars.

[72] Marjolin (1989) 176.

6

Federation, an American Recipe

It is essentially a question whether European countries should proceed to closer unity by means of inter-governmental arrangements or by steps leading to federation. . . . His Majesty's Government are not prepared to contemplate the entrance of the United Kingdom into a federal system confined to Western Europe. . . . His Majesty's Government . . . are not prepared to contemplate entering into a federal system composed of Western European states.[1]

Throughout the post-war years, successive British governments have regarded European federalism and European federalists with disdain. Supranationalism, however, was eventually deemed to be in a different category from federalism and has become more acceptable. The definition of an acceptable supranationalism is one which leaves ultimate national sovereignty, the right *in extremis* to say no, unimpaired because it is incorporated in a treaty rather than in a constitution.[2] By 1950 supranationalism had in fact been accepted by Britain in matters of security without calling it federalism. Britain wanted a commitment of American troops to Europe and an American General in overall command of NATO forces.[3] Even the UK would concede supranationalism for the purpose of ensuring its own security especially under American leadership. Lionel Robbins, a dedicated opponent of the Schuman Plan and of European federalism, was not alone in finding

---

[1] Sir Roger Makins to Ernest Bevin, 17 June 1950—Notes for debate on Schuman Plan: MS Attlee dep. 102.

[2] The three judges in the Queen's Bench Divisional Court in the case of William Rees-Mogg against the Treaty of Maastricht, while rejecting the Rees-Mogg appeal on the grounds that it had no merit, also made clear that 'In the last resort . . . it would presumably be open to the government to denounce the treaty or at least to fail to comply with its international obligations under Title V': *The Times* Law Reports, 31 July 1993. See also the discussion of the nature of treaties in Dell 88 and 92.

[3] This could by no means be taken for granted. At Yalta Roosevelt had foretold that two years was the most that US troops could be expected to remain in occupation of Germany: Bullock 144.

supranationalism under English-speaking leadership more acceptable than anything the continent of Europe could offer.[4]

The UK, as a condition of entry into the European Community in 1973, conceded to supranational management in accordance with the requirements of the Treaty of Rome as then implemented within the Community. Since entry the UK has come to accept that some supranationalism within Europe must be accepted in order to achieve certain economic ends such as a single market. For such purposes, it may even be desirable. It provides discipline against state aids. It is the only hope of creating that 'level playing-field' which governments and businessmen tend to require as a condition of free trade between nations. British governments have come to realize that supranationalism can advance *national* political and economic ends.[5] Sometimes supranational decision-making will require unanimity among the participating governments. Sometimes participating governments will permit themselves to be overruled by some form of majority voting.

Despite this shift in thinking, federalist sentiment has been scarcely detectable in the UK throughout the post-war years. It has remained undisturbed by Secretary of State Henry Kissinger's discovery that Europe had no telephone number. While supranationalism has been sanctioned for limited purposes, federalism is all-embracing, is, in intention, for ever and therefore is, for ever, barred. Thus, today, the UK's absolute and consistent objection to European federalism leaves open the possibility of an acceptable supranationalism. Too late, in the years after the Schuman Plan and after the Treaty of Rome, supranationalism became, for the British, a matter for judgement case by case in the economic field as it already was in matters of security. In 1950, outside the area of security, there appeared, in the British view, to be no concept of international governance in between federalism, which was damned, and intergovernmentalism, which could be acceptable.

THE AMERICANS HAVE A POLICY FOR EUROPE

In considering the big questions as they related to European integration, Britain might resist American policy but it could not be ignored. It was

---

[4] See Ch. 13 below.
[5] Alan S. Milward and Vibeke Sorensen, 'Interdependence or Integration? A National Choice', in Milward *et al.* 20.

a curiosity that the British government refused to become too deeply embedded in Europe because it preferred an Atlanticist stance, when the USA, which might be considered to have some interest in the Atlantic, would have preferred the UK to take the lead in European integration. Britain's policy put insufficient weight on the probability that its voice would be proportionately more influential in Washington the more deeply it was involved in European integration. But a major problem for the UK, and a major disincentive to getting too deeply involved in Europe, was that the Americans had a policy for Europe going far beyond what was needed for security and economic integration into the realm of constitutional structures. Britain saw it as at once naïve and a threat. It was a continuing source of friction between the two countries.

British ministers were compelled, for example, to fight to kill the extraordinary American notion of an OEEC, with supranational authority, led by the Belgian socialist and European federalist Paul-Henri Spaak.[6] The US Administration perhaps gained comfort from Monnet's support for their proposal. The question is whether Monnet's support for the idea more reflects his ignorance of European opinion or his cynicism. As late as 14 October 1949, just before Acheson finally accepted that Britain was not to be moved on the subject of European integration, he was again pressing upon Bevin the candidature of Spaak as Director-General of an OEEC with political powers.[7] The irony was that the US Administration saw, better than the UK government, that British interests lay in European economic integration. Unfortunately the Administration muddied its constructive influence by its counterproductive insistence on political structures for Europe which were neither practicable nor, if practicable, desirable.

The Americans believed they knew the secret of their own success. It lay in their large market and their federal system of government. Europe, they believed, should learn from both parts of this American experience. Having learnt the lesson, Europe should act on it. Americans had an undeniable stake in the future of Europe. They had been summoned once more to provide Europe with the security and stability it could not guarantee for itself. Despite earlier fears in the USA that

---

[6] 'The Paris conference gave Britain a unique opportunity to assert economic and political leadership in Europe, but the United Kingdom sabotaged the CEEC, the Organization for European Economic Cooperation (OEEC) that issued from it was stillborn, and the Marshall Plan thereby failed to become a vehicle for European economic integration': Gillingham 129.

[7] Bullock 730.

European federation and European economic integration would be damaging to American economic interests, the US Administration concluded on balance that their achievement was in American interests. The USA's economic pre-eminence now exceeded anything achieved by a single nation in that long past since the world economy became truly international. America was unchallengeable. Any cost from European integration could be absorbed. It would end once and for all the era of civil war in Western Europe, it would assist the recovery of the European economy and reinforce the alliance against Communism at home and abroad. A rich Western Europe, the Americans knew, was more likely to be a peaceful Western Europe. What had become quite as important was that it would be a strong Western Europe capable of accommodating Germany and of being an effective ally against the Soviet Union. The Americans would therefore offer Western Europe the remedy that had worked for them. Indeed they would press it even harder if Europeans did not respond sufficiently rapidly to their advocacy. They would employ whatever lever came to hand. Marshall Aid was one such lever and the ECA tried to use it sometimes beyond the bounds of acceptable diplomatic pressure.

The Americans were spending a great deal of time and money on Europe, and, in their view, what had to be done should be done quickly. By the autumn of 1949, the Planning Group of the ECA, assisted by Robert Triffin and Albert Hirschman, had produced a timetable for a currency union in Europe culminating in July 1952 by which time Marshall Aid would have ceased. The currency union would be controlled by a European monetary authority, the European currency unit would float against the dollar, and there would be simultaneous removal of all quantitative controls on dollar trade. National currencies would then be stabilized against the common currency. To all this would be added a central commercial authority.[8] The programme may have lacked something in credibility but nothing in imaginative power.

ECA attitudes towards Europe were elaborated further in an address by Edward T. Dickinson, delivered on 29 December 1949, before the American Political Science Association. Dickinson was Director of the Program Co-ordination Division of the ECA. As such, he was quite a senior official of the ECA as one would expect of someone invited to address so distinguished an audience. His views shocked senior Whitehall officials such as Sir Leslie Rowan and Sir Edmund Hall-Patch

---

[8] Milward (1984) 296.

among others.[9] Dickinson stressed that these were his personal views. But, given his position in the ECA, it appeared unlikely that the speech would have been made without approval. Indeed, his address carried intimations of what Hoffman might have wanted to say to the OEEC on 31 October 1949 had he been entirely free from political constraints. Under less political constraint than at a meeting of the OEEC, Hoffman, in an address to the National Association of Manufacturers on 7 December 1949, had said: 'Some people say that I ask for a United States of Europe. That is an oversimplification; hence inaccurate, though to be candid, I can think of nothing better for Europe.'[10] Here, before the American Political Science Association, was the monkey blurting out the contents of the organ-grinder's mind. In any event, Dickinson's views coincided with what had emerged, possibly presented more diplomatically, from other representatives of the US Administration. Such thoughts had been heard from Milton Katz, for example, and were certainly spreading in the State Department.[11]

For Dickinson, the American model was the model for Europe. The main question was how long a transition to constitutional bliss should Europe be allowed. Dickinson's address was long both on analysis and prescription. In fact it does him credit on all points except perhaps judgement, foresight, and sensitivity to the feelings of Europeans who were bound to become acquainted with what he was advocating at such length and in such detail. If any European feelings were hurt, they could be soothed by his careful reference to 'exceptions'. But he revealed his main insight with a minimum of circumlocution:

With exceptions, of course, and in varying degrees, it is evident that the West European national states in their present form would have been economically bankrupt and unable to maintain their political stability or independence for very long without continued, substantial external aid . . .

While the national governments of Western Europe may still be going concerns largely as a result of external economic and military aid, they have, with certain exceptions of course, ceased to be the focus of strong mass loyalties because they are widely recognized to be unable themselves to discharge the responsibilities of sovereign governments . . .

---

[9] Sir Leslie Rowan had been Attlee's Principal Private Secretary and was now a senior official at the Treasury. For Rowan's views of Dickinson's speech see FO 371/87136, letter from Rowan to E. A. Berthoud, 31 Jan. 1950.

[10] FO 371/87136, quoted by Edmund Hall-Patch in a letter to E. A. Berthoud, 20 Jan. 1950.

[11] Ibid.

This led him on to his first, and apparently logical, conclusion:

It is apparent . . . that in a world where the 'critical' size of independent existence is set by the powerful giants of East and West, the basic problem of
Western Europe is the fact that the required magnitude of the military and
economic unit necessary for successful survival is considerably larger than the
actual size of the existing political units, or sovereignties. Enough blurring of
the clear edges of national political sovereignties must therefore occur to establish in fact that unity of Western European society which now exists in
essence. . . . The deep fissures in this essential and desirable unity created by
obsolete national sovereignties must inevitably be welded together, peacefully
or by violence, constructively by the democrats or destructively by the communists.

From here he derived his prescription:

The stable political form which should result from a peaceful, democratic,
evolutionary transition would be a West European federation including not only
the metropolitan nations but their overseas territories as well. It does not seem
to me that any political structure less authoritative than a federation would be
adequate to fulfil the obligations of statehood . . .

These requirements cannot be met without some degree of central political
authority able to enact, execute, and enforce its law directly on individuals in
certain fields, particularly in the military field and in the realms of money and
credit, taxation and fiscal policy and commercial policy . . .

Despite American pressure on such devices as imperial preference, this
American observer incorporated in his concept of a West European
federation those bountiful overseas territories which were to ensure
Europe against a shortage of raw materials.

Dickinson underestimated the loyalty which nation states could retain even in face of limitations on their ability to discharge the responsibilities of sovereignty. He did not foresee that experience would
elaborate ways, alternative to federation, for repairing the fault lines in
national sovereignty, ways such as the creation of a community of
European nations prepared to work together in the exercise of their
sovereignty.

Dickinson's federation, he realized, could not be constructed at once.
It would take perhaps as much as ten years to achieve 'the ultimate
. . . objective in Western Europe . . . the creation of a real, federal republic'. Therefore there would have to be an 'intermediate (say five-
year) objective'. For the transitional period, 'there might have to be
some difference in economic arrangements for the continental countries

and for the United Kingdom, which could be bound somewhat more loosely to a continental economic grouping.' Nevertheless:

For the continent (including at least France, Italy, Western Germany, Austria, Benelux and, if possible, Scandinavia, the intermediate arrangements might be:

    (1) A common currency or its equivalent . . .
    (2) A central gold and dollar reserve. . . .
    (3) A central authority over inter-country trade policy and commercial policy with the rest of the world . . .

As an intermediate objective I can envisage that the Council of Ministers of the Council of Europe would assume the role of a top political body and that all other bodies would be in varying degrees subordinate to it and subject to its authority . . .

Only the USA had the commitment to achieve this European construction: 'I do not think that effective leadership toward these objectives is likely to come from the continental governments. Nor, alas, has there been any evidence that the United Kingdom is willing or able to play this role *in present circumstances*. Hence, the task falls to us.'[12]

Thus would the USA rebuild Europe in its own likeness. While Rowan and Hall-Patch were shocked, and others in the British government service did not know whether to laugh or to cry, E. A. Berthoud, of the Foreign Office, took it calmly. In a letter to Alan Hitchman at the Treasury, dated 26 January 1950, he suggested that not too much fuss should be made about a speech by a member of the group of 'dollar-a-year businessmen who are temporarily giving up their normal vocations, very often for patriotic reasons'.[13] Certainly, during his conversations with Bevin and Cripps in Washington in September 1949, Acheson had made no mention of a central gold and dollar reserve, a central authority over inter-country trade policy and commercial policy, or a common currency. In any case, he had come to believe that the United Kingdom should not be too closely tied to European economic and political developments.[14] The suspicion remained that the combination of insight, ignorance, and contempt demonstrated by the Dickinson speech was too close for comfort to opinion in the US Administration, and warranted caution on the part of the UK government as to how it should respond to American ideas on the future of Europe. The idea of giving executive power to the Council of Ministers of the Council of Europe would be a particular source of distress in London. The British

[12] FO 371/87136.
[13] Alan Hitchman was now Third Secretary at the Treasury.   [14] Leffler 316.

government was in constant battle to ensure that nothing was done by the Council of Ministers except by consensus and that the Consultative Assembly of the Council of Europe should achieve no higher status than as a talking shop with a very limited range of products on its shelves.

BRITAIN AGAINST FEDERALISM—THE INTERGOVERNMENTAL APPROACH

American pressure for federation was unwelcome in London. The British government wished to make its own choices free of American coercion and American misconceptions about what was practicable or desirable in Europe. Robert Hall reflected attitudes in Whitehall in his 'think-piece': 'Temperamentally, [the U.S. Administration] are against the Commonwealth and in favour of Britain in Europe—temperamentally also, they find compensation for not being able to plan their own economy in making detailed plans for other countries.'[15] But behind the joke there was real concern.

Many factors have, over the years, contributed to Britain's determined opposition to federalism. One was the British conviction that it was in a special position. The UK was different from other European nations. In the early post-war years, it saw itself not just as a European power. It was a global power and intended to remain so. A more permanent factor is the consciousness of a long independent history as a nation state. It was Stikker who observed that some of his collaborators in the construction of Europe were of uncertain national commitment. 'Schuman, although completely French, had, during the incorporation of Alsace in the German Empire, been a German subject, de Gasperi had in 1919 been a member of the Austrian Parliament, Adenauer had for some time favored a separate Rhine unit between France and Germany . . .'[16] It was easier for such people to think of a federal Europe than for a Briton who had known no other loyalty. British history could not just be swept aside for the sake of American dollars or American military forces, dearly as they were wanted. For Britain, this consciousness has probably been more important than the memory, for most people now distant, that Britain once possessed an empire. A European reason for British opposition to American pressure was that Europe is

---

[15] FO 371/87136.   [16] Stikker 177.

too diverse for American simplifications. The diversity embraces history, language, religion, culture, to mention nothing more. The evidence seemed to be that loyalty would remain to the nation state rather than to any synthetic construction at European level. Americans such as Dickinson found this difficult to understand. How could any informed person reject the American example? How could loyalty centre on a state unable to discharge the responsibilities of sovereignty?

Britain, at the time, had confidence in its ability to discharge the responsibilities of sovereignty. Where there were European problems that required collective action, it insisted on an intergovernmental approach. That approach enabled collective action while providing the protection for national interests that would be lost under federation. In the early post-war years the British insistence on intergovernmentalism was supported by the importance given to relations with the Commonwealth. Relations with the Commonwealth were informal and intergovernmental. With Europe they would be likely to be formal and binding. Robert Hall was, by origin, an Australian. In his 'think-piece', he attempted to answer the question why Commonwealth considerations made the UK cautious when it looked at European union. He concluded that,

apart from the facts that the Commonwealth is working now, and that it is a more suitable area for us than most of Western Europe, the main thing is probably that the sterling area and the Commonwealth have developed away from any written or formal arrangements and towards a system which depends almost entirely on tacit agreements. This can only be the result of a long growth and there can be little doubt that if anything is achieved in Paris [i.e. at the O.E.E.C.] it will have to be done with much more formality, so that on paper we might seem to be tied more closely to Europe than the Commonwealth, which we should very much dislike.[17]

In other words, in addition to the issues of substance which would impel the UK to prefer its own forms of discrimination against outsiders rather than accept those the Continent might wish to impose, Britain, with its unwritten constitution, favoured the informal, unwritten relationships characteristic of the Commonwealth to the formal, written relationships necessarily involved in supranational agreements. The informality of the Commonwealth, the absence of written arrangements, meant that in the end decisions lay with independent national

[17] FO 371/87136.

governments. That was the kind of informality which Britain wished to retain in its external relationships wherever possible.

The practical expression of this informality was 'functionalism'. For Britain, this meant a concentration on practical projects conducted on an intergovernmental basis. It denied constitutional visions. It was a case by case approach which left the future open and governments free to make their own decisions. Functionalists held that the process of European integration should be governed by decisions as to what *functions* could be better performed at the European level than at the level of the nation state. Those supporters that the Schuman Plan found in Britain claimed that it was an example of the functional approach and therefore entirely suitable for UK participation. To sustain their argument they were forced to discount the federalist verbiage with which the Plan had been presented to the world. Despite Monnet's emphasis on federalism, the Schuman Plan appeared to them exactly the kind of step-by-step, practical, movement towards European unity for which, it had been thought, British ministers had been pressing. Despite the continued harping in Washington on the desirability of European federalism there were, in the State Department, officials who, as the diplomatic correspondent of the *Manchester Guardian* put it, felt 'that much better results will be achieved by asking people whether they are ready to co-operate in this or that specific joint project rather than by asking them if they are ready to surrender their national sovereignty and political entity to a joint federal authority'.[18] These officials saw the Schuman Plan as exactly the kind of specific joint project which did not raise questions of national sovereignty in any serious way. That, indeed, is how Acheson saw it: 'The genius of the Schuman–Monnet Plan lay in its practical commonsense approach, its avoidance of the appearance of limitations upon sovereignty and touchy political problems.'[19] It conformed to the functionalist model and, if the UK was sincere about European unity, there was no reason why it should not join in.

But what did the functional approach really imply? There was a range of functionalist attitudes. It was quite clear that at one extreme, that habitually occupied by the British government, the functional approach would achieve little if anything by way of specific projects for European integration. In this interpretation, the functional approach was an excuse for inactivity, waiting for some idea to turn up which could

---

[18] *Manchester Guardian*, 24 May 1950.   [19] Acheson 384.

then be turned down. As Sir David Maxwell Fyfe later put it, 'Nothing can be worse than a functionalist without a function.'[20] At the other extreme the functional approach could verge on federalism. Denis Healey, International Secretary of the Labour Party, wrote a pamphlet *Feet on the Ground*, published by the Labour Party in 1948, which attempted to define the functional approach:

[I]n . . . functional co-operation the countries can choose the issues in which their common interest is agreed. Success in joint action on concrete economic and political problems will greatly weaken the force of sectional interests, creating such interdependence and mutual confidence that federation may finally become possible. Failure to solve these problems will make federation futile in any case. But it is possible that even a fully developed Western union will prefer an undefined and flexible association, like that of the Commonwealth, to a rigid written constitution.[21]

Thus Healey appears, in 1948, to have regarded the functional approach, through the multiplication of individual functional successes, as a possible route to federalism while leaving it open that, in practice, countries might prefer indefinitely a continuation of the functional approach. In this speculation, Healey was conceding a great deal to the federalists while claiming that his feet were still on the ground. It was significant of the success of European federalists at that time in leading the debate on the future construction of Europe.

Harold Macmillan was against the federal approach to European integration and in favour of the functional approach.[22] His ally on European questions, Duncan Sandys, offered as a definition that the functional approach 'involves no federal constitution and no irrevocable transfer of sovereign powers'.[23] Robert Boothby, Conservative MP, was a leading figure in the European Movement, a firm supporter of UK acceptance of the French invitation to the Schuman Plan negotiations, and one of the most enthusiastic 'Europeans' in the House of Commons. He claimed to be a committed advocate of the functional approach. Nevertheless, he would have been regarded in London government circles as a raving federalist. Boothby was prepared to contemplate degrees of integration that would horrify many Conservatives

---

[20] HC Debs. 13 Nov. 1950, col. 1489. Maxwell Fyfe was later Home Secretary in the Churchill Cabinet and, as Lord Kilmuir, Lord Chancellor under Harold Macmillan.

[21] Healey (1990) 72.

[22] *DBPO* 118, Hugh Dalton's note on the proceedings of the General Affairs Committee of the Council of Europe.

[23] HC Debs. 13 Nov. 1950, col. 1410.

even today. To prove his functionalist credentials, he emphasized that integration must be for 'specific purposes'. He told the House of Commons:

I do believe that there must be not so much a surrender as a merger or pooling of national sovereignty for specific purposes if we are to survive. . . . What are the implications? In the economic field it certainly involves the co-ordination of national monetary and fiscal policies and the acceptance of the principle of planned international investment, production and trade, and the abandonment of the principle of non-discrimination.[24]

In this we hear a pre-echo of fortress Europe. Nevertheless he assured the House of Commons: 'I have never for one moment at any meeting of the Council or Executive [of the European Movement] disguised from them the fact that this country as the centre of the Commonwealth cannot enter a European political federation and that our approach to the problem of European unity must always be functional rather than constitutional.'[25]

The European Movement was riven between the functionalists and the federalists. Boothby, in May 1950, wrote a paper for the European Movement warning it of the likely consequences of the split:

[T]he European Movement has been in a state of continuous and progressive disintegration; and as a result has ceased to give any effective leadership in the cause which we all have at heart. The cause of this is, in my opinion, the internecine disputes arising from the repeated attempts by our federalist friends to substitute a 'constitutional' for a 'functional' approach, as a result of which the Movement has literally been tearing itself to pieces. . . . If agreement cannot be reached, then the functionalists and the federalists should separate . . . or, alternatively, the Movement should be wound up.

The Schuman announcement, he wrote, 'makes the federation of Europe a declared aim, but adopts, without equivocation, the functionalist as against the constitutional approach'. In other words, Monnet's federalist rhetoric could be ignored. He went on to provide a definition of the functional approach which the sceptics of European integration would have found quite as objectionable as the clamours of the federalists. It was 'to break down national sovereignty by concrete practical action in the political and economic spheres'. This was reminiscent of Monnet's attack on the 'ramparts of sovereignty'. It was a long way from anything the British government had in mind. No wonder that Boothby

---

[24] HC Debs. 27 June 1950, col. 2121.   [25] Ibid., cols. 2116–17.

concluded his paper by emphasizing that 'the task confronting us is, in all conscience, formidable', and by issuing the plea: 'Must we make it even more difficult by superimposing hypothetical paper constitutions for which the Western world is certainly not ready?'

To the British government, functionalists of the Boothby variety were the thin end of the federalist wedge. Stikker comments: 'As a practical matter, the distinction between a functionalist and a federalist was often only a matter of championing a slower or a quicker pace of integration.'[26] Monnet was contemptuous of what he called 'pious "functional" hopes'.[27] He recalled that there were many in Europe who were pressing the functional approach. He mentions Paul Reynaud, André Philip, and Robert Boothby.[28] The merging of functionalism into federalism at the margin left it often unclear into which grouping a name should most appropriately be placed. Names such as Philip and Reynaud frequently appear in lists of European federalists. Monnet points out that nothing ever came of the functional approach. He refers to the resolution proposed by Kim Mackay, MP, at the Council of Europe in the summer of 1949 which read: 'The aim and goal of the Council of Europe is the creation of a European political authority with limited but real powers.' Monnet says, 'It was sent to the Committee of Ministers and there disappeared without trace.'[29] Of course, none of the names Monnet mentions were in government which somewhat limited their ability to move and shake. In government they might not have been so free with their nation's sovereignty. Nor had Monnet any good reason to be so caustic. An accumulation of functional authorities, of which his High Authority would be the first, appeared to be Monnet's own route to a European federation.[30]

The Schuman Plan alerted the British government to the fact that, in certain circumstances, the functional approach was itself unacceptable. Thus alerted, the government came out with a refined limitation to the acceptability of the functional approach. In the House of Commons on 13 November 1950, during a debate on the activities of the Council of Europe, Ernest Davies, Parliamentary Under-Secretary of State at the Foreign Office, said: 'The Government refuse to adhere in advance to an indefinite functional organization which is subject to a supranational authority whose composition and powers and the control of

---

[26] Stikker 188–9.   [27] Monnet 283.
[28] Reynaud was a former French Prime Minister, now regarded as very right wing.
[29] Monnet 281–2.   [30] Poidevin, *Schuman* (1986) 246.

which are unknown.'[31] He then added that as long as an organization retained the principle of the supranational authority 'it is still federation . . . and so the reservations have to be made whether the approach is a functional one or along constitutional lines'.[32] So anything that was supranational was also federal.

ROBERT MARJOLIN AND FEDERALISM

In pursuing its ambitions for Europe, the US Administration had allies among European federalists, none more effective than Jean Monnet. Well known and trusted in Washington, he was a committed, or at least an expedient, federalist.[33] He saw the value for France in agreeing with the Americans. Indeed, if Gillingham is to be believed, he combined statesmanship with cynicism.

For reasons of both principle and expediency, Monnet, and France, became the standard bearer of American policies of trade liberalization and political integration in 1948 and 1949. . . . The growing gap between New World ambitions on the one hand and Old World protectionism and nationalism on the other, gave Monnet a tailor-made opportunity to win American goodwill at very little cost. He could commend trade liberalization in theory without being expected to introduce it in practice.[34]

The Gillingham view does not comprehend the possibility that the Old World might perceive in the New World not merely ambitions but also its own protectionism and nationalism.

The UK might be the most outspoken opponent of American federal designs but it was an illusion to imagine that Europe was ready for federation or that Monnet spoke for Europe. There was another Frenchman, Robert Marjolin, Monnet's ablest aide, whose understanding of

[31] HC Debs. 13 Nov. 1950, col. 1403.   [32] Ibid., col. 1404.

[33] Richard Mayne, who knew Monnet well, questions whether he was a federalist. He says: 'I think this is an exaggeration, because he was never very systematic in his political thinking.' See Mayne, 'Jean Monnet, Europe and the British: A Witness Account', in Brivati and Jones. But other evidence, including the views of others who knew him well, suggests that, at the very least, he was an expedient, and bureaucratic, federalist. See Marjolin's view in Ch. 13 below.

[34] Gillingham 145–6. In this context Gillingham refers to Finebel, a French proposal in 1949 for an association short of a full customs union including Italy and the Benelux countries which 'never had a chance of working either politically or economically'. On the other hand it would be unfair to attribute this just to US influence. The idea had first been suggested by Hervé Alphand, head of the Economic Section of the French Foreign Ministry, as far back as 1947.

European realities far exceeded that of Monnet. Marjolin who, as the first Secretary-General of the OEEC, had much experience of American policies and pressures, and who generally approved of them, comments:

Originally, America's ambitions went very far, as far as the creation of a European federation. . . . They imagined, somewhat naïvely, a western Europe that would be an extension, as it were, of the United States in the Old World, inspired by the same values, following the same policy as they, relieving them of a responsibility they had always felt to be very heavy, that of defending Europe against all external aggression.[35]

Gillingham quotes Marjolin from an interview he held with him on 2 July 1971: 'If the British had wanted, in the years between 1947 and 1950 really to [direct] Europe towards union, they could have done it without problems. The French would have supported them, and all the others would have followed. That was an opportunity that was missed.'[36] It would, however, be wrong to deduce from this that Marjolin was a federalist. This quotation should be set alongside other Marjolin comments: 'Even in France, national sentiment was still too strong for the idea of a federation to have any chance of winning acceptance.'[37] Or again: 'I . . . thought that the nation state was not on the way out and that one could not expect the emergence of a European state in the foreseeable future.'[38] Or, yet again: 'Because the term "United States of Europe" creates illusions in minds that are ignorant of history, I have always refused to use it.'[39] Marjolin's view of Europe, as he himself acknowledged, had much in common with that of General de Gaulle.[40] He believed that Britain missed opportunities in not taking the lead towards a more integrated Europe. But in speaking of a more integrated Europe, he was certainly not thinking of a federal Europe. The correctness of Marjolin's appreciation of French opinion was confirmed when the attempt to convert the ECSC into a European Political Community (EPC), incorporating both the ECSC and an EDC, failed due to French opposition.

There are here questions of definition. When the Americans thought of federalism the majestic image of the American Constitution floated before their eyes. There is no doubt that many in the US Administration were looking for a Europe modelled on the American Constitution. It

---

[35] Marjolin (1989) 213.   [36] Gillingham 136–7.   [37] Marjolin (1989) 271.
[38] Ibid. 264. That these were Marjolin's views *at the time* is confirmed by George Ball. See ibid. 264–5.
[39] Ibid. 268.   [40] Marjolin (1981) 76.

is very doubtful whether even those Europeans who called themselves federalists had, at the time, any such conception of a federal Europe. It is doubtful whether most of those in Europe who advocated federalism in 1950 saw any inconsistency between national sovereignty and what they described as federalism.[41] It was no doubt in recognition of the truth of Marjolin's perception that, even at the time of the Schuman announcement, the French were busy redefining 'federation'. According to *The Times*'s Paris correspondent, reporting briefing from French sources, 'the word "federation" must no longer be taken in its usually accepted constitutional sense. It should rather be taken to indicate a growing network of common interests, jointly managed, among the countries of Europe.'[42] Monnet, in advocating the Schuman Plan, spoke of breaching the 'ramparts of national sovereignty'.[43] But Monnet was not standing for election and it is doubtful whether those European federalists, who were standing for election, wished to engage in such destruction. Rather, they were concerned to defend their national interest but believed that best done within a structured European context.[44] American policy might have been less naïve if the Administration had listened more to Marjolin and less to Monnet.[45]

BEVIN AND FEDERALISM

Bevin could never quite make up his mind whether he should take the federalist clamour at its own valuation or dismiss it. At times he derived comfort in his adherence to the intergovernmental approach by the thought that European federalism was really nothing more than rhetoric. Bullock says: 'The fact that "Europe" became identified with

[41] Milward writes of 'politicians who understood more clearly than their fellows that post-war reconstruction and survival of the nation state reposed on policies which might well require a certain surrender of national sovereignty for their effectiveness'. He adds that Schuman and Monnet may have 'reached the conclusion that the day of the nation state was closing but only when they had fallen from all political power': Milward, 'Conclusion: The Value of History', in Milward *et al.* 185.

[42] *The Times*, 22 May 1950.   [43] Monnet 296.

[44] Milward (1992), ch. 6, 'The Lives and Teachings of the European Saints', is of interest in this context.

[45] In Mar.–Apr. 1950 the Committee of Ministers of the Council of Europe rejected federalistic proposals for a supranational body in favour of Bevin's alternative of regular, informal meetings of the Assembly with ministerial representatives to resolve differences. They thus, once more, proved that more governments than Britain's disliked federalism: Young (1984) 143.

moves towards federation and the surrender of national sovereignty was a major stumbling block [to UK participation in the Schuman Plan]. . . . Bevin believed that this was so much rhetoric. . . .'[46] At other times, as we shall see, he took the threat of federalism more seriously. While he hoped that the federalist drive was just rhetoric, he actually feared its implications for Britain. There was thus confusion in the British understanding of what was happening in Europe. On the one hand, the Schuman Plan's supposed federalism was a bar to UK participation in it. On the other hand, the federalism was so much rhetoric. Yet, if the federalism was no more than rhetoric, there was no reason to be deterred by it and, by absence from the negotiations, to reinforce the conviction of increasing numbers of Europeans that they could make progress without Britain. If the Foreign Office at official level had shared their master's occasional opinion that federalist propaganda was no more than rhetoric, they might have thought more constructively about the Schuman Plan. In fact Bevin and his officials found enough substance in the federalist clamour to be diverted by it.

As the quotation from Makins at the head of this chapter illustrates, the view in London was that there were only two possible approaches to European problems, the federal and the intergovernmental. There was nothing in between. Yet it would have been possible to elaborate a treaty which was not federal because it preserved ultimate national sovereignty and yet gave greater incentive to common action than existed within such intergovernmental institutions as the OEEC. The evidence that such a treaty was conceivable is that one was eventually negotiated. It was called the Treaty of Rome. But to the British government at the time the Treaty of Rome, not being purely intergovernmental was, *ipso facto*, federal.

THE IRONY OF AMERICAN POLICY

The American urge to tell other peoples how to conduct their affairs was, so far as Britain was concerned, counter-productive. The outpouring of American money to Europe certainly gave them a platform. But it could have been used less raucously. There were many ironies in American policy. The UK had wanted to be treated separately from the rest of Western Europe in the planning of the ERP. By refusing the UK's request and thus forcing it to play a leading role in the CEEC, and

---

[46] Bullock 789.

subsequently in the OEEC, the Americans introduced a significant opponent to their intended use of the OEEC as the instrument of European federation.[47] They spent massively both in money and in energy pressing for European integration but, as the ECA warned, Marshall Aid by assisting recovery was entrenching the irrational boundaries of Europe's nation states.[48] Europe, they thought, needed a federal government and a unified European market. Yet Marshall Aid was saving European governments and economies from the need to face up to difficult choices.[49] Moreover, the more committed the USA became to the security of Europe, the less interested the UK became in European integration. More than anything else it was European civil war, and threats of war, that compelled the UK reluctantly to remember its geographical location. If, with the help of an American commitment to the security of Europe, European civil war could be consigned finally to an unhappy past, that would make the UK even less European, not more. It was a blessing, not just for Europe but for the USA, that American policy and pressure failed in its objective to create a federal Europe. The consequence was that in its security policy the USA could, as the years passed, depend on European allies strong in their national self-confidence. If it had had its way, it would have found itself in alliance with a European federal government which commanded no loyalty from its peoples and whose capacity to take decisions would have been undermined by the dissensions of the subsidiary nation states. American policy had been saved by its inability, in this respect, to enforce its will.

The final irony lay in American support for the Schuman Plan. It is not inconceivable that the British fear that the Schuman Plan had to be regarded not as functionalist but as federalist may have been enhanced by American support for it. Makins, in the quotation that heads this chapter, says that Britain would refuse participation in a federal system confined to Western Europe. Apparently a federal system that gave Britain access to the riches of North America would be nothing like as

[47] 'I still think [the CEEC conference in Paris] remarkable because I believe almost every national delegation came to feel a curiously vivid unity of purpose with the others, in spite of the diversity of national needs and national problems ... we were taking one step in the making of Europe': Franks 40.

[48] Bevin should have had some sympathy with this view. Speaking in the House of Commons on 24 Nov. 1945 he said: 'I cannot see a single frontier in Europe today that is economically sound.' He had held for many years the view that Europe needed a large single market. See e.g. his speech at the 1927 TUC Conference summarized Bullock's *Life and Times of Ernest Bevin*, vol. i. It was not surprising that he should return to this theme in the early days after the war, a time still of high hopes and idealistic visions.

[49] Milward (1984) 284–6.

objectionable. There were those in Whitehall and elsewhere who were prepared to entertain such dreams. But if that option was unreal, then Britain and British interests had to realize that they were under attack. The USA was on the attack against the Empire, the sterling area, and imperial preference. What would happen if British policy could be decided by a European majority which might be prepared to accept instructions from Washington? Washington might think that Britain no longer had special interests worth defending against a federal European authority. But Washington's view was self-interested and it was not, at the time, Britain's view. It was only as Britain's special interests declined even in Britain's eyes that its opposition to economic supra-nationalism, though never to federalism, also declined. These fears may seem today as unreal as the North American option. But Bevin in some of his moods was influenced by them.

Schuman had referred to his Plan as a step to federation. At the time his Plan was announced, the Labour Party was preparing a National Executive Committee (NEC) statement dealing with British policy towards the Council of Europe and the federalistic ideas appearing in the debates in that body's Consultative Assembly. The statement was eventually published under the title *European Unity*. It is discussed in Chapter 10. On 25 April 1950 Ernest Davies sent Denis Healey a paper headed *The Labour Party and European Co-operation*. Davies's paper was intended to help in the preparation of the NEC's statement. Davies told Healey that, in a minute the previous day, Ernest Bevin had asked that a paragraph should be included in the statement arguing that European federation could increase American influence over British policy. Davies provided Healey with a draft paragraph to this effect. It reads as follows:

A further and perhaps less obvious danger is that if there is any surrender of sovereignty to Europe an avenue of pressure through which the United States could influence Britain, through Europe, to accept its policies is thereby created. The Labour Party in particular is fearful of encroachment upon Britain's independence by the economic and financial power of the United States. All accept the necessity to co-operate with them, but do not wish to place themselves in a position to be dominated. If Britain had to accept the majority decisions made in the Council of Europe all the United States need do to impose its will on Britain would be to influence a majority of the European states there represented.[50]

---

[50] Ernest Davies Papers.

Neither this paragraph, nor anything like it, appears in the eventual NEC statement *European Unity*. On the contrary, the statement was fulsomely pro-American. It is not clear what intervened to prevent Bevin's views on this topic achieving immortality. It may have been prevented either by common sense in the International Department of the Labour Party or by quiet representations from the Foreign Office. The paragraph illustrates Bevin's resentment at American pressure on the UK to lead the way to a federal Europe. Resentment may have encouraged some people in the Foreign Office, following Bevin, to see the Schuman Plan as an instrument through which American hegemony could be exercised indirectly.[51] It is more likely that it was seen simply as an instrument of American demands for a European federation and that thereby British objections to participation in it were reinforced.

The US Administration watched the British government, in refusing to participate in the Schuman negotiations, cut off its nose to spite its face. The Administration's naïve federalist clamour bore some part of the responsibility.

[51] Ludlow, basing himself on Massigli, *Une comédie des erreurs*, says: 'it has become increasingly clear that the fear that the European Coal and Steel Community would be little more than an instrument of American hegemony was one of the more important factors influencing the British decision to stand apart from the Six in 1950': Ludlow 24.

7

'The Mess into Which They Have Landed Themselves'[1]

British diplomacy was rebuked by Schuman's announcement on 9 May 1950. The British government found itself bypassed. How should it react to what was undeniably a constructive French initiative, co-operatively or resentfully? For five years Western Europe had waited for Britain. Now France had acted. Should Britain work for the success of the French initiative or hope that it failed? Should it seek to prove by its behaviour that there was substance in its earlier talk about European unity or confirm the scepticism of its critics who believed that its words had no real meaning or intention behind them. One thing the British government dared not do. It dared not attempt to undermine the Schuman Plan. Unwelcome as was the French initiative, annoying as was the lack of consultation, the support which it had received from the USA put Britain on notice that, if it was not going to co-operate, at least it should behave. British reactions to the Schuman Plan were under close scrutiny in the State Department throughout the period leading up to the commencement of the negotiations in Paris on 20 June.

In the immediate aftermath of the announcement, it was bad temper and resentment that governed the British reaction to the announcement of the Schuman Plan rather than concern for the national interest. The initial response of the Attlee government was provided by Bevin. His outburst of bad temper was directed at both Paris and Washington. It was some mercy that this was in private. The more considered response combined blindness to the opportunities offered with failures in elementary diplomatic skills.

Bevin was in poor health. He had entered hospital on 11 April and had only returned to the Foreign Office on 8 May. This was just in time

---

[1] *DBPO* 31 Annex B, Makins to Bevin, 19 May 1950.

for the fourth session of the NATO Council in London. Kenneth Younger describes his condition:

He said himself that he is 'only half alive'. The doctors give him so many drugs that he often had difficulty in staying awake and in taking a proper grip of the meetings of which he has been chairman. . . . Personally I think it is something of a scandal that the PM has allowed this situation to develop. These talks have been heralded as 'the most important since the war', but they have been very largely futile, and Ernie's condition has been a big contributory cause.

Younger attended three out of four bilateral meetings between Bevin and Acheson, meetings which 'passed away as though they had never been'. He says: 'I . . . have seldom felt more embarrassed. Ernie was too ill to speak at two of them and could barely read out the agenda, let alone take charge.'[2] Massigli records that at the official lunch for the foreign visitors on 11 May, Bevin appeared weary in the extreme.[3]

Bevin's state of health probably did not improve his temper. He was furious with Acheson who, sworn to secrecy, had not been able to reveal, when he arrived in London from Paris, that Schuman had fore-warned him of the Plan.[4] According to Plowden, 'It took all Acheson's diplomatic skills to stop Bevin from immediately issuing a statement condemning Schuman's announcement.'[5] Acheson himself tells us that Bevin, when informed of the Schuman proposals, was 'very angry with me' and concedes that 'I had been stupid in not foreseeing . . . Bevin's rage at his apparent exclusion from the circle of consultation'.[6]

Within the British government, anger was not confined to Bevin. He had the sympathy and support of his officials in the Foreign Office. Such capacity for objective judgement as Foreign Office officials re-tained had been unhinged by resentment at French opportunism in acting without consultation. The resentment endured. In a brief to Bevin be-fore the House of Commons debate on the Plan at the end of June, Roger Makins wrote:

---

[2] Younger's diary, 14 May 1950. Acheson describes Bevin as he found him on 9 May: 'I found Ernest Bevin in distressing shape. . . . He had recently undergone a painful operation and was taking sedative drugs that made him doze off, sometimes quite soundly, during the discussion': Acheson 384.

[3] Massigli 198.

[4] At his press conference on 9 May 1950, Schuman said that 'The subject had not been broached in his talks with Mr Acheson yesterday, even in the "personal" conversation with which the day opened': *The Times*, 10 May 1950. This is confirmed by the Paris correspondent of the *Manchester Guardian*, 10 May 1950.

[5] Plowden 86.   [6] Acheson 385.

It would be appropriate to say something about the exceptional procedure adopted by the French Government in putting this idea forward, without consultation and without regard to the existing organisations which have been set up to deal with matters of common concern to Western European Governments both in the political and economic spheres, for example, the Consultative Council of the Brussels Treaty and the OEEC. We have recognized publicly why this procedure was adopted, namely in order to make the greatest possible impact on the Franco-German relationship, but at the same time we cannot be expected to act as though we had been consulted in advance.[7]

At the meeting of senior ministers under Attlee's chairmanship, the day after the announcement, it was considered that the French government had behaved 'extremely badly'.[8] At his press conference Schuman had suggested that the Plan would be open to the countries of Eastern Europe. This was a suggestion he was to repeat in giving evidence before the Foreign Affairs Committee of the National Assembly on 25 May 1950. The Plan, he said, was open to all European countries and Russia was in Europe.[9] Obviously he was anxious to demonstrate to French public opinion that his Plan was not a weapon in the cold war. Cripps, at the meeting on 10 May, took Schuman's invitation to Eastern Europe seriously. He expressed concern that it might lead to Russian influence on the European steel industry, oddly overlooking how unlikely this was, given that it would also lead to Western European countries exerting influence over Soviet coal and steel. Everyone present at the meeting agreed that the Plan 'showed a regrettable tendency to move away from the conception of the Atlantic community and in the direction of European federation'.[10] At the official lunch on 11 May, Cripps told Massigli that it was essential that the High Authority should not claim to dictate the economic policy of governments.[11] Thus the review of the options now facing the British government began with ministers and officials exhibiting bitterness about the manner and strong prejudices against the content of the Plan.

Resentment at the lack of consultation was not confined to the Cabinet or the Foreign Office or the Labour Party. A leading Tory, David Eccles, became a strong supporter of British participation in the Schuman Plan but even he resented the manner in which the French had

---

[7] Sir Roger Makins to Ernest Bevin, 17 June 1950—Notes for debate on Schuman Plan: MS Attlee dep. 102.

[8] *DBPO* 3.   [9] *The Times*, 26 May 1950.

[10] *DBPO* 3. The countries of Eastern Europe had not been given copies of the Schuman announcement.

[11] Massigli 198.

presented their proposal, without consultation and without prior notice. He did, however, find a more attractive way of expressing his resentment than did Bevin. In a letter to *The Times* he wrote: 'The French should have known that the British seldom fall in love at first sight. They should not have asked us to accept the engagement to marry before we had looked up the lady's family'[12]

One can find excuses for Bevin's fury. The question was whether it would be allowed to influence policy. There was substance in Bevin's suspicions of Acheson. It was not that he had visited Paris on his way to London just before the Schuman announcement and therefore had been given prior knowledge. This was a matter of chance.[13] What was not a matter of chance was that it had become settled American policy that, in default of British leadership in Europe, relations between Washington and Paris should become closer. Washington, in the absence of any move from London, *had* prompted Schuman into action. But it was no secret that the US Administration was intent on promoting deeper European integration and that Britain was resisting the pressure but had no ideas of its own.

There was justification in the suspicion that Acheson had, in effect, connived at lack of consultation with the UK over the Schuman Plan.[14] Schuman had announced a Plan affecting Germany without the appropriate tripartite consultations among the victors and occupiers. Acheson knew that Schuman was going to do it and did not attempt to stop him. All the evidence was there to suggest that Acheson was party with Schuman to an initiative designed, whatever was said to the contrary, to force Britain's hand. Moreover, Acheson's support for the Plan undermined Bevin's conception of post-war leadership. Bevin believed that Anglo-American agreement should precede all initiatives. His ground for being furious would, however, have been firmer had not the French experienced repeated occasions when Anglo-American decisions had ignored *their* declared interests. The proposition that all policy ideas had first to pass through an Anglo-American sieve could certainly not for long satisfy the French or Germans, not to speak of the USA itself. A more venial source of fury would have been Bevin's realization that

[12] *The Times*, 8 June 1950.
[13] This was not, in fact, particularly suspicious. Acheson was on his way back from Pakistan.
[14] Harvey, UK Ambassador, was informed by Schuman, together with other ambassadors, ten minutes before Schuman's press conference on 9 May. The notice that Massigli, French Ambassador to London, was allowed to give Bevin was only slightly longer: Massigli 188.

Schuman had stolen a march on him. For that, Bevin had to take the principal blame.

Whether venial or not, Bevin's outbursts of anger were futile. While his suspicions and fears were understandable, he should have saved his energy to devise ways of developing a constructive reaction to the Schuman initiative which avoided British isolation. For that there were many opportunities, all unfortunately wasted. The day after his announcement, Schuman visited London for the NATO Council. The visit was less happy than it might have been, given Bevin's outraged reaction to the fact that the French had shown the impudence to announce an initiative of their own without consultation. Bevin was reminded by Acheson, at a tripartite meeting with Schuman on 11 May, that the British had not given the French any but the briefest advance knowledge of the previous September's sterling devaluation.[15] This may have been a good debating point but it was one that would have appeared to Bevin as wholly irrelevant.

Schuman behaved very well. He had been, according to Massigli, astonished when warned by his ambassador that he must expect that his meeting with Bevin would be disagreeable. But then perhaps his appearance of astonishment was merely an aspect of his peasant cunning.[16] Schuman explained to Bevin and Acheson that French ministers had only been considering the Plan during the previous week 'though there had of course been studies on the subject by experts since long before the war'. It was a proposal, not a *fait accompli*. There was a need to break the deadlock in Europe caused by disagreements over the future of the Ruhr and by Law 75. The way to do it was by creating a 'European economic organization'. He accepted that the German part in any discussions would be dealt with by the High Commission because it 'was responsible for Germany's foreign policy'. He then offered 'his personal regrets for any embarrassment that might have been caused' to Acheson and Bevin.[17] He took every opportunity of emphasizing that he wanted British participation in his Plan. His courtesy lightened the atmosphere. But Bevin's mood and health remained an obstacle to mutual comprehension and the opportunity for a series of discussions about the Plan between Foreign Ministers was lost. Schuman did not leave London until 19 May. But from this point on there was no further substantial discussion between Bevin and Schuman about the Plan.

---

[15] Acheson 386.   [16] Massigli 197.   [17] *DBPO* 12.

A THIRD FORCE?

In London, any attempt at European integration was liable to be presented, even where it carried American support, as implying an intention to move the balance of European policy away from the Atlantic relationship in the direction of a neutralist European third force. The Schuman Plan was seen by some officials in the Foreign Office in London, and not in the Foreign Office nor among officials alone, as the product of third force neutralism. In some quarters on the continent of Europe and in some sections of the Labour Party, there was support for the idea of building Europe into a third force, neutral between the two Great Powers. Such an idea was attractive to many in France because of the strength of the Communists. French national unity was to be preserved by finding a middle way between the Great Powers of West and East. The idea of such a third force was supported in the British Labour Party by the far left in Parliament and, apparently, by a large section of the membership outside Parliament. For the left in Britain, the idea had the attraction of avoiding a choice difficult for those who put the USA and the USSR on the same moral level or who thought that the best way of helping the Soviet Union was to make Europe independent of the USA.[18] The British government sensibly rejected the third force option. There were many reasons. Perhaps the decisive reason was that a neutral third force Europe did not have the strength to defend itself.

But to rule out a neutralist European third force should not have ruled out a more integrated Europe of nation states. On the contrary, the dangers of European neutralism suggested that, if for no other reason than as a precaution, Britain should accept deeper involvement in European integration. Oliver Harvey argued that case in a memorandum to Bevin of 19 May. He advocated British support for the Schuman Plan precisely because it would move France in an Atlanticist direction:

The Schuman Plan . . . represents a turning point in European and indeed in world affairs. . . . If the Plan is adopted in its main lines, Franco-German

---

[18] In 1948 the Labour Party Conference approved a resolution moved by Benn Levy (MP for Eton and Slough 1945–50) which urged the Labour Party to 'co-operate with the European Socialist Parties in taking practical steps to enhance the United Socialist States of Europe (including the establishment of supra-national agencies to take over from each nation powers to allocate and distribute coal, steel, timber, locomotives, rolling stock and imports from hard currency countries) in complete military and political independence of the USA and the USSR'.

relations and in consequence Western European co-operation, the policy of Western Union and the Atlantic Pact should be set on a steady and hopeful course. If the Plan is rejected . . . it would have a paralysing effect on French statesmanship for years to come. It would seem inconceivable to French opinion that so bold a policy involving for France both forgiveness of the past and pooling of resources for the future, could be rejected for disinterested motives. It would strengthen anew those negative and insular tendencies of French policy fostered by that corrosive school of thought . . . against which Monsieur Schuman himself has now warned us, the neutrality school. A very powerful argument would be afforded to those, not only Communists, who favour appeasement of the Soviet Government.[19]

In fact, after the expulsion of Communists from the French government in 1947, and the establishment of NATO, a French betrayal of Western solidarity became much less likely though the possibility continued to worry the Foreign Office.[20] It was a pity that all Bevin could think of by way of a reaction to Harvey's eloquent appeal was to urge that he 'be instructed to continue to press our point of view on the French'. Dispatches favourable to the Schuman Plan were evidently not welcome in the Secretary of State's office.

The fears about a European third force were frequently based on misunderstanding rather than on a real threat of neutralism. There were neutralists. But advocates of European integration were not necessarily neutralist and did not necessarily question the Atlantic alliance. Much that was criticized as 'third force neutralism' was a natural wish, notably in France and Germany, that Europe should have a political personality of its own that was not simply taken for granted by the USA and the UK. The misunderstanding extended even to a journal as favourable to the Schuman Plan as *The Economist*. It complained that 'when Dr Adenauer supports the Schuman Plan . . . as a means of creating a neutral bloc between the quarrels of the two world powers, it is clear that something has gone awry in European thinking'.[21] Denis Healey, International Secretary of the Labour Party, informed the International Sub-Committee of the NEC: 'The Schuman proposals were immediately welcomed by the German Chancellor, Dr Adenauer, as creating the basis for a neutral Third Force in Europe.'[22] Both comments

[19] *DBPO* 33, Harvey to Bevin, 19 May 1950.

[20] Acheson clearly still had his worries. So had some members of the British Cabinet and some Foreign Office officials. See e.g. *DBPO* 3, 15, 17, and 31 Annex A.

[21] *The Economist*, 27 May 1950.

[22] In a note prepared as background in preparation for the International Socialist Conference on the Control of Europe's Basic Industries, to be held in London on 16–18 June 1950.

seriously misrepresented Adenauer's ideas. Adenauer had in fact said in a speech in Cologne on 21 May 1950: 'A united Europe with the inclusion of Britain will never be so strong as to endanger either of the two big Powers, the Soviet Union or the United States. It must, however, be strong enough to throw its weight on to the scales in favour of peace. Tensions between the big two may one day lead to an explosion exterminating Europe.'[23] As German Chancellor, Adenauer could hardly be blind to the fact that a war between the Great Powers would be fought on German territory.

But this did not mean that Adenauer was a neutralist. At a press conference on 9 May at which he welcomed the Schuman Plan, Dr Adenauer also announced the Federal Cabinet's intention to recommend to the Bundestag Germany's accession to the Council of Europe. He advocated the decision to join the Council of Europe as a gesture of solidarity with the West. He argued that 'the co-operation of the European countries is absolutely necessary to withstand pressure from the east'.[24] But he felt that Europe must have a voice.[25] The point was well made by Raymond Aron. He wrote: 'Politically to stand up to Soviet imperialism as well as in their own relations with their ally across the Atlantic, the European nations obviously need to be able to present a substantial and publicly proclaimed united front. The Schuman plan is a last attempt to do this.'[26]

The three principal people behind the Schuman Plan were Schuman, Monnet, and Bernard Clappier, Schuman's *Directeur de Cabinet*. As Harvey was to point out in June, none of them were supporters of a third force:

Though M. Schuman habitually has many mental reservations and though both M. Monnet and M. Clappier suffer from that excessive precision which is a characteristic of the French *Inspecteur des Finances* they are all three fundamentally men of good will, sincere, disinterested and patriotic. Moreover, none of them are partisans of the 'Third Force' in Europe, still less of neutrality. All of them believe in the necessity for collaboration with the United States and the United Kingdom.[27]

[23] Reported in *Manchester Guardian*, 22 May 1950. See also Adenauer 258–9.
[24] *The Economist, 17 June 1950.*
[25] Any neutralist tendencies in Adenauer's mind would be negated by what Sir Brian Robertson in a message to Younger described as 'the intransigence of recent Russian behaviour, culminating in an agreement between the East Zone Government and the Polish Government on the Oder–Neisse line': *DBPO* 108, 19 June 1950.
[26] *Manchester Guardian*, 30 May 1950.
[27] *DBPO* 103, message from Harvey to Younger, 16 June 1950.

Monnet, in his opening speech to the Schuman Plan negotiating conference, severely criticized all those who suggested that the Plan had
something to do with neutralism. On the contrary, the object was to
strengthen Europe, the exact opposite of neutralism. Neutrality was
based on fear and on the belief that war was inevitable. It was not
inevitable but it could be avoided only if the West was strong.[28] But the
suspicion in London was not so easily eradicated. It was yet one more
barrier to constructive thought about the Schuman Plan even though
Washington was giving it its support.

THE PUBLIC FRONT

Reconciliation between France and Germany was an objective of which
the UK government could only approve. Nor could it object publicly to
proposals presented as designed to improve the efficiency of French
and German industry. Nor could it take the least objection to the development of the African continent.[29] It was, at the time, actively promoting the groundnuts scheme in East Africa. When, as he occasionally
did, Bevin spoke of an Anglo-French union or an Anglo-French customs union, the idea of involving the African continent had always
been present. He regarded Africa as a source of raw materials which the
Americans would need and which the UK, as the imperial power, could
one day use as a bargaining counter with the USA.[30] Robert Hall, in a
minute of 11 May, wrote that even though there would be 'immense
practical and administrative difficulties' in implementing the Plan, nevertheless 'we would look very much of a dog in the manger if we
appeared to disapprove'.[31] In a statement in the House of Commons on
11 May, Attlee said: 'It is the declared policy of the Western Powers
to promote the entry of Germany as a free member into the comity of
European nations. The French proposals are designed to facilitate that
process and must consequently be regarded as a notable contribution
towards the solution of a major European problem.'[32]

Thus the public position of the British government was one of

[28] *DBPO* 113, message from Harvey to Younger, 22 June 1950.
[29] The sentence about Africa was added at the suggestion of René Mayer: Monnet 300.
At his press conference on 9 May 1950 at which he welcomed the Schuman Plan, Dr
Adenauer 'emphasized three times . . . those passages of the French proposal which related to the development of Africa': *DBPO* 5. See also nos. 21 and 25.
[30] J. Gallagher, *The Decline, Revival and Fall of the British Empire* (Cambridge
University Press: Cambridge, 1982), 146. Quoted Hennessy 221.
[31] *DBPO* 13.   [32] Cmd. 7970/3.

support for the French initiative though without any commitment to British participation. As ministerial discussion had already made clear, this favourable opinion did not enjoy the private support of Attlee's Cabinet. But it was the only possible public position if Britain was to avoid infuriating Washington or appearing, as Hall had warned, as a dog in the manger.

INTERNATIONAL ENTANGLEMENTS

International entanglements always bring an element of uncertainty into the conduct of economic policy. They threaten the exercise of national sovereignty. The Schuman Plan gave rise to more specific fears. It appeared to deprive the governments of member countries of control of their basic industries. The High Authority could make decisions which bound governments. There was, therefore, a threat to *national* economic planning. For *national* economic planning would be substituted planning on a *European* scale. Though the UK had no planning apparatus worthy the name, nor any expectation of creating one, there were, in Britain, exaggerated expectations from national economic planning. Only such exaggerated expectations could justify the feeling that the Schuman Plan threatened to deprive the British economy of the splendid future that national economic planning would create for it. But, even on the most optimistic assessment of the potentiality for planning, was the threat real? The Plan may have *appeared* inconsistent with an ideology of national economic planning and might prompt fears that something as important as national economic sovereignty was being sacrificed, but the obscurity of the words suggested enquiry before rejection. The only way of conducting such an enquiry would be by attendance at the negotiating table. It was not publicly suggested in London in connection with the Schuman proposals that there must never be any compromise of British sovereignty, only that the full significance of any compromise of sovereignty had to be assessed before the UK could commit itself.

There was an even more specific fear. There were those who believed that the High Authority could, without the agreement of member governments, shut down pits and plants. If this fear was justified there was reason to question the effects of this particular international entanglement on full employment. Attlee had established a Ministerial Committee, GEN 322, with himself in the chair, to consider the Schuman Plan. This fear was strongly expressed at the first meeting of GEN 322 on 11 May 1950.[33] A Treasury memorandum, dated 11 May, on the economic implications of the Schuman Plan for the UK steel industry, stated:

For the purpose of this study . . . we must assume that the Authority will arrange for steel to be made by the most efficient producer. . . . In those circumstances it is by no means certain that the United Kingdom would gain. In the short term the efficiency and recent modernization of the United Kingdom steel industry would operate in our favour. . . . In the longer term, however, the logical fulfilment of the process of economic integration . . . might be a large measure of concentration of European steel production in the Ruhr–Saar–Luxembourg area, where the presence of more easily worked coal coupled with iron ore deposits and water transport might give an advantage in costs over the United Kingdom.[34]

In his defence of the UK government's rejection of participation in the Schuman negotiations in the debate in the House of Commons on 26 June 1950, Cripps suggested that the 'supra-national high authority . . . could cause a whole coal field and steel centre to go out of production without any social or political responsibility for their action'.[35] This expressed a dread that was present throughout the preliminary examination of the Plan in London. Cripps appears really to have persuaded himself that such a thing could happen. The fact that no High Authority, however its powers were defined, would be able to take decisions to close down industries, or major parts of them, without the agreement of member governments was a matter of practical wisdom that escaped him. Other governments, including the French, would have exactly the same concerns and would ensure that there was no such danger. Given the low competitiveness of its industries, the risks being accepted by France far exceeded those that would have been taken by Britain. Of this, the French were entirely aware. As we shall see, they made perfectly clear to the UK government their intention that the High Authority's work would not prejudice full employment and would permit the reconciliation of full employment with rationalized production.[36] This was at least as important to France as to Britain. The Schuman

---

[33] *DBPO* 15.   [34] *DBPO* 18.

[35] HC Debs. 26 June 1950, col. 1940.

[36] Cmd. 7970/10. The Convention on Transitional Provisions, negotiated together with the Treaty of Paris establishing the ECSC, required the High Authority to prevent decreases in production and instability in employment due to sudden shifts in the established pattern of coal sales: Haas 65. What Belgium achieved for its high-cost coal-mines was an example of the recognition in the negotiations of the political realities: Diebold 66; Milward (1992), ch. 3, 'Coal and the Belgian Nation'.

Plan was not launched for the purpose of encouraging Communist subversion. Subsequent experience of the activities of the High Authority would confirm its respect, sometimes even excessive, for political realities.

A more sophisticated perception of the problem came in a letter in *The Times* on 10 June from four Oxford economists with Labour sympathies, Thomas Balogh, Dudley Seers, Paul Streeten, and G. D. N. Worswick. They argued that full employment was essential to the successful implementation of any plan to integrate the European economy. The letter also questioned whether the Schuman Plan could be effective once the power to control Germany was lost. It was a question in many minds. It was not, by any means, a specifically socialist question.

Full employment must be put first in any attempt to 'integrate' Europe. Until this is secured no country will permit the closing down of its own industries, however inefficient. . . . Thus without general full employment the 'pooling' of single industries is likely to take the form of an old-fashioned restrictive cartel so as to protect every existing enterprise. . . . It is rather naïve . . . to hope that the present proposals are worth more than the 'Ruhr Statute', the Potsdam Agreement or the Treaty of Versailles. So long as the allies are capable of enforcing their will nothing much matters. Once we lose control, no agreement is worth the paper it is written on.[37]

This letter presented a more realistic appreciation of the questions raised by the Schuman Plan than the exaggerated fears of Cripps and others that the High Authority might take a scythe to European heavy industry.

The economic recovery of France and Germany were prime American objectives. Yet the US Administration strongly supported the Schuman Plan. The Plan would hardly have had its support if the Administration had suspected damage to this prime political and economic objective. Important as European economic recovery was to the USA, it was certainly not less important to the countries of Western Europe which were proposing to take part in the Schuman Plan. They did not appear to perceive prejudice to their economic interests provided that they were present at the negotiating table to mould the Plan to accommodate their requirements, and present later to supervise the implementation of the treaty that would emerge. If the countries of Western Europe, including France with its Monnet Plan and its *Commissariat Générale du Plan*, did not fear the power to bind, why should

[37] *The Times*, 10 June 1950.

the UK? There was, therefore, reason to question whether dramatic language about the closing of pits and steel manufacturing without the consent of governments was really appropriate in considering the Schuman Plan.

More mature advice came from E. F. Schumacher, Economic Adviser to the National Coal Board (NCB):

I conclude . . . that from the point of view of the British coal industry there appears on balance to be no alarming economic or commercial danger in leaving the French and the Germans to come to any arrangement they please, without British participation. But I also believe that an important opportunity for achieving a far-reaching European co-ordination of import and export policies would thereby be missed and that the political consequences of staying outside might be very serious and disturbing.[38]

Thus it was Schumacher's view that it was staying out that could have the serious and disturbing consequences. This advice was not without influence in the NCB's sponsor Ministry of Fuel and Power. It may even have influenced opinion within the NUM. Certainly, the advice could be read in different ways. Economic advisers to major industries are not invariably advocates of free trade. Schumacher's use of the word 'co-ordination' might justify fears among economic liberals. A strong case could be made against the Schuman Plan on liberal grounds. But there could be no doubt that Schumacher's advice encouraged participation in any Schuman Plan negotiations rather than the opposite. And the ministers in the Attlee government were planners rather than liberals.

QUESTIONS

The Schuman Plan, it was repeatedly emphasized, had been sprung on the UK not just without previous consultation but with little if any detail. Dangers were read in every line, not to mention those suspected between the lines. Undoubtedly there were many legitimate questions to be asked. But so far as Britain was concerned the many questions only needed to be answered if participation in the coal and steel pool was to be seriously considered. If its interest was genuine, the British government would have to decide when these questions needed to be

---

[38] T 229/749, 18 May 1950.

answered. Did they have to be answered before it agreed to participate in the negotiations for which France was calling or could the answers await the meeting of the negotiating conference? As there was to be a negotiating conference in which other countries besides France would take part, and have a say, wisdom might have been thought to dictate patience until the conference convened. After all, French wishes might not, in all cases, prevail. There was yet another possible course of action. That was to pretend that participation was being seriously considered, to ask the French all kinds of questions, to insist that they be answered definitively before making the commitment even to participate in the negotiating conference, but without any sincere intention of actually taking part. It was this latter course that the British government actually adopted.

The first, and most important, of the legitimate questions was about the nature and powers of the High Authority. This question will be further discussed in Chapter 9. But there were other questions. One was whether the real intention behind the Plan was to re-create a cartel. At the time of the Schuman announcement there was already a steel glut.[39] The Economic Commission for Europe had forecast that, on present development plans, by 1953 crude steel production would have risen to 70 million tons whereas demand would be 62 million tons. Some industrial support might have been attracted to the Plan by the thought that the intention was the re-creation of the pre-war steel cartel. Monnet strongly denied any intention to create a cartel. But the US Administration, while strongly supporting the French initiative, was never totally convinced that that was not the purpose.[40] The British government had the same suspicions.[41] It was entirely reasonable to be suspicious. It was not to be expected that a proposal emanating from France and from Monnet would be an economic liberal's dream. The question throughout was whether the political gains from Franco-German reconciliation justified any economic cost. It would, moreover, be optimistic to imagine that, whatever countenance the High Authority would find

---

[39] It was reported to the Foreign Office that Luxembourg ministers were concerned that the steel industry on which everything in Luxembourg then depended was running at a loss. Future prospects were so black that any change that might be brought about by the Schuman Plan must inevitably be for the better: *DBPO* 66.

[40] The steel glut rapidly disappeared under the impact of the Korean War.

[41] See e.g. *DBPO* 65. Plowden says: 'I predicted wrongly that the setting up of a common authority as proposed would most likely lead to the formation of a cartel "of the more or less conventional type"': Plowden 86. Plowden should have held on to his suspicions.

it necessary to give to vested interests within the ECSC, they would receive less countenance if an ECSC never came into existence.

Kenneth Younger was uncertain whether to be more suspicious of an intention to create a cartel or of the influence of Catholicism. He noted his first reactions to the Plan in his diary:

In view of the political complexion of the French and German governments and their links with heavy industry, one cannot but expect that this will develop along old-fashioned cartel lines. It need not do so, however, and if we can get the scheme executed in a way which safeguards the public interest and limits the power of the vested interests in the international authority, then it *may* be a step forward. On the other hand it may be just a step in the consolidation of the catholic 'black international' which I have always thought to be a big driving force behind the Council of Europe.[42]

If he read *The Economist*, Younger might have noticed the description of German industrial leaders as 'the most cartel-minded people in the world'.[43] Nevertheless, Younger was prepared to reserve his judgement for the time being.

The Schuman announcement had stated categorically that the institution of the High Authority would not in any way prejudge methods of ownership.[44] It was a statement that would help to recruit industrial support. It would also safeguard the ambitions of those advocating state ownership of what were still believed to be the commanding heights of the economy. But if the intention of the Schuman Plan was not to create a cartel, and methods of ownership were not in question, that in itself raised questions as to how its actual purposes, for example of modernization and equalization of living conditions, were to be achieved. There was every justification in asking how serious the intention was to equalize living conditions, how it was to be managed and over what period. This was a question that would deeply concern British trade-unionists if the levelling was to be down rather than up.

The Schuman Plan had specified that the supply of coal and steel to all member countries should be *on identical terms*. This was a key French requirement. The French government and steel industry suspected discrimination in pricing in the supply of German coking coal to the advantage of the German steel industry. The announcement left it unclear, however, how these further purposes were to be achieved. In later press briefing, French sources indicated that it would not be the

[42] Younger's diary, 14 May 1950. See also Massigli 196.
[43] *The Economist*, 20 May 1950.   [44] Cmd. 7970/2.

function of the High Authority to fix prices. They were not proposing that it should institute a uniform delivered price throughout the area covered by the High Authority. The requirement of 'identical terms' apparently meant, among other things, no differential transport rates. Here too, clarification of objective and method would be necessary.

THE MILITARY VIEW

Monnet noted at the time that one reason why the UK distanced itself from the Schuman Plan was that it doubted the ability of continental Europe to defend itself.[45] To surrender control of the British coal and steel industries to a supranational authority could be incompatible with the objective of sustaining a capacity to stand alone if Western Europe was overrun. One source of good sense on this issue was, as it happened, the British Chiefs of Staff. At its first meeting on 11 May 1950, GEN 322 considered a paper prepared by the Chiefs of Staff on the defence issues associated with the Schuman Plan. The Chiefs of Staff were very favourable to the Plan. A Franco-German *rapprochement* could only strengthen Europe's defences. 'The strategical implications of the French proposal appear to be strongly in favour of Western European defence and at first sight we see no serious military disadvantages.' On further consideration they associated themselves with a statement that nothing should be done to diminish 'domestic self-sufficiency as regards special alloy steels and other speciality steel items essential to defence production'.[46] They appeared to think that such a proviso would be negotiable. The Ministry of Defence itself, on similar grounds, was concerned that the UK should not attach itself so closely to Europe, by joining the Plan, that it could not survive the fall of the Continent. The Ministry made a distinction between liberalization, which it approved, and integration, which it did not approve. Integration 'in the full sense' meant 'compulsory specialization'. Particularly under the control of a supranational authority, it could imply that 'we should abandon certain of our manufactures which were admittedly uneconomical'. As a result 'we might well find that our war potential was crippled because we were dependent on supplies from abroad, and these

[45] In some notes he made at the time, Monnet wrote: 'Britain has no confidence that France and the other countries of Europe have the ability or even the will effectively to resist a possible Russian invasion': Monnet 316–17.

[46] *DBPO* 129, memorandum by Minister of Defence, 1 July 1950.

supplies were not forthcoming'. The Ministry of Defence apparently considered that these uneconomical industries would survive liberalization, presumably on the basis of subsidy. But the key defence objective was to ensure that participation in the Schuman Plan did not prejudice Britain's ability to stand alone if it were ever again necessary. The Chiefs of Staff had indicated the necessary proviso. It would have seemed sensible to attempt to negotiate it. There can be little doubt that such a proviso would have been negotiable.[47] The Schuman Plan negotiations in Paris were largely concerned with satisfying member countries' provisos. As the weeks passed, the Chiefs of Staff did not change their immediate reaction to the Schuman announcement. In a paper dated 1 July, when the Ministry of Defence had had the opportunity for a more considered reaction, Emanuel Shinwell, Minister of Defence, put to the Cabinet a paper confirming the arguments that in May had led the Chiefs of Staff to take a favourable view of the Schuman proposals, subject only to the need to ensure the survival in Britain of capacity in special alloy steels and speciality steel items essential to defence production.[48]

MONNET'S VISIT TO LONDON

Monnet arrived in London on 14 May in an attempt to remove the mystery from the Plan. He did not succeed. The Foreign Office was always suspicious of Monnet's motives. There was too much evidence of his desire to draw Britain into Europe for the benefit of France. It was never quite sure how he should be treated. He did not seem to fit into any of the well-known categories. In British life, there were ministers and officials. Monnet was an official but he did not act like an official. Sometimes he seemed to have his own policies and his policies sometimes seemed to be more influential than those of ministers. By British standards, it was all rather irregular. Massigli, who kept his admiration for Monnet well this side of enthusiasm, appears to have felt that it would have been better if he had not come.[49] Massigli may have been right. Monnet's visit may have led British ministers to think that Monnet was the man to talk to rather than French ministers. Face to face discussion of the Plan was left to an undesirable extent to a

[47] *DBPO* 16 and 129.
[48] *DBPO* 129, memorandum by Minister of Defence, 1 July 1950.
[49] Massigli 199–200, 209.

dialogue between its most ideological supporter, Jean Monnet, and a group of senior British officials led by Roger Makins and Edwin Plowden.

It was too readily accepted that Monnet was the appropriate spokesman of the French government and that he spoke for the French government as a whole. At the first meeting of GEN 322 on 11 May, it was proposed that informal contact should be made with Monnet 'to ascertain whether the proposal represented an economic scheme which had been put forward at this juncture for political reasons, or whether the project was primarily political in character'.[50] Plowden was instructed to find out, in the course of his discussions with Monnet, whether Britain could participate in the negotiations without commitment.[51] Both questions could have led to valuable discussions. Those discussions could have helped to clear the air. But they should have been addressed by Bevin to Schuman, not by Plowden to, of all people, Monnet. If there had been no other effect, it would have compelled Schuman to think more carefully about what he was doing.

There was an encounter between Cripps and Monnet on 15 May. Cripps asked Monnet whether France would go ahead with Germany even without the UK. Monnet replied: 'My dear friend, you know how I have felt about Britain for more than thirty years. . . . I hope with all my heart that you will join in this from the start. But if you don't, we shall go ahead without you. And I'm sure that, because you are realists, you will adjust to the facts when you see that we have succeeded.'[52]

There are those who claim that Monnet's statement about the hope in his heart was totally insincere. Their principal arguments are the lack of consultation before 9 May and the ultimatum from Paris to London on 1 June which is discussed in the next chapter. But there are more intuitive arguments. The presence at the negotiations of another of the victor powers would have greatly diluted the influence of France and hence of Monnet. It might have prevented his getting the kind of High Authority he wanted. He could not possibly want the UK to be present. The question whether the French, or Monnet, actually wanted British participation in the Schuman Plan negotiations has only limited importance. Its importance for this book is that the allegation that they did not really want British participation is used as an excuse by those, like Sir Frank Roberts, who wish to defend the British decision not to participate.[53] The question will, therefore, be discussed in the final

[50] *DBPO* 15 .   [51] Plowden 87.   [52] Monnet 308.   [53] See Ch. 1 above.

chapter. Meanwhile it is enough to say, as is recorded in the next chapter, that the British government received an invitation from Paris and that it was the British government that decided to decline. The receipt of an invitation may usually be taken as evidence that there will be a welcome if it is accepted.

Cripps's immediate reaction to Monnet's statement was that in his personal opinion the United Kingdom should accept to negotiate at once on the basis proposed by the French, subject to clarification of certain points. 'He did not believe that the United Kingdom would ever be able to come in later on a scheme which had been worked out by France, Germany and Benelux and he thought, therefore, we should collaborate from the outset.' He added that 'he realised that the proposal might lead to political federation but thought this would not come until later'.[54] We have seen that Cripps, earlier, had expressed strong reservations about the Plan, notably about the powers of the High Authority. Contrary to his reputation, Cripps, at this stage of his career, exhibited a tendency to agree with the latest persuasive interlocutor whether from inside or outside the Treasury.[55] It may have been due to the poor state of his health. Cripps's reaction surprised Plowden who felt that he had to warn Monnet that Cripps was speaking for himself, not for the British Cabinet.[56] None of the points on which Cripps then said he would want clarification would have raised any difficulty. His instinct that Britain should collaborate in the Plan and his calm attitude towards Monnet's federalist dreams should have been a model for the whole government. The Schuman Plan, whatever Monnet may have claimed for it, was a long way from European federation. During the conversation with Monnet, Cripps was clearly persuaded that the Attlee government could influence the development of the Schuman proposals only by becoming part of the negotiations and that it should not be frightened away from the negotiating table by words.

The following day at a meeting of the Economic Policy Committee of the Cabinet, Cripps reported his conversation with Monnet. It appears that he had by this time thought better of his immediate favourable reaction to participation. He spoke of the need for assurances on 'preliminary political conditions' and suggested only the involvement of British officials. It was agreed that 'United Kingdom officials should take part in the elaboration of a detailed scheme—on the understanding

---

[54] *DBPO* 24.   [55] Gaitskell detected this phenomenon: Gaitskell 187.
[56] *DBPO* 24; Plowden 87–8.

that their association with this work would not commit the United Kingdom government to adopting, either in principle or in detail, the scheme evolved.' This was in accordance with Cripps's recommendations.[57] There is always a problem about how far ministers can be expected to commit themselves in advance to the outcome of official negotiations. It is a problem easier to handle if negotiators, while accepting the absence of commitment, which normally applies to all of them, have confidence in the sincerity of their partners and of their wish to be involved in the outcome if reasonable anxieties are reasonably met.

On 16 May, in the Hyde Park Hotel, there was a meeting between Monnet and Plowden, Makins, and Hitchman. Plowden discovered that Monnet's ideas on exactly how the mechanics of the Plan would work were 'vague in the extreme'.[58] The notes of the meeting show that there had been as many questions which Monnet could not yet answer as those which he could.[59] This was seen not as an opportunity but as an objection. The best that these officials could get by way of a written interpretation of the Plan was a letter from Monnet to Plowden. The letter, from Paris, was dated 25 May but apparently was only received on 30 May. Monnet's letter was still explicitly tentative and professed a willingness to discuss and to modify. It gives no guidance on how the problem of equalizing pay was to be tackled. Monnet expresses concern about low-wage competition from other countries. He fears 'social dumping' within Europe. But he gives no clue as to how he would aim to achieve the equalization of pay, probably because he had no clue to give.[60] The same question had occurred to other countries and was being discussed by them. Federal Vice-Chancellor Blücher, in conversation with the British representative on the IAR, Sir V. Berry, pointed to one difficulty. 'German miners' wages were higher than the French, output per man-shift [was] also higher and . . . German prices included the cost of much miners' welfare, which was an essential part of the German social structure.'[61] At a meeting in Paris on 25 May with French representatives, Benelux Ministers argued that there could be no equalization of wages and social services in one important section of the European economy without similar equalization in other sectors. The French had no answer to the problem.[62] In the course of the negotiations,

---

[57] *DBPO* 26.   [58] Plowden 89.   [59] *DBPO* 25.   [60] *DBPO* 45.

[61] Ibid. *The Times*, however, calculated that 'German wage limits, at the present exchange rate, are much below the French': *The Times*, 11 May 1950. There is a discussion of relative pay levels between France and Germany in Milward (1984) 374–5.

[62] *DBPO* 43.

the idea of equalizing wages had to be abandoned. In substitute the eventual treaty provided that wages should not be reduced to improve competitiveness except as part of a general *national* reduction in pay.[63] Presumably the British government would have been content with this had it consented to be present at the negotiations and assist Benelux representatives with the argument.

Monnet told Makins and Plowden that 'the French Government recognize that the establishment of [the High Authority] means the surrender of national sovereignty over a wide strategic and economic field and that they are prepared to do this in the interest of furthering European unity'.[64] Such a statement coming from such a source should have been tested by discussion with French ministers. They were unlikely to endorse it. During the following days there were other encounters between British officials and members of Monnet's team. On each occasion the question for British officials was whether any reliance could be put on what they were told as an expression of French government intentions What did become clear was that there was extensive room for British influence on the outcome if only Britain agreed to take part in the negotiations. The ideas of some of Monnet's coterie were many miles away from what French ministers would consider acceptable. Thus Étienne Hirsch, who was to be Monnet's successor as head of the *Commissariat Générale du Plan*, said, in discussion with Plowden, that it would be a matter of indifference whether steel production was sited in France or Germany because national frontiers would be wiped out; that members of the High Authority could be of any nationality, for example British, Swiss or American, because it would be their technical expertise that would be important. The naïvety of these views should have alerted British officials to the desirability of their ministers talking to French ministers to determine what was in *their* minds rather than in those of one singularly determined French official and his supporters.[65]

An official committee under the chairmanship of Edward Bridges was established to study the Schuman Plan. It was called the FG Committee, short for 'Franco-German'.[66] Plowden, after his various discussions with Monnet and his coterie, pointed out to a meeting of the FG Committee on 17 May that 'It would only be possible to find out whether the proposals, which were extremely nebulous at the present stage, would be advantageous to the United Kingdom by taking part in

---

[63] Milward (1992) 69.   [64] *DBPO* 25.   [65] Milward (1984) 401.
[66] Its full name was the Committee on Proposed Franco-German Coal and Steel Authority.

the initial discussions'.[67] The British government was to prove itself intent on ensuring that it did not find out whether the proposals would be advantageous to the United Kingdom.

By 24 May, Cripps was among those who wished to ensure that the UK should in no way be committed, or appear to be committed, by any involvement in negotiations.[68] By the time of the debate in the House of Commons on 26 June 1950, he had departed even further from his initial calm acceptance of the need for UK participation. He referred to the part of the Schuman announcement that stated that 'these proposals will build the first concrete foundation of the European Federation which is indispensable for the preservation of peace'. On this he then commented: 'This approach involves the partners in the scheme, not only in commitments in regard to coal and steel industries, but also in commitments in regard to the future political framework of Europe.'[69] Just as Monnet was obsessed with the need for European federation, British ministers and civil servants were obsessed by fears that they would be sucked along the federalist path. There was in fact no truth in the proposition that by accepting the invitation to participate in the Schuman Plan negotiations, the UK would become committed to a federalist political framework for Europe.

The British demand for interpretation of the various obscurities in the Plan became an excuse for quibbling and delay. Given the obvious urgency emanating from Paris, the determination that the UK must know more precisely the nature of the commitment before entering negotiations amounted to a rejection without all the palaver about federalism, supranationalism, Atlanticism, multilateralism, which the UK was to employ in an attempt to give a respectable cover to its refusal to participate.[70] Other countries did not insist on laborious investigation, or on a great deal of detail, before consenting to enter into negotiation. It was at the negotiating table that French intentions would be revealed and then moulded to the requirements of the various member states rather than those of the French alone. In their press briefing, the French expressed surprise at the British criticism of lack of detail. The criticism, they thought, was inconsistent with the British reputation for pragmatism. The French answer to the criticism was *solvitur ambulando*.[71]

Cripps's spontaneous and relaxed initial reaction to Monnet's

[67] *DBPO* 28.   [68] *DBPO* 41 n.
[69] HC Debs. 26 June 1950, cols. 1947–8.   [70] Plowden 88–9.
[71] *The Times*, 22 May 1950.

presentation might perhaps have led to a happier outcome had such views not been opposed by the Foreign Office. Schuman had, however, perhaps unwittingly, provided the Foreign Office with an excuse for inaction. He had accepted, at his final press conference before leaving London on 19 May, the possibility of British association with his Plan as an alternative to membership.[72] The idea of association suggested to the Foreign Office a satisfactory third way between membership and abstention. It did not, therefore, have to think seriously about membership. While the rest of Europe was making up its mind, the Foreign Office dawdled.

SCHUMAN AND MONNET DEPART FROM LONDON

Schuman probably left London with too optimistic an appreciation of the likelihood of British participation in his Plan. After enduring Bevin's initial explosion, Schuman's contacts at the French Embassy with both opposition leaders and British ministers had been friendly. R. A. Butler and Harold Macmillan told him that they regarded his Plan favourably. Hugh Gaitskell and Patrick Gordon Walker had not evinced any opposition in principle. Aneurin Bevan had been particularly warm in his congratulations.[73] At an Italian reception on 18 May, Attlee told Massigli that 'We must be in from the beginning'. These, says Massigli, 'were his exact words'.[74] It was all too good to be true but would Schuman realize that? Even Massigli who had warned against premature optimizm about British participation was beginning to believe that it might happen.[75] Monnet also appears to have been optimistic about the outcome of his visit. It was reported to Plowden that Monnet had told a journalist of the French News Agency that 'he thought he had completely disposed of British fears about the working of the Schuman Plan'.[76] There was an encounter on the evening of 18 May between Bevin and Schuman. Bevin was responding to a brief from the Foreign Office that 'it would be most valuable if you could find an opportunity of discussing the matter with M. Schuman before he returns to Paris'. Bevin

[72] Monnet comments that Schuman's offer of association was 'unwise, for experience has taught me that it is not good for the British to obtain special conditions and an exceptional position in their relationships with others, or even for them to cherish such hopes': Monnet 308.

[73] Massigli 199.   [74] Ibid. 201.   [75] Ibid. 202.

[76] T 229/749, Note to Plowden dated 19 May 1950.

confessed to Schuman that he had not had time to consider the Plan thoroughly or to discuss it with his colleagues. Schuman replied that he too had not had time to consider all the implications.[77] Schuman left London the following day. With this expression of mutual ignorance, the ministers principally concerned in the Schuman Plan parted.

MAKINS'S MEMORANDUM

The Foreign Office has frequently been criticized for having given Europe, in this era, too low a priority in its policy planning. But what was now to be displayed was a simple failure of diplomatic skills combined with an inability to handle an unwelcome initiative which should have been foreseen but was not. Schuman and Monnet had now left London. The opportunity for a thorough discussion of the Plan between Bevin and Schuman had been missed. The spirit of the Foreign Office's reaction to the Schuman announcement and all they had heard since is illustrated by a note from Sir Roger Makins to Bevin dated 19 May 1950. It breathes superiority and ignorance. It is in itself a damning indictment of the Foreign Office. It reads in part as follows:

The purpose of the scheme was Franco-German rapprochement, but the French have tried to negotiate with us before approaching the Germans. They have not thought out how their scheme will work and we could not accept it in principle as we do not know what it would involve. The French say they are prepared to go ahead with the Germans, but they have not done so, neither have they worked out their proposals any further than the communiqué. We shall have to do what we can to get them out of the mess into which they have landed themselves.[78]

The spirit of the note is that the French, having got themselves into a mess of their own making, were now turning to the British to help them out of it.[79] Nothing could have been further from the truth. The Foreign Office entirely misunderstood Monnet if it thought he would be

---

[77] *DBPO* 31.

[78] *DBPO* 31 Annex B. As Ambassador in Washington in 1955, Makins advised the State Department that the common market project seemed 'to have an air of unreality': Geoffrey Warner, 'Eisenhower, Dulles and the Unity of Western Europe, 1955–1957', *International Affairs*, 69/2 (1993), 324.

[79] 'There was some feeling ... that the French were counting on the hard working civil servants of Whitehall to figure out the means of putting their great ideas into practice': Diebold 49.

compelled to turn to the UK to get him out of a mess or even to fill in the details of the Plan. Events were to prove that the French were perfectly capable of taking the Plan forward without the British if British reluctance forced them to do so. The statement that the French were negotiating with the UK before the Germans was wrong. The French were not negotiating with the UK. The discussions, such as they were, about the Schuman Plan held in London with Schuman and Monnet between 10 and 19 May had not been a negotiation. The French were in fact about to invite the British, and other countries, to a negotiation. They intended to hold the initiative. The second sentence quoted above from Makins's minute was to become the principal formal obstacle to British participation in the negotiations although participating in the negotiations was the only way of finding out what would be involved. The last sentence must be counted among the most unfortunate but revealing of British post-war diplomacy. It underlined the conviction in London, not just among those hostile to the Schuman initiative, that there was no need to worry too much about it because the French could not manage it to success in any case. There *was* one aspect of the Schuman announcement that would cause trouble, the High Authority, Monnet's peculiar contribution to it. But so far from the British helping to unhook the French from this flight of fancy, it was to become a British objection to taking part even in negotiations and the task of unhooking France was left to its other partners.

PARIS, A CITY TOO FAR

Early in 1950 Bevin had travelled to Colombo, Ceylon, for a Common-wealth conference. He had visited Paris on his way back to London. But Paris, now, was evidently too far even for ministers in a better state of health than Bevin. During the critical period between Schuman's departure from London on 19 May and the French ultimatum of 1 June, there was no meeting between British and French ministers about the Plan.[80] Though only Bevin among the leading ministers was compelled, during this period, to enter hospital, they remained in London or on holiday, failing to make the necessary personal contacts with their

---

[80] Emanuel Shinwell, Minister of Defence, saw his French opposite number, René Pleven, in Paris on 13 May 1950. They discussed the Schuman Plan. Pleven emphasized that the idea behind the Plan was economic, concerned with the danger of French steel production being undercut by the Germans: *DBPO* 18 n.

opposite numbers either in Paris or Bonn even though it was known that in both capitals there was dissent from the pure milk of Monnet's ideas.[81] Apart from resolving any problems in the way of British participation in the coming negotiations, a ministerial visit to Paris would have forced French ministers to clarify their ideas, it would have shown interest and a desire to co-operate. If there was anyone in Paris who wanted to exclude the British, a ministerial visit would have made their task more difficult. The Quai d'Orsay was known to have serious doubts about whether it was sensible for France to go ahead with the Plan without Britain. Not all French ministers were happy at that prospect. The French socialists strongly disapproved of proceeding without British participation.[82]

The socialist newspaper, *Populaire*, while finding the Schuman proposals 'seductive' nevertheless saw a need to avoid the dangerous possibility of a tête-à-tête with Germany. It saw British membership as a desideratum on two counts. First, it would bring in non-German votes. Secondly, it would bring in socialized industries. Thereby would be solved *Populaire*'s other worry that socialized industries would come indirectly under capitalist control through the representation of private industry on the High Authority.[83] At the French Socialist Party Congress in the last days of May, the leading French socialist Jules Moch repeated the same message. He insisted that Britain must be a participant in the Plan so that France was not left face to face with Germany. Guy Mollet, like some other French socialists, was originally critical of the Schuman Plan. He at first saw it as little more than a scheme to shore up a decadent German and French capitalism and affront the British Labour Party. French socialists shared the same fear as British socialists, that of close association with countries that favoured economic liberalism. The best guarantee against this, they thought, would be the participation of the UK and a large say for workers' representatives in any controlling forum. Despite these doubts, French socialists came to support the ECSC Treaty. They continued to regret the absence of the UK.[84]

Schuman himself, despite provocation from Bevin, had shown

---

[81] Attlee was visiting the châteaux of the Loire. Cripps was also in France, staying at Briançon in the country home of Maurice Petsche, the French Finance Minister. Bullock's view is that 'Left to himself Schuman might have adopted a compromise' but that Monnet was determined not to permit it: Bullock 780. The only way to discover whether a compromise was available was a Ministerial visit to Paris.
[82] *DBPO* 92.   [83] *Manchester Guardian*, 12 May 1950.   [84] Haas 116.

considerable willingness to find a route whereby the UK might stay involved. On 23 May he felt it necessary to assure the Foreign Affairs Committee of the National Assembly that he was almost certain that 'no negotiation of any sort would take place without the participation of Britain'.[85] He took this reassurance further when, at his next appearance before the Committee on 25 May, he told them that the British government, far from being opposed to the Plan, was showing great interest.[86] On 29 May the Paris correspondent of the *Manchester Guardian* reported: 'The French Government would certainly wish to go before the Assembly when it discusses the plan next Wednesday with the assurance that the British Government is so far interested that there would be small danger of the pool becoming in practice a tête-à-tête between the French and the Germans.'[87] There was, therefore, in France a great deal by way of potential political support on which British ministers could have built if they had taken the trouble.

Adenauer, whose vital role in any negotiations should have been obvious to the Foreign Office, was ignored, although his doubts about the High Authority had been exposed in *Le Monde*[88] and Federal Vice-Chancellor Blücher, who was the German representative on the IAR, had given the clearest indication of the importance he attached to British participation and of his desire to meet any British difficulties.[89] British neglect of Germany gave Monnet every opportunity to exploit his own, recently established, relationship with the German Chancellor. Bevin clearly saw the need to incorporate Germany into the Western alliance and into the European economy. Nevertheless, his relations with Adenauer could never have been easy, given his deep hostility to the Germans which he was never afraid to express. Whereas Bevin's hostility was allowed to become counter-productive, Schuman realized that there was an inconsistency between insulting the Germans and trying to find a way of living peacefully with them. It was an inconsistency that Bevin, in free parliamentary flow, was inclined to overlook.[90]

Some part of these failures must be attributed to the ill health of the key ministers, Bevin and Cripps. It is understandable that civil servants, who did not think much of the Schuman Plan in any case, would not want to press foreign travel upon ministers who were barely able to get

[85] *The Times*, 24 May 1950.   [86] Ibid., 26 May 1950.
[87] *Manchester Guardian*, 29 May 1950.   [88] On 17 May. See Ch. 8 below.
[89] *DBPO* 21. For Adenauer's doubts, see Massigli 201–2.
[90] e.g. in the foreign affairs debate in the House of Commons on 28 Mar. 1950: Bullock 764.

to the office without distress. On 26 April, two weeks before the announcement of the Schuman Plan, Cripps had informed Attlee confi-
dentially that, on health grounds, he could not carry on as Chancellor
of the Exchequer beyond the summer.[91] Stikker, a critic of the way in
which the French were handling the matter, wanted to discuss the Plan
with Bevin in Paris. His friendly overture was repulsed, probably because Bevin would be in hospital on the dates suggested.[92] The high
cost of ministerial ill health had been amply demonstrated during the
extraordinary events preceding the September 1949 devaluation. At considerable cost to the reserves, firm decisions were delayed for weeks
while Cripps recuperated in Switzerland. A stronger Prime Minister
might have decided that the national interest could no longer be put at
risk by the incapacity of senior ministers to do their jobs. Bevin's
struggle to continue in office despite ill health was heroic. It was typical
of the man both in the heroism and in his conviction that he had become indispensable, a conviction encouraged by the fact that no one
else had been allowed to grow up under his banyan tree and by his
position as the longest serving Western Foreign Minister. Bevin had
shown himself Attlee's greatest support in times of trouble. Attlee was
repaying the loyalty. He would go on doing so until the last possible
minute.[93] A closer study of French behaviour might have taught him
that, in national affairs, there are higher priorities than gratitude.

[91] MS Attlee dep. 100.   [92] *DBPO* 47.
[93] Bevin was finally removed as Foreign Secretary one month before his death in Apr.
1951. He resented it and even more that Morrison was nominated his successor. Bullock
explains why Attlee left Bevin in office as Foreign Secretary after the Feb. 1950 general
election. No one else had Bevin's prestige both in international affairs and with the TUC,
there was no obvious alternative candidate, and, in any case, Bevin was the most 'European' of Labour Cabinet ministers: Bullock 757–8. If Attlee considered Bevin indispensable, it is not surprising that Bevin himself did. But, in view of Bevin's repeated
serious illness and his evident inability to concentrate during important international
meetings, Bullock's explanation says little for Attlee's forward planning. Younger notes
in a diary entry for 29 May 1950 that Bevin 'is not in a fit state to do a full job. . . . I
think what carries him on is his stupendous egotism. He really believes himself to be
wholly indispensable.'

8

Diplomacy by Telegram

In the absence of ministerial contact, everything depended on telegraphic exchanges of memoranda and on the goodwill of ambassadors.[1] Monnet found it extraordinary, as indeed it was:

There was something extraordinary about this negotiation by telegram. At one end, in Paris, were Clappier,[2] Uri,[3] Hirsch, and myself; at the other, Kenneth Younger, alone with the staff of the Foreign Office while Bevin was away ill. No messenger crossed the Channel; no ambassador or semi-official envoy played any part in the prolonged bout.[4]

Both the British Ambassador in Paris, Sir Oliver Harvey, and the French Ambassador in London, René Massigli, sincerely wanted the UK to participate. Both did their best. They reckoned without the Foreign Office. First it found objection to French ideas on procedure. Then it took its stand on an issue of principle on which all other participants were satisfied. The principle was whether the UK would commit itself to the Schuman Plan, however it might emerge from the negotiations, simply by entering the negotiating conference. The Foreign Office was persuaded that it would be committed. The Quai d'Orsay assured it that it would not. The Foreign Office claimed that supranationalism was not an obstacle as a matter of principle. The UK naturally wished, as did all other participants, to know more precisely what form it would take and where it would lead before it was committed. But, as all the other participants accepted, the only way to discover the answers was to enter the negotiations. The Foreign Office preferred to absent itself and remain ignorant. It preferred to complain about its ignorance of what was

---

[1] There is an extraordinary message dated 12 June 1950 from Younger to Harvey in Paris. It asks Harvey to explain the French refusal to compromise on their terms for British participation in the Schuman negotiations. It reads as though France was a far-away country of which we know nothing instead of a few hours away across the narrow channel: *DBPO* 98.

[2] Bernard Clappier, then Schuman's *Directeur de Cabinet*.

[3] Pierre Uri, then an assistant to Monnet.   [4] Monnet 312–13.

intended rather than to take the only step that would enable it to become better informed and to exercise influence.

ON TEACHING THE FRENCH TO SUCK EGGS

Until 25 May 1950, sixteen days after the initial Schuman announcement, the only substantial response by the UK to the French proposal had been Attlee's statement in the House. On 25 May Bevin directed Harvey to deliver to Schuman the following message about procedure:

I have now been able to give some thought to the organisation of further discussions about your proposal for a Franco-German Coal and Steel Authority, in which other European countries might participate.

I feel that the important thing is to get something started soon. The welcome given to your proposal and the effect which it has had on Franco-German relations lead me to think that no time should be lost in following it up. A full scale international conference to which no participating country could come without a great deal of preparation and some degree of commitment seems to me an inappropriate way of handling this affair in the next stage. In my view, the most desirable step would be the earliest institution of direct conversations between France and Germany. His Majesty's Government would like to participate in these from the outset, with the hope that by obtaining a clearer picture of how the proposals would operate in detail, they would be able to join the scheme.[5]

This message was dispatched by Bevin on the advice of officials and with the concurrence of the Chancellor. The advice was given on the explicit assumption that 'Ministers would be willing to agree to abrogate certain sovereign rights under suitable safeguards, provided a satisfactory scheme can be drawn up'. Apparently ministers were willing in principle to make the sacrifice. Whether ministers were in good faith in accepting the assumption and officials in good faith in proposing it will be discussed later.

This procedural proposal was not one which Schuman was likely to accept. It was made despite a warning from Monnet that such a response would greatly embarrass the French government.[6] It suggested a procedure entirely different from that mooted in the communiqué of 9 May. In the initial Schuman announcement, the French government

---

[5] Cmd. 7970/6. Sahm refers to a meeting between Bevin and Schuman on 23 May. This is an error: Sahm 22.

[6] *DBPO* 31 Annex A. See also T 229/749, draft note to ministers.

had said that it 'is ready to open *negotiations*'[7] in order to promote the realization of the objective it had defined. In the meeting at the Hyde Park Hotel on 16 May 1950, Monnet had emphasized that the French government intended to go ahead with the *negotiation* of a treaty.[8] Why should the French government accept advice from Bevin on 25 May that all that was appropriate in the first instance was a Franco-German *conversation* with British representatives present? The memorandum provided no reason, other than assertion, why Schuman should abandon the approach he had proposed. It could be interpreted either as an attempt to wreck or as a determination to teach the French how to suck eggs. The Foreign Office underestimated the accretion in self-confidence in Paris resulting from the immediate popular success of the Schuman proposal. It had been widely acclaimed. The British had not come forward with a comparable proposal. Why should Paris give way to British views on procedure?

During the exchanges between London and Paris over the following days, both sides vigorously briefed the Press in order to present their own actions in the best possible light. No doubt they also wished, through the medium of the Press, to inform the other side of reactions that would be inappropriate in an official memorandum. The French let it be known that they considered the London note of 25 May less helpful than Britain no doubt intended. There was no justification for confining talks to France, Germany, and the UK. Moreover, to warn the UK off any idea that it might be doing France a favour by considering involvement, French sources emphasized that they did not fear a tête-à-tête with Germany contrary to what had been suggested by some British commentators.[9] The Paris correspondent of the *Manchester Guardian* observed that 'the French Government at the present moment is being more polite than it feels about the hesitations of the British'.[10]

Bevin's memorandum was made particularly infelicitous by the progress France had already made in discussion with Germany. Monnet and Clappier visited Adenauer on 23 May.[11] This led to a joint

---

[7] Emphasis added.   [8] *DBPO* 25.
[9] *The Times*, 27 May 1950. It had also, of course, been suggested by many French commentators.
[10] *Manchester Guardian*, 29 May 1950.
[11] *DBPO* 92. Monnet gives a somewhat grandiloquent account of this, his first meeting with Adenauer, in Monnet 309–11. Naturally it was Monnet who put Adenauer at his ease. For Adenauer's account of the meeting, see Adenauer 263. Massigli gives his account of what happened at this meeting at which he was not present in Massigli 202–3.

communiqué of the French and German governments that both accepted the principles of the Schuman Plan. Adenauer agreed to the joint communiqué despite his doubts, reported in *Le Monde* on 17 May, about rushing into the creation of a High Authority.[12] Massigli criticizes him for forgetting so easily the concerns he had expressed to *Le Monde*.[13] But perhaps Adenauer had more realistic expectations about the actual powers of the High Authority as it would emerge from negotiations than either its advocate, Monnet, or its critic, Massigli. It is also possible that Germany, emerging into freedom, had a self-confidence in confronting such devices that Britain lacked.

Bevin's message crossed with one from Paris which Massigli presented to Kenneth Younger on 25 May. This referred to the outcome of Monnet's meeting with Adenauer. It read, in part, as follows:

[T]he Chancellor of the German Federal Government has informed the French Government that he agrees to engage in negotiations on the basis indicated, and that in consequence he accepts the terms of the attached communiqué.[14] The text has been transmitted to the Belgian, Netherlands, Luxembourg and Italian Governments with the indication that the French Government intends to publish it towards the middle of next week.

The French Government express the hope that the British Government for its part will be able to participate on the same conditions in these negotiations from the outset.

Draft Communiqué

The Governments of _____ are resolved to carry out a common action aiming at peace, European solidarity and economic and social progress by pooling their coal and steel production and by the institution of a new high authority whose decisions will bind _____ and the countries which may adhere to it in the future.

Negotiations on the basis of the principles and essential undertakings contained in the French proposal of 9th May last will open on a date which will be proposed almost at once by the French Government, with a view to working out the terms of a treaty which will be submitted for ratification to the respective Parliaments.[15]

---

[12] Massigli 201.   [13] Ibid. 202.

[14] The text of the draft communiqué had been cleared with Adenauer during the visit of Monnet and Clappier on 23 May: *DBPO* 92.

[15] Cmd. 7970/7. All the French memoranda quoted are in translation. The original French is in *DBPO* 42.

The Foreign Office was thus made to look exceedingly foolish. It was also exceedingly annoyed that a draft communiqué had been discussed with Adenauer before it was discussed with the British government.[16] It was bad enough that the original Schuman announcement was made without consultation. The Monnet–Adenauer meeting, followed by the draft communiqué, added to the resentment and the Press was vigorously briefed about the unacceptable behaviour of the French.[17] The Foreign Office had not been unaware of the fact that the French were in communication with Adenauer. It was their decision not to make their own approach to the German Chancellor.

This crossing of messages also led to total confusion as to what exactly the UK government meant. It had suggested Franco-German conversations at which British representatives would be present.[18] But by this time the Benelux countries and Italy were already closely involved in discussions. A fortnight had elapsed since the Schuman announcement and others' speed of reaction had been greater than that of the Foreign Office. Was Britain suggesting that their interest should simply be ignored? This was certainly no way to win the propaganda battle. The procedural point should not have been raised but, given that it had been raised, it was clearly appropriate now to drop it. Instead the Foreign Office showed its persistence in poor judgement. A memorandum was dispatched to Paris on 27 May which read in part:

His Majesty's Government appreciate that it would not now be possible to confine the conversations to a purely Franco-German basis if some of the governments which have been approached wished to participate on the same basis as the German Federal Government, and further, that it might be necessary to consult such Governments before agreeing to participation in the discussions of other Governments on a different basis.[19]

This contorted language left the French government either bemused or disbelieving. In a memorandum of 30 May, it responded:

---

[16] Makins to Bevin, 17 June 1950—Notes for debate on Schuman Plan: MS Attlee dep. 102. In his brief, Makins draws attention to the difficulty of reaching agreement when the French had already negotiated a communiqué with the German government.
[17] See e.g. the *Manchester Guardian* of 14 June 1950.
[18] Bevin assured Harvey in a telegram of 26 May 1950 that, contrary to French press briefing, it was not the intention of the UK to attend the Franco-German talks simply as observers but to make 'a practical and positive contribution': *DBPO* 49. Regarding the French impression that the UK were only prepared to be present at any discussion of the Schuman Plan as observers, see also *DBPO* 50 n.
[19] Cmd. 7970/8.

As the British Government recognized in their memorandum of 27th May, the agreement of other Governments to participate in the negotiation on the same basis as the German Federal Government already opens a new phase by broadening the scope of the discussions, which will, from the very beginning, be on a European basis. Nevertheless, in their memorandum of 27th May the British Government declare that, as regards their own participation, they must hold to the method suggested in their message of 25th May, which only referred to direct conversations between France and Germany.[20]

Instead of taking this new opportunity to drop the point which had no conceivable further usefulness, there was an exasperated response from London dated 31 May. The French had misunderstood, possibly wilfully.

There is one point in the French Memorandum as to which His Majesty's Government wish to dispel any misunderstanding. The French Memorandum suggests that in their Memorandum of 27th May His Majesty's Government have only offered to participate in direct conversations between France and Germany. It had been hoped that it was clear from . . . His Majesty's Government's Memorandum of 27th May that the observations made in their Memorandum of 25th May, about the participation of His Majesty's Government in the Franco-German discussions foreshadowed in the original French Memorandum, applied equally to any discussions which the French Government might arrange with other Governments willing to participate on the same basis as the German Federal Government.[21]

The French could be forgiven if they found this message incomprehensible or, at least, ambiguous. Did it mean that the UK government wished to participate in a series of bilateral discussions between the French government and other possible adherents to the Schuman Plan, or in a collective meeting of all possible adherents? The Foreign Office presumably knew what it was intended to mean but it was not clear on the face of their memorandum. From this point on, this procedural proposal was, reasonably enough, ignored by the French. There could be no better example of the costs of exchanging memoranda when what was needed was a face to face conversation between ministers. It would have been funny if the outcome had not been so tragic. Indeed, given the lapse of time, one can perhaps concentrate on the humour of the exchange. The Foreign Office did not merely fail to understand what was going on across the narrow waters, it could not even make clear to the French what it itself meant. The Bevin memorandum of 25 May had

[20] Cmd. 7970/10.   [21] Cmd. 7970/11.

been irrelevant when it was sent and had certainly not achieved greater relevance in the course of this exchange. In the circumstances, one can forgive the French for their determined refusal to understand what the British actually meant. It did not matter. As Bevin's proposal, whatever it meant, was inapposite, it did not require to kill it the intervention of Monnet who thought he understood perfectly well for what the British were angling. No doubt to make assurance doubly sure, he sent a note to the French government in which he said:

To accept British participation on these terms—i.e., in a special capacity—would be to resign oneself in advance to the replacement of the French proposal by something that would merely travesty it. Soon, if that happened, there would be no common rules and no independent High Authority, but only some kind of OEEC. In the end, a time would come when France would have to take the responsibility of breaking off the negotiations and incurring the blame.[22]

A QUESTION OF PRINCIPLE

It now emerged that the key question as seen by the British government was not one of procedure but of principle. The point of principle had been explained in the French memorandum of 25 May. It said:

From the outset, the French Government have been anxious that the British Government should associate itself with the French initiative. To this end, in the course of conversations which took place in London on 11th May and on the following days, the Minister of Foreign Affairs and M. Jean Monnet sought to give additional explanations to certain members of the British Government and to certain high officials. *They pointed out that if it were desired to reach concrete results it was necessary that the Governments should be in agreement from the beginning on the principles and the essential undertakings defined in the French Government's document,* but that the numerous problems which would arise from the putting the project into effect would require discussions and studies which would have to be pursued in common with the object of achieving the signature of the proposed treaty.[23]

To this the UK government responded in its memorandum of 27 May: 'if the French Government intend to insist on a commitment to pool

---

[22] Monnet 313. See also two other memoranda sent by Monnet to the French government around this time in which he emphasizes that if the UK is allowed to change the basis of the negotiation, Germany would be able to do the same and that the outcome would be a caricature of the Schuman Plan: Elgey 449.

[23] Cmd. 7970/7. Emphasis added.

resources and set up an authority with certain sovereign powers as a prior condition to joining in the talks, His Majesty's Government would reluctantly be unable to accept such a condition. His Majesty's Government would greatly regret such an outcome.'[24]

This was a crucial moment in the telegraphic exchanges. For the first time, the British government was threatening that it might not take part in the development of the Schuman Plan. The exchange has to be read in the context of the Franco-German draft communiqué. The draft communiqué recognized that the final outcome of the negotiations would require ratification by Parliaments.[25] Thus the French were insisting on a certain procedure and on a certain basis for the negotiations. They were not insisting, and could not insist, on a commitment to the outcome of the negotiations. That would require ratification by Parliaments. On 26 May Bernard Clappier, who had contributed personally to the drafting, such as it then was, of the Schuman Plan, had a conversation with Harvey. Clappier confirmed that Britain could leave the negotiating table at any time so long as supranationalism remained the basis of the talks. Harvey reported that

[Clappier] argued that by accepting the principles of the French plan and subscribing to the proposed communiqué a Government did not, in fact, commit itself to pool its resources or to accept the decisions of the new authority, because it was only the eventual treaty which would create obligations; and if in the course of negotiations any Government did not like the terms of the treaty, then it would always be open to that Government to decline to become a party to it.[26]

Thus the French position was clear. There would be no commitment until ratification of a treaty by Parliaments. The exchanges thus far raised the question whether British ministers were sincere in accepting that, in appropriate circumstances, they would be prepared to ask Parliament to abrogate certain sovereign rights under suitable safeguards. This was the point of principle that had been put to them by officials. They had accepted that they would be prepared so to do. If, in truth,

---

[24] Cmd. 7970/8.

[25] Treaties into which the British government enters are ratified under the royal prerogative. However, where they affect domestic law, Parliament is required to pass the necessary legislation before ratification. A treaty establishing a High Authority with supranational powers would certainly have required legislation before ratification.

[26] *DBPO* 50. On 25 May 1950 Parodi also made clear to Harvey that 'the fact of accepting the invitation would in no way necessarily bind [the UK] to accept the eventual treaty': *DBPO* 46.

that was not the case, then indeed the French terms were unacceptable. But in that case British ministers had entered the exchanges on a false basis. They should have told the French at the outset, without wasting time, that Britain would not participate.

On 28 May Massigli, who was keen on finding the way to British participation, called on Kenneth Younger at the Foreign Office. Younger reported the interview. His report reads, in part, as follows:

2. He [Massigli] asked if he was right in thinking that, while we are not prepared to commit ourselves now to the principle of pooling resources under an international authority possessing certain sovereign powers, we are not taking up an attitude of opposition to this principle but are prepared to enter into discussions with the object of finding a practical method of applying the principle.

3. I told him that I thought that roughly expressed the difference between us. We were certainly not proposing to go to these discussions with our minds set against the principle referred to, but equally we were not prepared to commit ourselves to the principle without having a much clearer idea than we have at present about the way in which it is to be carried into effect. The Ambassador said that he had always felt sure that this was our attitude but had thought it better to get it confirmed by me before passing this interpretation to his Government.

4. He said he found my explanation reassuring since it seemed to him that our reservations would not in any way limit our effective participation in the discussions.[27]

Younger, in this conversation with Massigli, assured the French that the British government was not opposing the principle of an international authority with certain sovereign powers. It merely wished to have a clearer idea of the way in which the principle would be put into effect before committing itself to the creation of such an authority. It was not the case that the UK government had such objections of principle to a High Authority with certain sovereign powers that, so far as it was concerned, the idea could be ruled out without further discussion. The difference between the French and British governments hardly now seemed unbridgeable provided the British government was sincere in its protestations. It was not. Massigli, with his sympathy for the British point of view, did not understand that the British government was not being sincere. In his memoirs, Massigli defines the different points of view as he saw them emerging. France and Germany would arrive at the conference saying that they had accepted the principles contained

[27] Cmd. 7970/9.

in the declaration of 9 May. The problem of the conference would be to see whether they could be put into practice. On the other hand, says Massigli, the British would arrive at the conference saying, supposing we accept these principles, let us see how we can put them into practice.[28] Surely, claims Massigli, this was not sufficient reason for Paris to break with London.[29] But this was not the difference at all. The truth was that, whatever Kenneth Younger had said, the British were not prepared to accept the principles under any circumstances. This fundamental truth will emerge as the story unfolds.

On 30 May 1950 Bevin entered the London Clinic and did not return to the Office until 27 July.[30] By 30 May it was publicly known that Italy had accepted Schuman's invitation. On 30 May there arrived a lengthy memorandum from Paris in which the French government set out with great care the rationale behind the Schuman Plan and the proposed procedure for the negotiations. It read in part as follows:

Knowing the practical difficulties which the discussions will have to surmount, it seems essential that they should constantly be guided by common principles. Only if the negotiations are clearly directed by agreement between participating Governments on the fundamental objectives to be reached, will it be possible to work out quickly the ways and means and the supplementary arrangements necessary for giving effect to M. Schuman's plan of 9th May . . .

6. The French Government particularly wish to recall once more the central inspiration of their proposal: it aims at substituting, on a limited but decisive point, a community of interest for the present divisions; it provides for the establishment of a high authority of a new character; it gives that authority the task of providing for a general rise in the standard of living.

7. The British Government are of course legitimately preoccupied with following a policy of economic expansion, of full employment, and of a rising standard of living for the workers. The proposed scheme, far from obstructing such a policy, is calculated in the view of the French government to avoid the dangers which may suddenly obstruct its course. For competition based on exploiting labour will be substituted a concerted rise in workers' conditions; for the restrictive practices of cartels, the development of outlets; for dumping and discrimination, the rational distribution of products. The policy of full employment only reaches its true objectives if it provides labour with the most productive occupations—and it cannot finally be carried out under pressure of the development of unemployment in other countries. The task entrusted to the high authority thus excludes the possibility of its work compromising the results achieved by this policy where it is already being carried out, and means

---

[28] Massigli 204.   [29] Ibid. 205.
[30] The Foreign Office announced that Bevin was going back into hospital on 23 May: Bullock 779.

that it will favour a general expansion, allowing rationalized production to be reconciled with the maintenance of full employment.[31]

Nothing could, on the face of it, have been more painstaking and helpful, especially to a Labour government. It even had the flavour of planning for prosperity and thus should have deflected critics within the Labour Party from their prejudice that, on the Continent, they believed only in *laissez-faire*. There might be room for some scepticism about the practicality of the French ambitions but not surely in a government such as that of the UK supposedly devoted, like the French, to economic planning. Nothing, however, could dissuade the UK government from its determination to make elaborate difficulties.

The Foreign Office did feel it necessary to placate Washington. It had heard that the French were putting it about that Britain was 'adopting an obstructive attitude towards mild and reasonable French proposals'. The Press were therefore briefed to the effect that, on the contrary, London was being practical not obstructive. The line to be taken with the Press and with Washington was defined as follows:

To proceed as the French suggest, namely by making advance commitments and hoping that the details will look after themselves is likely to lead to acute disappointment. We already have before us the example of the Franco-Italian Customs Union with respect to which a treaty has been concluded between France and Italy but which neither side shows any sign of implementing. There is also the Ruhr Authority which was set up in advance of the end of the control period in Germany at the request of the French and which finds itself without adequate functions. We do not want to see these experiences repeated in relation to a proposal of such outstanding importance as the Schuman Plan.[32]

This line of briefing proved more successful with the British Press than with Washington. The State Department indicated that it 'was inclined to deprecate the rather negative line' taken in the references to the Franco-Italian customs union and the Ruhr Authority.[33] As the French read the British Press they might have concluded that they needed no warnings from London about the dangers of 'acute disappointment'. They knew that the course they were taking was not without risks. They

---

[31] Cmd. 7970/10.

[32] *DBPO* 56. The Foreign Office briefing about the Franco-Italian Customs Union was reflected by *The Times's* diplomatic correspondent on 31 May. It was no doubt Schuman himself who had reminded the Foreign Office of the unhappy history of this customs union. At his press conference on 9 May, he had indicated that one of the hopes he had in mind when he suggested his Plan was that it would facilitate the realization of the Franco-Italian Customs Union: *Manchester Guardian*, 11 May 1950.

[33] *DBPO* 64.

thought they knew how to minimize them. As it turned out, it was the persistent attempt by the Foreign Office to teach the French how to suck eggs that was doomed to acute disappointment.

On 31 May the Foreign Office responded to the French memorandum of 30 May. Its response reads in part:

it remains the view of His Majesty's Government that to subscribe to the terms of the draft communiqué enclosed in the French Government's Memorandum of 25th May would involve entering into an advance commitment to pool coal and steel resources and to set up an authority, with certain supreme powers, before there had been full opportunity of considering how these important and far reaching proposals would work in practice.

It therefore proposed an addition to the draft French communiqué:

The Government of the United Kingdom will participate in the proposed conversations in a constructive spirit and in the hope that, as a result of the discussions, there will emerge a scheme which they will be able to join. But they cannot at this stage enter into any more precise commitment. They recognize the important and far-reaching character of the French proposal, and are in complete accord with the objective of pursuing a common policy aiming at peace, European solidarity and economic and social progress.[34]

The British government was still proposing a conversation and discussions, not a negotiation. By 1 June 1950 it was clear from Paris that Germany, Italy, Belgium, Luxembourg, and the Netherlands had all signified their acceptance of the French invitation.[35] Having received the assent of all other potential participants to negotiations, the French government was clearly losing patience. The French may also have noted that the British Labour Party delegation to the International Socialist Conference at Copenhagen on 1 June had taken the position that the Schuman Plan organization must be intergovernmental.[36] So far as the British Labour Party was concerned, there was evidently no question of accepting any form of supranationalism in the context of the Schuman Plan.[37]

On 1 June Schuman handed a further memorandum to Oliver Harvey.

---

[34] Cmd. 7970/11.   [35] *The Times*, 1 June 1950.

[36] *The Times's* report by its own correspondent in Paris on 3 June 1950 says that the French had noted this 'particularly'.

[37] See e.g. the minute from Sir Roger Makins to Kenneth Younger dated 31 May 1950. He raises the question 'whether we are, in principle, willing to surrender sovereignty over our iron and steel industries *if a scheme acceptable to us can be worked out*. We cannot answer this question without further Ministerial authority': (emphasis added) *DBPO* 60. But this question was supposed to have been decided on ministerial authority before the UK's memorandum of 25 May.

In doing so, he asked that the decision of the UK government should reach the French government by 8 p.m. on the following day, 2 June.

The French memorandum read in part as follows:

2. It appears that the text, which several Governments have already accepted, has through certain expressions used given rise to misunderstandings which have led to an exchange of notes between the French and British Governments, in which the intentions of those Governments have been more clearly defined. In order to clear away this obstacle, and because it seems extremely desirable that all Governments should announce in the same terms their participation in the negotiations, the French Government proposes the following new text, concurrence in which is being sought forthwith from all interested Governments.

This communiqué, in the opinion of the French Government, expresses the unity of view which is indispensable for the successful prosecution of the negotiations. If, contrary to the hope of the French Government, the British Government were unable to subscribe to it, the French Government would open negotiations on the stated conditions with the other countries which had accepted them as a basis. In that event, they would keep the British Government informed of the progress of the negotiations in their desire to enable the latter to join in whenever they felt able to do so.

ANNEX

Draft Communiqué

The Governments of _____ in their determination to pursue a common action for peace, European solidarity and economic and social progress have assigned to themselves as their immediate objective the pooling of coal and steel production and the institution of a new high authority whose decisions will bind _____

Negotiations, on the basis on the French proposal of 9th May last, will open at a date which will be proposed almost at once by the French Government with the view to working out the terms of a treaty which will be submitted for ratification to the respective Parliaments.[38]

Schuman explained to Harvey this final attempt to accommodate the UK. The communiqué no longer said that the governments had *resolved* to establish the pool and set up the High Authority. All that was now said was that they had the *immediate objective* of doing so. This change also helped to meet the reservations of the Dutch which had

[38] Cmd. 7970/12. The original French is in *DBPO* 58.

something in common with those of the British.[39] The French were also trying to ensure that if London remained recalcitrant despite this concession, the responsibility for failure should fall where, indeed, it truly lay, on the UK government.

On 2 June Sir William Strang, Permanent Under-Secretary of State at the Foreign Office, gave his categorical advice to Kenneth Younger. France's attempt to help was, he made clear, no help at all. The UK, he wrote, would still not be able to reject a draft treaty or a concrete and detailed scheme on the mere ground that it embodied the pooling of coal and steel resources and the establishment of an independent authority whose decisions would bind governments. In his advice Strang appeared to ignore the fact that the government had never rejected these elements as a matter of principle. It had said that it merely wished to know how such a scheme and such an authority would operate. Strang now turned to the real gravamen of his advice:

It has been the consistent advice of the Foreign Office and other departments, accepted by Ministers as a basis for policy, that we should not become involved in Europe in the economic sphere, beyond the point of no return. To contemplate, even in principle, an agreement to pool the British coal and steel industries with those of other Western European countries, and make their operations subject to the decisions of an independent European authority which are binding on HMG, would imply a readiness to accept a surrender of sovereignty on a matter of vital national interest which would carry us well beyond that point. The decision which the French are now summoning us to take is, in fact, the decision whether or not we are to bind ourselves irrevocably to the European community. Once we accept the French communiqué we shall have less ground for justifying the policy of caution which we have hitherto adopted in this sphere. We shall have tipped the balance against the other two elements in our world situation, the Atlantic Community and the Commonwealth. It is not for nothing that M. Schuman's original memorandum said in terms and repeatedly that his plan would be a step towards the federation of Europe.[40]

In face of advice of this character, Kenneth Younger's lone stand that the UK should be involved in the negotiations had little chance. In a minute which he wrote early on the morning of 2 June and which,

---

[39] *DBPO* 71. Harvey's translation of Schuman's words was the 'immediate aim' not 'objective'. The English translation of the French draft communiqué of 25 May used the word 'resolved' not 'decided'. In a telephone call of 2 June, Massigli told Strang that if the word 'immediate' in 'immediate aim' caused any difficulty, it should not be regarded as essential: *DBPO* 73 n. Monnet in his memoirs as translated by Richard Mayne uses the word 'objective': Monnet 313.

[40] *DBPO* 75.

later in the day, he sent to Strang, Younger set out the arguments in favour of British participation on the assumption that the other countries would reach agreement even if the UK was not involved.

5. We should be seriously criticised in Europe and the USA for rejecting the first imaginative proposal put forward for rationalising a key proportion of European heavy industry and for making Western Germany a good member of the 'Western Club'.

6. On the economic side our coal and steel experts view with some alarm the consequences of our having to compete with a powerful, integrated group of European industries formed without our participation.

7. While we might be able to join in the plan before it reached finality, we should, by failing to participate at the start, greatly reduce our chance of getting a scheme worked out on lines proposed by ourselves. . . .

8. The French would be seriously humiliated at the failure of their much-applauded initiative and would feel very bitterly towards us . . .

9. The only gesture of friendship made by France to Germany would have been frustrated by us. . . . The French feeling of inferiority and isolation, which makes them so hard to deal with, would be enhanced.

10. While Western Germany's reactions can only be guessed at, she would be bound to feel grave doubts about the sincerity of the West in professing to see her reinstated as an equal. . . . In particular she would be more than ever convinced that British policy was dominated by fear of commercial competition and not by security considerations . . .[41]

These were points of unequal importance but together they made a powerful case for British participation. In his diary Younger tells us how he interpreted the attitude of his senior officials:

I was very much impressed throughout with the importance of trying to make some scheme work, and consequently of finding some basis upon which we could participate from the start. In this I was virtually alone. Strang said frankly he thought the whole thing nonsense and a mere French attempt to evade realities. Makins, though less hostile, felt we should not get committed, that the Franco-German talks would inevitably break down sooner or later, and that we would then have a chance of coming in as *deus ex machina* with a solution of our own. In addition, Makins was the main protagonist of the view that the plan is largely designed to get away from the 'Atlantic' conception and to revert to a 'European third force neutral between [the] USSR and [the] USA.' I have no doubt there is some force in this view. Quite certainly that is the notion of one big group of Frenchmen and possibly also of the Germans.[42]

---

[41] *DBPO 82.*   [42] Younger's diary, 12 June 1950.

The problem for Britain, in the view of these officials, had nothing to do with the *working* of a supranational organization. They were opposed to European supranational organizations operating in the economic sphere *on principle*. They thought that the British government should refuse to depart from intergovernmental arrangements. The Schuman Plan was leading to federation and to a neutral third force. As Makins put it in his brief for Bevin in words already, in part, quoted:

10. It is essentially a question whether European countries should proceed to closer unity by means of inter-governmental arrangements or by steps leading to federation. . . . As far as His Majesty's Government are concerned the question of the pooling of resources of the European iron, steel and coal industry is one which they are fully prepared to discuss, but their approach is primarily economic and not political and constitutional. His Majesty's Government are not prepared to contemplate the entrance of the United Kingdom into a federal system confined to Western Europe.[43]

Younger was a man given to seeing both sides of any question without having very firm convictions on either side. His ability to see both sides of the question did lead him to argue the case for participation in the Schuman negotiations. Nevertheless, he himself continued to feel suspicious of the motives behind the Plan and he knew there was strong opposition to participation in the Plan both within the Foreign Office and among his political colleagues. In the circumstances, Younger's ambivalence is not surprising. His ambivalence and his suspicions are illustrated by the continuation of his diary entry of 12 June 1950:

On reflection I think we really had no choice and that seems to be the almost unanimous view of the press. Nevertheless it is unfortunate that we appear to be 'out on a limb' as usual, and no doubt we shall come in for a good many kicks as a result. What is more important is that no one has yet produced either a coherent explanation of how the French plan can be made to work, or any alternative proposal for eventually bringing Germany safely into the community of W[estern] Europe and the Atlantic. That major problem is still quite unresolved, and this French invitation, even if it was a bit haywire, offered and perhaps still offers a possible solution if only we can get it on a workable basis.

   Among all the numerous uncertainties is the uncertainty about the ideological implications of this type of plan. It could easily be a purely capitalist cartel with U.S. backing. In view of the reactionary nature of nearly all the governments concerned (and their strong Roman Catholic complexion) it would be

---

[43] Makins to Bevin, 17 June 1950—Notes for debate on Schuman Plan: MS Attlee dep. 102.

surprising if there were not at least an element of this in the conception. Moreover the most vocal support has come from thoroughgoing reactionaries like Reynaud, and on the German side there is even said to be a link up with Moral Rearmament and Dr Buchman. If this is so, it seems to be an argument for coming into the negotiations early and preventing the development at the start. If we do not, the probability is that there will be an industrial get-together anyway.[44]

Younger was not Secretary of State. He was simply Minister of State standing in for his sick master. He was not one of the political giants of the Attlee Administration. He was often out of tune with Foreign Office officials and, as Gaitskell put it in his diary the following February, he 'does not carry much weight'.[45] It would have taken moral courage of a high order for him to persist against such powerful opposition in advocating participation in the negotiations. Even if he had persisted, it is unlikely that the outcome would have been different. It is difficult to blame him for having, in the end, gone with the multitude despite his own doubts.

The high-flown and dramatic language of Strang's minute cannot conceal the fact that, if this was the position of the British government, then the exchange of memoranda with France since Schuman's announcement on 9 May 1950 had been conducted in bad faith throughout. The original British memorandum of 25 May had been drafted by officials on the explicit assumption that 'Ministers would be willing to agree to abrogate certain sovereign rights under suitable safeguards, provided a satisfactory scheme can be drawn up'. If ministers were not prepared to make that assumption, the implication was that another approach and another draft would have been necessary. It would probably have had to be a draft rejecting British participation from the outset. The assumption, of course, was private but that ministers accepted it was soon made clear to Massigli, the French Ambassador. When, on 28 May, Massigli had asked Younger whether he was right in thinking that the UK was not taking up an attitude of opposition to the principle of pooling resources under an international authority but was prepared to enter into discussions with the object of finding a practical method of applying the principle, Younger told him that he thought that roughly expressed the difference between France and the UK. The UK, Younger had said, was certainly not proposing to go to these discussions with its minds set against the principle. It merely wished to have a much clearer idea of how it was to be carried into

[44] Younger's diary, 12 June 1950.   [45] Gaitskell 229–33.

effect.[46] The British memorandum of 31 May said that the UK was not prepared to enter 'into an advance commitment to pool coal and steel resources and to set up an authority with certain supreme powers *before there had been full opportunity of considering how these important and far reaching proposals would work in practice*'.[47] What Strang's advice made clear was that, in his view, there were no circumstances at all in which the British government should be willing to join. It was not a question of finding out how the Schuman principles would work in practice. The British government was against the Schuman principles.[48]

If it had been acting in good faith, the Attlee government should not have wasted time but should have rejected participation in the Plan from the outset. It did not wish to take that course because international, and especially American, opinion was so strongly in favour of the Schuman proposals that the British government had to search desperately for some presentable excuse for absenting itself. Its attempt to find a presentable excuse failed. Subsequent British government protestations that it had acted in good faith were a further example of bad faith. The bad faith entered not just into the UK's discussions with Paris but with Washington and the British Press. Washington and the Press were given the impression that the problem was not the principle but how it would work in practice. Only press briefing could explain the language of *The Times*'s diplomatic correspondent who reported that 'The British Government are fully in favour of the principle of an international body to control the industries concerned, but they are not prepared to commit themselves necessarily to join any such authority without knowing how it is to be set up'.[49]

But Britain's objection was not the practice but the principle.

However much Massigli might deceive himself about the real British attitude, Washington was not deceived. And even within the government, some ministers were watching the manœuvres of the Foreign Office with impatience. Hugh Dalton recalled in his diary a meeting with the Prime Minister before Attlee's statement in the House on the Schuman Plan on 13 June. 'He showed me a draft. It was, I thought, rather flat. . . . We still seem to [be] living in a world of make-believe,

---

[46] Cmd. 7970/9.   [47] Cmd. 7970/11. Emphasis added.

[48] It was the view of some Foreign Office officials that the tergiversations of the UK government had left its attitude to supranational authorities unclear. See the minute of I. Mallet to Sir P. Dixon and Sir W. Strang, 20 June 1950, referred to in Ch. 10 below: *DBPO* 102 n.

[49] *The Times*, 31 May 1950.

not stating clearly that we could not hand over our key industries to any supra-national authority.'[50] Dalton also records that he consulted Bevin in the London Clinic about a declaration being drafted for the Socialist Conference taking place in London in mid-June. 'E[rnest] B[evin] wanted to be assured that our declaration didn't commit us to a supranational authority. He was satisfied that it didn't though he would have liked a declaration definitely *against* such an authority. But he understood that the French and Dutch would not have agreed to this.'[51]

That this was the real British attitude is confirmed by a minute from Sir Pierson Dixon, of the Foreign Office, to Sir Roger Makins dated 13 June. Bevin had been speaking to Dixon about the Schuman Plan. 'Mr Bevin said that on no account must HM Government come into any arrangement providing for an Authority independent of Governments.'[52] Though too much of the British Press was prepared to swallow Foreign Office briefing, not every journalist was blind to what was going on. The diplomatic correspondent of the *Manchester Guardian* referred to 'the ambiguity of the British Government's attitude towards a high authority'.[53] And J. H. Huizinga, then London correspondent of the *Nieuwe Rotterdamsche Courant*, in a perceptive letter published in the *Manchester Guardian*, wrote:

What has made us so critical is the persistent attempt to evade the issue by deliberately deceiving yourselves as to its real nature. . . . From the very beginning . . . the British Government, with the seemingly unanimous support of public opinion, has refused to give a straight answer. While it soon became clear that you would have nothing to do with the supra-national idea forming the essence of the Schuman Plan your Government continued to pretend—even after Mr Dalton had let the cat out of the bag—that it had not rejected the plan but only wanted more 'details' before it could make up its mind. And if that is not the most obvious self-deception I do not know what is.[54]

Mr Dalton had let the cat out of the bag by publishing Labour's statement, *European Unity*, a subject to which we shall return in Chapter 10.

A CABINET DECIDES

The French memorandum of 1 June faced the UK government with what was in effect an ultimatum. The sense of outrage with which this

[50] Dalton's diary (BLPES), 16 June 1950.
[51] Ibid., 18 June 1950. Dalton adds: 'He sounded sleepy . . . '   [52] *DBPO* 101.
[53] *Manchester Guardian*, 14 June 1950.   [54] Ibid., 24 June 1950.

ultimatum was received in London is admirably caught by Douglas Jay, at the time Financial Secretary to the Treasury, writing thirty years later. The sense of outrage has stayed with him through the years. 'The ultimatum is not explicable except on the assumption that the French were determined to keep future moves for so-called "European Unity" under French control, and exclude the British at least until such time as the whole arrangement had been so devised as to promote French interests and where possible to damage this country.'[55] Douglas Jay has combined long, and important, service to this country with bitter opposition to European entanglements. He has been consistent throughout. Neither at the time nor subsequently has he seemed to realize that there was nothing surprising or objectionable in a French government attempting to promote French interests and that the only way in which, at the time, they could seize control of the processes of European integration, and thereby damage this country, was if Britain, by its own desire, despite its invitation, insisted on abstention from the Schuman Plan negotiations. Jay's view appears to be that, as the French were so unreasonable as to promote their own interests and thereby damage Britain, the appropriate reaction was to let them do so.

It was the spirit that Jay has so accurately caught that informed the British response to the ultimatum. Herbert Morrison and Kenneth Younger went to see Bevin in the London Clinic on the morning of 2 June. Younger put the arguments he had advanced in his minute to Strang earlier that day but Bevin was in no mood to listen. He argued two new reasons for rejecting the French text. The first was that Schuman had sent an ultimatum and to submit to it 'would be to invite a repetition of this technique'. The second argument was that the French communiqué contemplated the drafting of a treaty. But if the main effort of the conference were devoted to drafting a treaty, the British government could, in the end, be faced with a request to sign it without knowing what the implications would be. This anxiety was not groundless. As is explained in the next chapter, Monnet wished to rush the negotiations through with a minimum of detail. There was indeed a question whether the treaty would provide all the necessary detail on how the Plan would operate and would therefore enable the government to explain all the implications to Parliament. The fact that British ministers could not yet be sure whether the eventual treaty would give all the answers for which they were looking was not a reason for

---

[55] Jay 200.

rejecting the French terms. While the anxiety was not groundless, there was, on this point, consolation. It would be reasonable to assume that Britain's negotiating partners would have the same anxiety and would require a great deal of detail before committing themselves. Britain would not be friendless at the negotiations. Bevin was not, however, looking for a way into the negotiations if they were to be conducted on French terms. The meeting at the London Clinic decided that the best way forward was to suggest a meeting of ministers of the countries interested at which the question of procedure would be examined and settled. The exchange of notes had, in Bevin's view, simply 'led to misunderstanding and delay'. It was time for ministers to meet face to face.[56]

An emergency meeting of the Cabinet was called for the afternoon of 2 June. The FG Committee under Sir Edward Bridge's chairmanship recommended rejection of the Schuman proposals 'not because we necessarily preclude . . . some surrender of sovereignty, but because we think it wrong to pledge ourselves on these matters without knowing more precisely the nature of the commitment'. The FG Committee drafted over the basic question. Was it really a question of knowing the precise nature of the commitment or was the British government against the pooling of resources and surrender of sovereignty on any terms? The paper said that it was settled policy not to 'commit ourselves irrevocably to Europe either in the political or the economic sphere *unless we could measure the extent and effects of the commitment*'.[57] Strang in his advice to Younger had been more emphatic: 'It has been the consistent advice of the Foreign Office and other departments, accepted by Ministers as a basis for policy, that we should not become involved in Europe in the economic sphere, beyond the point of no return' and that the Schuman Plan would take the government beyond the point of no return. Perhaps, by this time, officials themselves did not know what they really meant. The paper concluded that the real difference of view between Britain and France could not be 'glossed over by mere verbal ingenuity in the drafting of a communiqué'. Nor, apparently, could the confusion among officials.

The Cabinet met on the afternoon of Friday, 2 June under the chairmanship of Herbert Morrison. Attlee and Cripps were on holiday and Bevin was in the London Clinic. Cripps was represented by Douglas Jay. Younger explained the point reached in the exchanges with France. Morrison reported on the meeting that morning with Bevin. He

---

[56] *DBPO* 76.   [57] *DBPO* 77. Emphasis added.

recommended to the Cabinet Bevin's proposal of a meeting of ministers of the countries concerned. He emphasized that the government had been conducting its discussions with France in good faith. Neither Morrison nor Younger enquired of the Cabinet whether the objection to participation lay in the principle or in ignorance of the way the principle would work. Nor did either of them suggest their own answer to that question. Some ministers thought that attention should be drawn to the fact that Germany could not take part in the Schuman negotiations without the agreement of the occupying powers.[58] Sensibly, any such egregious obstruction was ruled out on the grounds that Attlee had welcomed the Schuman proposal in his statement in the House of Commons. It was therefore left that, at a later stage, it might be appropriate to make clear that Germany's adherence to a Schuman treaty would require the concurrence of the occupying powers. The ministers who were making these points clearly had an overblown idea of the capacity of the British government to obstruct progress on the Plan. Some ministers thought that the UK should be slow to accept the principle of the French proposal without consultation with the other members of the Commonwealth. Some were concerned at the likely reaction of American opinion.

The conclusion was to reject the revised French text. As an alternative, at this last minute, the UK government followed Bevin's thought and revived its procedural ideas in a more inclusive form. It proposed a ministerial meeting of all the interested countries. London's memorandum of 2 June read in part as follows:

After careful consideration [HMG] have come to the conclusion that there is still a difference of approach between the two Governments as to the basis on which the negotiations should be opened. . . . They earnestly hope that the French Government understand that His Majesty's Government are acting in good faith in the matter. They are anxious to do their best to see whether a workable scheme could be produced that is fair and just to all concerned and which would promote peace, European solidarity and economic and social progress. His Majesty's Government feel that this could have been achieved and could still be achieved by a meeting of Ministers of the countries interested at which the question of the most effective and expeditious method of discussing the problems at issue could be examined and settled.[59]

---

[58] The British High Commissioner, General Sir Brian Robertson, had made the same point at a meeting between Monnet and the High Commission when Monnet visited Germany to see Adenauer on 23 May. Monnet persuaded him that once the Federal government was authorized to negotiate it must do so as a sovereign power: Monnet 309.

[59] Cmd. 7970/13.

Understandably, the French government, after consideration, refused to have the negotiations delayed by the summoning of such a ministerial meeting. Schuman told Harvey on 3 June that such a meeting on so vague a basis would lead not only to delay in the opening of negotiations but probably to an impasse. Moreover, it would be impossible to hold such a meeting, with the possibility of Anglo-French divergences, in the presence of the Germans.[60] Schuman's reaction was hardly surprising. All the other participants were prepared to go ahead with negotiations. There was no reason to accept further delay. The essential commitment to the Schuman Plan had always been that of Germany, not that of Britain, and that Paris already had.

A COMMITMENT?

Would Britain, by accepting the language of the French draft communiqué, have been committed to any outcome of the negotiations however unacceptable? The answer must be that any such idea was absurd. The limit to the commitment into which the British government would be entering would be that they were honestly trying to negotiate an acceptable outcome. The French government repeatedly asserted that no country would be committed until the terms of a treaty had been submitted for ratification to the respective Parliaments.[61] In their memorandum of 30 May to the UK government they said specifically: 'As has already been made clear in the French Memorandum of 9th May, there will be no commitment except by the signature of a treaty between the States concerned and its parliamentary ratification.'[62]

By 'no commitment' they presumably meant no commitment except that commitment into which anyone enters when participating in a negotiation, honesty of purpose.

THE NETHERLANDS RESERVATION

The point that Clappier had made to Harvey on 26 May was repeated by Schuman to Harvey on 31 May. 'He did not believe that His Majesty's Government, in accepting the French invitation as set out in the communiqué, would be binding themselves to accept the eventual

[60] *DBPO* 85 and 92.   [61] See Cmd. 7970/7.   [62] Cmd. 7970/10.

treaty.... All that they would have agreed to was the final objective.'[63] It hardly needed reassertion. No participant in negotiations, including no country participant in negotiations, is compelled in advance to accept the outcome. The Dutch asked for specific reassurance on this point. They were assured that they could join in the negotiations without commitment. They agreed to take part in the negotiations subject to a specific reservation that they were not committed in advance to acceptance of the plan.[64] The Dutch reservation was spelt out by the Dutch Foreign Minister, Dirk Stikker, in a reply to a Parliamentary Question. Stikker's reply read in part as follows:

Although the Netherlands Government sincerely hope that the discussions which it regards as being of great importance to the future of Europe, will ultimately lead to satisfactory results, the Netherlands authorities considered it opportune to inform the French Government of the fact that they wish to reserve the right to withdraw their acceptance of these basic principles should the course of the discussions prove that the practical application of these principles meets with serious objections.[65]

If the Dutch could accept such reassurance, why could not the UK? There was a debate on the Schuman Plan in the House of Commons on 26 and 27 June 1950. The Tory motion on which the debate took place, and which was supported by Clement Davies as Leader of the Liberal Party, argued that the UK should accept participation in the Schuman Plan *negotiations* subject to the Netherlands government condition, namely that if the negotiations showed the plan not to be practicable, freedom of action was preserved. *The Economist* encouraged the government to accept the motion. 'It would be an act of statesmanship to accept the motion and to bring to an end the self-imposed isolation in which Britain stands ingloriously today.'[66]

The argument against accepting the Dutch reservation was elaborated by Cripps in replying to the debate for the government in what Dalton described as a 'very masterly' speech.[67] Cripps made three points. The first, essentially irrelevant, was that the Netherlands was a minor

---

[63] *DBPO* 59, Harvey to Younger, 31 May 1950.

[64] *DBPO* 67 n. The Dutch reservation became public through an inspired statement that they had agreed to take part in the talks subject to this specific reservation.

[65] MS Attlee dep. 102. Eden in the House of Commons, HC Debs. 26 June 1950, col. 1918, used a slightly different translation which referred to 'negotiations' rather than 'discussions'.

[66] *The Economist*, 24 June 1950.   [67] Dalton's diary (BLPES), 27 June 1950.

player in the European coal and steel industries. The Netherlands had $^1/_{40}$ of British coal production and $^1/_{150}$ of British steel production.

I can easily understand the Netherlands Government being prepared to take a risk in view of the small part of their economy that will be affected and accepting the principle without knowledge as to how it was to be applied or whether it could be applied, but I could not understand any British Government taking that risk with a major part, indeed, it may almost be said, with the whole, of its economy at stake.[68]

Cripps's second point on the Netherlands reservation was 'It does not entitle the Netherlands Government to do what we insisted we must be able to do, and that is to discuss whether in principle a new high supra-national authority could be made acceptable to our Parliament and people.'[69] The reply to this objection is that the Netherlands reservation did do precisely what Cripps claimed it did not do, that is enable the Netherlands to go back on the principle if it was shown to raise serious objections in practice.

Cripps's third, and most important, point was that 'It is, of course, by no means certain that the French would have been content with such a reservation from us'.[70] But representatives of the French government, such as Schuman, Clappier, and Parodi, had made it quite clear to the UK government that France would not regard Britain as committed to accept the outcome of the negotiations, and Massigli had gone even further in indicating that France would accept from the UK a reservation such as had been made by the Dutch.

On 21 June there was a ministerial meeting to prepare for the Schuman debate. Attlee was in the chair. Attlee asked 'whether it was not the case that the French Government had already refused to agree to our taking part in the negotiations on the same terms as the Netherlands Government'. He was told that that was not the case. All that had happened was that the French government had refused to accept the addendum to the communiqué which the British government had proposed in its memorandum of 31 May. Attlee asked Younger to provide him with the precise form of the reservation.[71] On 27 June, the day he spoke in the debate, Attlee was given some defensive briefing on the suggestion that the French government would like the British government to accept a position similar to that being taken up by the Dutch government. Attlee had started his preparation for the debate under the

---

[68] HC Debs. 26 June 1950, col. 1939.
[69] Ibid., col. 1938.   [70] Ibid., col. 1938.   [71] T 229/749.

impression that France had refused Britain the benefit of the Netherlands reservation. Just before his speech in the debate, he found that, on the contrary, there had been two informal suggestions that the British should, in effect, protect themselves by some action similar to the Netherlands reservation. The briefing read in part as follows

No such suggestion has been made to us officially by the French Government.

2. The possibility was, however, referred to twice in conversations between officials during the course of the negotiations. On May 25th Monsieur Parodi suggested to Sir Oliver Harvey that the acceptance of the invitation would not necessarily bind us to accept the eventual Treaty. . . . Sir Oliver Harvey was informed that it would be misleading for us to accept the scheme in principle.

3. On June 1st the French Ambassador in London called on Sir William Strang, not on official instructions but in a personal way. At one point in a long conversation he asked why we could not adopt the line of the Dutch. Sir William Strang explained why this was not possible.

4. No reference has since been made, even unofficially, to this possibility by any French representative.

5. As the Chancellor stated yesterday the Dutch reservation is not a reservation on the principle of a supra-national authority, but a reservation on the possibility of translating it into practice.[72]

The two meetings referred to in this brief are reported in the Foreign Office files. At the meeting between Strang and Massigli on 1 June, Strang replied to Massigli that 'we could not possibly adopt [the Dutch] line. . . . We would rather be blamed for taking this line now than run the risk of being blamed later on for wrecking the plan after negotiations had started.'[73]

Britain did not need to be invited by France to take the Netherlands reservation for its own. It was quite obvious that the French could not be expected to invite the British government *officially* to take advantage of the Dutch reservation and thereby expose themselves to a further rebuff. But what they could do to bring the British in, they did. The fact that it was done informally, even by two men such as Parodi and Massigli who clearly wanted British participation, is itself highly significant of the French desire for British participation. There was no reason for the French to return to the subject formally or informally after 2 June. The French government had repeated officially to the British government that there would be no commitment without parliamentary ratification. Despite its efforts, Britain had, on 2 June, refused

[72] MS Attlee dep. 102.   [73] *DBPO* 69.

participation in the negotiations and that was that unless Britain had a change of heart.

In the debate, Churchill said: 'I did not like the attitude of the French Government in springing this large question upon us so suddenly, or in making pedantic stipulations before sitting in council with their war-time comrades.'[74] The French did not deserve Churchill's accusation of pedantry.[75] But, he added with reason, 'this was no excuse for the British Government piling their own prejudices on the top of French pedantry.'[76]

It might be argued that neither Parodi nor Massigli were intimate with the thinking in Paris behind the Schuman Plan and that, therefore, their informal soundings were not to be relied upon. Schuman and Clappier, however, were intimate with the thinking, and had made essentially the same point. In any case, the French could not have prevented an independent interpretative statement from London carrying significance comparable with that of the Netherlands reservation. The Dutch had, in their reservation, explained their interpretation of the communiqué to which they had assented. They had made clear that their commitment to the Schuman Plan depended on the outcome of the negotiations. The French had accepted the position. If the British government had assented to the communiqué, it would have been compelled to issue an official explanation of its position. It would have been in the form of a statement to the House of Commons by the Prime Minister. The statement could have said that the British government, while accepting the immediate objective as defined by France and intending to work in good faith for its success, was not committed until the outcome of the negotiations was known. Its commitment, and its readiness to submit any treaty to Parliament, would depend on the consistency between the outcome and British national interests. The point would, no doubt, have been re-emphasized by the Prime Minister in his answers to supplementaries. The French could not have raised any objection. If the British government did not take this course, it could only be because it did not want to and the reason it did not want to was that it did not intend to have any truck with supranational authorities pooling coal and steel under any circumstances.

---

[74] HC Debs. 27 June 1950, col. 2141. But he went on to excuse the French by reference to the lack of consultation over devaluation and because of UK government opposition to the movement towards European unity.

[75] HC Debs. 27 June 1950, col. 2141.   [76] Ibid., col. 2143.

THE COMMUNIQUÉ OF 3 JUNE

At the last minute the UK government publicized its idea of a ministerial meeting, no doubt in the forlorn hope that this would rally France's allies to the UK side. It was just one more error of judgement in an unhappy history of errors of judgement. In a communiqué of 3 June, the UK government said:

His Majesty's Government are anxious to do their best to see whether a workable scheme could be produced that is fair and just to all concerned and they feel that this could best be furthered by a meeting of Ministers of the countries interested at which the question of the most effective and expeditious method of discussing the problem at issue could be examined and settled. If the French Government were prepared to reconsider their attitude and arrange a meeting of Ministers to reach agreement on the procedure for the opening of the negotiations, His Majesty's Government would be glad to participate and they have so informed the French Government.[77]

DEFINING THE DIFFERENCE

Reading the exchanges in May 1950 between London and Paris, it is hard to avoid the impression that the British government was striving to find an excuse not to be bothered which would be presentable to Washington. Because it did not wish to offend Washington more than was inevitable, it did not say outright from the beginning that it was opposed to British involvement in the Schuman Plan, but found other grounds for turning it down. Unfortunately Washington noticed that if the UK government had been honestly stating its attitude, it was only by splitting hairs, if at all, that it could explain its decision not to participate. The American Ambassador Douglas was very critical of this UK communiqué of 3 June and, indeed, of the whole British attitude. He wrote to Acheson that 'the British included in their public communiqué the proposal for a ministerial meeting as a challenge to the renaissance of French leadership on the Continent. . . . The British may have some good reasons for not participating in the negotiations. Some of the reasons they have advanced, are, however, I think no more than excuses.'[78]

Makins in a minute to Kenneth Younger on 6 June 1950 defined the difference with France thus:

[77] Cmd. 7970/16.   [78] *DBPO* 86 n.

the essential point on which the Franco-British negotiations broke down was the French insistence that we should accept the principle of an international authority with power to bind Governments, composed of neutral and impartial persons, in advance of any discussion, and secondly that we should set up such an authority by treaty before discussion of how it would work.[79]

If he had only realized it, the proposed system of treaty-making defined in Makins's second objection was abandoned by Monnet and the French government under pressure from their other partners.[80] It was true that Monnet himself wanted in negotiating the treaty to avoid technical and legal questions. Not surprisingly, the other participant countries refused to allow that approach. It was another example of the fact that the UK government would have found friends at the negotiating table if only it had agreed to negotiate. Monnet's ideas on treaty-making are discussed further in Chapter 9. Makins's first objection is the one perceived as the source of the breakdown by Monnet. In his memoirs, Monnet defined the question at issue between France and the UK as being: 'could anyone sit down at the negotiating table in order to question the very principle of establishing a High Authority?'[81] He was quite entitled to do so though the point had in fact been conceded to the Netherlands.

However, neither of these comments goes to the heart of the matter. If one tries to make sense of the difference between the French and British governments which led to the breakdown, the best interpretation is as follows. The French were asking for an assurance that if the negotiations led to a treaty which met the British government's anxieties about pooling and the High Authority, then it would sign. The British government, on the other hand, did not want to be committed in advance to signing *however great its success in influencing the treaty in the directions it required*. It was not sure, it had not made up its mind, its position was totally reserved. It was not even certain what the treaty should say if it was to meet its requirements. The problem, in other words, was not that the UK was refusing to commit itself until it knew how the scheme would work. That was the way the UK tried to present its position publicly and in Washington and it seemed logical. It was not, however, the truth. The true problem was that the UK was not prepared to give any assurance that it would commit itself to the scheme even if it knew how it would work and it was satisfactory in

---

[79] *DBPO* 92 n.

[80] Makins emphasized this point in his briefing for Bevin dated 17 June 1950—Notes for debate on Schuman Plan: MS Attlee dep. 102.

[81] Monnet 311.

so far as any supranational plan could, in Britain's view, be satisfactory.

This was a position which the French were quite entitled to reject. How could they, or indeed their negotiating partners, agree to meet British requirements if they could not be sure whether, even if they were met, the UK would join? This is not the only occasion since the war in which the UK has attempted to get in on a European negotiation on the basis that it would like to have its say, would like to influence the outcome of the negotiation, but would not commit itself to join even if its requirements were met. Nevertheless, so accommodating were the French in their desire for British participation that the UK could, without the least dishonesty, have agreed to the language proposed by France and have taken part in the negotiations. Any necessary safeguard would be provided by the independent explanatory statement by the Prime Minister reserving the government's position on the basis that it would negotiate with the intention of achieving agreement but could not be committed until ratification.

On 16 June the Belgian Ambassador in Paris told W. G. Hayter, the second man at the British Embassy in Paris, that

he and his government had the greatest difficulty in understanding [the UK's] attitude about participation in the talks. They did not regard themselves as in any way committed, by their signature of the communiqué, to accepting the principle of a supra-national authority or to any other feature of the Plan. They thought that by participating they were merely enabling themselves to work out a project which they hoped would make sense. But if no such result emerged they would regard themselves as entirely uncommitted in any way.[82]

Harvey wrote that the breakdown was 'a classic example of the difficulty of reconciling French cartesianism with British empiricism'.[83] British ambassadors occasionally take refuge in language of this kind. The British always pride themselves on their empiricism. But in this case a little clarity of thought and honesty of purpose would have served better.

Massigli is forthright in his denunciation of Monnet. It was Monnet and Monnet alone, he asserts, who, in the second half of May, prevented Schuman agreeing a reasonable compromise with London.[84] But once the initiative had been seized by France, any compromise would have had to involve a High Authority in some form. No compromise was available because London was not prepared to accept the High Authority in any form that Monnet would recognize. Massigli, who

[82] *DBPO* 106 n.   [83] *DBPO* 92.   [84] Massigli 209.

throughout had supported the British point of view without fully understanding it, concludes his account of these exchanges with a reproof to
both sides. 'No one had the right to be proud of the result.'[85]

THE ATTEMPT TO EXPLAIN

The British government was shocked at its condemnation by opinion in
the USA, Western Europe, and even the Commonwealth. In subsequent
weeks, it did everything it could to show that it had acted in good faith
and that its attitude had been reasonable. Ministers roamed the country
making speeches defending their decision. Typical was one made by
Sir Hartley Shawcross, Attorney-General, at Weymouth on 25 June:

[W]e did not feel able to tie ourselves down in advance to a plan which might
seem to contemplate that our Government would be subordinated to an outside
supra-national body. It is an odd commentary how some who are bitterly opposed to the British coal and steel industries being controlled by the British
public are yet willing to commit themselves in advance to a scheme which
might involve their control by some outside authority not responsible to the
people of this country at all.[86]

We can leave aside the obligatory political debating point. But if the
whole concept of the Schuman Plan was so objectionable, what had 'in
advance' to do with it?

Or as Hugh Dalton, Chairman of the Labour Party's International
Committee, put it: 'How could the British Labour Party consent, as a
sort of half-way house to Federalism, to giving up to some new High
Authority beyond the control of governments, and hence of national
Parliaments, the right to take decisions on matters such as the control
of our coal and steel industries, vital to our national life?'[87] Again, if
the whole idea was so outrageous, if the Schuman Plan really was a
half-way house to federalism, why had the British government toyed
with the idea for three weeks before turning it down on rather specious
grounds?

THE DURHAM MINERS

It may be argued that Britain's Labour government could not have
involved itself in the Schuman Plan because it would have provoked

[85] Massigli, 207.   [86] *Manchester Guardian*, 26 June 1950.
[87] Speech at Middleton-in-Teesdale, 22 July 1950.

opposition from its working-class supporters. The well-attested story goes that Herbert Morrison, in the absence of Bevin in hospital and Attlee and Cripps on holiday, was briefed by Kenneth Younger and Edwin Plowden about the French ultimatum of 1 June 1950. Morrison commented: 'It's no good. We cannot do it; the Durham miners won't wear it.'[88] Yet the objections of the Durham miners may have been a great deal less than Morrison feared, despite the opposition of the NCB to British participation in the Plan.[89] On 9 June Sir William Lawther, President of the National Union of Miners (NUM), was quoted as saying:

We want to know what we are signing our hands to. British miners enjoy the highest standard of living in Europe. We do not want to jeopardise this achievement by joining the Schuman Plan before knowing exactly what it is all about. . . . If M. Schuman or anyone else can prove that his plan will not push us back, then it is all right, but we want proof.

Lawther added that Labour should take part in working out the details of the Schuman Plan. 'The best way to have the details the way you want them is to be on the inside working them out.'[90] These sensible comments, coming from a man who had himself been General Secretary of the Durham miners, hardly sound like an irreconcilable objection which could not give way to the persuasions of a Labour government. Lawther's opinions may have been influenced by thinking in the Ministry of Fuel and Power which was the department of government most determined to find ways of achieving British participation in the Plan. Massigli believed that the Miners' MP, Aneurin Bevan, was genuinely favourable to the Plan.[91]

There need have been no fear, therefore, that British participation in the Schuman Plan would have encountered prohibitive political opposition from the Durham miners. The steel workers might, in fact, have been more difficult, reflecting the strong opposition to the Plan in the Ministry of Supply. Nevertheless, there is no reason to think that the political difficulties of the British government in participating in the Schuman Plan would have been greater than the political difficulties of the French government whose people had suffered invasion, oppression, and deportation by the Germans. If there had been a British initiative before the Schuman Plan, the politics would, certainly, have

---

[88] This story is authenticated by Geoffrey Warner who had an interview with Younger on 12 Dec. 1969. It is recorded in Donoughue and Jones 481, 639.
[89] Milward (1984) 402–3.   [90] *Manchester Guardian*, 10 June 1950.
[91] Massigli 206.

been easier. A British initiative carried more prospect of acceptability to the trade unions than a French initiative.

PROTECTING BRITAIN FROM OBLOQUY

In his conversation with Massigli on 1 June, Strang indicated his anxiety to protect the British government against obloquy if the negotiations failed. Britain, unlike the Netherlands, was too important to enter the negotiations and then leave. If it did so, it would then be accused of sabotaging a step towards European economic integration. On two counts, Strang's judgement was in error. It was absurd to be deterred by the possibility that it might be accused of sabotage if it was dissatisfied with the outcome of the negotiating conference provided only that it had honestly sought to get agreement. Nor did Britain escape obloquy by its refusal to participate. The suspicion remained in Europe that Britain *was* trying to sabotage the Plan.[92] But what was increasingly manifest was that Britain, though it might be accused of sabotage, could not achieve it if the other partners were willing to go forward. Throughout the exchange of memoranda with France, the British government acted as though its views must be respected. It was a disturbing experience to find that others were prepared to ignore them. The second count on which Strang's judgement was in error was even more important. He did not appear to realize, nor did he advise ministers, that the probability was that the negotiations would succeed.

The Attlee government allowed British participation in the Schuman Plan to go by default, happy in the unfounded expectation that the negotiations would fail.

[92] *DBPO* 137, letter from Sir I. Kirkpatrick to Sir D. Gainer, 11 July 1950, reporting a conversation with John McCloy, US High Commissioner, 10 July 1950.

9

The High Authority

Nothing had startled the British government about the Schuman Plan more than the concept of a High Authority with sovereign powers. Nothing Monnet could say during his visit to London, or in his letter of 25 May to Plowden, could dispel the astonishment that such an idea, so inadequately thought through, could have passed the French Cabinet and become French policy.

By way of possible comfort, the communiqué had said: 'Appropriate measures will be provided for means of appeal against the decisions of the authority.'[1] But the French were unable to imbue the sentence with any specific meaning. They had not yet worked out the grounds on which appeals could be based nor could they identify the judges. The minute of Monnet's meeting with Makins and Plowden on 16 May 1950 said that

The French have not decided whether Governments could appeal against decisions of the Authority only on the grounds that they were contrary to the provisions of the Treaty or on the grounds that it would be unreasonable for the Government concerned to have to carry them out. M. Monnet was clear that it would violate the whole purpose of the Authority if a Court of Appeal were to be set up which merely re-established the right of national sovereignty over the field which had been allocated by the Treaty to the Authority.[2]

In his letter of 25 May, Monnet speaks of governments having a right to demand a review of Authority decisions 'and in certain cases decisions could only be confirmed by the larger majority'. On juridical questions, appeal could be to the Permanent Court of International Justice. On 'fundamental questions', there could be arbitration. It was all vague and unsatisfactory.[3] In his letter, Monnet also explained that 'it seems to us that the Authority will usually be able to confine itself to indirect and general means of action without interfering in the management of the enterprises concerned nor directly determining which of

---

[1] Cmd. 7970/2.   [2] *DBPO* 25.   [3] *DBPO* 45.

them should be eliminated.' Monnet seems to have had in mind competition policy and the need to equalize the conditions of competition, for example in transport tariff rates. The spirit of the letter is not directly interventionist.[4] The British government could have derived some encouragement from the modesty of Monnet's ambitions in this respect.

But if this was to be the nature and purpose of the High Authority, why had it been presented to the world in language which was the very opposite of modest? The Schuman announcement had called for UN accreditation to the new authority. 'A representative of the United Nations will be accredited to the authority, and will be instructed to make a public report to the United Nations twice yearly, giving an account of the working of the new organism, particularly as concerns the safeguarding of its pacific objects.'[5] In the meeting at the Hyde Park Hotel, Monnet is reported as saying that 'It was felt that the appointment of a United Nations observer was essential if undue suspicion on the part of non-member countries [?and] of organized industry and labour throughout the world were to be avoided.'[6] This was hardly an explanation that would satisfy critical minds. Ambassadors from national governments as well as from the UN were to be accredited to it. What precisely was this new authority to be that required the accreditation to it of representatives of the UN and of sovereign states?

Massigli says in his memoirs that one thing about the Schuman announcement that had not surprised him was the High Authority. He comments on the frequency with which the idea of a supranational organization had been put forward in the context of the coal and steel industries.[7] But this was no ordinary supranational organization. Everyone was entitled to be surprised at the idea of a High Authority consisting of nominated personalities possessing sovereign powers in the exercise of which they could bind governments. Massigli himself rapidly came to realize that the undemocratic character of the High Authority could become a major obstacle to British participation in the Schuman Plan negotiations.

Monnet had experience as head of the *Commissariat Générale du Plan*. This may have informed his thinking about the functions of the Authority. But the *Commissariat Générale du Plan* was not a sovereign authority. It was subordinate to the French government with all the aggravation that could cause to anyone as single-minded as Monnet.

---

[4] *DBPO* 45.   [5] Cmd. 7970/2.
[6] *DBPO* 25. '[?and]' is in the original report of the meeting.
[7] Massigli 186.

No UN observer was accredited to it. Roger Bullen believes that the High Authority was modelled on the High Commission of the occupying powers. 'It was clear that in French thinking about Germany the High Commission of the occupying powers was the model for the High Authority of the Schuman Plan. It was adapted and modified but most of all it was transformed from a symbol of defeat into the ideal of co-operation.'[8]

But the High Commission consisted of three High Commissioners appointed by the occupying powers. They were not independent of their governments. They could be removed. The members of the High Authority, once appointed, were to swear oaths, however seriously they regarded them, of independence from governments. In the original Schuman announcement there was no way of removing them. They were sovereign and irremovable for the duration of their term of office. Even boards of directors of private companies can be dismissed by their shareholders. The independence of the High Authority can, perhaps, be compared with the independence of the Bundesbank. But the Bundesbank is not sovereign. It is independent *of the Federal German government* but not of the Bundestag. The Bundestag established the Bundesbank's independence of the government by law, and provided it with its remit. But it retained the power to recall what it had delegated. The High Authority did not embody the ideal of co-operation between governments. It was to bind governments. One may wonder whether the French Cabinet, in approving the Schuman announcement, knew what it was doing, indeed whether Schuman himself knew what he was doing, before they all found themselves committed to the High Authority.

Monnet hated the OEEC intergovernmental model of supranationalism. It was too subject to politics and to the veto of governments. In his letter to Plowden, Monnet argues that 'to entrust the Authority to a Committee of Government delegates . . . would amount to returning to our present methods, those very methods which do not enable us to settle our problems'. Repeatedly revealed in Monnet's life and in his memoirs is his impatience with the compromises required by democracy. It led him to the idea of a High Authority and to the proposal that decisions should be left to 'quite a small number of men of real stature . . . capable of rising above particular or national interests'. Of course they would consult with all manner of people, including governments, but *they* would take the decisions.[9] Among Monnet's blind spots

---

[8] Bullen, in Bullen *et al.* 195.　　　[9] *DBPO* 45.

was a failure to appreciate the legitimacy that comes from democracy. He wanted 'the power of decision' to be 'entrusted to institutions serving the general interest and applying the will of the majority in a system of common rules'.[10] But he regarded himself as a better interpreter of the will of the majority than any elected leader. As for elected leaders, he used them but he was not in love with them.[11] He had a similar attitude to the technocrats upon whom he called to convert his inspirations into drafts. He was the apotheosis of the meritocrat who, while expecting there to be a technocratic solution to every problem, nevertheless believes that the technocrats should be on tap, not on top. Massigli describes him as a technocrat but also an autocrat.[12] In its introduction to the public in the Schuman announcement of 9 May 1950, the High Authority was to be free of any element of democratic control.

At the Council of Europe on 8 August, Harold Macmillan put forward an intergovernmental version of the Schuman Plan as a counter-proposal to French ideas. He was rewarded with the following written comment from Monnet: 'The indispensable first principle of these [Schuman] proposals is the abnegation of sovereignty in a limited but decisive field and . . . in my view, any plan which does not involve this indispensable first principle can make no useful contribution to the solution of the grave problems that face us.'[13] Monnet always appeared to believe that the only question raised by the High Authority was the readiness of European states to abnegate sovereignty. But this was by no means the only, and perhaps not the most important, problem with it. Monnet, according to Massigli, was surprised when, in London on 14 May, it was explained to him that the British would not accept an Authority free of any form of parliamentary control.[14]

Schuman, when he understood the criticism, appeared to be searching for an answer, partly perhaps because the point was being taken also in the French Cabinet.[15] At the MRP congress at Nantes on 21 May, he was reported as saying that the new organization would be subject to the Council of Europe.[16] However, speaking on 7 June to the Anglo-American Association, he had modified his position. First, he appeared to contemplate the possibility that the Authority would

---

[10] Monnet 370–1.   [11] With apologies to the Marquis of Halifax.
[12] Massigli 200.   [13] Monnet 316.   [14] Massigli 200.
[15] In conversation at lunch with Edmund Hall-Patch on 16 June 1950, Maurice Petsche, the French Finance Minister, described a High Authority not under control by ministers responsible to Parliament as 'franchement inconcevable': *DBPO* 95 n.
[16] *The Times*, 22 May 1950.

acquire its powers only gradually, meanwhile being subject to a governmental right of veto. Then, in answer to a question, he recognized that the Authority should be responsible to some other body. This was necessary, he foresaw, to meet contingencies such as the madness or corruption of a member of the Authority. For such reasons members might have to be dismissed. He could not, however, foresee what this body to which the High Authority should be responsible would be. He did not think it would be the Council of Europe in its present form. But if the composition of the Council were altered, in various ways which he would rather not define at that stage, it might meet the case. It had in any case to be a supranational body.[17]

The idea that the High Authority should be made subject to the Council of Europe was an idea in widespread discussion. Kim Mackay repeated it during the House of Commons debate on the Schuman Plan though by that time other proposals were emerging at the negotiating conference in Paris: 'I would suggest to the Chancellor of the Exchequer that the Council of Europe provides a proper authority to which the board for the coal and steel industries of Europe under the Schuman Plan could be responsible.'[18] Debate in the House of Commons allows MPs to enjoy the luxury of recommending a better way for the world even where the British government is in no way involved or, as in this case, has decided deliberately not to be involved. A fundamental problem with the idea of responsibility to the Council of Europe was that the membership of the Council differed from the likely membership of the ECSC. Britain itself was a member of the Council of Europe but did not intend to join the ECSC. Another problem, from Monnet's point of view, was that a High Authority that was responsible to some other, outside, body would not be sovereign. If it was not sovereign, it would not be effective.

Other French answers to criticism of the undemocratic nature of the High Authority were provided in press briefing. It would be subject to a mandate authorized by national Parliaments. This would be a guarantee against arbitrary and irresponsible decisions. It would be in the position of a trustee bound to give prime consideration to the interests of the trust. Governments, although bound by Authority decisions, would be the bodies that gave them executive force. Although the delegation of sovereignty to the High Authority was irreversible, any government

---

[17] *The Times*, 8 June 1950: quoted in *DBPO* 104.
[18] HC Debs. 27 June 1950, col. 2127.

could initiate discussions leading to the amendment of the covenant. The proposed authority would be concerned neither with management nor with ownership but solely in framing policy in accordance with the covenant.[19]

None of these responses met the criticism that it was intended to establish a sovereign body of considerable power which lacked any form of democratic accountability. Yet the French government, without having undertaken sufficient, or indeed any, study on the subject had committed itself to the creation of such a High Authority. On that commitment, Franco-German reconciliation was to be built. If there was any ground for the British government to turn down the Schuman initiative, it was this, that it was being asked to accept the principle of a High Authority lacking any element of democratic legitimacy but with, in theory at least, vast powers over major industries and governments. In presenting the High Authority in this way Schuman gave a powerful handle to all those who did wish to oppose supranationalism. Macmillan told the Council of Europe that the British people were not going to hand over to any supranational authority the right to close their pits and steelworks.[20] Attlee was on firmer ground when, on the final day of the debate on the Schuman Plan, he made a distinction between the High Authority and the surrender of sovereignty to bodies like the OEEC, the Atlantic Charter, and the UN: '[I]n every instance that surrender is made to a responsible body, a body of people responsible to Parliaments, not to an irresponsible body appointed by no one and responsible to no one.'[21] To claim that the High Authority was to be 'appointed by no one' was oratorical licence. Attlee would have been right if he had said that, in the form in which it was originally presented to the public in the Schuman announcement of 9 May, the High Authority could be dismissed by no one. But the central point of Attlee's criticism was entirely justified. He had made the same point in a private conversation with Massigli on 7 June.[22]

Why did the British government not put this objection in the forefront of its arguments with the French and in its briefing of the Press and Washington? Instead of splitting hairs about the degree to which it

---

[19] *The Times*, 22 and 24 May 1950.   [20] Horne 329.

[21] HC Debs. 27 June 1950, col. 2164. The lack of democratic control over the High Authority was a point that worried Younger. 'There is a draft French plan which uncompromisingly insists upon a supra-national authority, with very little democratic control. We could not possibly accept that': Younger's diary, 6 July 1950.

[22] Massigli 208–9 . Attlee's less detailed account of the conversation is in *DBPO* 94.

might be committed by joining in negotiation, it could have turned the propaganda battle against the French. It could have argued that it was not against supranationalism, simply against the undemocratic nature of the supranational institution that the French proposed to establish. Instead of highlighting the undemocratic character of the High Authority, it allowed the French to win the propaganda battle by stressing that the issue was supranationalism and by underlining the British government's reluctance to pool sovereignty. The only explanation of this tactical failure is that the French were in fact right. For the British the question really was supranationalism, and the undemocratic nature of the High Authority was secondary. The British were pretending that they were not against the principle of supranationalism, only attempting to discover how it would work before committing themselves. The truth was that they were against supranationalism in this instance however it would work and even if the High Authority was democratically controlled. If they had put the undemocratic nature of the High Authority in the forefront, they might have been embarrassed to find the French co-operative in solving that specific problem.

If the British government had been honest in claiming that it was not against the principle of supranationalism, the undemocratic nature of the High Authority would have remained a serious problem. Nevertheless, in assessing this major hurdle in the way of participation in the negotiations, the UK government should have set against it the great value of the element of Franco-German *rapprochement* in the Schuman Plan and the probability that the High Authority would emerge from negotiation as rather a different beast from the way it entered. It might enter the conclave as Pope but was more than likely to emerge as cardinal or, perhaps even less, as bishop.

At his meeting with Plowden, Makins, and Hitchman at the Hyde Park Hotel, Monnet is reported as saying: 'It was the intention that the Treaty should be drawn up in general terms and be signed before the detailed operating clauses have been settled.'[23] This caused dismay in London because it seemed to mean that even if it took part in the negotiations, the government might not know, when invited to sign the treaty, how in practice it would operate.[24] In his memoirs Monnet recalls his initial attitude in preparing the Schuman Plan negotiations: 'I was convinced that progress towards a united Europe would be easier

[23] *DBPO* 25.
[24] Makins conveyed his concern about this matter in his brief for Bevin, dated 17 June 1950—Notes for debate on Schuman Plan: MS Attlee dep. 102.

if we could exclude from the new Treaty the legal and technical formalities that normally burden such agreements.'[25]

Of course this is what Monnet wanted. A rapid negotiation, which excluded 'the legal and technical formalities', presented him with the best chance of getting away with his version of the High Authority untrammelled by constraints of a democratic variety. But his negotiating partners would not permit it and he had to concede a proper negotiation. In his memoirs, immediately after the sentence just quoted in which he registers his convictions about the best method of proceeding in the elaboration of the Treaty, he makes a virtue of necessity: 'For the Schuman Plan, things did not work out that way; but in the end we made a virtue of our disappointment. We used the long, painstaking negotiations to draw up an entirely novel Treaty, in which future generations will no doubt look for models of how to pool resources and bring nations together.'[26]

On the contrary, future generations would look away from the High Authority model, not towards it. At the outset of the negotiating conference, Monnet 'asked that the word "negotiations" should not be used to describe our meetings. Instead, for ourselves as for the public, they should be known as the Schuman Plan Conference.'[27] Despite Monnet, it was a negotiation and, in negotiation, the independence of the supranational High Authority came under close scrutiny by the negotiators and they insisted on amendment. As Roger Bullen says, 'most of the other European states had expressed some private misgivings about the nature and power of the High Authority and it was well known in London that the French government was also divided on the question.'[28] Schuman and Monnet realized that, in the form presented in the 9 May announcement, the High Authority would be acceptable neither to their partners nor even to the French Cabinet. In a paper put to the negotiating conference by the French government, the powers of the High Authority were defined in a way which made them far less terrifying than they had originally appeared. Indeed the *Manchester Guardian*, when it heard of the French proposals, commented: 'Much of the powers which, it seemed, was to be vested in the supra-national body will remain firmly in the hands of the Governments. The authority has thus become an advisory and planning council.'[29]

Under the new French proposals, the High Authority would collect

---

[25] Monnet 321.   [26] Ibid.   [27] Ibid. 323.
[28] Bullen, in Bullen *et al*. 201.   [29] *Manchester Guardian*, 20 June 1950.

information and would strive to protect the consumer against discrimination and to eliminate unfair trade practices. By making appropriate recommendations to the governments or enterprises concerned if the level of wages appeared abnormally low, it would endeavour to ensure that competition and the adjustment of enterprises did not operate to the detriment of wage-earners. It would give guidance to enterprises on the establishment of their own production and modernization programmes. It would be empowered to make investment loans to enterprises and to make grants as well as loans for the necessary conversion and the development of new enterprises. A compensation fund would be established in order to provide temporary assistance to those enterprises whose adjustment to a single market required a certain delay. Thus would the bitter edge of competition be blunted in the interests of social harmony.

Perhaps the decisive point in the French proposals was that coal and steel enterprises would remain responsible for their investments and for financing them. It was the fact that responsibility was left to enterprises, as was indeed inevitable, that ensured that the High Authority should be to a large extent advisory.[30] Apart from this, the French government proposed a Common Assembly, consisting of members of existing national Parliaments, which would meet once a year, to which the High Authority would report, and which could in certain circumstances compel its resignation. This was a nuclear weapon which was unlikely to be used but it gave some semblance of democratic control to the peoples of the six member countries. But, during the negotiations, a more important concession was forced from the French. It was decided that a Council of Ministers should be constituted, as part of the ECSC, charged with the duty of harmonizing the policies of the High Authority with those of member governments.[31] Massigli comments that the ministers were no less ministers in their national governments for the fact that the Council of Ministers was part of the ECSC.[32] Though it was required to be unanimous, the Council of Ministers would by its nature be very powerful. The evidence suggests that Monnet opposed the creation of the Council of Ministers. In his view, to bring ministers

---

[30] There was a sense in which the High Authority had control over investment. Projects had to be submitted in advance and, if disapproved, this had the effect of prohibiting the enterprise concerned from resort to resources other than its own funds for the purpose of implementing the project.

[31] The course of the negotiations is described in Diebold 60 ff. and Gillingham 239 ff.

[32] Massigli 227.

into the picture would simply re-create an intergovernmental machine.[33] But the Benelux countries insisted and there was a compromise though one which conceded the main point argued by Benelux. It was now the ECSC to which the member states had made their limited delegation of sovereignty.

Thus the High Authority emerged from the negotiation a very different animal, to which the term 'sovereign' no longer accurately applied, though, within its heavily limited scope, it remained the exclusive source of executive power.[34] Monnet had included in his original plans neither an Assembly nor a Council of Ministers. Thus by the time that Macmillan made his counter-proposals to the Council of Europe, the High Authority had been placed under some formal democratic constraint. But that was not what the original Schuman announcement had proposed.

One can only speculate how much further compromise might have taken the structure of the eventual ECSC if Britain had not renounced its opportunity to be present. In the cause of constraining the High Authority, the UK would have found allies, in the Netherlands as might have been expected from the doubts publicly expressed by the Netherlands government, but also from Belgium, concerned to secure guarantees for its uneconomic coal-mines, and within the French and German governments. The problem for the Benelux countries in negotiating limitations on the sovereign powers of the High Authority was that, if necessary, the Plan could proceed without them. It was essentially a Franco-German project and although France would move some way to meet Benelux, its need to move was limited as long as Germany was kept on board. If the UK had been involved, the problem for France in resisting sensible compromise would have been qualitatively different.

In his memoirs, Monnet writes as though the outcome of the negotiations was exactly what he wanted. He records how he made the following statement to the negotiating conference on 12 July 1950:

I have to admit that there was a gap in our original draft, which Spierenburg and Suetens have suggested ways of filling. We can now distinguish two types

---

[33] *DBPO* 115, Hall-Patch to Younger, 23 June 1950.

[34] The High Authority had nine members. No more than two were to be from any one country. Eight were chosen by agreement among the governments. The ninth was chosen by the eight. In theory, a member country might not be represented on the High Authority. Each country had one vote in the Council of Ministers. It sometimes needed unanimity, more often a majority. A minority which included France and Germany could block action.

of problem: those which the Treaty, by a collective decision of our national Parliaments, will expressly entrust to the High Authority; and those which spill over into the responsibility of Governments, and in which Governments should be empowered to intervene, provided that they act collectively. In such circumstances, well defined in advance, the High Authority and the Governments could hold joint meetings. We have just made a great step forward.[35]

One might say, some gap, and after nine drafts! It was clear from the beginning that the exercise of the High Authority's supposed independent sovereignty would spill over into the responsibilities of governments. It was, therefore, clear from the beginning that the High Authority, in the form proposed in the Schuman announcement, was unacceptable. Monnet's statement conceded defeat for his conception of the High Authority. Schuman himself appears to have believed that, by the end of August, the supranational character of the High Authority had been so attenuated that the principal obstacle to British participation had been removed.[36] If he believed that, it may well have been because he was being advised by an ambassador in London, René Massigli, who had himself failed to understand the real nature and depth of British opposition. Massigli, uncritical friend of British policy, himself sums up the situation that had been created. 'The Authority established by the Treaty was no longer unaccountable and it did not have to any degree the disposal of the economic powers of the participant countries; however, England remained on the sidelines . . .'[37]

REFLECTIONS ON THE HIGH AUTHORITY IN PRACTICE

Denis Healey, at the time International Secretary of the Labour Party, reflected at leisure many years later that 'The Schuman Plan for coal and steel now operates by fairly effective bargaining between states'.[38] In short, it was effectively intergovernmental. It is a pity that that perception of what was, in fact, inevitable did not permeate Labour

---

[35] Monnet 331–2. Dirk Spierenburg was of the Netherlands Ministry of Economic Affairs and Chairman of the OEEC Council at official level. He led the Dutch delegation to the Schuman negotiations, became one of the first members of the High Authority and, in 1994, was joint author of a major history of the High Authority. Monnet describes him as 'the living incarnation of Dutch stubbornness, and a very tough debater': Monnet 324. Maximilian Suetens was head of the Belgian delegation.

[36] Massigli 224.   [37] Ibid. 229.

[38] Healey (1990) 78. Lecture at the Bologna Center of the Johns Hopkins University, 10 Nov. 1987.

government thinking in 1950. Marjolin's appreciation of the history of the High Authority was that it was constrained in the exercise of its powers 'by the fact that any decision of consequence in regard to coal and steel had repercussions in other areas of the member countries' economies. As a result, close cooperation had become a practice between the High Authority and the Council of Ministers.'[39] Elsewhere he wrote, putting a more positive gloss on the High Authority: 'though the High Authority did not live up to its ambitions, it demonstrated what a group of independent minded men, moved by a common ideal, could achieve in spite of lack of real power.'[40]

Diebold observes that

on very many issues the Treaty required the High Authority to consult governments and interest groups before it acted, even when the power of decision was its alone. As a matter of policy the High Authority went further. It tried to get as wide an area of agreement as possible before it acted, even when it had legal authority to move without the assent of the others. . . . On many matters the governments had the power of decision; the High Authority was unlikely to carry much influence with them if, in its own sphere, it ignored their interests and views. The High Authority was new, and not as powerful as it appeared in Treaty law . . .[41]

Haas, after a close analysis of the powers that could be exercised independently by the High Authority and those subject to consultation with or the agreement of the Council of Ministers, concludes:

in all matters relating to the routine regulation of the common market, the High Authority is independent of governments. As regards measures to be taken in a crisis situation, however, as well as in areas not clearly part of the coal–steel complex, the controlling capacity of the member governments remains potent if not dominant. *Hence, ECSC is a far from federal structure with respect to the crucial criteria of executing decisions and expanding tasks.*[42]

Haas adds:

The member states have yielded their former ability to control—actually or potentially—the production, pricing, marketing and distribution of coal and steel, as well as the forms of organization adopted by the enterprises engaged

---

[39] Marjolin (1989) 274–5.
[40] Ibid. 234. This judgement was taken from Marjolin (1981) 34.
[41] Diebold 596, 597.
[42] Haas 55–6. Author's emphasis. In a manifest crisis the High Authority could impose equitable production quotas.

in these pursuits. Yet, they clearly have *not* yielded their ability to control the economic conditions under which coal and steel are produced and sold: monetary, fiscal, foreign economic, wage and social welfare policy. . . . If the division of functions is heavily weighted on the side of national states, the same is true in the field of powers of control and manipulation.[43]

Nothing of what Haas writes should have been a surprise to the British government, fearful that British sovereignty would be abrogated by participation in the Plan. As early as 24 June 1950 William Strath of the CEPS reported to Sir Edwin Plowden on a conversation he had had with Duncan Burn, the great authority on the steel industry.

Mr Burn recognizes as we do that a coal and steel authority can really do very little to affect the *demand* for coal and steel, which really depends on the general level of economic activity. . . . The real power, therefore, lies in the hands of those organizations, i.e. Governments, which are able to influence the level of economic activity as a whole, and not with sectional organizations like the proposed coal and steel authority.[44]

It was the good fortune of the High Authority, when at last established, that it was born into a world in which, with some pauses, economic expansion helped to avoid major clashes with national governments.[45] But there was no question but that, when major decisions had to be taken, for example when problems of serious overcapacity in coal and steel did emerge, governments had to be involved in the solution. Recently the work of Spierenburg and Poidevin has confirmed the deference of the High Authority to national governments combined with an excessive respect for vested interests in the coal and steel industries supposedly under its control.[46] None of this was unexpected either before or after Monnet's ideas had been processed through the fire of the Schuman Plan negotiations. Fears in British political circles that the High Authority would have the power to close pits and steelworks without the concurrence of governments was a convenient nightmare with which to frighten anyone rash enough to be thinking of supporting the Schuman initiative.

---

[43] Haas 58.   [44] T 229/749, Strath to Plowden, 24 June 1950.
[45] The Korean War had given a helpful impetus to demand after 1950. 'The temporary easing of demand for steel in 1957 and 1958 was not marked or long enough to create any serious problems for the Community.' The problems with coal in the same period were much greater and were met by government action as well as action by the High Authority: Diebold 683 ff.
[46] Spierenburg and Poidevin, *History of the High Authority*.

A BLIND ALLEY

Monnet's idea of a sovereign High Authority completely independent of governments took supranationalism into a blind alley. It was not a model that could conceivably have been applied in the construction of the EEC. But it was, no doubt, of educational value to the member states of the EEC to be alerted to what people such as Monnet would hold out for them if they were not on their guard. It was a model that led, not to federalism as Monnet hoped, but nowhere at all.

In his memoirs, Monnet also comments: 'We had [made a great step forward]: the Council of Ministers of the European Community had just been born.'[47] A Council of Ministers already existed as an institution within the Council of Europe. The Council of Europe predated the ECSC. It would be untypical of Monnet had he allowed priority in institutional inventiveness to the intergovernmental Council of Europe rather than to the supranational ECSC. Nevertheless, his claim, that the ECSC gave birth to the Council of Ministers of the EEC, reveals Monnet's misunderstanding of the institutional structure of the EEC. A few years later, when the Treaty of Rome was being negotiated, it was the Council of Ministers that led the development of the Community, there was no High Authority, only a Commission with very limited powers. Under the Treaty of Rome, the Council of Ministers of the EEC constituted its legislative body. The power, in other words, was located in the representatives of democratic governments. The existence of the Council of Ministers underlined the key role of governments and the fact that governments would have to take the responsibility before their electorates. The institution of the Council of Ministers of the EEC represented the rejection of the High Authority model, not its acceptance and not even its development. It demonstrated that integration within the EEC would take a path entirely different from that of the ECSC.[48]

Equally misguided is Monnet's comment on the memorandum of the negotiating conference dated 5 August 1950 which set out the institutional structure of the future ECSC: 'Not only had the High Authority emerged unscathed from the ordeal [of negotiation], but the very constraints which had sought to limit its independence only emphasized the

[47] Monnet 332.
[48] Even so, the German Ministry of Economics was not too happy with the arrangement, wanting more power for the Council of Ministers: Gillingham 346–8.

federal nature of the institutional system which it headed.'[49] On the contrary, the imposition of the constraints was the first indication that the six countries of the ECSC were unwilling to accept the Monnet model for their further integration and that, in future, they would seek a different model. The Treaty of Paris could not emphasize the federal nature of the institutional system headed by the High Authority because it did not have a federal character. It was a hotchpotch. It was the outcome of efforts by the governments of member countries, which had entered the negotiations committed to the principle of a High Authority, to provide a guarantee against irresponsible behaviour by the High Authority. This was achieved by ensuring that the real power remained with the national governments. The result was in no sense federal.

It was naïve to imagine that, whatever the wording of the treaty, a supranational High Authority would not be subject to national vetoes if anything went seriously wrong.[50] Nothing illustrates the continuing supremacy of the national over the supranational better than the transitional protection that had to be conceded to Belgium and to its uncompetitive coal industry in order to bring them into the ECSC.[51] It was the nation states of Europe that held and would retain democratic legitimacy. They had no power to delegate that democratic legitimacy to artificial 'supranational' creations. The High Authority's lack of democratic legitimacy proved a major constraint on its freedom to act independently or to bind governments on issues where they thought it important to take a stand. Indeed it is arguable that the High Authority's lack of democratic legitimacy was counter-productive. The power it could be permitted was less than was needed in the interests of European integration.

That major constraints would be put on the powers and independence of the High Authority was foreseeable. The pity was that the UK government had not foreseen it. Oliver Harvey, in a minute of 6 June to Kenneth Younger, reviewing the fruitless negotiations with France which had led to the British refusal to take part in the negotiating conference, wrote:

It may be doubted whether the surrender of sovereignty in so vital a sphere as national heavy industry with all the military, economic and social consequences

---

[49] Monnet 333.

[50] Professor Reuter held that the juxtaposition of national and federal powers in the ECSC made it 'pre-federal': Haas 34.

[51] See Milward (1992), ch. 3, 'Coal and the Belgian Nation'.

involved, will prove acceptable to the parties concerned, particularly if Great Britain is absent to act as a counter-weight to Germany. . . . It may be that His Majesty's Government will feel able to participate even in a supra-national Authority as the details become clearer.[52]

In fact, it was the judgement of officials, when the outcome of the negotiations was known, that the British government would not have been prepared to accept the High Authority even in its modified form known as the 'Dutch compromise'.[53] The fundamental problem remained that the British government rejected any form of supranational control of its basic industries however limited.

The Schuman Plan proved to be the high point of Monnet-type supranationalism. Little Europe began the retreat from the elevated ideas of Jean Monnet during the Schuman negotiations. In 1954 France rejected the EDC which had been proposed by René Pleven four months after the Schuman announcement. This shock played its own part in instilling in the minds of European statesmen caution in the creation of European federal structures. The negotiations for the EEC confirmed the future irrelevance of the Monnet model. It was a retreat from Monnet's conception of what was appropriate in a democratic Europe. It was also a retreat from federalism which, indeed, Monnet's model, though in no sense federal, may have done something to discredit. It was pragmatic supranationalism based on the nation states of Western Europe that characterized European integration in the following years.

Schuman himself, in 1953, addressed the question how far supranationalism implied federalism:

The question of a supranational authority does not necessarily mean a federation, that is to say the creation of a federal state, a super-state, a geographical entity with a legislature and a government working like an ordinary state. We consider that it is possible to begin, and that one must begin, by having supranational institutions whose authority is confined within strictly determined limits. We can thus have a supranational authority to control certain industrial undertakings and certain types of production. This is what we have done for coal and steel. We can have a communal army, obeying a supranational authority created by the associated states. But all this does not create a federal state. The competence of these supranational institutions applies, then, to technical problems rather than to functions which involve the sovereignty of the state.[54]

---

[52] *DBPO* 92.
[53] *DBPO* 149, minute from Mr Stevens to Ernest Bevin, 27 July 1950.
[54] Schuman 20.

He went on to confess that 'it is not always easy to define the limits'. But he concluded:

The powers of the High Authority are clearly defined and limited; it has to ensure loyalty and free competition, which is the essential principle of this community (because there is no control but freedom of competition); it has to prevent the practice of double prices within the community; it has to forbid and prevent cartels and agreements which might aim at interfering with the free movement of prices; and then to a certain extent it must control investments. These are the powers of the High Authority, powers which are admittedly very important, but do not constitute those of a government with full authority.[55]

There was nothing in the powers of the High Authority as it emerged from the negotiations that a British government should not have been prepared to accept. But the changes made no difference to the Attlee government. At the Consultative Assembly of the Council of Europe on 21 November 1950 Hugh Dalton, leading the British delegation, could do no better than to repeat the old refrain:

we are outside the stage of the formal discussions because we were not prepared to accept—and we are not prepared to accept—the principle of handing over the coal and iron and steel industries of Britain to a supra-national authority not responsible to our Government, to our Parliament, to our trade unions or to the broad masses of our people.[56]

On 30 March 1951 the new Foreign Secretary, Herbert Morrison, had a meeting with Massigli. Morrison made his own note of the conversation: 'M. Massigli said he hoped very much that the Schuman Plan would be studied once more in its present form. It was now profoundly different from the original draft and was, he thought, much more palatable to us. There was now no supreme authority. I said that we had to be careful not to deprive Parliament of its constitutional rights.'[57] One can be too careful.

CONCLUSION

An attempt might be made to argue that the criticisms made in this chapter of the High Authority are unfair because, admittedly, the

[55] Schuman 21. Regarding prices, the High Authority had the power to prohibit unfair and discriminatory practices. Price scales and conditions of sale had to be public.

[56] T 230/180.

[57] *DBPO* 245, Morrison's note of the meeting on 30 Mar. 1951 in message to Harvey. See also T 230/182.

Schuman announcement had been rushed out without every detail being considered in order to create a major impact on German thinking and in order to meet a timetable imposed by the London meeting of the Foreign Ministers of the occupying powers. Such an attempt at rebuttal would have to overcome certain well-known facts. There was time for nine drafts.[58] There could have been nothing more obvious than that, as presented in the Schuman announcement, the High Authority lacked any kind of democratic legitimacy. In addition there was nothing more obvious than that the High Authority as planned in the announcement was exactly what Monnet wanted. It was only under multiple pressure that Monnet gave way. That pressure came from within the French Cabinet and from the other five participating governments. Even when Schuman and Monnet had had the time between 9 May, the date of the original announcement, and 20 June, the date at which the negotiating conference convened, to assess their proposed High Authority in the light of the public and private reactions to it, their concessions were still insufficient to carry their negotiating partners with them. Certainly they had scaled down very substantially the powers that the High Authority could independently exercise. They had proposed a parliamentary assembly with certain ultimate rights as against the High Authority. There was still the 'gap' which Monnet was forced to acknowledge in the negotiating conference. And there was still no proposal for a Council of Ministers. The Council of Ministers completed the institutional composition and conferred an element of democratic legitimacy.

Monnet had been obliged to accept the politicians. He had been left with no alternative but to accept or admit the total failure of his enterprise. Rather than make any such admission, he preferred the rather empty eminence of the Presidency of the High Authority within a Community still supposedly sovereign. Monnet, apparently, himself came to realize that he had been wrong in his approach to the High Authority. Richard Mayne records that at a celebratory lunch after the British referendum in 1975, Monnet spoke of the early days when there was so much discussion of supranationalism and the High Authority. He said: 'We were wrong in those early days to talk about a power above nations, the High Authority, as a supranational power. What eventually emerged, even in the Coal and Steel Community days, was a dialogue between the independent body, which was the High Authority, and the

---

[58] Monnet 297.

Ministers representing the Nation States.' Mayne comments: 'It was that dialogue that Monnet believed to be the motor of integration, and he said that we were wrong in those early days because we had a very simplistic view of the way things would work.'[59]

Monnet was, deservedly, the first President of the High Authority. He had worked to invent the job. It was only right that he should fill it even though it had turned out no more than a shadow of all he had hoped. The High Authority met for the first time on 10 August 1952. On 9 November 1954 Monnet announced his intention not to seek reappointment when his term of office as President expired on 20 February 1955. The High Authority, he had found, had only limited functions which it could not go beyond. He now wanted to 'be free to act as I saw fit'.[60] He had not even been permitted his federal district.[61]

[59] Mayne, 'Jean Monnet, Europe and the British: A Witness Account', in Brivati and Jones 29–30.

[60] Monnet 399. Monnet stayed five months beyond the terminal date of his appointment waiting for the selection of his successor, René Mayer. Diebold comments that the appointment of Mayer 'comported well with the need to carry on a policy that emphasized negotiation and persuasion': Diebold 598.

[61] Monnet describes the manœuvres by which he was deprived of his pretentious idea of a European Federal District in Monnet 369–71. See also Stikker 304.

10
The Labour Party and Europe

It is no accident that in their approach to European unity since 1945 the socialist parties of Britain and Scandinavia have been most conservative—for they have most to conserve. Economic factors reinforce the trend towards nationalism in a governing socialist party: in a world predominantly capitalist, national economic planning may often be inconsistent with forms of international co-operation a *laisser-faire* government would be quite willing to accept.[1]

Behind the arguments of high policy, however valid, and probably more important than any of them in its influence on the British government, was the Labour Party's view of Europe and of the effect that European entanglements might have on economic policy. That view is eloquently expressed in the quotation that heads this chapter. But there was yet more to be said about Labour's view of Europe than could be respectably accommodated in a New Fabian Essay, and it was not particularly socialist. Britain had its niche in the world. It was a large niche and yet, psychologically, it remained a niche. It was constituted by kinship and history. It was called the Commonwealth and, on the assumption of peace in Europe, it provided all that the English-speaking people of Britain could reasonably require. If that people was compelled to look beyond its niche, it would be to the English speakers of North America that it would turn, not to Europe. For Labour there were, in addition, two immediate concerns in assessing the merits of any European economic entanglement with which it might, unfortunately, be threatened. The first was that British wages were higher than continental wages. British trade unions would fight any entanglement that threatened to reduce British to continental wage levels. The second was the effect on full employment. The perception that the continentals

---

[1] Healey, 'Power Politics and the Labour Party', in Crossman 168. At the time of the Schuman Plan, Healey was International Secretary of the Labour Party. By the time of publication in 1952, he was MP for Leeds, South-East.

were insufficiently Keynesian remained a fundamental problem with European integration.

There was a key fact which British socialists, in their enthusiasm for Keynesian economics, were inclined to disguise perhaps because it was politically inconvenient. It was brought out in David Eccles's letter to *The Times*. He wrote: 'Professor W. Arthur Lewis recently pointed out what nonsense it is to believe that the British Government have discovered some secret weapon which by itself can prevent unemployment in Britain. We now know that the only way to maintain a high level of employment in one free country is to maintain it in all free countries.'[2] Or as *The Economist* put it:

it is simply not true that planning and nationalisation have maintained full employment in Britain in the last five years. Full employment here—as in France and Switzerland, or Scandinavia or the Commonwealth—has been maintained partly by Marshall Aid, partly by the level of postwar demand and partly by the phenomenal prosperity of the United States. . . . In 1949, a mere five per cent fall in the level of American business activity was enough to bring Britain to the brink of financial disaster.[3]

British socialists could hardly have failed to appreciate the dependence of full employment on the state of the international economy. The UK had suffered enough from the 1949 American recession to show that the success of Keynesian policies in Britain could not be guaranteed in an unfavourable international environment. Keynesianism had become another excuse for insularity.

'EUROPEAN UNITY'

The Labour Party's view of Europe was elaborated in a statement entitled *European Unity*. That view was none too friendly. *European Unity* appeared on 12 June 1950 just before the publication of a White Paper in which the UK government gave what appeared to be a measured reaction to the Schuman Plan as something which could still be considered and was not to be rejected out of hand. The statement was presented at a press conference by Hugh Dalton, Chairman of the International Sub-Committee of the National Executive Committee, and the most dedicated opponent of European entanglements. It was announced as 'the first full-length statement in the fields of foreign policy

---

[2] *The Times*, 8 June 1950.　　　[3] *The Economist*, 17 June 1950.

by the NEC since the war'. *European Unity* made a major impact but not of the kind its authors had expected or hoped for. According to *The Economist*, its publication demonstrated the Labour Party's 'almost phenomenal gift for bad timing'.[4] The *Manchester Guardian* referred to it as 'one of those lamentable fatuities of which the Labour Party . . . is capable'.[5]

The first draft of *European Unity* had been prepared weeks before the announcement of the Schuman Plan. It had been intended as a rebuttal by Labour Party policy-makers of federalist proposals emanating from members of the Consultative Assembly of the Council of Europe. That body, whose members were nominated from existing national parliaments, was disinclined to keep to the narrow brief on which the Attlee government had insisted, and was regarded by too many of its continental members as an incipient European Parliament, as a first step towards a federal Europe. Consequently its activities caused great annoyance in London both in the government and in the Labour Party. *European Unity* was to be the Labour Party's riposte to all this federalist nonsense.

In between the first and second drafts, the Schuman Plan was announced and it was decided, at quite a late stage in its preparation, to include passages commenting on the Plan. In other circumstances *European Unity* might have passed little noticed by the international or national Press. The government's rejection of British participation in the Schuman Plan negotiating conference changed the public prospects of the statement. It was now bound to attract attention. The Press was certain to focus on any views emanating from the Labour Party which explained what had been found inexplicable overseas, the government's rejection of participation. On the Schuman Plan itself, what the statement said was in line with government policy and hence welcoming, even though the UK did not intend to take part on existing conditions. That welcome was submerged by unhappy wording which was widely interpreted as clarifying the British attitude to the Plan.

The words that caused the furore were as follows:

Any such representative body in Western Europe would be anti-Socialist or non-Socialist in character. In the Consultative Assembly [of the Council of Europe] itself the Socialists number only one in four. The proportion would be even further reduced if Communist opinion was represented in a European Parliament. . . . No Socialist Party with the prospect of forming a government

---

[4] *The Economist*, 17 June 1950.   [5] *Manchester Guardian*, 13 June 1950.

could accept a system by which important fields of national policy were surrendered to a supranational European representative authority, since such an
authority would have a permanent anti-Socialist majority and would arouse the
hostility of European workers.[6]

This was taken as implying that Britain's Labour government would
co-operate only with European socialists, or European socialist governments. With a triumphant air of discovery, opponents and critics of the
Labour government announced that it was for this reason that the Labour government had refused its participation. It was not the intention
of the passage to imply any such thing. The Labour government was
prepared to co-operate with European governments of a different political orientation provided that it was on an intergovernmental basis. But
anyone happy to find fault with Labour could easily read it as a bar on
any form of co-operation with non-socialist governments. Foreign
Office officials had warned against this passage but too late to secure
any alteration.[7] Dalton did not help. As he told his diary, at the press
conference 'I refused, in particular, to say if there were more Socialist
governments in Europe, we should be more willing to enter into closer
arrangements'.[8] His failure to deny the interpretation which unfriendly
journalists wished to put upon it gave them the necessary encouragement to do so. Kenneth Younger attributed the bad reception of the
statement not to its argument but to Hugh Dalton:

On the whole the pamphlet is good, but unfortunately it was ineptly launched
by Hugh Dalton at a press conference where he was so rude to all the foreign
journalists that they went away determined to make trouble for him. They
picked out odd sentences from the text and gave the impression that the Labour
Party would cooperate only with socialist governments in Europe . . .[9]

Foreign Office Ministers were not entirely without responsibility for
the misfortune. Ernest Davies, Parliamentary Under-Secretary of State,
had been asked by Bevin to prepare a memorandum on the government's attitude towards the Council of Europe. Amended after Bevin
had commented on it, it became a paper entitled *The Labour Party and
European Co-operation*. It was dated 25 April 1950. Ernest Davies sent
the paper to Healey under cover of a letter also dated 25 April, saying
'my sole purpose is to present this for your consideration in drafting the
paper you are preparing for the Executive on this subject'. It was a

[6] *European Unity* 8.   [7] Ernest Davies Papers.
[8] Dalton's diary (BLPES). 16 June 1950.   [9] Younger's diary, 6 July 1950.

private communication, intended for guidance but not for attribution. Davies's paper contained the following passage: 'With the governments of Scandinavia alone socialist, and the rest of Europe apparently moving further away from Britain in respect of economic planning and favouring in some cases "laissez-faire", Socialist Britain could not commit herself in the economic field to the majority rule of a largely non-Socialist Europe.'[10] Thus encouraged, the Labour Party issued its sectarian prejudices to a world less amazed by the sectarianism than by the honesty of the confession.

The intended message in Ernest Davies's paper was clear enough even though toned down from an earlier draft:

Our policy can and should be to participate fully in the Council of Europe but always and only on the understanding that Britain's special requirements as the chief partner of the Commonwealth and centre of the sterling area, and its special relationship to Canada and the USA make it necessary to reserve the right to limit participation when it would endanger the fulfilment of obligations arising from her special position.[11]

The earlier draft, dated 22 April, had, more bluntly, 'reserve[d] the right to contract out of any specific issue which conflicts with our responsibilities towards the Commonwealth and our special relationship with Canada and the United States'.[12] There was nothing new in this, however disagreeable sight of it would have been to federalists in the Consultative Assembly.

The misfortune of the Labour Party's apparent socialist sectarianism aside, the statement illustrated all that was sensible and all that was misguided in Labour Party thinking. Sensibly, there was the expected firm opposition to European federalism. A federation would face massive practical difficulties due to differences in language, traditions, and customs. It argued, therefore, that intergovernmental co-operation through the OEEC was sufficient to the needs of Europe:

It is far better that unity should continue to be pursued as at present through co-operation between governments by mutual consent. . . . It is highly doubtful whether at the present time any European government would submit to a majority ruling against its profound conviction on an issue vital to itself. Any attempt to establish majority rule would wreck the atmosphere of confidence which

[10] Ernest Davies Papers.   [11] Ibid.
[12] Ibid. The 22 Apr. version had also stated that 'The British system of Cabinet responsibility to Parliament is not compatible with the delegation of powers to a supranational authority where the national representatives would be in a minority'.

already exists and revive ancient jealousies and suspicions. Co-operation between governments must be based on mutual consent.[13]

It is a pity that, in the light of this highly perceptive judgement about the probable behaviour of European governments, a Labour government should have permitted itself to believe that the Schuman Plan would be allowed by member governments to breach so fundamental a rule of policy.

The statement strongly rejected the neutralism so prevalent at the time in Western Europe: 'Western Europe neither could nor should attempt to constitute a geographical Third Force. For some time to come its economic stability and strategic defence will depend on close co-operation with the USA.'[14]

What was said directly about the Schuman Plan was so favourable that the reader might have been led to think that the Labour Party would have liked to see the Labour government involved in its planning. On 25 May 1950 the Labour Party had published a pamphlet on the international control of basic industries which was to be among documents to be discussed at the International Socialist Conference at Copenhagen, 1–3 June. The drafting of the pamphlet was obviously influenced by the Witten conference which had taken place two months before.[15] Unlike *European Unity*, the pamphlet was not a statement of party policy. It argued that some approach to inter-European organization of basic industries was essential if a price war, unemployment, and the depression of workers' standards were to be avoided. International control would be possible only if there were planning for full employment and if the industries concerned were subject to national control in each country. This would be possible even among socialist and capitalist countries though not as satisfactorily or effectively as in an entirely socialist Western Europe. It suggested that the existing committees of the OEEC should be modified to form new authorities for coal, steel, electricity, and transport.[16] The bias of what was said in *European Unity*, published three weeks later, was different but not very different.

European Unity began by painting in the background:

The European Socialist Parties have repeatedly emphasised the need for co-ordinating Europe's basic industries. . . . Continuous study has convinced them that international planning of iron and steel is the key to economic unity. But such planning will be worse than useless if it is inspired, like the cartels of the

---

[13] *European Unity* 10.   [14] Ibid. 9.   [15] See Ch. 3 above.
[16] *The Times*, 25 May 1950.

past, exclusively by the desire for private profit. . . . This means that any industries concerned in European planning should be subject to government direction in their own country. Otherwise a government which has accepted certain obligations in an international organisation will have no means of carrying them out. . . . The Labour Party is convinced that nothing less than public ownership can ensure this fully. Control without ownership can only be effective for negative purposes.[17]

Surely, if the need for co-ordinating Europe's basic industries was so great and the danger of the revival of cartels so imminent, Labour must involve itself in the Schuman Plan. The statement continued:

There is no doubt that at this moment Europe's private industrialists fear overproduction and will try to reorganise restrictive cartels as in the past. They will seek to pervert the Schuman proposals for their own selfish and monopolistic ends. . . . It is the duty of all who have European unity at heart to see that the Schuman proposals are shaped in the interests of the peoples as a whole. The decisive part in co-ordinating Europe's basic industries must be played by the governments as trustees for their peoples.[18]

The Labour government professedly had European unity at heart. But how was such a government to help shape the Schuman proposals and prevent their perversion if it was to be absent from the negotiations? It was not enough to say by way of excuse that the High Authority could bind governments when the statement had already proved to its own satisfaction that governments would not allow themselves to be bound contrary to their wishes on matters of vital national interest.

Denis Healey's first draft of *European Unity* was based freely on a pamphlet published under his own name in January 1950 by the Canadian Institute of International Affairs, and entitled *Western Europe— The Challenge of Unity*. But the passage that caused such violent objection to *European Unity* did not appear in Healey's earlier pamphlet. That pamphlet was clearly intended for a North American readership. No doubt overworked and underpaid, Healey sensibly reused the text he had composed for *Western Europe—The Challenge of Unity*

---

[17] *European Unity* 11. Apart from the advocacy of public ownership, these ideas found their echo in the thinking of Robert Boothby about the Schuman Plan. In his May 1950 memorandum to the European Movement, he wrote: 'the Schuman Plan spells the doom of the free market economy so far as the basic industries are concerned; and some means other than competition will have to be found to produce the requisite efficiency in production.'

[18] *European Unity* 12. Herve Alphand expressed 'great disquiet' about this paragraph: *DBPO* 100.

as the basis for his first draft of European Unity. The language of the two documents is often virtually identical.

One example is Healey's argument that majority rule in Europe would have proved fatal to Britain's position as banker of the sterling area. In words virtually reproduced in *European Unity*, the earlier pamphlet says:

A good example [of the need to avoid majority decisions] is the long argument in OEEC between Britain and most of the other countries about the second Intra-European Payments Agreement. If Britain had been obliged to accept the majority view she would have been committed to a plan which would have exhausted her remaining reserves of gold and dollars within a few weeks or months.[19]

This was really dredging for arguments. No consideration was given, in either pamphlet, to the possibility, later encapsulated in the Treaty of Rome, whereby matters of major national importance would be subject to unanimity and only questions of lesser importance to qualified majority decision. That issues varied in importance was not an insight that had to await the Treaty of Rome.

Healey's earlier pamphlet dismissed German rearmament as unacceptable. As part of his argument against third force ideas, Healey wrote: 'If Europe were isolated from the United States she could achieve military parity with the Soviet Empire only, if at all, by rearming Germany on a large scale. For obvious reasons this is unthinkable. An attempt to rearm Germany would wreck European union at the outset.' By the time of *European Unity*, only a few months later, German rearmament was no longer unthinkable. It was very much on the agenda and the British were adapting their minds to American pressure even if the French were still horrified by the idea. Two years later, and the problem of how to deal with an ever more powerful Germany was looming ever larger in Healey's mind:

It has been fashionable to see the answer in integrating Western Germany into some form of West European union. Britain herself has been unwilling to join such a union for fear of losing her independence outside Europe. But it is already obvious that if European unity is built without Britain it will be dominated by Germany. As Germany revives Britain may be compelled to integrate herself more deeply with Europe than is compatible with her other economic and political interests.[20]

[19] See *European Unity* 9.
[20] Healey, 'Power Politics and the Labour Party', in Crossman 177.

It was a period of flux and not everything could be foreseen even by Denis Healey, probably the most sophisticated International Secretary the Labour Party ever had. Nothing that Healey wrote, even if plainly mistaken, was ever less than the output of a powerful intellect. However, this courtesy of understanding about the difficulty of foreseeing the future was not extended by him to continental European countries. These, he appeared to hold in some contempt. 'Unfortunately many European countries were totally unable to predict their future economic activity.'[21] A quarter of a century later, as Britain's Chancellor of the Exchequer, Healey was to find the future similarly unpredictable.

Apart from the few sentences which caused such an uproar, *European Unity* could not have been a more faithful representation of British foreign policy and of the arguments that sustained it. This Labour government enjoyed a loyalty from the International Secretary of the Labour Party and its International Sub-Committee which few other Labour governments have experienced. *European Unity* contained all the well-known British objections to participation in European economic integration unless based on international planning for full employment. Along with distrust of continental economic policies, the statement expressed a dislike especially of what its authors considered to be continental *laissez-faire* in economic policy, a curious criticism given French *dirigisme* and the proposals for regulated markets emerging in much of Western Europe.[22] 'The Labour Party believes that its policy of full employment and fair shares is vital to British recovery, and that if the whole of Europe followed the same policy many of its problems would disappear. The price of economic liberalism today is class war and social unrest.'[23]

The Labour Party's fear that Britain might be robbed of its full employment if it associated too closely with Europe is clearly expressed in the statement. It says: 'The Labour Party's socialist principles demand that the movement towards European unity should be such as to permit the continuation of full employment and social justice in Britain and the extension of these benefits over the rest of Western Europe.'[24] To emphasize the point further, the statement added: 'We could not afford to have one out of ten workers idle, like Belgium, Germany and Italy.'[25] Europe was also rebuked for making such a poor comparison with the USA. 'Outside Britain and Scandinavia there is no government

[21] Healey (1950) 15–16.   [22] See Ch. 13 below.
[23] *European Unity* 8.   [24] Ibid. 5.   [25] Ibid. 7.

with a more progressive domestic or foreign programme than the present US Administration. Ever since 1931 America has pursued more advanced policies than most of the European countries.'[26] How the USA had achieved this even though it was not exactly a socialist country was not further explained. It may be that the Democrats in the USA were grateful for this tribute though gratitude did not shine forth from the Administration's reaction to *European Unity*. The risk that Republicans, who were about to be asked to vote the UK's next allocation of Marshall Aid, might not appreciate this tribute was, apparently, ignored.

The Labour government was for multilateralism as well as for imperial preference, for open markets as well as for discrimination. The contradiction was reflected in *European Unity*. The statement argued for unity in the whole of the non-Communist world, not just one part of it, an aspiration conveniently impossible to fulfil. The Labour Party's internationalism has always been utopian, convenient as a banner wrapping deep nationalist instincts but for no other purpose.[27] The statement's emphasis that Britain was a world power, with links to the USA and the Commonwealth, not just a European power, was frequently on the lips of Ministers both in their private colloquies and in their discussions with foreign powers. It would be equally on the lips of Conservative ministers when their turn came.

Britain is not just a small crowded island off the Western coast of Continental Europe. She is the nerve centre of a world wide Commonwealth which extends into every continent. In every respect except distance we in Britain are closer to our kinsmen in Australia and New Zealand on the far side of the world, than we are to Europe. We are closer in language and in origins, in social habits and institutions, in political outlook and in economic interest. The economies of the Commonwealth countries are complementary to that of Britain to a degree which those of Western Europe could never equal. Furthermore Britain is also the banker of the sterling area.[28]

Thus *European Unity* even found room for that most extraordinary of arguments justifying British coolness to any form of European economic integration, that European economies were competitive with that of the UK, not complementary to it. It was not actually clear that those Commonwealth countries most illustrative of kinship had the economies

---

[26] *European Unity* 9.
[27] The Labour Party's 'Keep Left' Group was in favour of a neutralist European Socialist Alliance based on the UK and France: Bullock 395–6. But there were not sufficient socialists in France (or the UK) for the purpose.
[28] *European Unity* 4.

most likely to be complementary. They might supply non-dollar raw materials but they were a drain on the sterling area dollar pool. Compressing the two arguments into a single paragraph maximized the chance that such questions would be overlooked. It was not the least oddity of *European Unity* that, like the government, it was both against cartels and in favour of the organization of the world economy on a complementary basis.[29]

European Unity claimed that

There has recently been much enthusiasm for an economic Union based on dismantling all internal barriers to trade, such as customs duties, exchange controls and quotas. Most supporters of this policy believe that the free play of economic forces within the Continental market so created would produce a better distribution of manpower and resources. The Labour Party fundamentally rejects this theory. Market forces by themselves could operate only at the expense of economic disturbances and political tensions which would throw Europe open to communism.[30]

The authors of the statement feared that the benefits of devaluation might be put at risk by further liberalization:

The main positive argument for devaluation was that it increased the relative attractiveness of dollar markets. Any further liberalisation of intra-European trade will tend to offset the benefits of devaluation by making it easier to sell in Europe. A complete economic union would undoubtedly create a protected high-cost European market and greatly hinder the solution of the dollar problem.[31]

The concern was clearly that, following liberalization and devaluation, goods would be sold to Europe that should have been earning dollars by sale to hard currency markets. That might require greater effort but was more germane to the UK's problems. These passages echoed Otto Clarke's warnings about European economic integration already quoted in Chapter 5. The Labour Party in government had access to the most expert advice. It had not yet caught up with the fact that, following devaluation, the advice was changing. The statement was still following Gaitskell and Jay rather than those officials in the Treasury and the Economic Section who had become more liberal since devaluation and were endeavouring to liberalize the minds of Gaitskell and Jay.[32]

---

[29] The statement had, in the course of discussion in the International Sub-Committee, become somewhat repetitive. This was a point that it was evidently felt desirable to repeat in case it had been missed. 'The national economies of Western Europe are parallel and competitive rather than complementary. Much of the specialisation which is possible has already taken place.'

[30] *European Unity* 6–7.   [31] Ibid. 7.   [32] See Ch. 5 above.

The statement said that even under a Conservative government planning and controls would be vital in Britain: 'even under a Conservative government Britain could not afford the degree of economic *laisser-faire* practised in Italy or Germany. By planning and control Britain has gone twice as far towards bridging the dollar gap as all the E.R.P. countries together, including Britain.'[33] By the end of the year, the Korean War would have plunged Britain back into a dollar crisis.

There was a great deal of support on the Continent for the thesis that there were serious risks in relying too much on market forces. On the Continent, too, enthusiasm for the unregulated removal of trade barriers was declining. Increasingly there was fear of the employment consequences. That was what the Stikker Plan, explained in Chapter 13, was essentially about. It was not only in the UK, under Labour leadership, that full employment was treasured. The continental countries of Western Europe were also democracies and had to be concerned. It was not a thesis that necessarily separated Britain from Europe. The real barrier lay in the attitude illustrated by Healey's admission to Hugh Dalton that 'I do not think there is really anything in European economic co-operation anyway, I am afraid'.[34]

TEACHING THE CONTINENTALS

One way of diverting the Consultative Assembly of the Council of Europe from its unrealistic speculations on an unattainable federal future would have been to suggest to it something useful that it *could* discuss. In this way, perhaps, *European Unity* could serve some purpose. In an attempt to be helpful, Ernest Davies, in his paper *The Labour Party and European Co-operation*, listed some possibilities that might distract the members of the Consultative Assembly from dangerous topics. They included the harmonization of economic development, the co-ordination of investment, the formulation of schemes for European civil aviation or hydroelectric development, exchange and co-operation in the cultural and social fields, and freedom of travel. These, according to Davies, 'might well be fields in which the idea of close co-operation could be fruitfully pursued' provided, of course, that it was on an intergovernmental basis. The Foreign Office had laboured

[33] *European Unity* 7.
[34] Healey, letter to Dalton, 3 May 1950: Dalton Papers.

and had produced a mouse. Healey considered these ideas too technical and unappealing. The only proposal from Foreign Office ministers with any political resonance was promotion of human rights. Ernest Davies had acknowledged in sending his paper to Healey that 'the paper reads somewhat negatively, but I fear its conclusions are none the less correct'.[35] Herbert Morrison, Lord President of the Council, wrote in a letter of 5 May that Ernest Davies's paper was 'rather more negative than is necessary to safeguard the position of the Government and the Party'.[36]

Healey, ever creative, and certainly more so than the Foreign Office, had a better idea. In sending his first draft of *European Unity* to Hugh Dalton on 3 May, Healey commented:

The Foreign Office I know would like [the Consultative Assembly] to discuss harmless issues like European civil aviation, the exchange of students etc. But such suggestions are insulting to the Assembly's *amour propre*. It is, after all, a political not an expert body. Most of the expert work it attempted last year was ludicrously incompetent. . . . I think if we try to rub their noses in full employment and fair shares we could, as a Labour delegation, completely capture the initiative from the Tories and Right Wing groups in the Assembly.[37]

Thus, his own idea was for the Labour Party to put full employment and social justice on the agenda of the Council of Europe. *European Unity* says:

though every country in the Council of Europe is pledged to pursue full employment and social justice, even a superficial glance at the present situation will reveal glaring failures to redeem these pledges. There is no work which the Assembly could more usefully perform than to consider ways and means of obtaining their further observance.[38]

The Foreign Office might not have many ideas of its own but, occasionally, it could appreciate a good idea when it heard of it, especially if it would help to dislocate a few continental noses. Healey's idea was considered a good wheeze. It would show the rest of Europe that the UK could spring surprises and not just the French.[39] Although a better idea than anything that had emerged from the Foreign Office, it was not one to capture the imagination of Europe as had the Schuman Plan. Though followed up in the next few months, it did nothing to soften the adverse impact of *European Unity* on foreign opinion.

[35] Ernest Davies Papers.   [36] Ibid.
[37] Dalton Papers.   [38] *European Unity* 14.
[39] Minute by C. A. E. Shuckburgh in the Ernest Davies Papers.

THE INTERNATIONAL REACTION

Healey comments: 'Dalton got the National Executive to insert a number of passages which overemphasised the obstacles which the supranational approach would present to the economic programmes of a Labour Government. His press conference on the statement was even more aggressively sectarian.'[40]

Dalton in his diary confesses that Healey's first draft was 'modified a good deal' before publication.[41] But it was not arguments about supranationalism that caused the problem. The problem was that *European Unity* lent itself to the interpretation that the Labour government was only prepared to collaborate with other socialist governments. That interpretation could not easily be repudiated even though the Labour government might insist that it was perfectly prepared to co-operate on an intergovernmental basis. The quotation from Healey, two years later, printed at the head of this chapter, demonstrates that the critical reaction was not just Dalton's fault.

Monnet saw *European Unity* as justifying his recent policy towards Britain.[42] Nor was he alone. Sir Oliver Harvey reported: 'M. Jacques Bardoux, Vice-Chairman of the Foreign Affairs Commission of the Assembly, who last week severely criticized . . . the tactics of the Quai d'Orsay in connection with the conference on the Schuman Plan, has now publicly stated that the Labour Party's pamphlet supplies full justification for M. Schuman's attitude.'[43] Schuman's immediate comment on *European Unity* was that he could hardly believe it was true and that he felt sure it would be disavowed.[44] On second thoughts, he became altogether more tolerant. As an elected politician he understood the difference between political parties and national governments. But he was probably motivated mainly by the need he saw as Foreign Minister to preserve relations with Britain despite every provocation.

Speaking on the eve of the House of Commons debate on the steel and coal pool, I believe I am in a position to state that neither the Government nor the Labour deputies will take as negative an attitude as that adopted by the statement of the Labour Party Executive. I have difficulty in believing that so absolute an attitude has been definitely adopted.[45]

---

[40] Healey (1989) 116–17.   [41] Dalton's diary (BLPES), 16 June 1950.
[42] Young (1984) 159–60.   [43] *DBPO* 102.   [44] Ibid.
[45] *Manchester Guardian* and *Financial Times*, 13 June 1950.

Acheson interpreted the significance of *European Unity* in his own way and it was no more helpful to Britain's international relations:

In a party pamphlet entitled *European Unity*, the trouble for doctrinaire social-ists with the plan was shown to lie just where Schuman had suspected it would: in the binding effect of the high authority's decisions. The issue was the sov-ereign right of a Labour Government to pursue democratic socialism. Important but secondary was the national policy of special ties with the Commonwealth and the United States.[46]

An American Committee on United Europe had been established in Washington. Though a private initiative, it was believed to have the support of the State Department. Massigli comments that it would need some naïvety to believe that this committee was established without the knowledge of the State Department and without its instructions.[47] Its chairman was General William Donovan, and its members included Allen Dulles, brother of John Foster Dulles, Senator Herbert Lehman, and Robert Patterson, a former Secretary of War. On 20 June it issued a statement. The statement welcomed the Schuman Plan. It regretted *European Unity* but noted that the British Labour Party was not speak-ing for the socialist parties of Europe. It added that *European Unity* had put the USA on notice that initiatives on European unity must come from the Continent.[48]

Owing to its anti-European tone, the government found the publica-tion of *European Unity* deeply embarrassing. Cripps was critical of the statement and of Bevin's part in it.[49] As busy ministers will, Bevin had given only the most cursory attention to what, after all, was only a party statement. He could be forgiven because he was not merely busy but very sick. Bevin's judgement of the statement, as conveyed by a minute from his Private Secretary dated 21 June, was as follows: 'The Secre-tary of State commented that apart from questions of timing and per-haps presentation, the real mistake had been to revise the Labour Party statement so as to include references to the Schuman Plan.'[50] Bevin had not seen the second draft modified to take account of the Schuman announcement. On 15 June 1950 Attlee admitted to the Commons that

---

[46] Acheson 387. However, after a press conference which he gave in Washington on 16 June 1950, Acheson was understood to have urged journalists 'to use moderation and pointing out that there was much to be said for the point of view expressed in the Labour Party's statement, although he deprecated its timing and presentation': *DBPO* 105, Sir O. Franks to Kenneth Younger, 17 June 1950.
[47] Massigli 168.   [48] T 229/750, 20 June 1950.
[49] Young (1984) 160.   [50] Ernest Davies Papers.

the statement was ill-timed. Dalton records that Attlee 'refused, flushed and embarrassed, to say whether he had seen [*European Unity*] or not before publication'.[51]

The following day, Attlee summoned to see him both Lewis Douglas, the US Ambassador, and René Massigli, the French Ambassador. Attlee knew that *European Unity* would be the subject of dispatches to their capitals. He therefore wanted to do what he could to ensure that the right message was conveyed. Massigli recalls their conversation. Attlee said that he had asked to see Massigli to disperse a misunderstanding. The statement was deplorable. Although he had known that such a statement was in preparation, he had known nothing of the details and even less of the positions adopted in the statement. The policy of the government was that which he had stated publicly. There was no other.

In reply to questions from Massigli, Attlee said that he was willing to contemplate compromises of British sovereignty not only within the Atlantic Pact. The implication was that Attlee was prepared to contemplate sacrifices of British sovereignty within the context of the Schuman Plan. Massigli then asked the specific question, 'Can I say to M. Schuman that you retain the desire to cooperate in his enterprise if a satisfactory solution can be found on the subject of the Authority?' According to Massigli, Attlee indicated assent. This conversation served several purposes. It helped Attlee to disembarrass himself of an awkward political fact which appeared to show that the French had been right in their judgement of the British position on European integration. It enabled Massigli to persuade himself that, despite *European Unity*, and indeed much other evidence, he had been right in his support for the British government in the Schuman exchanges and in his criticism of the policies and attitudes of his own government. He followed his conversation with Attlee by adjuring Paris once again to find ways of making the Authority acceptable to British public opinion. But the French government was persuaded that it had understood the British position better than its ambassador in London.[52] Unfortunately it was right.

Attlee was less successful with Lewis Douglas. In a memorandum of 26 June 1950 to his government, Douglas wrote: 'My own interpretation of the pamphlet and my conversation with Attlee is that at last there has been brought out into the open the real inconsistency between

[51] Dalton's diary (BLPES), 16 June 1950. HC Debs. 15 June 1950, cols. 552, 554–5.
[52] Massigli 211.

socialism as a part of an international order, except as it may be wholly and completely socialist, and the socialist state as an instrument for internal planning of the economic life of a nation.'[53]

BEVIN EXPLODES

The reception of the statement in the USA gave rise to an explosion of resentment that was never far below the surface of Bevin's relations with his ally. The critical comments in the American Press and in Congress were hard to bear. Senator William Knowland, Republican from California and a member of the Appropriations Committee, commented: 'Perhaps the time has come to give British Socialism a chance to demonstrate its ability to function on its own feet without being encumbered by dollar aid.' The *New York Times* spoke of 'a new form of insularism'. The *Washington Post* claimed that 'the Labour Party is now under the domination of economic planners. . . . Planners don't like to share control. They are the boss of society.' The *New York Herald Tribune* spoke of 'monumental ineptness'.[54] The reaction in the *Daily Express* was that if a suggestion such as that for a High Authority had been made to the American Congress, there is no doubt what the response would have been.[55]

One democratic country cannot complain to another about the views of a free Press or the words of free parliamentarians. All that had to be taken on the chin. The final straw was that a report on *European Unity* in the *New York Times* had led Paul Hoffman to tell a meeting of the Joint Senate Foreign Relations and Armed Services Committees that the pamphlet was 'one of the most deplorable examples of isolationism in the worst possible form'. For good measure he added that *European Unity* was 'one of the most detrimental statements that could have been made'.[56] No doubt Washington's patience with London, already all but exhausted, had been shortened yet further by the British reaction to the Schuman Plan. Bevin read Hoffman's comments in the *Daily Telegraph*. It was one thing to have been forced to accept, during the UK's exchanges with Paris on the Schuman Plan, the humiliation of justifying every move to the State Department and being told whether it approved

---

[53] *Foreign Relations of the United States* (1950), iii. 1654. I am grateful to Geoffrey Warner for this reference. The conversation with Attlee was on 16 June.

[54] These quotations come from the *Manchester Guardian* of 15 June 1950.

[55] *Daily Express*, 17 June 1950.   [56] *The Times*, 16 June 1950.

or disapproved.[57] After all, the State Department was fighting for the continuation of Marshall Aid on which the UK still depended. But Hoffman's comments were too much. He, after all, was head of the ECA and thus part of the US Administration. The USA was supposed to be the UK's friend and ally.

On 16 June 1950 Bevin dispatched an angry telegram to Sir Oliver Franks, UK Ambassador to Washington:

I shall be glad if you will see Hoffman, and ask him on which precise passages in the pamphlet he bases his statement, if indeed he said this or anything like it. Since reading his remark, I have read the pamphlet through carefully and I can see no justification for it. I find it regrettable particularly in view of the close relationship we have with the United States Administration and of all the efforts we ourselves have made jointly with Mr. Hoffman in the interests of closer European collaboration, that remarks of this kind should be made by men in responsible positions, apparently on the basis of Press reports only and without reference to the full text of the document itself. It is hard enough to hold the West together and make it strong without accusations like this.[58]

So, apparently, American reactions were imperilling the North Atlantic Alliance.

Before Bevin's anger could be conveyed to him, Hoffman had recanted. He let it be known that his earlier remarks had been based on press reports. He had now read the whole text. He had now concluded that 'It is a perfect diplomatic statement'. It contained sentences showing that the Labour Party favoured European unity as well as sentences showing 'deplorable isolationism'. In any case what was said by the Labour Party was not as significant as what was said by the British Prime Minister on the Schuman Plan in the House of Commons.[59] However, by the time he recanted, Hoffman had already promised the Senators that he would secure from the UK, informally, a 'clarification' of British policy towards Europe. This was necessary so that he could persuade Senators who believed strongly in European integration to vote a further tranche of aid under the ERP. *Amour propre* had then to be satisfied on both sides of the Atlantic. The British government did not respond to demands from Congress but Congress wished to be better informed. The 'clarification' was provided in a letter to Hoffman from Franks. It had been amended and authorized from London but was

[57] See Ch. 8 above.   [58] FO 371/87165, Telegram no. 2772.
[59] *The Times*, 17 June 1950.

described by Franks as being 'my views as British Ambassador to the United States'. The letter was bland enough. It ended:

Britain is a power with world-wide interests, responsibilities and commitments. Just as cooperation with her Western European neighbours and the vigorous promotion of unity in Europe is a vital necessity for Britain so her associations in the Commonwealth and in the Atlantic Community are also vital. The foreign policy of Britain rests upon and draws strength from these vital relationships with Europe, the Commonwealth and the Atlantic Community. It is the aim of British policy so to reconcile these relationships that they perpetually reinforce each other and by their complementary strengths add vigour and resource to the free world.[60]

In private conversation, Franks made Hoffman feel the full intensity of Bevin's resentment. 'During our conversation I said "isolationism" as applied by Americans to the British was too near a fighting word. We had waited three years in 1914 and two years in 1939 for them.'[61] The outbreak of the war in Korea on 24 June, and the prompt British offer of support for the Americans, did something to restore relations between London and Washington. In American eyes, the British effort was, as usual, inadequate. In British eyes, however, Britain was once more aligned in arms with the USA in defence of freedom. Europe slipped further into the background of policy. Another consequence was that Britain became a supplicant in Washington for defence aid once again.

THE FUNDAMENTAL TRUTHFULNESS OF *EUROPEAN UNITY*

Hugh Dalton could not understand the criticisms of the statement precisely because it did follow the British government's official position on Europe. Sir William Strang considered that 'The Labour Party statement, though ill-timed and in places ill-expressed, is in its main thesis along the true line of British policy'.[62] A less exalted Foreign Office official wrote:

---

[60] FO 371/87165, Franks to Hoffman, 21 June 1950.

[61] FO 371/87165, Telegram no. 1707.

[62] *DBPO* 102 n. A letter from Sir Philip Nichols, UK Ambassador to The Hague to Sir William Strang, 27 June 1950, mainly about 'the deplorable impression made in Holland by the Labour Executive's statement', also said: 'I agree with you that in its essentials [*European Unity*] is a sound statement of British policy: it only goes wrong in those passages where the party machine gets going!': FO 371/87165.

Most of the outcry about this document is artificial & put on in order to discredit the Labour Party or to boost the idea of European Federalism. Such attacks will therefore continue whenever a convenient excuse is offered. I have long thought that there was only one way of preventing such attacks, & that that was that the S. of S. or the P.M. should once & for all make clear our attitude towards a federal Govt. or a supra-national authority in Europe.[63]

So this official thought that the Labour government had left its attitude to federalism and supranationalism unclear. Any such thought would be surprising were it not for the exchanges of memoranda between London and Paris discussed in Chapter 8 which had suggested a tolerance in London of the idea of a supranational authority in Europe which did not in fact exist.

In fact *European Unity* revealed the true feelings within the Labour Party not just about European integration but about European socialists. There was a deep reluctance to co-operate with them. Socialism at the time really meant a distinct social order. It was not simply, as it became later, capitalism modified to protect the poor and the weak. It really was a new concept of society and the Labour government was beginning its construction in Britain. In addition to the great issues of federalism and Britain's global links on which such emphasis was placed in official arguments, the fact was that the Labour Party, and not the left alone, distrusted their continental comrades. Their socialist principles were questioned. Many were federalists. They entered into coalitions with middle-class parties. They were not the real European socialists.

For the left of the Labour Party, the real socialists were to be found within the European Communist parties, regrettably close to Moscow perhaps, but genuine socialists for all that. The genuineness of their socialism was proved by their early exclusion from the post-war coalitions. When, therefore, the statement noted that socialists would be in a minority in a federal Europe, some of its readers on the left of the Labour Party would be thinking not just arithmetically but ideologically. This was not Bevin's position. Bevin's position was that many French socialists were beyond the pale as federalists and that the continentals, whether socialist or not, were just too incompetent to be worth the trouble of co-operation. He would have shared Healey's presentation of this latter point in his earlier pamphlet *Western Europe—The Challenge of Unity*:

---

[63] *DBPO* 102 n., I. Mallet to Sir P. Dixon and Sir W. Strang, 20 June 1950.

The aim of state intervention in [Britain and Scandinavia] is to provide a decent economic standard of living for all citizens, to ensure that scarce goods are shared fairly, to guarantee full employment, and to balance trade with the outside world. In most of the other countries [of Western Europe] the governments are either unwilling or unable to control the national economy. Even when most of the government parties favoured planning, as in France in the years immediately after the war, attempts to apply planning broke down against the traditional obstacles of administrative inefficiency and civic irresponsibility. Thus classical methods of deflation and laissez-faire have been adopted instead.... Unemployment is rife in Belgium, Germany and Italy.... Moreover the French and Italian governments have failed to grapple seriously with their basic economic problems; their failure has been camouflaged only by large injections of American aid.

Britain, of course, had received its own large injections of American aid but that, apparently, had camouflaged only Britain's success. Healey also referred, as a substantial disincentive to co-operation in a federal Europe, to the 'congenital failure of other European peoples to pay taxes'.[64] In the light of this it is not surprising that pleas from European socialists that the Labour Party should interest itself in European unity cut little ice in London.

The distaste in London for French socialists was now reciprocated. *European Unity* was severely criticized in France. The French Socialist Party was as critical of the Labour Party's statement as were other French commentators.[65] Bullock comments that Bevin 'was quite unmoved by the appeals of French socialists like Guy Mollet'.[66] Mollet was not regarded as among the worst of French socialists. Dalton attended the Consultative Assembly of the Council of Europe in Strasbourg in August. In a letter from there, on 21 August, he informed Bevin that 'whatever may be said of Mollet, he is, anyhow, better than André Philip'.[67] Philip was also a socialist but more definitely a federalist. But this, evidently, was to damn Mollet with faint praise. At any rate he was not able to make any progress with Bevin. On 1 November 1950 there was a meeting in London between Mollet and Bevin. Mollet

[64] Some years later, in H. F. Havilland, Jr. (ed.), *The United States and the Western Community* (Haverford, Pa., 1957), 41–2, Healey wrote: 'It is very difficult to mix countries which for national reasons must exercise a large degree of state control over their economy with countries which for various reasons cannot do so even if they want to.... France after the war, even under a socialist government, found she was incapable of doing so because the country did not have the necessary level of civic responsibility': quoted by Milward (1984) 405 n.

[65] *DBPO* 102, Harvey to Younger, 15 June 1950.

[66] Bullock 786.   [67] Dalton Papers.

had come to London in an attempt to co-ordinate plans among European socialists within the Council of Europe. He departed from London a disappointed man. He left it to the French Ambassador Massigli to give Ernest Davies his impressions of his visit. Davies told Bevin in a minute of 1 November that Mollet had left with 'the impression that we were "handing over the baby of Europe". He thought we were abandoning Europe, turning to America and the Commonwealth.'[68] Mollet concluded from his visit that British socialists could not be dissuaded from letting continental socialists down.

The German Social Democratic Party (SPD) was also distrusted in London. Neither its ambivalence about the Schuman Plan nor its opposition to German rearmament was sufficient to persuade those within the Labour Party who shared that opposition that they could find in the SPD a genuine socialist interlocutor. Despite the evolution in Germany of a democratically elected federal government, too much attention was given on the British left to nationalist and revanchist statements by some German politicians. Germany was still the enemy even if continental Europe, which had suffered from the war even more, had decided to find a *modus vivendi* with it. Kenneth Younger was by now prepared to contemplate German rearmament because he was very doubtful about French morale, and especially civilian morale, if there were a Soviet attack. Yet he still shared the deep distrust of Germany. On 6 July 1950 he minuted Bevin: 'If . . . we are planning a defence against a full scale Russian attack, it seems clear that we must be able to count upon a large and immediate contribution from the United States or Germany or both. . . . As regards Germany, great as the political difficulties are, her rearmament seems essential if Western defence is to be real.' The political difficulties he foresaw were not only with the Labour Party. 'Such a course will probably put paid to any real democratisation of Western Germany since it will put the nationalists and militarists back in the saddle.'[69]

If there were any doubts about Labour Party attitudes to Europe they would have been removed by a speech in the country made, on 2 July 1950, by John Strachey, Secretary for War.[70] He appears to have referred to the Schuman Plan as a 'plot' on the part of the great capitalist interests of Europe to avoid nationalization of their industries,

---

[68] Ernest Davies Papers.   [69] Ibid.
[70] Younger considered it 'a rather silly speech . . . in which he, in effect, attacks the Schuman plan as a reactionary plot designed to prevent the public control of European industries': diary, 6 July 1950.

'comparable to the efforts of Montagu Norman to propose a European central bank'.[71] With more reason, but with questionable understanding of the political realities, he suggested that it was unacceptable for Britain to agree without negotiation to a scheme which would 'put real power over Europe's basic industries into the hands of an irresponsible body free from all democratic control'. European unity, he thought, was not enough. The Commonwealth and the USA had to be 'in it', because the US government was

in many ways, a much more progressive one than many of the Governments of central Europe. . . . I would much rather be in a combination which contained the US than a mere West European Federation. . . . [Also] whatever federation will ultimately be joined, [it] must have a really democratic federal government . . . in the meanwhile, we are not going to have any bogus federation by which the real powers of democratically elected parliaments are surrendered in the name of bogus internationalism to irresponsible, undemocratic and reactionary super-national bodies.[72]

The anti-European tone of the speech led to a debate in the Commons. Attlee had publicly to repudiate Strachey just as he had *European Unity*.[73] Strachey was forced into a humiliating apology in the House for 'the tone of some of the expressions which I used about the Schuman Plan'.[74] But Attlee still had to pay attention to his party's attitudes and neither he nor Bevin, advised by a Foreign Office that saw little wrong with *European Unity* except perhaps bad timing, possessed sufficient energy or insight to attempt to change their party's attitudes. So to reasons of high policy for refusing to join the movement towards European economic integration were added reasons of low policy, feeding the party's prejudices and keeping it happy at a time when much else was making it unhappy with the policies which external necessity was forcing upon the government.

---

[71] Attlee, on the basis of assurances from Strachey, insisted in the House of Commons that the word 'plot' referred not to the Schuman Plan but to 'the manœuvres in the House of Commons of the party opposite': HC Debs. 5 July 1950, cols. 472–4. See also Attlee's replies, HC Debs. 6 July 1950, cols. 630–4. This interpretation was confirmed by Strachey during a debate on the adjournment on 11 July 1950, HC Debs. col. 1156. The opposition did not accept Strachey's assurances on this point and claimed to believe that he had deceived Attlee.

[72] This account of Strachey's speech is taken from Thomas 262. Thomas's account is based on notes issued by Strachey to the Press beforehand. Extensive quotations from the speech are also to be found in the debate on the adjournment on 11 July 1950, cols. 1155–221.

[73] HC Debs. 11 July 1950, col. 1166.   [74] Ibid. col. 1158.

Meanwhile Healey had been briefing the International Sub-Committee in preparation for the International Socialist Conference on the Control of Europe's Basic Industries, which was being held in London on 16–18 June 1950. In his briefing, he referred to the virtual certainty of a steel surplus arising in 1953 which could lead to 'cut-throat competition'.

It is therefore greatly in the interests of British and European Socialists that the Schuman proposals should be developed into a plan based on increasing consumption within a full employment economy. . . . Only the governments working together can raise the effective demand for the products of Europe's basic industries in Europe and the world as a whole. An authority confined to organising the basic industries alone cannot ensure the required expansion of demand.

So the Schuman Plan would not be enough. There would be a need also to ensure the existence of sufficient demand for steel by means of intergovernmental co-operation. It is certainly true that the Schuman Plan without adequate demand would have been a poor thing economically. That was not necessarily a reason for the British government to exclude itself from the most intimate circle of European economic co-operation. Though the Schuman Plan could not create effective demand or full employment, there was no evidence of any wider circle of European economic co-operation which could secure the required result, certainly not the OEEC.

CODA

If *European Unity* had had the success hoped for as a considered statement of Labour Party foreign policy, many people would no doubt have claimed its parentage. As it was, Hugh Dalton was left to carry the responsibility alone. Everyone seemed to have some excuse. Either they could not remember seeing it, or if they had seen it they had not read it, or if they had seen it and read it, it was the first draft before the inclusion of the paragraphs on Europe's basic industries. And even if none of these excuses really served, the whole thing had proved extremely embarrassing due to the timing of its publication.

The sorry story is told by Dalton in his diary. He records that he was summoned to a ministerial meeting at No. 10 on 13 June where he found the PM 'in a bit of a fuss'. Attlee said of the statement that 'I

don't remember ever seeing this before!' This was odd because Attlee
had suggested about the only amendment to come from a member of
the NEC not also a member of the International Sub-Committee. It was
a suggestion about horticulture which had, in fact, been included, rather
awkwardly, in the final draft. Dalton continues: 'I reminded him that he
had sat next me at NEC when it was passed. . . . He then queried whether
the paragraphs on Basic Industries were in. I explained that they were,
and reminded him that Shinwell had asked whether we had taken
account in the draft of Harry Douglass's views.'[75] Attlee then accepted
and

indeed he could do no other—the fact that he had seen and agreed it all before.
He then said that it was very embarrassing to have it published that morning
when he had to make a statement that afternoon on the Schuman Plan. This was
the first I had heard officially of any such statement . . .

The discussion which followed was quite friendly. H[erbert] M[orrison] admitted formally his share of the responsibility but said he hadn't read the paper
carefully—he had so many papers to read and, as this seemed to be about
Strasbourg questions, he had left it to me. S[tafford] C[ripps] said that it would
make his job very difficult in future negotiations. He didn't disagree with the
general line but, if he had seen the draft, he could have suggested a few
amendments which wouldn't have changed the sense but would have made it
read more acceptably. I told them that I had kept in close touch with E[rnest]
B[evin] and the F[oreign] O[ffice] and they agreed the line. S[tafford] C[ripps]
said he has always found the F[oreign O[ffice] difficult from his point of view.

Dalton found consolation where it really mattered, in the support of
the party and in the quality of the statement. On 25 June 1950 he
recorded in his diary: 'I think I have very solid support in the Party and
some sympathy on the ground that some colleagues, especially P.M.,
seem to be trying to evade their share of responsibility. . . . *E[uropean]
U[nity]* is a first class document. Maybe a couple of sentences might
have been put differently.'

It said, after all, what the party believed.

---

[75] Harry Douglass of the Iron and Steel Workers Union. Douglass succeeded Lincoln
Evans as General Secretary in 1953. Dalton gives the date of the meeting with Attlee as
14 June. It was in fact 13 June, the date given in the text.

11

Could Britain Have Taken the Initiative?

> His Majesty's Government have been criticized for not taking the initiative in the field of European integration. But as the main objective of M. Schuman's original proposal was the placing of Franco-German relationship on a new basis, it was in present circumstances impossible for any Government other than the French Government to take the initiative . . .[1]

Whether Britain should or could have taken part in the Schuman Plan is an important question. But there is an earlier question. If, in the years after the war, the UK had conducted itself differently in European affairs, could it have avoided the difficult crunch it faced when presented with a French plan embodying supranational features which raised misgivings? Could the Attlee government have developed its own ideas before Schuman? Could it have given Europe leadership without prejudicing its relations with the Commonwealth and without committing itself to federalism and to supranational authorities of a kind which for good reasons it rejected? Or was Britain's only course to wait and watch while France stole its role in Europe?

After the rejection by the UK of participation in the Schuman Plan negotiating conference, the Foreign Office began anxiously to analyse the significance of the Schuman announcement for French policy. Sir Oliver Harvey, Ambassador in Paris, provided the simple and accurate explanation of what the French were about:

the main objective of the Plan seems to be an attempt to substitute for repressive institutions such as the High Commission or the Ruhr Authority, whose effectiveness is thought to be diminishing, a new organization which would have some chance of being permanently accepted by the Germans because they would have within it equal status with the French.[2]

---

[1] Sir Roger Makins to Ernest Bevin, 17 June 1950—Notes for debate on Schuman Plan: MS Attlee dep. 102.

[2] *DBPO* 103, message from Harvey to Younger, 16 June 1950.

Would it have been possible for the UK government and the Foreign Office to show comparable imagination?

In opening the debate on the Schuman Plan in the House of Commons on 26 June 1950 Anthony Eden said: 'we ought to have been better prepared for that French initiative and . . . we ought to have been ready with proposals of our own . . . we should have taken the initiative ourselves some time since. . . . The matter [of the Schuman Plan] was no more than the projection of a trend clearly marked out in recent years through the interplay of Franco-German ideas.'[3] Boothby was right to say in the same debate: 'It could and should have been our initiative long ago. From an economic point of view there is nothing very original or startling about it.'[4] It is easy to attribute these criticisms to the spirit of opposition which dominates parliamentary politics. But this criticism rings true especially in the light of the history of Europe's coal and steel industries, of the various proposals for dealing with them that had come from public figures over the previous two years, and of the comments of people such as Hayter, Hall-Patch, and Stikker already quoted.

Foreign Office Ministers had been inclined to indulge themselves over the years by deriding the impractical schemes thought up on the Continent. It was a constant theme of their speeches. On 22 January 1948 when Bevin was making one of his most 'European' speeches, his so-called 'Western Union' speech, he nevertheless found it necessary to say:

It is easy enough to draw up a blueprint for a united Western Europe and to construct neat looking plans on paper. While I do not wish to discourage the work done by voluntary political organisations in advocating ambitious schemes of European unity, I must say that it is a much slower and harder job to carry out a practical programme which takes into account the realities which face us, and I am afraid that it will have to be done a step at a time.[5]

In this passage, Bevin was casting scorn at European federalists with their impractical dreams. It was a theme to which Kenneth Younger, Minister of State at the Foreign Office, returned on 28 March 1950 in a Foreign Affairs debate: 'We do not believe that the unity of Europe can be achieved by coining slogans or by formulating paper schemes before a practical basis of co-operation has been worked out.'[6] The trouble was that neither in 1948 nor in 1950 was any action being taken

---

[3] HC Debs. 26 June 1950, col. 1913.   [4] HC Debs. 27 June 1950, col. 2117.
[5] HC Debs. 22 Jan. 1948, col. 395.   [6] HC Debs. 28 Mar. 1950, col. 214.

by the British government to work out some practical basis of co-operation that took the realities into account, would not deserve the epithet of 'a paper scheme', nor require the coining of slogans. It was Richard Crossman who responded to Bevin in the January 1948 debate by saying, 'It is no good telling us that it is difficult. Of course it is.'[7] Crossman then went on to list various possibilities which he considered practical including the joint planning of heavy industry. He evoked no reaction. So far as ideas that would provide a practical basis for co-operation were concerned, Whitehall was a desert.

One man in Whitehall did have an idea. This was Otto Clarke, Under-Secretary at the Treasury. He had been inspired by the Marshall Plan to consider what forms of European co-operation might be advantageous to Britain. His overwhelming concern was how to solve Britain's and Europe's dollar problem, whether or not Marshall Aid came on stream. It is worth quoting at some length a minute from Clarke dated 27 February 1948. The 'continuing organisation' to which he refers is the organization which became the OEEC. He wrote:

What we want the continuing organisation to do is to see what means are possible of securing dollar saving and dollar earning by co-operation between the European countries. . . . Take steel. The European countries as a whole will, for many years to come (on present form) be dependent upon the supply of US steel. We should raise this on the continuing organisation and there would be discussions between the steel industries with a directive stating that they had to plan what was the most economical way to produce the amount of steel which Europe needed for its own purposes and for export to the outside world. . . . This is the sort of concept which we have in mind for the development of European economic co-operation. This visualises very practical action, commodity by commodity, on a rather empirical basis, treating every problem on its merits in the light of the major objective and dealing with it by whatever administrative means are practical. This is vastly more promising than the attempt at a grandiose 'general' plan like a customs union which might even make the problem worse rather than better. . . . A great advantage of the empirical means of approach is that it avoids all the difficulties about the Commonwealth, for it would be perfectly easy for the sterling Dominions to co-operate with UK and Europe on this basis without raising any problem of imperial preference. Moreover it would be possible to resist the examination of certain specific commodities which might create difficulty for the Dominions.[8]

---

[7] HC Debs. 23 Jan. 1948, col. 566. Another idea was joint commodity boards. He suggested, by way of a question, that 'unless we resolve to say as a bloc that we must be able to discriminate against the outside world, there is no reality in Western union?'

[8] Clarke, Document 24 minute to Sir Wilfrid Eady, 27 Feb. 1948.

Here, in embryo, was the Schuman Plan, but a plan designed to be developed through the OEEC and on an intergovernmental basis. It would have been a plan involving no significant problems for imperial preference or for the Commonwealth. With the addition of a little political imagination, it could have been developed into a British proposal which provided the reassurance for which France was craving in respect of Germany as well as perhaps yielding the economic benefits foreseen by Clarke. The imagination to produce such a British initiative was lacking.

Otto Clarke's minute shows that hindsight is not necessary for providing an answer to the question whether there could have been a British alternative that would have run. Presumably what the French government service could do, that of Britain could do better. It would thereby prove the advantage of having a stable government and a professional, and permanently learning, civil service, undisrupted by foreign invasion. If the French could imagine the Schuman Plan, the British surely could imagine a Schuman Plan without unacceptable supranational elements. A Schuman Plan run by a commission subject to an intergovernmental Council of Ministers was an idea that the British could have run had it not been their sole European policy to hear what their European neighbours wanted to do and then attempt to shoot it down. All that was required was for the Cabinet to come to the same conclusion before the announcement of the Schuman Plan that it did come to after the announcement of the Schuman Plan.

The British public service had been given furiously to think by the announcement of the Schuman Plan. The response demonstrated the expected critical power of British civil servants but a lamentable absence of creativity. But what they now had to propose would have looked much better before the Schuman Plan than it looked after it. On 24 May 1950 the FG Committee appointed a Working Party, FG (WP). In the chair was William Strath of Plowden's CEPS. The terms of reference were, 'To consider practical measures for implementing the French proposals for the pooling of the coal and steel industries of West European countries on the assumption that the coal and steel industries of the United Kingdom would eventually be brought within the projected scheme.'[9] FG (WP) worked with great speed. Unlike the Schuman Plan as it had been first announced, their report did not suffer from any lack of detail. They proposed the creation of an 'International Authority'. There would be a Council of Ministers meeting once a

[9] T 229/749.

month which had to be unanimous; an Executive Council consisting of from six to twelve whole-time leading figures from industry; and an Advisory Council representing employers, workers, and governments.

Consultation had already taken place with, among others, Plowden's Economic Planning Board (EPB), the NCB, the British Iron and Steel Federation (BISF), and the unions.[10] There was far more intensive consultation with interested parties about FG (WP)'s phantom ideas than there had been before the government rejected participation in the Schuman Plan negotiations.[11] In the consultations, there was general approval of what was proposed. The EPB decided that 'There were economic advantages to be gained from some international regulation of iron and steel and coal in Europe, and in addition political advantages would accrue'. Some members were even prepared to allow the International Authority some mandatory powers. 'The Board considered that the United Kingdom could accept such abrogation of sovereignty as would be involved if the mandatory powers mentioned above were conceded.'[12] The NCB gave long, detailed, and generally favourable consideration to the FG (WP) ideas. It decided it was prepared, in principle, to accept the abolition of dual pricing provided dumping (i.e. dual prices in reverse) was also eliminated. Looking to the future, the NCB said that 'The elimination by member countries of tariffs and quantitative restrictions on imports of UK coals would be an undiluted advantage to the Board when we have more coal available for export'. The fly in the NCB ointment was the steel industry. 'The UK steel industry, on the other hand, appears to be greatly concerned about adequate protection for the home market.' The NCB feared that the insistence of steel on protection would lead to the continuance of European restrictions on exports of UK coal.[13] Their general conclusions were that 'Subject to the general consideration that UK membership of

[10] Younger reported to Attlee on 20 June 1950 on a rather inconclusive meeting he had had that morning with Sir Vincent Tewson, General Secretary of the TUC, Arthur Deakin, General Secretary of the Transport and General Workers Union, and Lincoln Evans, General Secretary of the Iron and Steel Workers Union. Both Tewson and Evans were members of the EPB but were on this occasion representing the TUC. They were not yet at liberty to reveal the Working Party's document to their colleagues and therefore could give only personal opinions: T 229/749.

[11] T 229/749, note to Plowden of 16 May 1950. Cripps had suggested that Monnet, while in London, should see Tewson and Evans. Plowden considered the idea 'most unwise' and Monnet 'was horrified at the thought of the likely effect in France'. It did not happen.

[12] *DBPO* 109, 20 June 1950. See also T 229/750.

[13] Western Europe accounted for less than 5% of British steel exports.

a Group with the objectives and functions described in the Working
Party Report might limit the Board's commercial freedom at a time
when we need it most, we think in general that the Working Party's
proposals would, in the long run, operate to the advantage rather than
the disadvantage of the Board.'[14]

The BISF had first considered the Schuman Plan at a meeting of its
Executive Committee on 16 May. Some of the steelmasters present
thought that the government might use the French proposal as an argument for state ownership of the steel industries. Others thought the Plan
would give the Attlee government an opportunity to climb down from
nationalization. Sir Andrew Duncan, Chairman, thought it unlikely that
British adherence to the Schuman Plan would encourage nationalization. He pointed to the fact that the French and German steel industries
were not nationalized and that Bevin had failed in his attempt to nationalize the Ruhr industries. However, he expressed dislike of the *dirigiste*
bent of the Schuman Plan and the idea of anti-cartel measures. At the
end of the meeting a noncommittal statement was issued stating that
'the proposals give the Committee no ground for consternation'.

There was a more thorough discussion of the Schuman Plan at the
BISF Executive Committee on 13 June when it also had the opportunity
of expressing its view on the ideas of the FG (WP). Its decision was
clearly against participation in the Schuman Plan as it was. They attached much more importance to their position outside Europe than
inside. Its final statement said: 'The British industry could not contemplate access by Europe to British scrap at British home trading prices
since this would jeopardize the United Kingdom price structure.' It was
also thought unacceptable for Europe to have access to the 'limited
reserves of Durham coking coal, since these were a vital factor in the
further operation of the industry'. These reservations were important
because the competitiveness of British steel prices was largely, if not
entirely, due to the costs at the steelworks of coke and scrap which
were kept lower than those paid by its European competitors. Concern
was also expressed that, because of exchange rate instability and dumping, 'it is unsafe to rely on complete freedom of trade'. However, the
Executive Committee was prepared to support the FG (WP) proposals
for an International Authority provided that, for the time being, its
powers were to be 'almost entirely advisory'. One of the steelmasters,
Sir John Craig, said that the proposed organization 'should be as near

[14] T 229/750, 23 June 1950.

as possible to that which obtained under the Cartel, which was sound in every principle'.[15] A more recent comment is that of Ruggero Ranieri: '[T]here seems now, as indeed there seemed at the time, a good case for asserting that the [steel] industry suffered from a degree of artificiality and overprotection and that joining the Community afforded an opportunity to amend these flaws.'[16]

Given the nature of its consultations, it was, perhaps, not surprising that FG (WP) ended up with a proposal that was worryingly like a cartel. As Strath put it to Plowden, describing the proposals of his Working Party, 'The proposed Authority is, in essence, an international producers' association of a special kind acting under government supervision'.[17] At a ministerial meeting which considered FG (WP)'s proposal, a note of warning was recorded that the scheme could be presented 'as a producers' cartel designed primarily to regulate production under conditions of falling demand'.[18] Indeed that was the way the proposal was interpreted both by the NCB and in the steel industry. Strath was forced to protest about the interpretation emerging from those sources. When C. H. de Peyer of the Ministry of Fuel and Power reported to him the thoughts of the NCB, Strath replied in some indignation comparing the NCB's ideas with those of the BISF. He emphasized that it would be 'impossible to set up in Europe a protected market for the coal of Germany and the UK in which the other members undertook to buy agreed tonnages at producers' prices'.[19]

Basing itself on FG (WP)'s report, the FG Committee, on 20 June 1950, told the Cabinet that 'it is our view that there is a case for concerted international action on economic grounds in regard to the coal and steel industries of Europe, that the more we depart from scarcity conditions, the more imperative the need for international action will become and that, therefore, the sooner a suitable organization is established the better'. For this purpose an 'International Authority' would be required:

We consider that the Authority itself should, as far as possible, consist of independent people, that it should be responsible to an inter-Governmental body consisting of Government representatives only and that it should start by having only advisory functions, though we recognize that later on in the light

---

[15] Ranieri 119, 136, 140–2.   [16] Ibid. 129.
[17] T 229/750, Strath to Plowden, 3 July 1950.
[18] *DBPO* 132, Cabinet CM (50) 42 of 4 July 1950.
[19] T 229/750, Strath to C. H. de Peyer, 13 July 1950.

of experience certain functions of a mandatory character might be entrusted to
it, particularly in respect of approval of commercial agreements between national industries . . . and in relation to investment . . .[20]

Some members of the Committee would have been prepared to concede
mandatory control of investment from the start.

On 22 June the Cabinet reacted cautiously but without hostility to
what was proposed by officials. A Ministerial Committee consisting
of Cripps, Harold Wilson,[21] Philip Noel-Baker,[22] George Strauss,[23] and
Kenneth Younger was appointed to consider the official recommendations and to report further.[24] The FG Committee's ideas were, in all
essentials, supported by the Ministerial Committee and, on 4 July,
endorsed by the Cabinet.[25] But they would not see the light of day
because Britain had pledged itself to France not to propose any alternative to Schuman unless the Schuman negotiations broke down. In its
communiqué of 3 June, the British government had said, by way of
warning or encouragement: 'They themselves are actively engaged in
working on proposals inspired by the French initiative of 9th May, in
order that they may be ready to make such a contribution.'[26] As a result,
there was an expectation that the British government would be an-
nouncing ideas of its own, and that this might still lead to British
participation in the Schuman Plan. The expectation, indeed, helped to
divert some criticism from the government. The statement proved to be
misleading and the expectation was disappointed. The British government let France know that it would not table any proposals of its own
unless French ideas proved unacceptable to its negotiating partners. In
his statement to the House of Commons on 13 June, Attlee said: 'There
is no question of putting forward any alternative British proposal at
the present time. It would not be right to take any step which might be
regarded as a diversion or as an attempt to modify the course which the
French and other Governments have decided to take.'[27] In other words
the British government would do nothing that might lead to its being
accused of procuring the failure of the Schuman Plan. It may have been

---

[20] *DBPO* 109 Annex 1.   [21] President of the Board of Trade.
[22] Minister of Fuel and Power.   [23] Minister of Supply.
[24] *DBPO* 112.
[25] *DBPO* 128, Report of the Ministerial Committee, 1 July 1950; *DBPO* 132.
[26] Cmd. 7970/16.
[27] For the full statement see HC Debs. 13 June 1950, cols. 35–8. The Foreign Office
continued to advise against injecting any British proposals into the Paris conference even
when Massigli suggested that it might be opportune to do so: *DBPO* 121 and 122, 28
June 1950.

hoping for failure but it wished to ensure that it was not blamed for failure.

Roger Makins throws light on this decision in his briefing note for Bevin. In it he revealed to his master that the British government had been trying to help all along.

8. It was made perfectly clear from Paris that the submission at the present stage of any proposals by His Majesty's Government which were not on the basis of the French conditions would be unwelcome to the French Government and would be regarded as an attempt to create a diversion and indeed to sabotage the French initiative. Since the policy of His Majesty's Government is to help and not to hinder the fulfilment of the French objectives, His Majesty's Government not unnaturally decided to take no initiative and to await information as to the progress of the negotiations in Paris.[28]

There is another explanation of British reticence. Washington was already sufficiently annoyed that the UK government had refused participation in the Schuman negotiations. To have appeared to undermine the Schuman Plan by advancing alternative ideas while there was yet hope for the Schuman Plan could have caused a major confrontation with Washington.[29] Bevin clearly hoped that the dissensions among French ministers and the criticisms by the other national delegations at the negotiating conference would be enough to return them all to reason without the UK exposing itself further.[30] But, in any case, Bevin was concerned that anything he proposed would look unimaginative as compared with the Schuman Plan, as indeed it would.[31]

At the end of June and early July what, if anything, Schuman should be told about British ideas became the subject of debate in London. There had been a government crisis in Paris. Cripps was going there for an OEEC Ministerial Council. On 1 July he tried to persuade Bevin that he should go prepared to say something to the new French Prime Minister and Schuman 'if they indicate that they would like our help'. There were also others who might be interested. 'Stikker, too, whose friendship is of considerable importance as chairman of OEEC and who is known not to like the Schuman proposals is almost certain to ask me in connection with the discussion of his own plan, how we regard the

[28] Makins to Bevin, 17 June 1950—Notes for debate on Schuman Plan: MS Attlee dep. 102.

[29] See *DBPO* 137, letter from Sir I. Kirkpatrick to Sir D. Gainer, 11 July 1950, reporting a conversation with John McCloy, US High Commissioner, 10 July 1950.

[30] DBPO 123, record of conversation between Bevin and Sir R. Makins, 29 June 1950.

[31] *DBPO* 111, minute from Bevin to Younger, 21 June 1950.

possibility of entering the Schuman Plan.'[32] Bevin and the Foreign Office were adamantly opposed to revealing anything. After much discussion of the question in and out of Cabinet, the Cabinet concluded on 4 July that Schuman should be told, first, that his proposals elaborated in the French working document for the negotiating conference already in progress in Paris were unacceptable to Britain because it retained the principle of a supranational authority, and, secondly, that nevertheless the UK did not intend to table alternative proposals because to do so might imperil or prejudice the outcome of the negotiating conference. The Cabinet also decided that Schuman should not be told about the ideas for an international coal and steel authority that had been developed in London.[33]

There is, perhaps, another reason why the Cabinet was so anxious to act properly and avoid embarrassing the French government in the midst of its negotiations. The possibility cannot be ruled out that the government did not really like even the intergovernmental ideas developed by officials. To turn them down would be difficult given all that had been said about British support for European unity. But to press them enthusiastically would imply a stronger endorsement than anyone in the Cabinet was really prepared to give. Thus the decision to avoid publicizing any British proposals was, in every respect, and on every hypothesis, self-interested. This decision did not bring the work of FG (WP) to a halt. Their proposal was considered in Whitehall from every angle. What effect would it have, when implemented, on the OEEC? Paper accumulated. It was as though Whitehall was convinced that the negotiations in Paris would collapse and it would be the proposal of the Strath Working Party that in the end would be implemented. In fact the Paris negotiations did not collapse and the work of the Strath Committee proved to be so much wasted time and paper.

So the UK remained silent as its leadership role in Europe slipped away. But it would probably not have made much difference even if the government had publicized its views. Sir Oliver Harvey and Sir Edmund Hall-Patch were of the opinion that once the UK government had confirmed its position that it would be prepared to enter a coal and steel organization constituted on an intergovernmental basis, Schuman should be told. They added:

We would like to add, however, that we do not think that there is any likelihood of M. Schuman modifying the plan to meet us as regards the supra-national authority or the federal principle as things are at present. He undoubtedly believes he can succeed in setting up the plan based on these features although no doubt with some modification. He also believes and hopes that even if His Majesty's Government cannot participate, means can be devised for associating them with it.[34]

Duncan Burn, the authority on the steel industry, wrote to Edwin Plowden on 21 June: 'I think [the Schuman Plan]'s promise is illusory and its objects can be better achieved in other ways. . . . This country cannot insulate herself from Europe economically, and it would be dangerous to do so politically; she should therefore offer a constructive alternative to the Schuman Plan, which can take advantage of the emotional reaction which this plan has evoked.'[35] Burn realized that the Schuman Plan had made a great impact on world public opinion. The opportunity, he thought, could be used by Britain to produce a better plan and thereby avoid isolation from Europe. It was a widely held illusion that it was still possible to start from scratch with a British initiative. It blinded genuinely wise men like Burn. They did not perceive that, once the Schuman Plan had been announced, the only option for avoiding British isolation was participation in the Paris negotiations.

Roger Bullen complains that, 'apart from M. Schuman himself, little credit was given to the British Government for its refusal to make a counterbid for the leadership in Western Europe by offering terms for an Iron and Steel Community more attractive to the Germans and the Benelux States than those offered by the French.'[36] Little credit was given because little was deserved. If the British government had wanted an Iron and Steel Community and had thought of the idea without the inspiration of the Schuman Plan, it would no doubt have proposed it months before. Now it was too late. It had failed to make any proposal of its own in time and it had failed to take the opportunities offered by the French invitation.[37]

AN INTERNATIONAL AUTHORITY

Presumably if an International Authority such as the FG Committee was now proposing would have been useful on 22 June 1950, something of the kind, less like a cartel, would have been useful on 22 June

---

[34] *DBPO* 127.   [35] T 229/749.   [36] *DBPO* Preface, pp. xii–xiii.
[37] See also *DBPO* 111, minute from Bevin to Younger, 21 June 1950. Bevin's fear was that anything he proposed would look unattractive as compared with the Schuman Plan.

1949 if anyone in the UK government service had been thinking creatively about European problems. The FG Committee's ideas were inspired by the Schuman Plan. Inspiration by the Schuman Plan should not, however, have been necessary. The existence of the IAR could itself have suggested the creation of an *effective* European coal and steel organization. The ideas belatedly suggested by the FG Committee did not go far enough to meet French anxieties about German economic and military power. But it would have been possible, without a significantly greater concession of sovereignty than that contemplated within the FG Committee, to produce a viable initiative which would have sufficiently met French concerns. Any such initiative might not have had the appeal of the Schuman Plan to the more ideologically federalist elements in European and American political society, but that would have been more than compensated in the eyes of most potential participants by the involvement of the UK. The Americans, despairing of progress for their own federal ideas, might even have welcomed it provided only that the new intergovernmental European Coal and Steel Authority did not act as a cartel. They would have seen in it at least some movement in a direction that they could approve and the involvement of the UK would have had in their eyes the benefit that it would eliminate any remaining risk that the new alignment would turn in a neutralist direction.

How would such a body have differed from the IAR? First, it would have been a serious body with serious purposes, not just, as was the IAR, a conciliatory gesture to France conceded without thought as to its real functions. Those purposes would have included most, if not all, the real functions of the Schuman High Authority. Secondly, it would have covered the coal and steel industries of the whole of Western Europe, including the Saar, not just the Ruhr. This would have removed one source of German resentment against Allied policies. As a British proposal it would have done something to improve Anglo-German relationships. Thirdly, it would have been a European body, not an Allied body.[38] Fourthly, it would have offered Germany from the

---

[38] Until the Federal German government entered into office, the German vote in the IAR was exercised by the occupying powers. On 16 Sept. 1949 the Allied High Commissioners agreed that, following the election of the first Bundestag on 14 Aug. 1949, Germany should be represented on the Authority by full voting members. However, it was not until after the Petersburg agreements of 22 Nov. 1949 that the German representative on the Authority served as a full representative. The German representative was Franz Blücher, the Vice-Chancellor, while the other powers had appointed technical personnel.

beginning a position of equality. It could, therefore, have been proposed immediately the Federal German government came into existence in September 1949. The UK would have been able legitimately to claim that, by its proposal, it was making a contribution to Franco-German reconciliation under its own guarantee.

How would it have differed from the ECSC as it eventually came into existence? Its constitution would have had more resemblance to that of the OEEC than to that of the Schuman Plan. It would have operated through a Commission, not a supposedly independent High Authority.[39] The Commission would have been subordinate to a Council of Ministers. It would, therefore, have acted by consensus. But, as the history of the High Authority right up to the present day shows, on all ordinary matters of political sensitivity, consensus is essential. Thus the difference from the ECSC would have been more apparent than real.

Would such a body, acting by consensus, have given the French the assurances that they were looking for from the High Authority, specifically that never again would the Ruhr resources be employed by Germany for aggressive purposes? The first point to make in answer to this question is that international treaties do not and cannot provide absolute guarantees about the behaviour of signatories and in this the Treaty of Paris as it was eventually negotiated was no different from other treaties. A High Authority with sovereign powers that could bind governments sounded majestic indeed. The reality would be a great deal less majestic.[40] The second point is that the addition of a British commitment to any ECSC would have offered a better guarantee than anything provided in the Treaty of Paris. But the real guarantee came, in any case, from the presence in Europe of American forces and the USA was not a signatory of the Treaty of Paris. The third point is that to mitigate French fears, which in 1950 only five years after the end of the war still had resonance in France and indeed elsewhere in Europe, it might have been appropriate to agree in negotiation that a certain limited number of carefully delineated issues, concerned with security and defined in ways which did not overtly discriminate against Germany, would have

---

[39] An idea of this kind had been put forward by Oliver Harvey on 6 June 1950: see *DBPO* 92.

[40] 'It is doubtful if anything done by the Community has made it "materially impossible" for [France and Germany] to go to war against one another': Diebold 664. This was also the view of Marjolin who wrote that the Schuman Plan 'did not make war "materially impossible"': Marjolin (1989) 234.

been subject to a veto. These issues could have included the location of speciality steel production.

Would such a body, acting by consensus, have been in a position to assure France of fairness of treatment in the supply of coking coal for its steel industry? First, the Commission would have established the facts which were by no means clear. Secondly, the answer must be severely practical. At a time of expanding demand, fairness between competing industries of different nations is easier to achieve than at times of recession whatever the institutional arrangements. Publicity can take one so far. But, equally, the power of so-called High Authorities is in practice limited by political imperatives.

ONLY THE FRENCH?

Schuman said in London, at the meetings in May 1950, that his Plan could only have been put forward by the French. Coming from any other government it would not have been accepted by the French and would not have produced the requisite change in psychological atmosphere.[41] There was at least this point of agreement between Schuman and Makins, as can be seen from the quotation that heads this chapter. Certainly it was convenient for Schuman to argue that way and as one of his problems was to carry French public opinion there was advantage in its being a French initiative. For different reasons it was convenient for Makins to argue that way. But there was little other logic in Schuman's claim. The French had long been begging for some sign of British leadership in Europe. They did not want to be left alone in Europe with Germany. To have been assured of effective international supervision of the European coal and steel industries, specifically of the German coal and steel industries, if only by an intergovernmental Council of Ministers, must have represented for them an attractive opportunity, much more attractive than the IAR. Intergovernmental arrangements can also be supranational. Certainly a French gesture towards Germany had great psychological significance. But a British gesture would have had great significance as well, especially as it would have represented the long looked for act of British leadership in Europe, and there would have been fewer hang-ups on the British side such as featured in the Pleven Plan. Such a gesture might even have been more acceptable to

[41] Bullock 774.

the Germans than was the Schuman Plan. There were many Germans who, emerging into sovereignty, saw no reason why they should sacrifice any part of it on the altar of Monnet's theology.

Many members of the French Cabinet would have welcomed such a British initiative. When Maurice Petsche spoke to Stafford Cripps in Paris on 10 June he said that not merely he himself but Bidault and René Mayer had grave misgivings about placing French industry under a supranational authority. He would clearly have been satisfied with rather more modest ideas coming from the British.[42] Indeed he wished to keep in touch with Cripps on the Schuman Plan informally but this idea was rejected in London as it could have had the appearance of British interference in internal French politics.[43] Robert Marjolin was clearly of the opinion that, if the British had led, the French would follow.[44] Some Frenchmen might well have complained at a typical Anglo-Saxon betrayal but France, unlike Britain, would not have excluded itself, for where else would it go?

THE TORIES IN OPPOSITION AND IN GOVERNMENT

It was not Labour alone, nor the Foreign Office alone, that lacked the qualities necessary to keep Britain in the heart of Europe. The Tory advocacy, at the Council of Europe Assembly in August 1950, of an intergovernmental alternative to the Schuman Plan could only look like attempts to sabotage the French initiative.[45] Moreover, it conceded nothing to the French fear that the Germans must not be allowed, by national vetoes or otherwise, to escape from their obligations under whatever treaty eventually emerged. The behaviour of the Tories had some resemblance to that of Labour in the late 1980s and 1990s. They played Europe against the UK government but without sufficient conviction actually to live up to what they had said when they arrived back in office. Indeed the behaviour of the Tories raises questions about

[42] Petsche made similar points at lunch with Edmund Hall-Patch on 16 June. 'He fulminated against M. Monnet's successful attempt to rush Ministers into decisions without adequate time for reflection': *DBPO* 95 and 95 n.

[43] *DBPO* 95 and 96. Harvey reported 'it is far from certain that Bidault ... or any other French politician really regards himself as committed to the details of the plan': *DBPO* 117, Harvey to Younger, 24 June 1950.

[44] See Ch. 6 above.

[45] Macmillan was the principal Tory spokesman. Bevin told Massigli on 31 Aug. 1950 that he was opposed to the Tory move and that he would do nothing to undermine the Schuman negotiations then in progress: Bullock 800.

Acheson's identification of 'doctrinaire' socialism as the reason for the UK's rejection of the Schuman Plan.[46] Harold Macmillan, addressing a group of industrialists on 1 June 1950, highlighted the possible consequences of the failure of the Schuman Plan. He said that if the Plan went wrong they could never revert to the situation which had existed before the proposal was made. If the Plan was not successful the situation might be the turning-point. It would create one of two hideous results—either people would lose confidence in Western Europe as a whole, or the plan would operate under a Germany not controlled by Britain and America, a Germany of the wrong kind. They might see a German Schuman Plan in the next five years which might be akin to a Ribbentrop–Stalin pact.[47] Yet despite the hideous prospect of a Germany, uncontrolled by Britain and America, dominating the Schuman Plan, the Tory government of which Macmillan would shortly be a prominent member did nothing to prevent it.

Opening the debate on the Schuman Plan in the House of Commons on 26 June 1950, Anthony Eden had dramatically posed the key question: 'Would we be prepared to enter discussions as a result of which a high authority would be set up whose decisions would be binding upon the nations who were parties to the agreement? My answer to that question would be yes, provided that we were satisfied with the conditions and the safeguards.'[48] Hailsham describes how, in June 1950, he was invited by Churchill to make the final speech for the Conservative Party from the back-benches at the end of the first day's debate on the Schuman Plan. His attitude 'given me orally by Winston' was 'a wholehearted support of Schuman's invitation'. He describes the government's attitude as 'a disastrous piece of political blindness characteristic of the Labour Party's attitude towards the European idea'.[49]

Nevertheless, as demonstrated by the Macmillan–Eccles motion put before the Consultative Assembly of the Council of Europe in August, the Conservative Party itself showed little understanding of the motivations behind the Schuman Plan. Macmillan himself describes his scheme:

Our scheme differed from Schuman's in three respects:

1. The experts who coordinate the coal and steel industries will be responsible to a Committee of Ministers and therefore the link with the underlying Parliaments is kept.

[46] Acheson 387. See Ch. 8 above.   [47] *The Times*, 2 June 1950.
[48] HC Debs. 26 June 1950, col. 1915.   [49] Hailsham 255–8.

2. The basic social, economic and strategic interests of each country are safeguarded from encroachment by the experts.

3. Any member can withdraw on giving 12 months notice; and any member can be expelled by the others.[50]

Thus the difference between Macmillan–Eccles and Schuman was not simply the difference between an intergovernmental scheme and a supranational scheme. It could hardly be attractive to France that Germany should be able to escape at twelve months' notice from such control of the Ruhr as the Schuman Plan would establish. Macmillan–Eccles also provided that the voting powers of the members of the Authority should be in proportion to the production and consumption of coal and steel in the member countries, another provision that, while of advantage to the UK, would create problems for France. Indeed, if this was the best that the Conservative Party could offer, it removes any justification from their onslaught on the government.[51]

When Churchill returned to office in 1951 it was open to his government to make an application for membership of the ECSC. Safeguards against the irresponsible power of the High Authority had been inserted during the negotiations leading up to the Treaty of Paris. Instead Churchill circulated to his Cabinet colleagues a memorandum dated 29 November 1951 which read:

We should have joined in the discussions and, had we done so, not only a better plan would probably have emerged, but our own interests would have been watched at every stage.

Our attitude towards further economic developments on the Schuman lines resembles that which we adopt about the European Army [Pleven Plan]. We help, we dedicate, we play a part, but we are not merged and do not forfeit our insular or Commonwealth -wide character. I should resist any American pressure to treat Britain as on the same footing as the European states, none of whom have the advantages of the Channel and who were consequently conquered.[52]

It was a little too soon for Churchill to resile from his view, when in opposition, that the UK should have taken part in the discussions, and

---

[50] Macmillan 202.

[51] Ibid. 202–3. Macmillan–Eccles included a series of other clauses safeguarding the conditions of workers, collective bargaining, and Imperial Preference, enabling stock-piling by governments if there was a surplus, and limiting the powers of the Authority in regard to capital investment to advice. It also expressed a preference for separate boards for coal and steel for which British industry had indicated a preference.

[52] Bullock 787.

it may indeed have been that a better plan would have emerged. But the hypothetical difference between what might have emerged and what did emerge was quite inadequate, if properly understood, to have justified the failure of the Tories to apply for membership of the ECSC as soon as they returned to office if their protestations of European commitment had had any real substance. The truth is that, despite the brave European vapourings of Churchill and his colleagues while in opposition, there was in practice nothing to choose between Conservative policy towards Europe and Labour policy towards Europe. The fact that Churchill exploited Europe against Labour naturally added to Labour suspicion of all things European but Labour suspicions were already deep enough.[53] The Conservative Party's attitude in opposition was one of unprincipled opportunism. It began a tradition in which, with considerable damage to British interests, opposition parties exploit the European question against the government of the day by making speeches and proposals to which they have no intention of living, once back in office. Macmillan himself, when back in government, refers to the views of the Foreign Office in early 1952 as showing 'a degree of myopia which a mole might envy'.[54]

Nevertheless the Conservative proposal for an intergovernmental alternative to the Schuman Plan, though faulty in its lack of understanding of French fears, shows that a non-partisan initiative of the kind described here would have been open to the UK government provided only that it had been made before 9 May 1950. By the same token, Conservative policy on Europe would have protected Labour from any fear that support for the Schuman Plan could be exploited against it in the general election that was bound to come in view of its small majority after the general election of February 1950.

[53] Geoffrey Warner points to the annoyance caused in Labour circles by the invitation to Churchill to chair The Hague Congress in 1948: Warner 67.

[54] Macmillan 468. The Foreign Office was commenting on a proposal for the complete union of the Schuman Plan countries.

12

The Press and the Schuman Plan

THE PRESS

The Press has two important functions. The first is to inform and the second is to comment. In neither function should it become simply part of the propaganda apparatus of government. Here we examine how four leading organs of information and opinion, *The Times* of London, the *Financial Times*, the *Manchester Guardian*, and *The Economist*, together with the *Daily Express*, the organ of Lord Beaverbrook's opinions, fulfilled their role during the events leading up to the convening of the Schuman Plan negotiating conference in Paris on 20 June 1950.[1] This coverage is not comprehensive. But it is illustrative. It helps to illumine the character of the contemporary debate, such as it was.

The Times was far from being a wholehearted supporter of the Labour government. The *Guardian*, on the other hand, was a liberal paper inclined to give the government the benefit of the doubt wherever it could. Its editor, A. P. Wadsworth, was a great admirer of Ernest Bevin. The *Financial Times*, in 1950, was purely a business paper with little of the wider coverage of news and the arts that it contains today. The *Daily Express* was a campaigning newspaper. Generally, it supported the Conservative Party, but it could not be relied on when Conservatives drifted away from Lord Beaverbrook's ideas on the primacy of the Commonwealth and Empire. *The Economist* was as it ever has been, independent and arrogant, but with some tendency to try to please an American readership. While initially friendly to the Attlee government, it had become disillusioned with the passage of time.

Comment on foreign policy involved considerations different from those on domestic policy. In foreign policy there was a general tendency to give the government the benefit of the doubt. This was particularly

---

[1] The *New Statesman* of 10 June 1950 dismissed the Schuman Plan as the product of a conspiracy headed by the Vatican, the Ruhr industrialists, and the *Comité des Forges*: Morgan (1984) 393.

the case because British foreign policy was dominated by the reliable figure of Ernest Bevin, by 1950 the longest serving Foreign Minister in the free world. The *Daily Express* was probably not alone in thinking that he was now long past his prime, but he still commanded sympathy and respect.

Despite the tendency, on foreign policy, to give the government the benefit of the doubt, it might have been expected that, in assessing government reactions to the Schuman Plan, all these journals would bring to bear such critical faculties as they possessed. There is little evidence of it in *The Times* and the *Manchester Guardian* during the crucial weeks after the Schuman announcement. On the contrary, the columns of both show clear evidence of domination by Foreign Office briefing. Where would such respectable journals turn for advice if not to the experts of the Foreign Office who were evidently very ready to help? Any hope that the debate about British participation might be enlightened or enriched by the independent judgement of these two newspapers was to be disappointed. The *Financial Times* failed to give the government the benefit of its advice until all the key decisions had been taken. Until that time, it devoted more space to the concurrent negotiations towards the EPU than to the Schuman Plan. Once the decisions had been taken, it swamped its editorial columns with its doubts and hesitations which, it appeared to think, made any decision about the Schuman Plan impossible. As no decision was possible, the government had been right to choose abstention. The *Daily Express* alone was happy at the outcome. For this happiness, there was a simple reason. Foreign pressure in favour of European economic integration had been resisted.

The Times had a flourishing letter page. It carried the arguments of many distinguished advocates of participation in the Schuman negotiations.[2] Of all the letters arguing that case, the most remarkable was that from David Eccles already several times quoted. The *Manchester Guard-ian* also had a flourishing letter page. But the Schuman Plan does not seem to have interested its readers. Letters on the Schuman Plan were virtually absent from its correspondence columns.[3] This absence of reader comment occurred despite the fact that its editorials on the Schuman Plan were long, and frequent, and that its news coverage was quite as full as in *The Times*, in some respects fuller. It also carried interesting articles on the topic from W. W. Rostow and Raymond

[2] Stephen Spender welcomed the Schuman Plan in a letter to *The Times*, 3 June 1950.
[3] There was a letter from Stephen Martin, Hon. Sec. of the Liberal Liberty League denouncing the Schuman Plan on free-trade grounds: *Manchester Guardian*, 9 June 1950.

Aron. But none of this, apparently, could stir its readers. It must have been of some comfort to the government that the readers of the *Manchester Guardian* could not be stirred. There was no suggestion here of any strong European sentiments in the industrial heartland of Britain.[4] The *Financial Times* also published letters but its readers were not spurred into expressing views on the Schuman Plan.

Hardly ever did the editorial judgements of *The Times* differ from those that were determining policy within the Foreign Office. This was the more remarkable in view of the attitude being taken by the opposition. The only difference in the *Manchester Guardian* was its tendency to hedge bets, to accept Foreign Office arguments but suggest that the question could have been better handled and that there was still another way. This, too, was remarkable in view of the strong support for the Schuman Plan offered by the Liberal Party.[5] This had no influence on the *Manchester Guardian* other than to muddy its editorial judgements with unrealizable hopes after decisions which ruled them out had already been taken. *The Economist* was very different. The quality of its journalism was a whole category higher than that of any of the newspapers. Its judgements can stand critical appraisal even today. Of course it is a weekly and its journalists had more time to think. This is not to say that Foreign Office briefing was kept entirely at bay. But throughout, the editorial pages of *The Economist* saw the main point in the debate and unswervingly supported British participation in the Schuman Plan negotiations.

FIRST ASSESSMENT

The first editorial reaction of *The Times*, published on 11 May 1950, was cautiously supportive of the Plan. *The Times* found much to comfort it in the French presentation of the Plan. It went so far as to find

---

[4] Gallup, then the only polling agency in Britain, investigated public opinion in June 1950. It found that 77% had heard of the Schuman Plan, 17% had not, and 6% did not know. 27% thought it a good idea, 21% a bad idea, and 29% did not know. The sample was not asked whether Britain should join. That question was not put until Jan. 1952. 23% then said we should, 47% said we should not, and 30% did not know. I am grateful to Geoffrey Warner for this information.

[5] Not by Dingle Foot, Liberal Party Vice-President. On 9 June 1950 the *Daily Express* quoted, with approval, Foot's words: 'We cannot place ourselves in a position in which we might not render military assistance to one of the Dominions, or invest our capital resources in our own Crown Colonies, or decide our attitude towards a dispute affecting, say, India or Australia, without the leave of a European authority. . . . We cannot abandon the existing British Commonwealth for the sake of a hypothetical United States of Europe.'

it 'much closer to Mr Bevin's functional approach' than had been previous French policy offerings. Moreover, what was proposed was certainly logical.

The French and German coal and steel industries are, of course, intimately connected. France has the largest reserves of iron ore in Europe—low grade ores but cheap to mine—but has to supplement her coal supplies from the Ruhr. The Ruhr draws some of its ore, and might use more, from Lorraine. The French have argued since the war that Germany should import French crude steel and make it into the more highly finished products characteristic of Westphalia; this, in the French eyes, would give security since the basic product, crude steel, would be made in only limited quantities in Germany.

Perhaps the Foreign Office mandarins and their ministers were, at this stage, too occupied with the London conference to bother with press coverage of the Schuman Plan. One comment does suggest Foreign Office briefing. 'Neither Britain nor the United States could have suggested it without French approval and a German proposal on these lines could not easily have been accepted by the French. It was for France and France alone to take the step.'

On the same day, the *Manchester Guardian* found the Plan attractive to continental opinion. It was the outcome of a long period of gestation. Its diplomatic correspondent recorded that 'Dr Adenauer has long held the view that German adherence to the Ruhr Authority would be much more easily accepted if its role were extended to cover the basic industries of Western Europe.' Editorially it recalled that, as long ago as December 1948, Schuman had said that the question of the Ruhr could only be solved on a European basis. 'It has, in short, been a long time in the air. But it has never been put so formally, or with such authority, as by M. Schuman.'

The *Manchester Guardian* then proceeded to miss the political message for Britain:

The attraction to British opinion is perhaps less strong, or at least less direct. If the British coal and iron industries were to come into the pool . . . it would be on economic grounds only, not also or even mainly on diplomatic grounds. . . . But that is no reason for not examining the economic case for participation fully and frankly, and with the knowledge that the Americans will watch with a critical eye any arguments based on the desire to shield nationalised industries against efficient competition from across the Channel.

The *Financial Times* also ventured an editorial on 11 May. It saw the political point but it gave no view as to how the UK should react. Its main worry seems to have been that the Plan would turn into a cartel, a concern to which, during the subsequent weeks, it returned.

From the political point of view, there is no doubt that [Schuman's direct approach to Germany] was precisely what was needed. It should do much to strengthen Dr Adenauer's hand in his effort to obtain a large parliamentary majority for Germany's proposed entry into the Council of Europe and will help to remove some of the bitterness caused by the Saar incident. . . . Perhaps . . . the main value of M. Schuman's initiative—apart from its immediate political aspect—is that it may make the Americans face the practical implications of their policy of European economic integration. As the OEEC itself is in process of discovering, this inevitably means, if it is to have any practical effect, agreements between combinations of national enterprises. . . . Real integration can only be achieved if the producers themselves are willing to tie themselves by international agreements. Do the Americans want this or not?

There was not the least equivocation in the stand taken by the *Daily Express* on 11 May, and from that stand it never wavered.

[The Schuman Plan] is a proposal which, if accepted, will end British independence. . . . No country which loses national control of coal and steel can retain national freedom. This threat to our sovereignty is not accidental. . . . It is part of a deliberate and concerted attempt to force Britain into a United Europe. . . . What strength will be added to the free world if this country deserts the Empire and joins instead with a Germany which has already waged two aggressive wars in this century and may well wage another? What stability will be secured by uniting with a France whose Governments for five years have tottered from one crisis to another? . . . Be sure too that the standard of living of Continental peoples would not be raised to ours. Ours instead would be dragged down to equality with theirs. . . . The way to that peace lies not in an uneasy union with the Continent of Europe. It lies instead in strengthening our comradeship with the Commonwealth and Empire. The British Empire is potentially the wealthiest and strongest Power in the world.

If Lord Beaverbrook believed that last sentence, he would believe anything. It says something about the state of opinion in Britain that such ideas did not simply provoke laughter.

By 12 May 1950 *The Times*'s parliamentary correspondent was finding that the Schuman Plan drew its inspiration from ideas put forward much earlier by that experienced foreign policy expert, Anthony Eden. No doubt the memory of the parliamentary correspondent had been refreshed by some interested interlocutor who himself chose to remember how wise and far-sighted he had been. He referred to Eden's arguments in December 1948 that there should be closer collaboration between the Ruhr and the complementary industries in France, Belgium and Luxembourg.

Mr Eden has also advanced the argument that the integration of the heavy industries of western Europe as a whole, extending from the Ruhr to Lorraine and the Saar, could put international control on so wide a basis and interweave so many mutual interests that there would be neither scope nor opportunity for purely nationalistic plans.

By 15 May the *Manchester Guardian* had changed tack and was becoming censorious. '[T]he British technique of waiting for others to make suggestions, then trying to make them work, has seemed inconspicuous by contrast [with the French initiatives]; and because we have in this way failed to give much public impression of "European feeling" we shall be all the more insistently pressed to make up for that by our actions.' Thus criticism of British lack of ideas on European integration was combined with echoes of the Foreign Office theme that it was the British who had to find ways of making the ideas of foreigners practical.

By 17 May *The Times* too was becoming critical of Britain's failure to lead. It praised Bevin for resisting the more outlandish proposals emerging on the Continent. 'Mr Bevin deserves more credit than he usually receives for this lonely crusade for realism.' But then came the whiplash.

It remains true . . . that in the planning and discussion of the more distant future of western European collaboration Britain has never taken the initiative although the western European peoples have always looked to her for a lead in giving content and shape to the powerful, urgent and increasingly widespread aspirations which the phrase 'western union' expresses.

The Foreign Office could take greater pleasure in *The Times*'s qualifying assertion.

No good can come from trying to conceal that if Britain were ever faced with the harsh alternatives of entering a European federation, and in the process weakening if not altogether destroying her ties with the Commonwealth, or remaining outside, with all the attendant risks of isolation from the Continent, she would be obliged to prefer the Commonwealth to western Europe.

But any pleasure that the Foreign Office could derive should have been diluted by the consideration that even the most enthusiastic supporters of British participation in the Schuman Plan would have conceded that point. Whatever might have been said in the Schuman Plan announcement, it was common ground among British supporters that the reference to federalism did not have to be taken seriously at this stage. As already indicated, there was good reason to think it was not being taken particularly seriously in France either.

Meanwhile *The Economist* had been weighing its words. On 13 May it contented itself with the observation that, as the West was increasingly looking to Germany as a partner in defence, there was an urgent need 'to get European opinion into a new mood and above all to put an end to the sullen discontent prevailing at Bonn'. When its more considered thoughts emerged on 20 May, they were expressed without equivocation. So powerful were its arguments, and so slight their influence in London, that they are worth quoting at length.

Politically, the Schuman offer stands or falls on the question whether it strengthens or weakens the Atlantic link, and whether it makes easier or more difficult an effective defence plan for Europe. . . . No one should underestimate the sense of defeatism and neutrality that exists in some parts of the Continent . . . the mood exists and . . . it is strong in France and Germany. . . . Fortunately there is every reason to suppose that the mainspring of the Schuman offer—certainly in M. Schuman's own mind, though one cannot be so sure about its appeal to some other sections of French opinion—is the straightforward and entirely reputable desire to draw Germany into closer and more confident relations with the west and to counter the drag of the east with its promises of unity and markets. . . . [The Plan] may offer a solution for one of the unresolved riddles of western rearmament. The western powers have naturally set their faces against any prospect of renewed German armament making. Yet to defend Europe— and Germany—without any contribution from German industry might place a load of unproductive industrial activity upon the heavy industry of Germany's neighbours and leave the Ruhr with a very considerable competitive advantage. If, however, genuine control and integration are established in the Ruhr–Rhine– Lorraine complex, a balanced solution of this problem becomes a possibility. . . . On political grounds, there would seem to be an immensely strong case not only for Britain's approval but for its active participation in the new authority. . . . Its presence on the new authority would ensure, as could nothing else, that the political aims of the new organisation were sound. . . . But [the Plan] will stand or fall by its economic implications, which are the real test of its merits.

The main economic question to be asked of the Schuman proposal . . . is whether it would be more than a governmental façade for an old-fashioned cartel . . . the strongest point of the whole scheme is the proposal that there should be absolutely free trade in the products of heavy industry, that neither

coal nor iron ore nor steel should be made the subject of either customs tariffs
or import quotas by any of the participating countries . . . it is impossible from
so general a statement to decide whether or not the proposal is an old cartel
under a new title or a genuinely new departure. . . . But, at least until there is
proof to the contrary, it should be accepted that there is a genuine intention to
press forward to higher productivity and that the new authority would give
priority to efficiency, lowered costs and more rational production . . . it is in
France, where postwar expansion has been pressed to some extent irrespective
of cost, that the first redundancies are likely to occur . . . is it certain . . . that the
French Government will accept the decision of an independent body on matters
which directly affect the livelihood of its own electorate and the interests of the
labour unions? . . . Who . . . will accept the added cut in steel production which
further German output may make necessary? . . . A functional economic body
may advise but it cannot enforce decisions. In a word it cannot usurp the
political authority which belongs to governments alone. . . . there will only be
disappointment ahead if the planners of the new scheme cherish the illusion
that purely economic and industrial proposals can persuade governments to
refrain from exercising their sovereignty in what they conceive to be their
national interests. . . . For economic reasons as well as political, Britain should
participate in the scheme. . . . At present, the British coal and steel industries
are certainly competitive with their French and German opposite numbers.
British steel producers stand to gain by the rationalisation of future European
development, the elimination of the marginally inefficient and the curbing of
excessive development plans. The Coal Board can still secure a higher price for
exports than for domestic sales; it need not fear free trade in coal. . . . Cautious
hesitation has become too invariable a factor in the formulation of British
policy. On this occasion, at least, no ground should be given for any accusation
of 'dragging the feet'.

The Economist adhered to this strong line throughout the subsequent
weeks. But together with the firmness of its recommendation that Britain should participate went sophisticated scepticism about the reality of
the sovereignty that would in practice belong to the High Authority.

DOUBTS AND CERTAINTIES

While *The Economist* was thundering, the *Manchester Guardian* remained deep in doubt. The best it could say editorially on 23 May was:
'Whether the main purpose of the scheme would be better achieved
with or without direct British participation is still a matter for discussion. But there can be no doubt that it is in our best interest to help
to make the plan a success.' On the same day the *Financial Times*

succeeded in writing an editorial on 'Steel Lessons' without mentioning the Schuman Plan.

It was at this point that the Foreign Office, freed from the burdens of the London conference, began both serious consideration of the Schuman Plan and serious attention to its other important objective of bringing the Press into line. *The Times* readily responded to Foreign Office briefing. Its change of tone is striking. The first British memorandum of 25 May was celebrated in a strong editorial on 26 May. 'The Government clearly cannot commit themselves to approve, let alone take part in, a scheme which, even after M. Monnet's explanations, remains extremely shadowy both in its aims and its functions . . . the idea [of the Schuman Plan] cannot properly be judged until more is known.'[6] From that point on, *The Times* converted itself, with only occasional backsliding, into a Foreign Office newsletter.

The *Daily Express* was, for once, pleased with the government. On 30 May it wrote: 'There can be only one criticism of the Government's refusal to commit Britain to support of the Schuman plan. It is not couched in sufficiently strong terms. Why leave the way open for further discussion . . . ? The whole senseless project should be rejected out of hand.' On the other hand, it was very displeased with those Tories who were supporting the Schuman Plan. 'These Tories must make up their minds quickly whether they stand for Empire and an increasing standard of life for every citizen of Britain. Or for union with Europe and equality of misery with the people of the Continent.'

On 31 May the diplomatic corespondent of *The Times* passed on to its readers the pure milk of Foreign Office propaganda: 'The British Government are fully in favour of the principle of an international body to control the industries concerned, but they are not prepared to commit themselves necessarily to join any such authority without knowing how it is to be set up.' Editorially, *The Times* advised its readers: 'The French Government . . . cannot expect the British Government to commit themselves to an idea, no matter how attractive, without first considering how it is to be put into practice, what its political and economic implications will be, and how they will affect the interests of this country.'

---

[6] There was one minor dissent. It related to the proposal conveyed to Paris that HMG would like to participate in direct conversations between France and Germany. 'The British Government apparently assume that the conference will be restricted to Germany, France and Britain, but there is a strong case for inviting the other nations of western Europe that would be affected by such a scheme.'

The *Manchester Guardian* at last had something hard to hang on to. It may not have been able to make up its editorial mind on whether Britain should participate or not, but it could now join in condemning French tactics. On 2 June, when it was already too late to exercise any constructive influence, it ventured so far as to give its blessing to Foreign Office briefing. It did so in ignorance of the fact that the French had made one last concession, the substitution in the draft communiqué of the words 'immediate objective'.

There is no doubt now that the declaration which the French required of us was an impossible one. It would have committed us publicly to joining the scheme: to putting our coal and steel industries under an International Authority whose decisions would be binding although its nature was as yet uncertain. Other countries may have accepted with mental reservations and it was implied that we should too; but if only for the reason that we are most exposed to criticism such deception would have been impossible. . . . That the original announcement of the plan had to be a surprise was easily understandable; but it is harder to see why the invitation too, and the proposed declaration, should have been sprung on us, especially if (as seems likely) it was found possible to discuss them with Dr Adenauer.

Thus in the view of the *Manchester Guardian*, shared with the Foreign Office, the British had the right to resent not just the original Schuman announcement, made without consultation, but the fact that France had been in discussion with Germany. But, from the beginning, the French had made it clear that, although they wanted British participation, the prime target of their policy was *rapprochement* with Germany. Britain, having neglected the opportunity to take the lead, now had to find a role in France's play.

By the following day, 3 June, the *Manchester Guardian* was aware of the last French concession. That knowledge introduced a little hedging into its editorial judgement. It seemed to be climbing back on the fence.

One can say that by insisting on our making a too elegant gesture, the French have jeopardized all chance of our practical co-operation. One can also say that the gesture would have been a fairly empty one and that the Government might have swallowed its prejudices and given it. The choice between these two possible verdicts depends in the first place on one's estimation of the chance, in the second on the binding force of the gesture. But the assessment of responsibility now hardly matters. . . . [I]t would be better if the scheme, irrespective of our practical participation, did not remain exclusively Franco-German in conception and elaboration. In other words, the plan could succeed without our industries, but it does need our interest. A way of expressing this can still be found.

The idea that a way of expressing British interest could still be found referred to the communiqué issued that day by the British government which said that it was 'actively engaged in working on proposals inspired by the French initiative'.[7] Awareness of that fact helped to modify an editorial judgement that might otherwise have been far more critical. Apparently the British government was still in the game. It was just a matter of waiting for it to play its cards.

By 5 June 1950, after the breakdown in negotiations between France and the UK, the *Financial Times* decided that it was time to let its readers have the benefit of its advice.

It is in the highest degree unfortunate that the British Government has felt unable to agree to direct participation in the coming international con-ference . . . on the Schuman Plan. This plan had fired the imagination of the peoples of Europe, and, what is equally important, of the Americans. . . . Yet it must be admitted that the French requirement that each country participating in the coming international conference should commit itself in advance to the principle of pooling its steel and coal resources under a new high authority whose writ would run beyond that of the participating Governments is an uncommonly exacting requirement. . . . To surrender national control of two basic industries, the magnitude and pattern of whose production are absolutely vital both to national security and to the smooth functioning of the national economy, is a proposition to which any British Government would be reluctant to assent without foreknowledge of the precise powers of the new authority. It can be accepted, however, that the British Government is anxious that a work-able scheme shall be evolved. . . . It may well be that as the negotiations over the Schuman proposals proceed, the outline will emerge of a scheme of inte-gration to which this country will be able to subscribe without serious misgiving . . . meanwhile, it is difficult to condemn the Government's reluc-tance to subscribe at this stage to the far-reaching declaration of intent required by the French Government.

Thus the *Financial Times* succeeded, after its long period of thought, in embracing a complex of views the principal one of which seems to have been that, with some extramural assistance from the British gov-ernment, but in its understandable absence from the negotiations them-selves, a workable scheme might emerge. It was accepted as given that the continentals were unlikely to know how to fashion a workable

---

[7] Cmd. 7970/16.

scheme without the aid of the British. In the circumstances, it is difficult to understand why the *Financial Times* so easily accepted the
absence of the British from the Paris negotiations.

On 5 June, too, *The Times* was also ready to name the guilty party.
But *The Times* too was looking for a way back into the game and found
it in the British government's announced intention to develop alternative proposals.

The British Government were entirely right in declining to undertake this prior
commitment. . . . [The British Government] would be put in a false position if
they committed themselves to the plan in principle and then, after examination,
had to withdraw from their undertakings. It would nevertheless be wrong to
suggest that the British Government decided as they did solely on a point of
scruple. The real question is why the six other Governments have felt able,
without any sense of falsely committing themselves, to accept the plan as a
working project while the British Government hold back at this stage. To that
question there is a cogent answer dictated by this country's way of thinking, its
ties with the Commonwealth countries, the pattern of its export trade and its
geographical position. . . . For this country it remains true that although the
material advantages of associating with a co-operative plan are not so apparent
as they are for France or western Germany, they are none the less great. The
sooner the British 'positive proposals' are prepared and have their impact on
the six-Power conference the better.

The discovery by *The Times* that the UK government had not been
acting 'solely on a point of scruple' did suggest a dawning awareness
that perhaps the government had been telling less than the whole truth
in its suggestion that they were not querying the supranational principle, merely the way it would work. It was now realized that there was
a great deal more to it than that.

By 9 June *The Times* appeared to be getting worried. The previous
day it had published the powerful letter from David Eccles, in which
he argued for British participation. 'The more profound cause for our
reluctance to join the steel talks is that, not having been occupied or
defeated, our ideas about national sovereignty are out of step with those
on the Continent.' Eccles's letter seems to have come near influencing
the Editor. *The Times* editorial of 9 June quoted with approval what
Eccles had said about employment in the UK being dependent on the
welfare of the international economy.

This country has an interest second to none in any new arrangements to break
through the restrictions of economic nationalism and so contribute to stability,
prosperity, and peace. It is the British view that these decisions have to be made

on the basis not of general hopes and hypotheses but of practical proposals which can be weighed and measured. Such proposals, it is to be hoped, are being busily fashioned.

Thus, though worried by the thought of British exclusion, *The Times* was still finding comfort in the thought of proposals being framed in Whitehall. It was, in typical Whitehall mode, deriding the 'general hopes and hypotheses' which made continental initiatives of such dubious value. It also allowed itself to be diverted from the issue of British participation by another piece of Foreign Office briefing, that, as *The Times* called it, 'a special form of association' could be a useful substitute for membership.

The Economist of 3 June had gone to press too early to pronounce on the final communiqués of the two parties. It confined itself to a Note of the Week which questioned French tactics while reaffirming its view that the British government should participate wholeheartedly.

M. Schuman should know his Foreign Office better by now than to imagine that the British would sign a declaration accepting 'in principle' the idea of setting up for the two industries a common authority whose decisions would be binding on governments. It should have been obvious that a Labour Government—or indeed any British government—would want to know more details about ways of reaching and enforcing decisions which would affect 1 ¼ million British workers in basic industries. . . . M. Monnet and his assistants left the impression that a brilliant French idea still required a great deal of working out in detail. None the less, the misunderstanding at this juncture is unfortunate. The British cannot be excused for showing once again their lack of *flair* for the generous gesture and the eloquent phrase which keeps a good idea before the public while the experts think out all the difficulties . . . Second thoughts reveal no reason for revising the view expressed in *The Economist* two weeks ago: that 'solid reasons,' both of general policy and of economic interest exist, that should lead the British Government to join wholeheartedly in the examination, drafting and establishment of the proposed council.

By its next edition, that of 10 June, *The Economist* was prepared to thunder again. In an editorial entitled 'Inverted Micawbers', it wrote:

The negotiations designed to give effective shape to M. Schuman's proposal . . . are to go ahead without British participation. That is the upshot of as sorry a piece of diplomatic muddling as the world had ever seen . . . there were really two points at issue—first, whether a commitment should be made to enter a scheme before it is known what the scheme amounts to; and secondly, whether governments should surrender any of their sovereignty to 'independent' (which presumably means non-responsible) supra-national bodies. On both these specific issues, if the argument be confined to them, there is a great deal to be said for the British Government's attitude. . . . If this were all that is to be said, then the answer to American criticism would be to enquire when the United States has been willing to accept any commitment without the lengthiest examination in Washington, or to accept any derogation of American sovereignty even with it. Indeed, on the matters formally at issue—the visible portion of the iceberg—the British case is so strong that one is compelled to enquire why the French took a course which they must have known would lead to the result it did. . . . The French passionately want British participation in the scheme when it is set up. But British participation in the negotiations that precede its setting up may be, in their eyes, another matter. They have had plenty of experience in recent years of British skill in deferring and emasculating projects that have been accepted in principle. . . . It is difficult to find anyone on the Continent or in America, or even in unofficial circles in this country, who has not by now been driven to the conclusion that the British Government's desire is to sabotage any moves towards European economic unity under cover of accepting them in principle. This is a hard thing to say of any government. So far as this journal is concerned, we are not yet convinced that there is any bad faith, or that the explanation cannot rather be found partly in terms of real difficulties inadequately explained, and partly in those of personal vanity, personal fatigue and personal stupidity. But what must be recorded as a fact is that world opinion believes that Labour Ministers approach all these matters (as Philip Guedalla once said of the Baldwin Government's attitude to the League of Nations) like inverted Micawbers, waiting for something to turn down. . . . In last week's affair, for example, had there been an active desire to push forward, it ought not to have been very difficult to find a formula for acceptance of the French Government's invitation with the qualifications which are assuredly in the minds of the governments that did accept. . . . One can regret that the issue was brought up by such unworthy tactics. One can regret that so mighty a principle as the pooling of sovereignty was invoked, and such high hopes of permanent pacification aroused, in support of a proposal which only those versed in its formidable technicalities can really understand—and whose actual practical accomplishments may yet turn out to be small. One can be deeply distrustful of the French and American leaning to the dangerous and difficult principle of federalism, and disappointed at the failure to realise how much sovereignty has already . . . been pooled in defence matters. . . . But when all these things have been said, the fact remains that at the bar of world opinion the Schuman proposal has become a test. And the British Government have failed it. . . . Fortunately the chapter is not closed. An interdepartmental committee is charged with working out the British attitude to the French proposals. It is still possible for the Government to take its place at the negotiating table. But it will take some hard work to erase the impression left by last week's performance. Those who are charged with responsibility for representing this country might do well to remember that what is now most urgently in need of reconstruction is not the European iron and steel industry, but the world's confidence in Britain's willingness to play a constructive role in world affairs.

Thus *The Economist* joined with *The Times*, the *Financial Times*, and the *Manchester Guardian* in accepting the Foreign Office line that the manner of the French invitation was deplorable. What all these journals failed to understand was the confidence generated in Paris by the enthusiastic world response to the Schuman announcement. In these circumstances, to water down further, for the benefit of the British, drafts that had been accepted by their other partners would have suggested lack of resolve. Where *The Economist* differed from its contemporaries was in suggesting that, despite the French tactics, the British should have ensured their involvement. The note of anger at one more British failure of leadership was loud enough.

The comments of these journals also illustrated the success of the Foreign Office in diverting anger by suggesting that the establishment of the interdepartmental committee held out hope of a British re-entry. It was a highly effective ploy. These journals appear not, at this stage, to have realized that the French were being informed that the British counter-proposals would be held in reserve and would only be brought forward if the negotiating conference failed. If it succeeded, as was probable, the British counter-proposals would be left on the shelf and Britain would remain excluded. They were thus a means of re-entry only in a disaster scenario which was likely to cause such ill feeling on the Continent that a considerable time would have to elapse before anything useful could be said again on the theme of *rapprochement*. We cannot know what these journals would have said, at this stage, if they had realized that they had, in fact, been tricked. It was not until 13 June that, with Attlee's statement in the House, they were told about the Britain's intended reticence.[8] What none of them suggest is the excuse for non-participation that became accepted later, that for political reasons, whether it was the views of the Durham miners or otherwise, it was quite impossible for the British to take part in this continental escapade. All were writing on the basis that participation was a politically feasible option for the government.

---

[8] On 29 June Bevin told Sir R. Makins that the correspondents of the 'most important newspapers, e.g. *The Times*, *Manchester Guardian* and the *Scotsman*', should be urged to play down the Schuman Plan for the time being while being assured that the UK government was 'on the alert to see how far we can help on the Schuman initiative and the cause of European unity generally': *DBPO* 123.

EUROPEAN UNITY

European Unity provided the press with an easy opportunity for denouncing the Labour Party. The journals exploited the opportunity in their various ways. The *Manchester Guardian* of 13 June commented editorially:

The document is much weakened by this assumption of superior virtue over the benighted Europeans of the Continent . . . the Labour Party is all for union if everybody will be like the British! . . . The implication is that the Schuman proposal can receive Labour support only if it is based on nationalised industries and that in this international coordination of industries Governments will play 'the decisive part'. . . . It is time [British Labour] realised that very few people in Europe or America share the childlike assumption that 'Socialist' Britain is the most perfect of countries and that only if Europe is first remade in our own image can we begin to co-operate fully.

The *Manchester Guardian* appeared unconscious of the fact that it itself might be accused of an 'assumption of superior virtue over the benighted Europeans of the Continent' in its attitude to British participation in the Schuman Plan.

For the *Daily Express* of 13 June, the main welcome fact about *European Unity* was its rejection of the Schuman Plan. It did not, however, approve all its reasons. The bad reason was that 'they cannot join with non-Socialist Governments. No Schuman Plan until Schuman becomes a Socialist!' The good reason was Labour's emphasis on the world-wide Commonwealth of which Britain was the 'nerve centre'.

The Times devoted two editorials to *European Unity*, on 13 and 16 June. 'What is politically suspect is the assumption that co-operation . . . is impossible because "many European Governments have not yet shown the will or the ability to plan their own economies."' The attitude that it was impossible to work with non-socialist governments in plans for Europe was 'anathema'. Apart from this criticism, *The Times* found 'much good sense in the statement'. For example, it commended the pamphlet's opposition to European federalism.

If the impression has been given abroad that this country would in any circumstances favour the federation of Europe—an impression which the new revelations are alleged to have brusquely dispelled—the blame belongs not to the Government but to a small knot of politicians, mostly, but not all, on the Opposition side, who have let their enthusiasm run beyond their countrymen's views and interests.

The *Manchester Guardian*, in a second attempt on 17 June, also found something favourable to mix with its criticism:

> The main part of the Labour document ... was not a turning of the back on 'European unity' but a critical examination of the half-baked ideas that are now running among the federal enthusiasts ... the document seems tragically to encourage some British myths—the impertinence of foreign interference with our sacred egoism, whether State, private capitalist, or trade union; the enviousness of less happy lands of our 'full employment' and 'planning'.

On the same day, 17 June, *The Economist* also found commendation to mix with its criticism. Under the title 'Socialism *Contra Mundum*' it said:

> To call it isolationist is nonsense. ... What the document does—surely very sensibly—is to put its weight behind the confederal principle as opposed to the federal principle of association. ... In the last analysis the indignation which the Labour Party's document has aroused is due to its outstanding lack of modesty. No party and no nation know all the answers. Planners who have no plan, and progressives who wish to avoid change, should not feel surprised if the world rejects with indignation the assumption that their own infallibility must be the starting point for co-operation among nations.

The editor was untypically modest in refraining from claiming that whereas no party and no nation had all the answers, *The Economist* did.

THE WHITE PAPER—CMD. 7970

The *Financial Times* treated *European Unity* simply as a news item. It did, on 14 June, comment on the White Paper containing the exchanges with Paris leading up to the Attlee government's decision to excuse itself from participation. It found its previous comments justified. It concluded that the UK's refusal to make the commitment requested by the French was right. 'In spite of the obvious danger that this attitude invites the accusation that Britain is once again "dragging its feet" most observers here support the British Government.' The paper still suspected that what the Schuman Plan was really about was the creation of a cartel to deal with the steel surplus. 'In spite of the French protests to the contrary, this has led many people to suspect that the scheme would, in fact, turn into a new cartel.'

The Times of 14 June was now confident again in its support of the Foreign Office:

The documents, which were published yesterday, give no evidence of any reluctance by the Government to go forward with France—and Germany—in this enterprise. They show that the Government had good and entirely honest reasons for not accepting the procedure suggested by the French for negotiating a treaty on coal and steel. . . . The British Government do not simply say that they will not accept a supra-national authority for coal and steel until the project has been thrashed out in discussion; they also say, or at least imply, that they are not ready to regard a supra-national authority as the right or practical solution . . .

In other words, though *The Times* does not say this, the government had been thoroughly dishonest in pretending that it might go along with a supranational solution to the problems the Schuman Plan intended to address. Even now, it was only *implying* its distrust of a supranational solution. It is astonishing that *The Times* still felt it possible to suggest that there was no 'reluctance'.

By 16 June the editor of the *Manchester Guardian* was almost in tears:

It is most unfortunate that the British Government's attitude towards the Schuman Plan should be misunderstood by everybody outside this country. The quite substantial grounds for caution in taking the French gift-horse at its face value have been quite lost in the pother about the Labour Party Executive's document of 'European Unity'. . . . Mr Dalton must be tethered to a post in one of his National Parks and kept strictly out of European affairs. . . . We must produce our alternative plan quickly.

The *Manchester Guardian* seemed unaware of Attlee's statement in the House of Commons on 13 June that the UK was not intending to put forward any alternative plans at that time.

The *Daily Express* was, as ever, robust, particularly with the USA. On 17 June it showed its contempt for American pressure. 'If the Americans feel that Britain's rejection of the plan gives them a just grievance, they can do something better than scold the British Government. . . . They can . . . integrate the coal and steel industries of the United States in the project which M. Schuman has presented and Mr Acheson has blessed.' If there were any faint hearts who feared that outraging the Americans would lead to a loss of Marshall Aid, the *Daily Express* had a message for them. On 22 June it wrote: 'Britain has never been in need of the Marshall dollars and can do very well without them now. She can, and she should, rely on the inherent strength of her own trading position with no dollars save those she can earn.' It was true that, whatever the UK's past need for Marshall Aid, it was now diminishing. The current account of the balance of payments had been improving following the devaluation of September 1949. Paul Hoffman was discovering that the UK required a smaller allocation than he had originally estimated.[9] Marshall Aid to Britain ceased as from 1 January 1951.

THE HOUSE OF COMMONS DEBATE

The next opportunity for comment came with the Conservative–Liberal motion put down for debate in the House of Commons on 26 and 27 June. *The Times* gave its view on 22 June. 'The analogy of the Netherlands is misleading for the Dutch are frankly prepared to accept a federal solution if, in the case of coal and steel, it can be shown to be practicable.' *The Economist* on 24 June put the other point of view. 'It would be an act of statesmanship to accept the motion and to bring to an end the self-imposed isolation in which Britain stands ingloriously today.'

By 26 June the *Manchester Guardian* had recovered the courage of its unfortunate convictions.

Everybody wishes that the Government had played its cards better and had not put itself in the wrong with European and American opinion. But all the same it is hardly contested that the Government was right in its reluctance to accept blindly the terms of the French invitation—a commitment in advance to an extremely vague proposition. . . . The Conservative–Liberal motion would have us make a 'gesture' by dropping our former objections and joining in the negotiations on the same terms as Holland. . . . The idea has its attractions since it so happily makes the best of both worlds. But it contains an element of danger. If we entered the negotiations and they broke down it is quite certain that the odium of failure would fall on us. . . . The Government therefore deserves support if it is able in the debate to prove that its aim is not obstructive, that it has constructive proposals, that it is not hostile to European integration and is prepared to join in a scheme that is not restrictive.

The *Manchester Guardian*, like the Foreign Office, was more consumed with the risks of failure than with the opportunities for success. Moreover, it rapidly forgot all those matters which the government

[9] *Financial Times*, 30 May 1950.

should be able to prove if it was to deserve support. It could, of course, prove none of them.

In its advice to the debaters on 26 June, the *Financial Times* thought it should draw their attention to all the formidable difficulties yet to be solved, as well as assuring them that all this talk about the sovereignty of the High Authority was really nonsense, though it is less clear whether the paper thought that fact good or bad. It did not deny that, even though the difficulties might lead to failure, it might, as a matter of political judgement, be better to fail with the Six than to enjoy their failure from outside.

[T]he protagonists seem to have overlooked the point that if the economic mechanism, which they tend to treat as a subsidiary issue, does not in fact function successfully, then the final result may well be worse than useless. If the individual participants find that the economic objectives they are trying to foster are at cross purposes with the decisions of the proposed European authority, what will have been created will be simply a further source of international bickering. There is little doubt that the surrender of a portion of their sovereignty to the authority—if they do, indeed, make this surrender—will still leave them with sufficient power to pursue their own separate ways if they are determined to do so. . . . Neither of these two basic industries can be organised in isolation from the other sectors of the economy that they serve. And the OEEC's attempts to co-ordinate European investment have shown clearly that even if the will is there, the administrative mechanism for joint planning of production on any useful scale, is lacking. . . . The Schuman Plan . . . bristles with potential difficulties of an economic kind, some of which might well provide the means of exacerbating existing conflicts among the participating nations. . . . A good argument could perhaps be made out in favour of our association with even a false start towards the ideal of European unity so that on a future, more auspicious, occasion there will be no suggestion that a tradition of British isolation can be taken for granted. But we ought in that case to have no illusion about our real motives. On purely economic grounds, the case for British participation in the Schuman Plan has still to be made out.

The *Financial Times*, which had been so reticent earlier, was now losing no opportunity to restate its firm view. It was all very difficult and it was impossible to make up one's mind because no one yet knew what it was all about.

If any clear impression is left at all it is that the whole scheme is still fatally hampered by the vagueness of its central idea and by the failure of anyone to look with any degree of realism at the kind of decisions that would have to be taken by a Common Authority. . . . What is more disappointing . . . is that the authors of the plan themselves are also apparently shying away from the essential difficulties. Yesterday's summary of the working document submitted by the French to the Six-Power conference in Paris last week is largely a sketch of the Authority itself. . . . But the passage which outlines the objectives of the Authority, in the economic sphere, is still the vaguest of all. . . . Essentially the difficulty of passing a judgement on the Schuman Plan remains what it was . . . we still do not know what the Schuman Plan contemplates in practice.

On 29 June the *Manchester Guardian* delivered its verdict on the House of Commons debate:

The debate has done no harm, for it has clarified a good many views, and not least those of the Government. It is useful for it to be reminded that, while most people are sceptical about submitting our fortunes to scratch 'supra-national' authorities, they do care a good deal about our strengthening our European ties and about the maintenance of British leadership in all forms of European co-operation. But equally they will not agree to the subordination of our Commonwealth and American ties to any European schemes. The present events in the Pacific [the Korean war] are reminder enough of the width of our vital interests.

The *Manchester Guardian* might well care about 'strengthening our European ties and about the maintenance of British leadership in all forms of European co-operation'. Unfortunately, under Foreign Office guidance, it had supported a course of action that had seriously weakened Britain's European ties and which had undermined any possibility of British leadership in European co-operation.

13

The Road to Association

The announcement of the Schuman Plan released a valve. A debate had been in progress in Europe for months following the American recession of 1948–9. The problem under consideration was how to insulate Europe against the consequences of a further American downturn. Now the ideas generated by the debate were converted into specific proposals and issued forth from the Netherlands, from Italy and, once more, from France. All were based on some form of European economic integration. All were concerned to regulate the degree and timing of integration with a view to the preservation of employment. All were submitted for discussion at the OEEC, being in this respect distinct from the Schuman Plan which, reflecting Monnet's distaste for inter-governmental organizations, had ignored the OEEC.

Dirk Stikker, Netherlands Foreign Minister, was the first to take the stage. He proposed for discussion in the OEEC the idea of an integrated European market planned to ensure that the current policy of trade liberalization did not result in mass unemployment. He was building on the Dutch reaction to the French proposals of November 1949. His Plan, first circulated informally at the beginning of June 1950, was formally announced under the title 'Plan of Action' on 15 June, five days before the opening in Paris of the Schuman Plan negotiations. It had already been agreed in the OEEC that, by the time the EPU came into effect, members of the OEEC would free 60 per cent of their private account trade with one another from quantitative restrictions (QRs). The achievement of this was anticipated for the summer of 1950. The Council of the OEEC was charged with deciding what further progress could be undertaken during 1950, the objective being to raise this percentage to 75 per cent by the end of the year. The 75 per cent was already a compromise suggested by Robert Marjolin, Secretary-General of the OEEC. It compared with the ECA's wish that

Western European trade should be entirely liberalized by the end of 1950. Stikker was of the opinion that 75 per cent was as far as it was politically possible to go by current methods. His idea was that, from the 75 per cent point on, further integration should be planned industry by industry. Industries would be selected in accordance with their expected contribution to Europe's viability. In the selected industries, both QRs and tariffs inhibiting trade within the OEEC would be removed. The process would begin with the basic industries and agriculture, and also those processing industries whose products played an important part in international trade both intra-European and intercontinental.

In a speech at Oslo on 8 June 1950, Stikker said:

There is no doubt that the removal of trade barriers is essential for the eventual well-being of Western Europe as a whole . . . but I consider that right now attention should be paid to the other side of the picture: the harmful consequences which any sudden and immediate abolition of barriers in itself may in some cases carry with it for certain members of the European family. As a result of a freer flow of goods deficits in their balance of payment might increase, some local industries might be seriously affected and unemployment might rear its ugly head again. Thus the creation of one European free-trade-area, although indispensable in the end can in itself, without adequate safeguard against adverse effects in countries with vulnerable economies, obviously not be regarded as an immediate solution . . .

He went on to insist that unemployment was a European problem, not just a problem for some national governments:

No longer can the internal developments in the political, economic and social fields within the frontier of each separate country be considered as a matter of concern for that nation alone . . .

All of us take the most energetic action, for instance, to fight unemployment within our own countries. But what common effort do we make to help solve the same problem in our neighbour's territory? How many of us are ready to admit that the two million unemployed in Western Germany and the two million more in Italy are not a national problem for those countries alone, but are also our joint European problem? . . .

At the moment we are living in a period of relative prosperity; in most of our countries there exists full employment and a high level of demand and production. But let us not forget that . . . the existing situation is a momentary one.[1]

---

[1] FO 371/87161.

In addition to integration sector by sector, Stikker proposed the creation of a European Integration Fund, financed by contributions from the members of the OEEC. The Fund would grant loans to countries which suffered dislocation as a result of sectoral integration. These loans would be used to modernize affected industries, to foster new investment, or to finance the re-education of displaced workers. Stikker also considered that it would be necessary for the participating countries to enter into consultation on budget policy and pointed out that the Integration Fund could contribute to economic stability if its investments were accelerated in times of declining economic activity.

Stikker implied that his plan represented the application to other industries of much the same procedure as Schuman intended for the coal and steel industries. There were, however, differences of approach. Both contemplated measures of financial compensation; but, whereas the Schuman Plan envisaged integration of two industries under the guidance of a specially constituted High Authority, the emphasis in Stikker's proposals was rather on giving play to the forces of free competition on a progressive industry by industry basis. In the upshot this difference in approach might not have amounted to much. What did seem clear was that, in view of its prospective scope, the compensation requirements to which Stikker's Plan of Action gave rise would probably be rather large.

Whatever else was said about the Stikker Plan, the description *laissez-faire* so often attributed to continental ideas by British socialists would have been entirely inappropriate. *The Economist* was surprisingly warm about the Plan. 'The Stikker Plan', it said, 'may offer some hope of breaking the age-old deadlock between national self-interest and international integration.' According to *The Economist*, it provided 'a framework within which Britain could, if it wished, show that it supported international expansion as ardently as it now advocates national planning and employment policies'.[2]

Stikker's ideas did not have a similarly warm welcome in official circles in London. He had realized that his Plan would create difficulties for the UK because, in the selected sectors, it involved the total abolition of tariffs between the member countries of the OEEC and was therefore inconsistent with imperial preference. The Dutch made clear privately to the British government their understanding of the difficulties this might cause and their readiness to find solutions:

[2] *The Economist,* 24 June 1950.

Spierenburg told Roll yesterday that although the references to tariffs in the Stikker paper appear to involve complete abolition in selected sectors of industry this was not to be taken literally. In particular, the Dutch were very conscious of our problem regarding Imperial Preference and they would be quite prepared to consider modifying their proposals in such a way as to remove any difficulties that our co-operation in them might encounter owing to the existence of Imperial Preference.[3]

British objections to the Stikker Plan followed well-worn paths. The proposals were not consistent with the aim of achieving a multilateral world trading system. The abolition of tariffs was inconsistent with imperial preference. Any reduction in tariffs would have to be made on a non-discriminatory, not simply an OEEC, basis. No government would wish to reduce tariffs unless in return for compensatory reductions by other countries. There was no provision in the General Agreement on Tariffs and Trade (GATT) for a partial customs union such as would be created by an industry by industry approach to liberalization. The assessment of contributions to and claims on the European Integration Fund would be extremely complex. If it were large enough to be of any use, it would constitute a heavy tax on the resources of each member country. Such a Fund would represent a step towards a federal budget.[4]

The only question for London was how to be dismissive courteously, to scotch the Plan but not make more enemies.[5] The international reaction to Britain's refusal to participate in the Schuman Plan had already provided evidence that sensitivity was required if continental initiatives were to be rejected. Fortunately for the Attlee government, other governments too had their doubts. Other continental countries were beginning to contemplate other forms of regulation which they thought might be of advantage to their industries. Their ideas did not, however, correspond with Stikker's ideas. Giuseppe Pella, Italian Minister of the Treasury, politely commended the Stikker proposals, but he insisted that the difficulties of implementing them would be formidable. Most countries lacked sufficient control over private investment to carry them out. Integration on the lines of the Schuman Plan might be feasible for a few basic industries but, without a vast apparatus of official control,

---

[3] FO 371/87161, telegram from OEEC UK Delegation to Foreign Office, 18 June 1950. Spierenburg was speaking to Eric Roll, later Lord Roll of Ipsden.

[4] FO 371/87161.

[5] A letter from G. J. MacMahon, Board of Trade, to Alan Hitchman, Treasury, 12 June 1950, says in part: 'We do not think the Stikker proposals should be accepted but if they cannot be scotched in Paris the aim must be, I suppose, to adopt a procedure which will take them out of the limelight for as long as possible': FO 371/87161.

the same ideas could not be applied to other industries which produced a wide range of products in a multiplicity of small establishments.

Instead, Pella revealed a set of ideas to take account of what he considered was Italy's poor factor endowment.[6] This required permanent compensation. Europe, he argued, needed an expanding economy, an increase in her exports to the dollar area, and a larger free market for her industries, conducing to specialization and lower prices. He therefore suggested that the OEEC should consider the establishment in Europe of a preferential tariff zone. The members of the OEEC would enter into multilateral tariff negotiations to reduce their tariffs against each other as much as possible. Progress towards the abolition of QRs would be facilitated and this, in its turn, would require the elimination of dual pricing and other discriminatory measures, including those applied to invisible trade. Payments within the group would have to be freed for a prolonged period and, to achieve this, American aid would be required. In place of Stikker's European Integration Fund, Pella proposed a European Investment Fund. F. C. Everson, of the Foreign Office, commented acidly, that the Pella plan 'also rides the usual Italian hobby horses such as the need for aid after 1952,[7] for substantial investment in the South and centre of Italy, and for a greater flow of migration from over-populated European countries'. The Board of Trade added, 'We are doing our best to discourage "mendicant mentality" in OEEC.'[8] Provided it received sufficient aid, Italy, apparently, would be prepared to contemplate freer trade. Nevertheless, the Pella proposals had for the UK one advantage as compared with Stikker. As there was to be a low tariff rather than no tariff, it did not rule out the possible continuance of imperial preference though, inevitably, it would reduce the margin of preference. Indeed ministers were advised that the Stikker Plan would be more acceptable if it had spoken of a low tariff rather than no tariff. The advice emphasized that ministers should not, however, suggest the change to their Dutch colleagues. There were too many other objections to Stikker.

Maurice Petsche, France's Minister of Finance, was a critic of the Schuman Plan. He also disliked both the Dutch and Italian initiatives. He therefore made his own diversionary contribution to the debate in the OEEC by reverting to the French proposals of November 1949 and

[6] FO 371/87161.   [7] When Marshall Aid was planned to end.
[8] FO 371/87161.

proposing a European Investment Bank with access to private capital. But, in London, even the Petsche proposal was suspected of federalism. Indeed British officials seemed incapable of freeing their minds of an obsession with federalism. Even the independent-minded Edmund Hall-Patch commented that 'the Stikker, Pella and Petsche plans were economic manifestations of this [federal] tendency, and would undoubtedly, if realized, constitute steps toward federation'.[9]

DISCOMFORT IN LONDON

The Schuman Plan was thus proposed and negotiated within the context of much other similar thinking. It was unique in advocating regulation of an industrial sector through a High Authority but the idea of a regulated rather than unregulated integration had become popular. It was unique also in the contribution it made towards the objective of Franco-German *rapprochement*. But, as a warning to the Attlee government, ideas that might involve the exclusion of the UK from the construction of Europe were not being rejected on that ground alone.

With France, Italy, and the Netherlands in the field with ideas for the construction of Europe, it became even more embarrassing that Britain had only questions to raise and criticisms to utter, but nothing to propose. Bevin and Hall-Patch were getting bored with the plaintive song that was all that was ever audible in London. On 29 June E. A. Berthoud, of the Foreign Office, reported to his colleague Sir Roger Makins on discussions on what guidance should be submitted to ministers on the attitude they should take at forthcoming OEEC meetings in Paris at which the various plans submitted to it were to be discussed:

Sir E. Hall-Patch laid lurid stress on the difficulties which would arise in Paris if we were wholly negative.... He doubted whether O.E.E.C. would survive. Without going quite so far, I said that the Secretary of State was beginning to think that it was time we took some initiative in the European economic field, or anyhow that we should not continue to be only destructive.[10]

The government might have noticed that, compared with these other plans, Schuman had considerable advantages from the point of view of the UK. It did not impact in any serious way on imperial preference.

---

[9] T 232/194. Meeting at the Treasury, 14 July 1950.   [10] FO 371/87161.

In so far as it impacted at all, arrangements could no doubt have been made to accommodate it.[11] It was arguable that, as a partial customs union, the proposal to eliminate customs tariffs on coal and steel between member countries was inconsistent with the most favoured nation provisions of the GATT and other international treaties. But it would clearly be much easier to secure agreement to the necessary derogations, notably from the USA, for a partial customs union of this limited character than for that proposed by Stikker. And although it was to raise a levy on coal and steel production so that it did not depend on government subsidies, at any rate, unlike Stikker, it did not aim to establish a European Integration Fund which would have had to be massive to perform the responsibilities that Stikker wished to place upon it.

As it turned out, there were found to be at least two problems with extending regulated integration to industries other than coal and steel. The first was that such an extension was not favoured by the German government and, after the Schuman Plan and the acceptance of German rearmament, there was no longer sufficient political benefit accruing to the Federal Republic to persuade it to abandon its point of view. Erhard preferred liberalization. Indeed, he himself preferred liberalization to the Schuman Plan.[12] By October 1950 the Federal German government was faced with protests that the speed with which it was decontrolling trade was wrecking the EPU because it was leading to large deficits in the German current account.[13] The second problem was the impossibility of agreeing to which industry, other than agriculture, sectoral integration could next move. As experience within the EEC was to show, even agricultural integration would encounter serious political difficulties. Sectoral integration appeared to be an attractive idea. Experience was that differences in national interest obstructed implementation whatever acceptance the idea had in principle. The British government had relied on these differences of national interest to ensure

[11] In a memorandum to the Cabinet dated 1 July 1950, the Secretary of State for Commonwealth Relations referred to the preferences accorded by the UK to imports of pig-iron from India and semi-finished and finished steel from Canada: *DBPO* 130. Duncan Burn, in his submission to Edwin Plowden on 21 June 1950, added his own view that 'The issue of Imperial Preference is not raised seriously by the Schuman Plan': T 229/749.

[12] Erhard detected in the ECSC Treaty the conflicting principles of *dirigisme* and free competition. His object became to support the latter principle against the former: Haas 129. Erhard opposed a wider common market equipped with supranational institutions: Haas 135.

[13] Milward (1984) 431.

breakdown of continental initiatives. It failed to notice that coal and steel might just be the exception, or the increasing evidence of continental readiness to go ahead without Britain if a project in which interests were sufficiently at one could at last be identified.

COULD THE OEEC SURVIVE THE SCHUMAN PLAN?

The British government was becoming worried about the future of the intergovernmental OEEC upon which it had based so much of its European economic policy. The OEEC appeared threatened by the Schuman Plan. In the view of Edmund Hall-Patch, as we noted above, it appeared threatened by the negative British reaction to the other ideas emerging in Europe. On 1 July Eric Roll had a conversation with Robert Marjolin. Marjolin was a close friend of Jean Monnet and had been his principal aide. Now he too, and not just the British government, had territory to defend in his role as Secretary-General of the OEEC. As we have seen, Marjolin was no federalist but he could not but be aware of the prevalence of federalist ideas in Europe, whatever federalism in practice turned out to mean. He wanted the federalist drive to be diverted from the economic sphere to the political, from his patch to that of the politicians.

M. Marjolin expressed to me his deep disquiet about present French policy and in particular about the Schuman Plan. He thought that to apply the principle of federation in the economic field first, and especially to so important a sector as coal and steel, was bound to fail in practice, whatever the public results. In any case, if the French plans prevailed, the end of OEEC was in sight. . . . In expanding on this thesis, M. Marjolin said that we had to bear in mind the almost universal despair of France, and of many Continental countries, of the European future. There was a serious lack of confidence and all the responsible statesmen in France were desperately looking for some wider unity in which to merge themselves. He believed that this was a strong tendency also in Holland and to some extent in Belgium and Italy, and accounted for the frantic search for devices in the economic sphere, e.g. the Stikker proposals and the Pella paper. He also said that as far as France was concerned some form of union with Germany seemed the best and, indeed, the only major immediate step forward, particularly in view of the great difficulty which the French would experience if they had to engage in a considerable new defence effort. He thought, therefore, that the movement towards federation should not be discouraged but should be directed into the political and away from the economic sphere so as to avoid serious divergence with us [i.e. the U.K.], as well as with the growing cooperation in the economic field with the Americans. . . . In this latter context, M. Marjolin feared that the Americans who had so light-heartedly given vociferous approval to the Schuman Plan, had not yet appreciated that it was leading to a preferential discriminatory system in Europe which ran counter to the ideas of world multilateralism espoused by the Americans. . . . At the end I asked M. Marjolin why he thought M. Monnet had espoused the federal principle. M. Marjolin said he was not at all sure that M. Monnet had, in fact, espoused the federal principle; he had espoused a new idea; he probably did not care what the consequences were.[14]

NO COMMONWEALTH VETO

How much of a problem was the Commonwealth? In the debate in the House of Commons on the Schuman Plan on 26 June 1950, Anthony Eden was able to quote Robert Menzies, the Australian Prime Minister, as saying: 'a peaceful and prosperous Europe would be a godsend to British people the world over. I, for one, am not, therefore, hostile to the basic idea of European union, but friendly to it and hopeful for it.'[15] Kim Mackay, MP, was an enthusiastic 'European' and a prominent member of the Consultative Assembly of the Council of Europe. He was an Australian by origin which gave him experience of a federal constitution and, perhaps, sharpened his insight into Commonwealth affairs. He said of himself, 'I have spent two-thirds of my life in the Commonwealth and only one-third in Great Britain.' As a federalist he was frequently in conflict with British policy though he did make efforts, naturally unavailing, to find accommodation with the Foreign Office on projects that could be regarded as specific or functional rather than constitutional. He declared his faith firmly. '[T]here is really no great hope for an improved standard of living for the people of this country except in so far as we take part in an economic integration of Europe.'[16] Mackay questioned the argument that the UK could not integrate with Europe because of responsibilities to the Commonwealth.

Great Britain has more investments outside the Commonwealth than she has inside the Commonwealth. She has a greater trade outside the Commonwealth than inside. The Commonwealth as a whole cannot sell its raw materials inside the Commonwealth. . . . Therefore, the Commonwealth as an entity is not self-sufficient, but there is no real conflict in the interests of the United Kingdom

---

[14] T 229/750.   [15] HC Debs. 26 June 1950, col. 1912.
[16] HC Debs. 27 June 1950, cols. 2122–3.

and the other members of the British Commonwealth and Western Europe. . . . No one has ever suggested any Western Europe integration which should develop otherwise than with the Commonwealth coming in.[17]

He continued by quoting a resolution of the General Affairs Committee of the Council of Europe passed in December 1949:

That the Committee on General Affairs expresses its unanimous wish that the President of the Assembly should establish contact with the British Government to request that it arrange for informal talks to take place between representatives of the countries in the British Commonwealth and representatives of the Council of Europe with a view to seeing how the Commonwealth can co-operate in the political and economic field with the Council of Europe.[18]

Despite Mackay's imaginative analyses and proposals, and Menzies' typically friendly words, there was no single Commonwealth attitude to British participation in European economic integration. Some Commonwealth countries had grave doubts about a European customs union and how UK membership of it could be made consistent with their interests. They had their preferences and change was risky. They certainly had doubts about UK participation in a scheme, such as the Schuman Plan, involving supranational authorities with powers that could bind governments and about any proposal to incorporate Britain in a European federation. Nevertheless there was clearly concern in a number of Commonwealth countries such as Canada, Australia, and South Africa about the wisdom of the UK's decision not to participate in the Schuman negotiations.[19] The Schuman Plan was not a European customs union, Commonwealth interests might well not be prejudiced by British participation in it, and, in any case, how could one know if problems were insurmountable except in the course of negotiations.

WATCHING PARIS

Under the nervous eyes of the Foreign Office, the negotiations in Paris progressed. For those sceptical about French ability to carry through any project, it was encouraging that the Bidault government collapsed on 24 June 1950 four days after the commencement of the Schuman

---

[17] HC Debs. 27 June 1950, cols. 2124–5.   [18] Ibid., col. 2125.
[19] Memorandum by Secretary of State for Commonwealth Relations, 1 July 1950, *DBPO* 130 and Annex B.

Plan negotiating conference.[20] Forming a new government proved difficult and time-consuming even though there was a new crisis in the outbreak of the Korean War on the very day the Bidault government fell. So far as the British government was concerned, there was nothing unexpected in the irresponsibility then demonstrated in political circles in Paris. The attitude to these events in London is illustrated by an exchange of telegrams between Bevin and Oliver Harvey, British Ambassador to Paris. Harvey advised Bevin: 'This prolonged crisis at this critical moment in international affairs is undoubtedly irritating. But it should not be taken too tragically, that is the way French democracy functions, and this reshuffling of politicians has little real effect on the workings of the French state.'[21]

Bevin considered Harvey too optimistic. 'That at such a decisive moment France should be without a Government is a tragedy not only for France herself but also for her associates.' According to Sir William Strang, Bevin then continued by pouring out all the grievances, and the sense of ingratitude, to which the Schuman Plan had given rise in his mind and which he could not forget:

The Secretary of State cannot forget that since the days of the Treaty of Dunkerque he has urged upon our Parliament and people the need for close association and solidarity between ourselves and France and has called upon them to enter into commitments to France in the series of international instruments to which both countries are parties. It would be disastrous if our public should come to think that the confidence which we have reposed in the French has been misplaced.[22]

Harvey's assessment was to be confirmed when Schuman survived as Foreign Minister and the Schuman Plan negotiating conference continued little disturbed.

Edmund Hall-Patch reported on a meeting with Bevin at the London Clinic on 30 June, at a time when there was no French government and dissensions appeared to be emerging among the Six, with Benelux countries leading the criticism. Bevin clearly saw his opportunity coming. The French would see that their conditions 'were unacceptable, not only to us, but to others'. Schuman might be 'seeking a way out of the

---

[20] The successor government, that of M. H. Queuille, was formed on 1 July and was defeated on 4 July. A government was then successfully formed by René Pleven on 11 July. Schuman remained Foreign Minister throughout.

[21] *DBPO* 36 n.   [22] *DBPO* 136 and 136 n.

impasse'. Therefore, with due reservations and great care because he did not wish to be accused by the French of sabotaging the Schuman proposals, Bevin might be prepared to act to rescue the French from the consequences of their follies: 'If M. Schuman were prepared to drop his impossible conditions, and so make negotiation possible, but was in such a difficult position that he could not say so openly, Mr Bevin might be prepared to help him out by making suggestions from our side.'[23]

This was as serious a misreading of the situation as that of Makins the previous month. Edwin Plowden informed a US Embassy official on 30 June:

It might be that the French and the Germans would be successful in coming to an agreement about a supra-national authority, in which case we would probably hope to become associated with it in some way, while not becoming members of it. On the other hand, we recognized that if they were unable to come to any agreement the time would probably then be propitious for us to put forward our suggestions which we, of course, realize would be modified in the course of discussion.[24]

When, on 25 July 1950, Schuman announced that the Six agreed on all major issues, the Economic Policy Committee of the Cabinet, on Bevin's recommendation, decided to await approval by the French Assembly and then negotiate association.[25] There was still some comfort to be found in the hope or expectation that the French National Assembly would reject the treaty. Bevin informed the Economic Policy Committee that the accord 'might well fail to obtain the approval [of the National Assembly] even when it had been agreed between the parties to the Paris discussions'.[26] Roger Makins retained similar hopes or expectations. On 3 August he minuted: 'it remains to be seen whether the Treaty will in fact be ratified when it goes to the French Parliament.'[27] Macmillan also thought that when the French Parliament and people realized that the agreement meant going in without Britain, they might shrink from handing their rather weak and largely obsolescent industry to German control.[28] The desperate assumption that the French National Assembly would rescue British foreign policy was to be disappointed.

[23] *DBPO* 124. Cripps showed a similar desire to 'help' in a letter of 1 July explaining his attitude to Bevin: *DBPO* 126. See Ch. 11 above.
[24] *DBPO* 125.   [25] Young (1984) 164.
[26] *DBPO* 150.   [27] *DBPO* 151 n.   [28] Macmillan 204.

FEDERALISM REVISITED

It was considered in London that the Schuman Plan required a re-
appraisal by the FG Committee of the phenomenon of European federalism, and its implications for the UK. The result was presented in a
joint Foreign Office/Treasury paper dated 19 July 1950.[29] The exposi-
tion and analysis in the paper did not lead to any modification of British
policy. The opening section of the paper was drafted by Sir Roger
Makins. It reads:

There is in Western Europe at the present time a movement of opinion in
favour of forms of association in the economic and political spheres having
federal implications. The reasons for this movement are complex. The feeling
of disillusion with the efficacy of governments and of inter-governmental action; a belief, derived partly from occupation by the enemy and the consequent
national divisions, in the weakness of the national unity and the desire for some
wider association or loyalty; a desire to get away from the disagreeable consequences of existing policies, such as liberalization, and, in the case of France,
the progressive relaxation of allied controls in Germany; a corresponding feeling among the defeated countries that the federal path offers the fastest way
back to equality of status; a genuine feeling for European union and solidarity
as an intellectual concept; and, finally, on a lower plane, a feeling that this is
what the Americans want. These tendencies have been accentuated by the fears
aroused by the outbreak of the Far Eastern crisis. The corollary of this movement has been a turning away from the inter-governmental methods of co-
operation which have been strongly favoured by the United Kingdom, and
which find their outstanding expression in the OEEC.
    2. The principal manifestation of this trend at the moment is the Schuman
Plan.[30]

In the same paper, the Committee restated Britain's economic policy:

[O]ur economic policy is to work towards multilateralisation of our trade with
the whole world through the medium of the Havana Charter and the GATT and
by the elimination of quantitative restrictions on imports from all countries
from which we could afford to buy more freely; and we should like the European countries to adapt any schemes for integration to fit into these same
policies and the principles of inter-governmental co-operation which are inherent in them.[31]

---

[29] T 232/194; *DBPO* 144. The paper was entitled *Consequences of Contemporary
Movements in Western Europe towards Forms of European Integration having Federal
Implications.*
[30] The reference to the Far Eastern crisis is to the Korean War.
[31] The meeting was held on 14 July 1950.

Officials derived comfort from the endless reiteration of multilateralism as British policy when their own practice was quite different. It was particularly comforting to discover that intergovernmental forms of organization, which gave Britain a veto, were inherent in multilateralism. The Schuman Plan failed on two key counts, as a step to federalism and as a move away from multilateralism towards economic regionalism.

It was the interpretation of the Schuman Plan as a step to federalism that principally inhibited constructive thought about it in Whitehall. Such an interpretation was encouraged by the wording of the Schuman announcement and by American support for it. Yet it was perfectly possible to regard the Schuman Plan as functionalist rather than federalist and at the acceptable end of the functionalist spectrum. In Whitehall, fear of federalist tendencies in Europe had become obsessive and almost everything that was proposed in Europe other than on an intergovernmental basis was suspected of the disease of incipient federalism. We have already seen that the Petsche proposal for a European Investment Bank was so regarded.

Richard Crossman, summing up as a back-bencher on the government side in the House of Commons debate on the Schuman Plan, was well in line with official thinking when he declared: 'The amount of enthusiasm for federal union in any country is a measure of its defeatism and of its feeling of inability to measure up to its own problems.'[32] There was some truth in this. Dickinson had pointed to the alleged inability of European governments to discharge the responsibilities of sovereignty. Makins wrote of disillusion with the efficacy of governments. The great problem according to Dickinson, Crossman, and Makins was about the efficacy of government. But the British government, in 1950, despite frequent applications for financial help from the USA, considered itself very efficacious. It saw no reason to abandon what it had in search of speculative solutions for problems that it thought it had not encountered. The strength of European federalist sentiment *has* varied with the degree of self-confidence felt by the individual states of Western Europe in their ability to manage their future successfully without the abandonment of national sovereignty. So far, Crossman was raising a real and worrying issue.

But Crossman allowed himself to be misled by the attraction of a clever sentence. He was guilty of a considerable over-simplification. European federalist sentiment has not been solely a phenomenon of the

[32] HC Debs. 26 June 1950, col. 2039.

early post-war period. It has survived the debates and controversies of that period. It has survived the recovery of the European economies and of European self-confidence. It has never been quite clear what European federalism means to its supporters or how far it should be taken as replicating the American model. But, whatever it means, it has survived as a trend in European political thought. Within Western Europe, it has been encouraged by the sense that this cradle of civilization has lost status as compared with the two superpowers. Many Germans have seen, and continue to see, European federation as a necessary protection against an over-mighty Germany.

For British governments, European federalism was a problem but not one to which there appeared to be any answer. The federalistic tendencies emerging in Europe were disliked but there was, apparently, little that the UK could do about it. The Continent could not be denied it if that was what the continental peoples actually wanted. It would be better if they could be dissuaded from an adventure likely to turn out badly. It would, however, be counter-productive if the UK was too active in the cause of dissuasion. Life might dissuade even if British diplomacy was too diplomatic to make the effort. Britain could not influence continental developments unless it was prepared to become engaged in the European future. If it was committed to Europe it could hope to influence the structure of Europe, but not otherwise. In 1950 the UK did not intend to take part in any form of European economic integration which endangered imperial preference and its relations with the Commonwealth. The question for the UK was not whether it would participate but simply whether it would look on such developments benignly or seek to undermine them. The conclusion was that the right attitude was one of benevolence provided that they did not, by high protective tariffs or otherwise, damage British interests.

This last proviso reflected an undercurrent of feeling in Whitehall that the continentals were really out to damage the UK. It led to a riposte from Robert Hall:

I think it is quite likely that a high preferential tariff system on the Continent would adversely affect our interests. But it is a great deal less certain that an integrated system would do so. If the main result of this system were to strengthen the direct competition with our own exports, it would probably be damaging to us. But in general it is a fallacy to suppose that we are likely to be poorer because our neighbours get richer. Both on general economic grounds, and on historical evidence, one is more likely to prosper in a prosperous world than in a poverty stricken world. And, in any case, we could not possibly even hint publicly at objecting to anything designed to make other countries more efficient.[33]

Britain could not prevent European federation even if it tried and that, perhaps, was the most powerful reason for not trying. As was said in the paper *Consequences of Contemporary Movements in Western Europe towards Forms of European Integration having Federal Implications:*

It would be a heavy political responsibility for the United Kingdom to seek to prevent forms of closer association which were generally desired by other Western European countries, simply on the ground that we ourselves, in view of our world wide obligations and responsibilities, could not participate in them. Even if we wished to shoulder this responsibility, it is doubtful whether we would have the power to prevent the development of such forms of association.[34]

There was always a chance that the Europeans themselves would see the error of their ways and turn aside from so improbable an escapade. Denis Healey, International Secretary of the Labour Party, reported to Ernest Davies, Parliamentary Under-Secretary of State at the Foreign Office, that, at a Socialist Conference in London in October 1950, he had been told by Spaak and Mollet that they had been 'frightened at [the UK's] present policy of putting no obstacle in the way of partial federation. Both Spaak and Mollet made it quite clear that they would consider federation without Britain disastrous and were therefore most anxious to find a way whereby we can remain a full participant in the Council of Europe.'[35]

Such reports were heartening to the Foreign Office. They confirmed it in its continuing conviction, despite the evidence, that Europe could get nowhere without Britain which could therefore stultify all European development by refusing to participate. But, even if Healey's report reflected accurately the sentiments of Spaak and Mollet, any influence exercised by British abstention from European projects was an expiring asset. If the UK was not going to take part it could hardly expect, in the long run, to exert influence against federal structures. Its influence would expire more rapidly because of Britain's failure to participate in the Schuman Plan. Once the continentals found how comfortably they could work together without Britain, they would place far less value on British participation and would fear British absence far less. Britain

[33] T 232/194, R. L. Hall, 19 July 1950.   [34] T 232/194.

[35] Minute from Davies to Bevin, 27 Oct. 1950: Ernest Davies Papers.

would learn, too late, that abstention is not a good way of influencing European developments. Continental countries did learn by experience that federalism was not then an option and that, on this topic at least, Britain had sense on its side. Even without the friction of British participation, Monnet's federalist dreams were far from the reality of European economic integration. The failure of the EDC, rejected by the French National Assembly on 30 August 1954, was to move European federalism even further off the agenda of practical European politics. The trouble with such wisdom is that even if the lesson is learned, the absence of the original teacher, however wise, leaves him forgotten, unacknowledged, unthanked, and irrelevant. If Europe has, in the end, disdained federalism, it is not because of British influence but because of the native good sense of its peoples.

LIONEL ROBBINS

The eminent liberal economist, Lionel Robbins, was a leading campaigner against participation in the Schuman Plan. Robbins's views are of interest not just as those of an eminent economist but because they carried the support of Prime Minister Attlee. Robbins's letter to *The Times* published on 16 June 1950, when the UK government had already excluded itself, gained the honour of first position.

Surely two things are now very clear. First, that at no stage in the discussions have sufficient details been divulged to permit a proper judgement on the structure and working of the proposed pool. Like the public in the days of the South Sea Bubble, we are being asked to subscribe without reserve to an undertaking the nature of which shall hereafter be revealed. Secondly that, if the various French statements mean anything at all, they do mean that in a situation from which the danger of war is unfortunately not to be excluded, we are asked to consent to the volume of our steel production being determined by a tribunal composed in part of representatives of a nation (Germany) which, under present arrangements, is not even to rearm, let alone be pledged to fight on our side.[36]

Robbins was not particularly felicitous in his choice of analogies but, in reality, it was the politics rather than the economics of the Schuman Plan that alienated him. A few days later he demonstrated further his distrust of all things continental. He was not against federation, only a

[36] *The Times*, 16 June 1950.

European federation. In a further letter to *The Times* he wrote that if we entered a European federation,

> our capacity to rally to the aid of Canada [if it were attacked from the north] would depend on the absence of a defeatist (or collaborationist majority) in [the Western European Cabinet or Congress]. . . . Personally . . . I would be quite willing in principle to see us enter a federation of the English-speaking world and western Europe, but I would not be willing to see us enter a western European federation from which the United States and the British Commonwealth nations other than ourselves were absent.[37]

In other words, a federation including the UK was acceptable on two conditions. The first was that it must be impossible to achieve; the second that it must be dominated by the English-speaking world.

Robbins supplemented his views of Germany in an article published in *Lloyds Bank Review*. The article is quoted here because it was sent to Attlee in advance of publication and strongly approved of by him.[38] The sense can be derived from the following extract:

> [R]ealism compels us to admit that, for a long time, the influence of good Germans has been at a discount and that, although national characteristics may change over time, they do not usually change overnight and there is no evidence in Western Germany that any such marked transformation has actually taken place. Because we are now confronted by dangers much greater than any which are likely to come from a defeated Germany, and because we should very much like to believe that no trouble is likely to come from that quarter, it is surely very naïve to forget altogether what has happened in the past and to act as if we had to deal with a population with sensibilities and aspirations similar to our own. Any disposition that way can easily be checked by the realization that, even now, Germans frequently desecrate Jewish graves in German cemeteries.[39]

The strong feelings about Germany expressed by Robbins were entirely understandable and were widely shared. It cannot be pretended, however, that Britain had suffered more than the occupied countries of Western Europe. They had decided that German prosperity was essential to European prosperity. They did not need to forget. But they had to think about the future. The deep bitterness after the First World War had led to the Treaty of Versailles and that, arguably, had led to the Second World War. They were determined now to find a better path.

---

[37] *The Times*, 23 June 1950.   [38] MS Attlee dep. 102.
[39] *Lloyds Bank Review*, 3 July 1950.

THE TREATY OF PARIS

The Treaty of Paris establishing the ECSC was signed on 18 April 1951 by the six countries that, later in the decade, were the founder members of the European Economic Community, France, Germany, Italy, and Benelux.[40] Even with the UK absent from the negotiations, the Schuman Plan had been so modified that there was little, if anything, which a British government, alert to realities rather than paralysed by words, could not have accepted. The wording of the Treaty was intentionally obscure. It occasioned much discussion in Whitehall, among lawyers and others, as to what, in places, it actually meant. The reasonable conclusion was that differences among the negotiating partners had been fudged and that the ECSC would operate much more like an intergovernmental conference than a dictatorship by the High Authority.[41] The debate on ratification in the French National Assembly showed that French legislators had concerns comparable with British and that they were prepared to ratify the Treaty only because they were satisfied that there would be little impact on national sovereignty.

There were considerable disagreements on who had done best out of the negotiations establishing the ECSC. Kurt Schumacher, leader of the German Social Democratic Party, regarded the outcome as hardly better than a Franco-American plot at the expense of the German worker. He also claimed that the Schuman Plan was 'putting the economic strength of Germany . . . in the service of French diplomacy'.[42] But the SPD had been ambivalent about the Schuman Plan from the beginning and, in the end, voted in the Bundestag against ratification of the Treaty of Paris. In fact the Germans, despite some concessions particularly on antitrust questions, had done well. Its partners in the negotiations knew how dependent they were for their own prosperity on German prosperity. France, perhaps, had reason to regret the absence of Britain as the balance of power within the negotiations moved towards a resurgent Germany. If, as has been argued, Adenauer himself was not enthusiastic for British participation, it is understandable that he had his reasons.[43]

---

[40] In addition to the Treaty itself there was a Convention concerning Transitional Provisions which was to govern the ECSC in the first five years. The ECSC Treaty was not ratified by France until Dec. 1951.

[41] See T 230/182 for the discussions in Whitehall about the meaning of the Treaty.

[42] Quoted by Bullen in Bullen *et al.* 197.

[43] Younger 25. Nevertheless, in his speech to the Bundestag, 13 June 1950, Adenauer expressed his 'profound regret' at Britain's absence and his 'hope that in the course of discussions Great Britain would come to a more favourable view of the Plan': Adenauer 264.

LONDON DEBATES ASSOCIATION

It was not until 1 March 1951 that the UK government finally received a draft of the Treaty of Paris. On 12 March 1951 the Foreign Office sent a telegram to Paris supporting the Schuman Plan as a way of solving the German problem and hoping for association with it. There was, however, less than total conviction behind the message. Criticism that the British had stood outside the Schuman Plan negotiations had been deflected by the suggestion that, even if membership was not possible, there was the alternative of association. But when the Treaty of Paris was at last signed, it became apparent that the Foreign Office had little more enthusiasm for association than it had had for membership. The Foreign Office continued to have many anxieties about any kind of relationship with the ECSC. There was the question whether the Treaty would be ratified. It was always possible that it would not be and that, therefore, there would be nothing with which the UK could associate itself. This was a consideration that the Foreign Office naturally cherished.[44] It was the rescue for which they were hoping. It would justify all their doubts and criticisms. On 24 April 1951 Kenneth Younger answered a question from E. L. Mallalieu, MP. 'There can be no question of formal discussion on the possible association of the United Kingdom with the Schuman Plan organizations until the Treaty is ratified.'[45] A battle then broke out in Whitehall about the nature of Britain's future relationship with the ECSC. Among the options debated were partial membership and formal association. Neither could be specifically delineated pending negotiations with the ECSC. Both implied a range of possibilities from something very near membership on the one hand to something little more than diplomatic relations on the other. On the assumption that the government would, in the end, decide to seek some kind of relationship with the ECSC, officials turned to the task of defining British preferences.

In this battle, the Economic Section of the Cabinet Office carried the banner for the fullest possible participation in the ECSC. The FG (WP) which had developed Britain's alternative ideas was now required to watch developments in Paris and elsewhere in the incipient ECSC. The Economic Section's representative on FG (WP) was David Miles Bensusan-Butt (hereafter Butt). Butt was a man of strong views. Robert Hall, Director of the Economic Section, confided to his diary that Butt

---

[44] See e.g. *DBPO* 305, Duncan Wilson to Morrison, 4 June 1951.
[45] HC Debs. 24 Apr. 1951, cols. 49–50 WA.

'hates the idea of tempering the truth as he sees it, and will not admit that there is a limit to what Ministers can take or will do'.[46] Butt was, in other words, exactly the type of adviser ministers need.[47]

Among Butt's strong views was that the Schuman Plan was of great political importance and that Britain should be a partner in it primarily to ensure that it succeeded. He understood that such political considerations were for the Foreign Office rather than for him. But as he knew he was right, and felt the issue deeply, he saw no reason why he should not acquaint his colleagues with his opinions, the more so as he had, in Robert Hall, a supportive boss. Butt knew that Britain had made a grave error in refusing to participate in the Schuman negotiations. On 17 August 1950, having observed the progress of the negotiations in Paris, he wrote:

[M]ight we not remember that our objection is fundamentally not to the supranational principle but to subscribing to any mystical principles of vague import at all? Our real objections all along have been the empirical one that a supranational authority might compel us to do things we do not want to do; if it cannot, or may reasonably be expected not to, surely our objection fades. We can omit the word Love in this marriage service if we want to insist that this is merely a marriage of political convenience.[48]

Like others in London, he was by no means convinced that the continentals could carry it off by themselves, so complex were the problems. He was, therefore, angry in September 1950 when the Foreign Office responded to a hint from Schuman by refusing, without consultation, to put forward any British ideas 'unless Schuman insists'. This, in Butt's view, went beyond the policy that had been laid down on non-intervention in the Paris negotiations.[49] In a minute to Hall on 4 November 1950, when the Six were still wrestling with their manifold problems, Butt wrote that he was convinced 'that they'll never get through the technical difficulties of getting the thing going unless they have us in, helping with impartiality and administrative nous'. He added that 'politically it is vastly important that it works well'.[50] On the other hand he was less impressed by the economic arguments for participation. He wrote that 'economically it doesn't much matter whether we're in or not'. Against that comment, Russell F. Bretherton of the Economic

[46] Hall, 2 Sept. 1948.
[47] For confirmation, see D. M. B. Butt, *On Economic Knowledge: A Sceptical Miscellany* (Canberra: Australian National University Press, 1980).
[48] T 230/180, D. M. B. Butt to W. Strath, 17 Aug. 1950.
[49] Ibid., Butt to Hall, 11 Sept. 1950.   [50] T 230/180.

Section minuted, 'On a long view, I think we should risk a lot if we stayed out.'[51] Later Bretherton, when at the Board of Trade, was unjustly criticized for his supposed role in Britain's failure to sign the Treaty of Rome.

In a letter to D. B. Pitblado of the Treasury towards the end of 1950, Butt argued that the UK should at least keep an open mind on the possibility, and even desirability, of full membership of the ECSC. Any idea of keeping an open mind was at once repudiated by the Foreign Office. Duncan Wilson wrote to Pitblado: 'The general feeling in this Office is that any such possibility is now pretty well ruled out in the minds of Ministers.'[52] In a paper on the Schuman Plan written on 14 April 1951, when all hope of membership had passed, and Butt was fighting instead for the closest possible relationship with the ECSC, he nevertheless declared his own convictions without equivocation: 'My own feeling, which I confess to be somewhat emotional, is that the balance of advantages, political and economic, is to join with full membership only qualified by something as near *carte blanche* as we can get for our Commonwealth relations.'[53]

Association was discussed in a paper dated 30 April 1951, written by Duncan Wilson:

There are . . . powerful arguments against sacrificing sovereignty to a body which is avowed by the French to be only a first step towards a Western European federation. . . . There is one further objection to any form of association . . . which involves an important sacrifice of sovereignty . . . the UK tends to live up to its international obligations even when they involve disagreeable consequences and . . . to judge by experience in OEEC, the same can hardly be said of the other participant countries.

The paper concluded that the arguments in favour of association were not so powerful that:

(i) we should press for association on political grounds alone, and in the absence of substantial economic arguments in favour of association

(ii) we should regard it as desirable to accept association on terms which would conflict with our major political or economic interests in other fields

(iii) we should think it necessary to engage in the laborious and perhaps

[51] T 230/180.
[52] T 229/751, Butt to Pitblado, 28 Nov. 1950; Wilson to Pitblado, 4 Dec. 1950.
[53] T 230/181, paper on the Schuman Plan by D. M. B. Butt of Economic Section EC (S) (51) 9, 14 Apr. 1951.

fruitless task of negotiating arrangements for association before the Plan is ratified . . .'[54]

Within the Economic Section, Butt and Hall exchanged their comments on this paper. Butt's comment was 'Damp'. Hall, more mildly, wrote: 'It seems that you will have to think up some good economic reasons as clearly the F.O. are determined to sit on the fence.'[55]

Finding such economic arguments was not made easier by the Board of Trade which contributed to the discussion with a paper on 3 May:

> The present trend of opinion in the Board of Trade is that from the general trade point of view it would not be in the best interests of the United Kingdom to enter into economic association with Europe in a manner which would require us to give our European partners a priority preference over our interests and responsibilities elsewhere. . . . Present indications are that the Ministry of Fuel and Power see considerable advantages in our having close association with the Schuman community but would not wish to insist on full participation; the Ministry of Supply considers that it would be preferable to remain out of the Group and the Foreign Office would not press for association on political grounds alone. We for our part are not aware of any special considerations in the trade field which would make it necessary to join the Plan . . . we would consider that the United Kingdom should not become a full partner in the Plan.

Naturally the Board of Trade also drew attention to the fact that the Schuman Treaty contained some provisions contrary to the GATT and that therefore a waiver would be necessary.[56]

The Foreign Office was worried that any form of membership, even partial membership, whatever that turned out to mean, could cause problems for Britain's relationship with the Commonwealth. British steel enjoyed preferential tariff treatment in Commonwealth and imperial markets. About 50–60 per cent of British steel exports went to those markets in the years between 1949 and 1953 whereas the share going to European markets was very modest.[57] Here, Butt seems to have secured a victory. On 3 May 1951 he suggested to Duncan Wilson that 'there is no reasonable doubt that the Community might give us concessions to meet our position as both Europeans and members of the Commonwealth'.[58] Wilson responded that that 'seems to me still a rather

[54] *DBPO* 278. See also T 230/181.   [55] Ibid.
[56] T 230/182, Board of Trade paper FG (WP) (51) 20 of 3 May 1951 to FG (WP).
[57] Ranieri 133–4.
[58] *DBPO* 282, Butt to Wilson, 3 May 1951. See also T 230/181.

large hypothesis'.[59] Butt was becoming increasingly impatient with the Foreign Office. On 29 May he told Pitblado of the Treasury of his 'feeling . . . that the UK was becoming unduly gingerly and hesitant'.[60] However, by 25 June 1951, when Wilson was reviewing the options in a note to the Economic Section, the Commonwealth seemed less of a problem. 'We do not think that . . . our Commonwealth relationship would be prejudiced by accepting the general obligations of the Treaty.'[61] The problem with the Commonwealth was not, in fact, of such dimensions that it should have deterred association with the ECSC or even membership.[62] It is the view of Ruggero Ranieri that, on the subject of Britain's preferential markets, 'it was conceivable that some appropriate agreement could be found with the ECSC . . . although the question of retaining Commonwealth markets was used during the debate as an argument against joining the Six'.[63] It was, nevertheless, certainly true that, such was the loss of British influence with the Six, as a result of the refusal to participate at the outset, that the whole range of British problems had become more difficult to solve than they would have been had Britain been present in the negotiations in Paris.

Duncan Wilson's note of 25 June 1951 made other concessions. He had pointed out that 'We should need, particularly for strategic reasons, to retain the right to take special measures to prevent our steel industry being reduced, by the effect of the free market, below a safe level.' He also insisted that the UK would require no major change in the basic principles and methods of working of the nationalized industries. However, he concluded that it was quite possible that the ECSC would be

---

[59] *DBPO* 284, Wilson to Butt, 5 May 1951. See also T 230/181. In a memo of 22 May 1951, Butt suggested to Pitblado how the Commonwealth problem might be dealt with. See T 230/181.

[60] T 230/182. Pitblado's correspondent is actually unidentified in the file but the context makes it clear that it was Butt.

[61] T 230/182.

[62] On 5 Dec. 1952 Sir Cecil Weir, the first UK Ambassador to the ECSC, assured Anthony Eden that if the UK changed its policy and opted for membership, 'we could obtain consideration for the special problems inherent in our relationship with our Commonwealth': *DBPO* 520.

[63] Ranieri 137. Ruggero Ranieri, in his essay 'Attempting an Unlikely Union—the British Steel Industry and the European Coal and Steel Community', in Stirk and Willis 119, says: 'It soon became apparent that Australia had embarked on a massive build-up of her steel capacity, so that not only would she soon be able to provide her own needs but would presumably be able to outbid the British in New Zealand. In [Canada and South Africa] preferential duties had been whittled down to practically nothing and, in face of strong competition in Canada from American producers and in South Africa mainly from European ones, British steel was just managing to hold on to particular market niches, such as to the one for rail products.'

prepared to accept these points. He now had a new difficulty on which to insist. Under the Treaty, Britain would be deprived of control of coal and steel exports in times of shortage. He could not see what permanent arrangement, to defend British interests, would be accepted. 'At most we might be able to secure some temporary protection by means of special transitional provisions.' C. H. de Peyer, of the Ministry of Fuel and Power, questioned whether the Treaty did have the implications perceived by Wilson.[64] But it did not much matter who was right as the Attlee government had, in any case, no intention of signing the Treaty, or even of joining in forms of partial membership or association which might mean accepting parts of the Treaty. At least, however, Wilson did now see advantages in seeking a noncommittal form of association. 'The advantages of such a formal association are that we should establish a basis of friendly cooperation without having to decide here and now to subject our industries to the general jurisdiction of the Community.'[65]

In the light of all these hesitations, it is hardly surprising that the British government remained suspect of hostility to the Schuman Plan. On 25 June 1951 W. G. Hayter of the Paris Embassy warned the Foreign Office: 'There is no doubt that we are still believed to be hostile to the whole Schuman Plan idea, and not only by the French.' He went on to refer to 'American suspicion and dislike of our attitude to the Schuman Plan'.[66] On 4 July 1951 Butt gave Hall his own assessment of the situation then reached. He was unrepentant about his desire for full membership:

The Ministry of Supply have a curious belief that they can do deals with the Community which would get all the advantages but have none of the disadvantages of membership. They hanker after a cartel agreement combined with a tariff agreement on the pre-war model, by which we would have agreed to admit up to about half a million tons of steel but thereafter shut it out with a hefty tariff. They also feel, in my view quite naïvely, that imperial preference will retain our steel export markets *ad infinitum*, and that these are the only export markets that are really vital. . . . The Foreign Office seem to me to be very short-sighted about the political aspects both as regards control over Germany and as regards Franco-German relations, mainly, in both cases,

[64] T 230/182, de Peyer's letter to Wilson, 1 May 1951 and his note to the Economic Section of the Cabinet Office of 2 May 1951.
[65] T 230/182, Duncan Wilson to Economic Section of the Cabinet Office, 25 June 1951.
[66] *DBPO* 323, W. G. Hayter to R. B. Stevens, Foreign Office, 25 June 1951.

because they seem to have a fear that a successful supra-national and quasi-federal body will strengthen 'third force' ideas in Europe. I cannot find the evidence for this belief, which seems to be just the opposite of what one would have expected. My own feeling is very strongly that the potentialities for good of a body which will really take a grip on the coal and steel industries on the Continent, and do it much more effectively than all the international inter-allied machines of the last five years, are so great that it would be very short-sighted not to get right in.[67]

This was a message well beyond the limits of what ministers could take. But by July 1951 senior ministers such as Cripps's successor Hugh Gaitskell, as well as Philip Noel-Baker and Alfred Robens, were inclining to the view expressed also by J. C. R. Dow of the Treasury that Britain should at least consider 'partial membership' of the ECSC.[68]

ASSOCIATION AT LEAST

The British government was the first foreign government to appoint an ambassador to the ECSC. It did so immediately on the constitution of the ECSC in 1952. The High Authority at once responded to Section 13 of the Transitional Convention which required it to 'undertake negotiations with the governments of third countries, and particularly with the British Government'. Britain still had some political significance for France. On 21 December 1953 Monnet told Sir Cecil Weir, the British Ambassador to the ECSC, that if it were known that the British government intended to associate with the ECSC, twenty more votes would be cast in favour of the EDC in the French Assembly.[69] Exactly a year later, on 21 December 1954, a Treaty was signed associating Britain with the ECSC.[70] It entered into force on 23 October 1955. Massigli says of the Treaty that it represented little more than an expression of good neighbourly relations.[71] The Treaty created a Council

[67] *DBPO* 329. See also T 230/182.
[68] Morgan (1984) 420–1, based on a report by J. C. R. Dow dated 23 July 1951 and a memorandum of views of Gaitskell, Noel-Baker, and Robens dated 24 July 1951. Robens had become Minister of Labour following the resignation of Bevan.
[69] Ranieri 145.
[70] The Treaty was approved by the House of Commons in Feb. 1955 with substantial support from both sides. Community countries were slower to ratify. The Treaty did not come into effect until Sept. 1955: Diebold 502, 506. The EDC had been turned down by the French Assembly on 30 Aug. 1954.
[71] Massigli 231.

of Association made up of representatives of the British government and of the High Authority. The main commitment of the Treaty was to discuss. There were two other provisions of substance. One required the Council of Association to study barriers to trade between the UK and the Community with a view to proposing reductions. The other stated that if new restrictions on trade between the UK and the ECSC were contemplated because of shortages or a decline in demand, the British government or the High Authority should bring the matter before the Council of Association with a view to considering co-ordinated action. Diebold comments that 'Neither of these provisions seriously restricts national action, but they point a direction.'[72] The most substantial accomplishment of the association was the steel tariff that went into effect in early 1958. Diebold's summary of the evidence is that 'the Council of Association . . . cannot be thought to have had a major effect on the economic relations of Britain and the Community'.[73] Ruggero Ranieri comments that 'By the end of the 1950s trade [in steel] between the United Kingdom and the Six had fallen to its lowest ever level.'[74]

One problem in negotiating an association agreement with any substance was that the Six were afraid of British competition in their market and the British were afraid of competition from the Six in their market. It is unclear whether anything more substantial could have been negotiated. Ranieri says that,

If the word [association] were to mean anything, it would mean that the British steel industry would shed most of its protection against the Six and demand from them a set of guarantees about prices and dumping. . . . In other words, what was required was an act of faith, an attempt to make the new institutions abide by their own principles and stated objectives, after which other bonuses might follow: more reciprocal trade with the Six, a healthy degree of liberalization, more competition.[75]

The necessary act of faith was not offered on the British side and it may not have been on offer by the ECSC. The irony was that the minister charged with the negotiation of the association agreement was Duncan Sandys, Minister of Supply. Sandys, in opposition, had been an enthusiastic supporter of the Schuman Plan. Now, in 1954, he was insisting that there was no question of grafting the principle of a common market on an unwilling British steel industry.[76]

---

[72] Diebold 508.   [73] Ibid. 515.
[74] Ranieri, 'Attempting an Unlikely Union', in Stirk and Willis 122.
[75] Ranieri 136–7.   [76] Sandys had been Secretary of the European Movement.

The illusion that something of value could be achieved from association had encouraged the decision in London that Britain could not honourably accept the invitation to participate because it had been conditional on a prior commitment to a supranational High Authority. The illusion proved to be totally counter-productive in France as well as Britain. It helped to reconcile French opinion to its tête-à-tête with Germany. It persuaded British opinion that there was a *via media* with substance that did not involve acceptance of the principle of a supranational High Authority. Association was delayed until long after the inauguration of the ECSC and then was achieved on a basis containing little of economic or political significance. As Massigli puts it, 'insensibly, the gulf between England and the continent widened'.[77]

CONCLUSION

Britain suffered few short-term economic losses from its absence from the ECSC and, at first sight, few political losses either.[78] Its absence was not seriously felt, on one side or on the other. The British steel industry was dependent neither on French ores nor on German coal, and British coal played no part in the Ruhr–Lorraine complex. About 75 per cent of British steel exports were delivered to countries outside Europe.[79] The Monnet Plan for the reconstruction of the French economy placed great emphasis on the coal and steel industries and the Schuman Plan reflected that emphasis.[80] Yet, despite the illusions at the time, in the UK as well as in the rest of Western Europe, coal and steel, as it

---

[77] Massigli 232.

[78] The iron and steel industries in Belgium, France, Germany, and Italy initially opposed the Plan: Milward (1984) 418–19.

[79] Robert Hall came to the conclusion from an assessment of the economic advantages and disadvantages of participation in a scheme such as was proposed by the FG Committee that the gains would outweigh the losses though adding the cautionary note, expected from any economist, that 'we cannot really be certain about anything . . . we might just as well lose as gain by non-participation': *DBPO* 110, Calendar; memorandum by Robert Hall, *The Schuman Proposals for Coal and Steel*. Referred to also by Morgan (1984) 418.

[80] Gillingham whose admiration for Monnet knows few bounds nevertheless says: 'The Monnet Plan . . . met few of its targets, wasted money on a grand scale, helped create runaway inflation, and had to be abandoned in all but name in 1952.' However, apparently it ensured that 'improvements in productivity, economic growth, and living standards . . . became the supreme national priorities they have since remained': Gillingham 137–8. Milward says: 'The Schuman Plan was invented to safeguard the Monnet Plan': Milward (1984) 395.

turned out, were not the commanding heights of the European economy. Such supranational control of the Ruhr industries as was provided by the ECSC gave the French psychological comfort, which was important, but, by 1952, or even 1950, the danger to European security did not come from the Federal Republic of Germany or from the Ruhr.

For the participants the gains were political rather than economic, and the political gains were more from the creation of the club of Little Europe than directly from the Schuman Plan itself. Whatever ground was won by the Schuman Plan for European federalism was barely perceptible at the outset and was rapidly eroded. But the Six had agreed to talk together in launching, and subsequently managing, the Schuman Plan. The intimacy and trust thus created eased the elaboration of future plans for European reconstruction. Though Monnet's ideas were modified in the negotiations, the ECSC did give the participants experience of the working of 'supranationalism' and, in the next stage of European integration, they would turn even further away from his conceptions of the European future. All this was of greater significance than the Schuman Plan itself. Unfortunately Britain had excluded itself and was not present to learn that supranationalism could be consistent with national sovereignty.

14
Conclusion

I think WSC made a fool of himself over the Schuman Plan. He
is apt to plunge in without considering the consequences. It is
generally thought that we had the better of the debate.[1]

It was for Britain, if it wished for leadership in Europe after the war,
to take more sympathetic account of the concerns of its ally France.
Leadership involves understanding. Too little effort was directed in
London to understanding the anxieties of a country which had been
invaded three times by the Germans in a matter of seventy years. Those
anxieties could not be sensibly assuaged by returning to the policies of
Versailles. Having secured the American commitment to the security of
Europe, what was required from Britain was an initiative towards Franco-
German *rapprochement* guaranteed by its own participation. It should
not have been too difficult to identify the Ruhr as the core of any such
initiative or to perceive that, if it was going to have prospects of survival, any initiative on the Ruhr must not discriminate against the
Germans. Nor should it have been too difficult to reconcile such an
initiative with Britain's wider interests, real and supposed.

Unfortunately the necessary imagination was not to be found in
London. Britain was then confronted by the Schuman Plan. Even looked
at selfishly, the Schuman Plan had attractions. It represented a giant
step towards Franco-German *rapprochement* and yet Britain could involve itself without serious prejudice to any of its wider interests. The
argument of this book is that, having failed to find its own initiative,
Britain should have entered the Schuman Plan negotiation, and used its
influence which at the time was considerable. The probability must
have been that Britain, on a mature appreciation of its own interests and
those of Europe, would have been content with the outcome. That
probability justified any risk. Confidence in that probability was warranted by knowledge of the many allies Britain would have found at the

---

[1] Letter from C. R. Attlee to his brother Tom Attlee 30 June 1950: Attlee Papers.

negotiating table. Instead, by dint of a massive policy failure which has profoundly influenced the whole of Britain's post-war history, Whitehall and Westminster rejected participation in the Schuman Plan.

THE EXPECTATION OF FAILURE

British policy towards Europe has frequently been influenced by the expectation that the initiatives of its continental partners would fail. This expectation has not always been disappointed but any such assumption needs a more secure foundation than existed in this case. It was certainly possible that the Schuman negotiations would collapse. There were many conflicts of interest around the negotiating table. The Schuman Plan was bitterly attacked by vested interests on both sides of the Rhine. The French were forced to guarantee the Italian iron and steel industry, supplies of mineral ore from French North Africa.[2] The Germans were compelled to compromise on their opposition to the decartelization of the Ruhr industries.[3] The problems of the European coal and steel industries were sufficiently complex to make success difficult. American insistence on German rearmament following the outbreak of the Korean War created tensions which came near undermining the negotiations. The problems that arose fed the government's hopes that nothing would come of it. Throughout the negotiations the Foreign Office remained sceptical, considered itself very wise in its scepticism, and took every opportunity of comforting ministers with adverse information about the progress of the negotiations. Even the UK Embassy in Luxembourg played its part. On 13 February 1951 it informed Attlee of 'the growing feeling of distaste in the Grand Duchy for the Plan'.[4] This was two months before the Treaty of Paris was signed.

The Foreign Office and the British government should have assessed more accurately the political pressures making for success. In his briefing note for Ernest Bevin before the debate on the Schuman Plan in the

---

[2] T 230/182, Ambassador in Rome, Sir Victor Mallet, to Foreign Office, 19 Feb. 1951: 'The eventual agreement gave the Italians about half what they originally asked for, but they seemed quite satisfied.'

[3] Law 75, now Law 27, was at the centre of this controversy. A meeting in the Foreign Office on 29 Jan. 1951 concluded that 'it seemed quite possible that this question [Law 27] was the main obstacle in the way of the signature of the Schuman Plan treaty': T 230/182.

[4] T 230/182, R. T. Laudale (UK Embassy in Luxembourg) to Attlee.

House of Commons, Roger Makins discussed three possible outcomes from the Paris negotiations. The first was complete success. This, he wrote, following Attlee's original statement in the House, would be welcome to the government. The second possibility was the emergence of a rather different plan. In that event the government would naturally study whatever plan emerged with the object of seeing how far it could join in or adhere to it. The third possibility was the emergence in the discussions of difficulties of such a nature that they might make some fresh approach to the problem desirable. It was to be hoped, wrote Makins, that this third contingency would not, in fact, arise. In any event it was too early to define the government's reaction to whatever course the conference might take.[5] All this was defensive material for a debate in which the government would be under attack. For that purpose, the briefing note was both adequate and reasonable but only on the assumption that it had been sensible for the British government to refrain from participation in the negotiations and therefore deny itself influence in modifying the Schuman Plan. It can be compared and contrasted with Younger's account of the views of Strang and Makins quoted in Chapter 8. What was missing from the brief to ministers was an explanation why this Plan, unlike previous French initiatives, was highly likely to succeed. That the probability of success was not put to ministers demonstrates a remarkable failure in the Foreign Office to understand the contemporary European political dialogue.

Had such a brief been written, it would have been likely to contain the following arguments. First, the end of war had created a determination to guarantee peace in Western Europe. The road had not yet been found but the Schuman Plan was a likely step on the way. Secondly, Acheson had encouraged Schuman to take an initiative towards European unity through reconciliation with Germany. The US Administration must be expected to place all its weight behind a successful outcome of that initiative. Thirdly, if the Germans agreed to sign, no other of the Six was likely to take dissent to the point of isolating itself.

The probability was that the negotiations once started would not collapse. The key had always been Germany, regarded throughout continental Europe as essential to its economic prosperity. For Germany, the Schuman Plan implied costs. Yet it also offered the prospect of an increase in German steel production to a figure in excess of the

---

[5] Roger Makins to Bevin, 17 June 1950—Notes for debate on Schuman Plan: MS Attlee dep. 102.

11.1 million tons a year then permitted. The establishment of the High Authority would render Law 75 largely nugatory or obsolete. The IAR, seen as discriminatory, might go by the board. The French did in fact agree, after a struggle, that the IAR should disappear when the Schuman Plan came into operation.[6] Though the German coal industry had to pay a levy to assist less competitive industries, the probability was that, with time, German coal would gain markets in Belgium and France.[7] Proposals for public ownership of the Ruhr industries would be side-tracked. The international status of Germany had already been greatly improved by the creation of the Federal Republic, by the invitation to join the Council of Europe even if only as an associate member, and by proposals for German rearmament emanating from Washington which, after hesitation, would be supported by London.[8] Everything was going Germany's way even without the Schuman Plan. Yet Germany still wanted equality and international acceptance. Though it had its federal government, its independence was still limited by the Occupation Statute. The Schuman Plan represented a further step on the road to equality and international acceptance. It was not a negligible consideration that it re-established a link between Germany and the Saar and thus, in Adenauer's words, 'one cause of tension between France and Germany will be removed'.[9] On 24 June 1950 the outbreak of the Korean War

---

[6] The UK government was happy to see the IAR disappear as long as it was not as a present from France to Germany. In other words, there must be a tripartite conference at which the UK was properly consulted. Much to the annoyance of London, the British attitude was leaked to the Press and the disappearance of the IAR, to which the USA was very willing to agree, did appear as a French present to Germany. The British steel industry wanted a guarantee of continued scrap supplies from Germany. As a result, tripartite agreement on freeing Germany from controls on its steel industry was not signed until 19 Oct. 1951: Young (1984) 179–80.

[7] Milward (1992), ch. 3, 'Coal and the Belgian Nation'.

[8] An analysis of the German reasons for accepting the Schuman Plan was given by General Sir Brian Robertson in a message to Kenneth Younger on 19 June 1950. Robertson comments that, in addition to the considerations listed here, the Germans would be motivated by the thought that 'in any combination in which France and Germany are the only two great powers', Germany would be the dominant: *DBPO* 108. Acheson points out that US proposals for German rearmament led to the Germans 'dragging their feet in the Schuman Plan negotiations'. The US threw its weight behind the French and thus helped to secure the eventual agreement: Acheson 389.

[9] Adenauer 260. See also Marjolin (1989) 273. In Feb. 1950 France began negotiations with Saarland under which it retained financial and customs authority and was given a long lease on the Saar coal-mines. Saarland was to have autonomy and to remain separate from Germany. Adenauer described the convention as a 'decision against Europe'. At the same time he indicated a readiness to negotiate an association between French and German industries on equal terms or even a Franco-German economic union: *DBPO* 17 n.: Milward (1984) 390; Young (1984) 142. Reunion between Germany and the Saar had to wait until 1956.

would further emphasize Europe's need for unity in the defence against Communism. In this, for geographical reasons apart from any other, the participation of Germany was essential. Thus, despite the opposition of Erhard, Adenauer would be likely both to value the political benefits to Germany and to listen to Washington which, with whatever hesitations, saw the Plan as at least some advance in European integration.

The probability of success was reinforced by the decision of the British government not to reveal its own proposals. During the Schuman Plan negotiations in Paris, British officials came under considerable pressure from the Dutch to declare their hand. The Dutch were particularly anxious to know whether the UK would come in if there was an intergovernmental Council of Ministers. Spierenburg told Roll that an affirmative answer to that question might make a considerable difference to the outcome of the negotiations. Officials could give no reply to such questions because of the British decision to do nothing that might lead to Britain being accused of a desire to sabotage the French proposals.[10] British abstention left Benelux no alternative path and made more likely the decision of all Six to join, having achieved the best terms they could. In any event, there were other motives propelling the negotiations towards success. For example, the Belgian coal and Italian steel industries wanted some respectable cover for the continuation of subsidies for their industries.[11]

For the UK to place so much reliance on failure was worse than an error. The Schuman Plan held out the prospect of Franco-German *rapprochement*. That was an objective which, whatever its offended feelings, the UK government should have wished to see achieved. Precisely because there was a risk of failure, the Attlee government should have striven to be present to help towards success. Roger. Bullen regards as unfounded the charge that the British government 'sought the failure of the negotiations'.[12] That may well be true. Apart from any other consideration, if the British government had actively sought the failure of the negotiations, it would have caused a major row with the US Administration. But the British government did expect failure and even hoped for failure.

The hope that the negotiations would fail was also very unwise. It was absurd to imagine, as the Foreign Office too readily did, that if the Schuman Plan negotiations failed, it would be an easy matter to revive

[10] *DBPO* 135, Hall-Patch to Younger, 6 July 1950.
[11] For the politically sensitive way in which the Belgian coal industry was treated see Milward (1992), ch. 3.
[12] *DBPO* Preface, p. xii.

the project of Franco-German *rapprochement* on the basis of a British afterthought such as was being rapidly assembled in the recesses of Whitehall. There could be no confidence that, once this first attempt had failed, another, a British variety, could be easily launched. It showed little understanding of the effect on French opinion if their own great gesture of reconciliation with Germany collapsed.[13] It is therefore no excuse that part of the UK government's planning for failure was the preparation of alternative plans.

NO PRIVATE AND CYNICAL INTENTIONS

If the British government had been present in the Schuman Plan nego-tiations there would have been much to play for as the eventual out-come showed. Monnet might try to impose conditions. What he could not prevent were the compromises on his ideas that emerged from the actual negotiations.[14] Richard Crossman, the final back-bench speaker on the government side in the House of Commons debate on the Schuman Plan on 26 June 1950, said what was probably in the mind of the British government: 'The purpose of the Schuman Plan politically is to tie the Germans up so tightly that they will not be a menace to the French, but what ties the Germans up so tightly that they cannot be a menace to the French might tie this country up so tightly that it could not do its service to the world.'[15] Whatever that service might be, it seemed to escape Crossman that other countries too might be reluctant to accept ties so tight that their own service to the world might be denied them.

Kenneth Younger recalls 'a number of individuals criticizing the Government on the ground that [the French conditions for participation in the negotiations] should have been accepted with the private and cynical intention of sabotaging the supranational aspects of the plan at

[13] Harvey thought that if the difficulties of the Schuman Plan proved too great, the UK government would then have an opportunity to 'enter the scene with their own version of the plan': *DBPO* 92.

[14] 'The European Coal and Steel Community that came into being on 10 August 1952 was a profoundly different organization from the one first proposed on 9 May 1950': Gillingham 228.

[15] HC Debs. 26 June 1950, col. 2038. In a letter to *The Times* on 13 May 1950, strongly supporting the Schuman Plan, W. W. Rostow had made the same point in a rather more friendly way: 'France has accepted now another historic fact, if German sovereignty is to be limited it will require a virtually equal limitation on the sovereignty of other states.'

the conference table. I always thought this advice disastrous and such a course was never contemplated by the Government.'[16] Kenneth Younger's scruples did him credit. But it could not have been a British interest to deprive France of the essential benefits of its initiative. There was no good reason why the UK could not accept supranationalism within a coal and steel community and then work within the negotiations to ensure that the form would be politically acceptable. Moreover, as Kenneth Younger himself seems to have discerned, there could have been a role for the UK in the negotiations which had nothing to do with 'sabotaging' supranationalism. It was to help ensure that the negotiations succeeded, despite the difficulties, thus assuring for the future that *rapprochement* between France and Germany which Britain did see as a major objective of policy.[17] Britain had an even more direct interest. When France needed help in the negotiations it would look to the USA not to the UK. When the question arose of how far German steel companies should be allowed to own coal-mines, a question of considerable interest to Britain, it was the Americans that forced the necessary compromise between France and Germany.[18] On 21 March 1951 D. B. Pitblado of the Treasury wrote to Plowden: 'Our policy of avoiding interference in any way with the Schuman negotiations led to these vital German issues being discussed and in effect settled between the Americans, the French and the Germans.'[19]

France had real concerns and it was those concerns, rather than just Monnet's federalism, that led Schuman to propose a High Authority with binding powers. The British objective in this case would not have been to 'sabotage' supranationalism, or even the High Authority, but to make them workable and consistent with the real interests of the member states. That is what the Six successfully achieved in the Schuman negotiations and they moved a good deal further from Monnet's conception of supranationalism when they came to found the EEC.

It was hardly conceivable in the atmosphere of the time that the negotiating partners would not have been prepared to accommodate Britain in all reasonable respects once they were convinced that doing so would lead to its membership of the new Community. The UK had succeeded in sucking federalism out of early proposals for the Council of Europe and the OEEC. The OEEC and the Council of Europe were created as intergovernmental organizations and the Assembly of the

---

[16] Younger 26.   [17] Ibid. 27.   [18] *DBPO* 233–6.
[19] T230/181, Pitblado to Plowden, 21 Mar. 1951.

290 The Schuman Plan

Council of Europe was nominated and consultative. This outcome was not due to Britain's prestige or diplomatic skill alone. Two other factors were important. The first was that the UK did intend to take part if its concerns were reasonably met. Its European partners therefore had a motive to accommodate its arguments. The second was that it was not only the UK that was opposed to federalism. Britain's doubts were shared even in France. They were shared within the French government. A few years later, under de Gaulle, France was to become the staunchest adherent of the national veto. Britain's objective in the Schuman Plan negotiations should have been, not to sabotage supranationalism, or the High Authority, but to negotiate reasonable controls, and it would have found strong supporters at the negotiating table.

'THEY DON'T WANT US, CALLAGHAN'

James Callaghan, then a junior minister at the Admiralty, wrote to Attlee to say that Britain should participate in the Schuman Plan negotiations. Callaghan regarded the Schuman Plan as corresponding to the 'functionalist' approach to European integration, that is integration by the creation of specialized authorities. He was summoned by Bevin only to be told 'They don't want us, Callaghan'.[20] The 'they' in question were, presumably, the French government. One can understand the mountain of resentment that lay behind Bevin's lament, the feeling of rejection by France, for which he thought he had done so much. Callaghan believes that Bevin had good reason for his suspicion. Massigli was of the same opinion. In his memoirs he wrote: 'having to choose between an Authority with limited powers in a community which included England, and an all-powerful High Authority, the technocrat [Monnet] chose the all-powerful.'[21] This is a further example of the way in which an ambassador too sympathetic to the views of the government to which he is accredited can actually become a liability. It would have been more conducive to the British participation which Massigli so ardently desired if he had used his position in London to inject a modicum of scepticism into the idea that, under any circumstances, Monnet would get his all-powerful High Authority. In any

---

[20] Callaghan 79. Callaghan also explains the position he took on the Schuman Plan in the Council of Europe
[21] Massigli 203.

case, Massigli, to his own great annoyance, was not in the decision-making loop on the Schuman Plan and was therefore not in the best position to know the real intentions of his government.

Ernest Davies reported to Sir Pierson Dixon of the Foreign Office on Bevin's meeting with Guy Mollet on 1 November 1950. 'In referring to the Schuman Plan the Secretary of State expressed regret at the manner in which it had been presented to us without prior consultation or information. M. Mollet said that had been intentional to make it impossible for us to come in as those responsible did not really desire our co-operation.'[22] Mollet, regarded in some quarters in London as no better than a federalist, was, on this occasion, trying to make a friend of Bevin. He told Bevin how he had won 'a victory over the federalists' such as André Philip and Paul Reynaud in the Council of Europe. It may well be that in his statement about the Schuman Plan he was simply saying something that he knew Bevin would like to hear. In any case Mollet was no more a primary authority on the intentions of the French government at the time of the Schuman Plan than was Massigli. Bevin's exchange with Mollet is evidence rather of his continuing resentment at Schuman's lack of consultation with him than of Schuman's views on British participation.

Others favourably inclined to participation, such as Kenneth Younger, also came to the conclusion that the French did not really want British participation. He subsequently wrote: 'Governments which seriously hope for an agreement to a major new proposal rarely, if ever, launch it publicly without private preparation.'[23] Younger appears to have overlooked the fact that, despite the absence of private preparation, the French did achieve agreement with all their expected partners except Britain. The French view was that the surprise element in the Schuman announcement was important in winning it public acceptance and in ensuring that it was not drowned in detail before it was born. There is no doubt that the announcement did achieve rapid public acceptance and it is not impossible that the surprise element contributed to that result. Even if one discounts this as an excuse for lack of consultation, it is perfectly understandable that the French government would have wanted the main credit for its initiative.

Poidevin says that Schuman and Monnet were influenced by their experience of the way the UK had distorted the construction of the

---

[22] Ernest Davies Papers.
[23] Younger 25. See also Sahm 17–18 for his view on Monnet's real wishes on the subject of UK participation.

292 The Schuman Plan

Council of Europe. They therefore took the precaution of shutting the door to the manœuvres of London because they wanted a supranational authority and, they suspected, Britain did not.[24] It was always clear that Schuman and Monnet would insist on a supranational authority. This does not mean that they were seeking to close the doors to British participation in the negotiations provided Britain accepted the objective of establishing a supranational authority as the basis of the negotiations. They may have been at fault in equating supranationalism with federalism but diplomats should be capable of detecting the realities behind the words.

Bevin's lament to Callaghan, and the suspicions of others, were probably mistaken. Foreign Office officials may well have led Bevin to believe that 'They don't want us' but the probability is that 'they' did want 'us' but 'we', for a series of reasons we were not ready to face up to honestly, were turning them down. The argument that they did want us can be summarized as follows. First, it really is difficult to explain Monnet's repeated efforts, in London, in his letter of 25 May 1950, and on the telephone to Plowden, to persuade the British government to participate if he did not want the apparent objective of his exertions. He was diligent in the cause beyond the bounds of duty. His persistence suggests that he wanted to find a way round the difficulties even though they were being made by the British through a failure to distinguish between what was imperative in the French position and what was negotiable. Monnet met nothing but discouragement. Bevin, according to Massigli, regarded Monnet's efforts after he left London as an attempt to bypass the Foreign Office.[25] The French should stick to channels.[26] Monnet talked to Plowden who, as Chief Economic Planner, was his opposite number. But Plowden was in the Treasury, not the Foreign Office, and the lead on the Schuman Plan lay with the Foreign Office, not with the Treasury. Bevin's store of grievances mounted even higher. But it was Bevin who failed to conduct serious talks about the Plan during Schuman's visit to London.

And, as no minister was prepared to travel to Paris to discuss the matter throughout the crucial two weeks between Schuman's departure from London and the French ultimatum of 1 June, Monnet was doing his best in the circumstances. It was perfectly possible that he wanted the British government to be present at the negotiations even though it

---

[24] Poidevin (1986) 277.   [25] Massigli 200.
[26] See, e.g. *DBPO* 32, 45, and 55. The Foreign Office disapproved of Monnet's telephone calls to Plowden. '[T]hings ought to be kept in the proper channels': *DBPO* 69.

had not been granted the favour of prior knowledge. Monnet had an honourable record of trying to involve Britain in the process of European integration. He had persisted despite the absence of any positive response. Oliver Harvey wrote that 'he is known to have been personally extremely anxious to bring us in'.[27] It would have been understandable if Monnet had not wanted UK participation. In fact the evidence available to the British government was that he was doing his best to secure it provided only that what he saw as the essential elements in the Plan were safeguarded. Nor should these have represented an insurmountable obstacle.

Secondly, there was intense French political interest in British participation. Much of the French political Establishment did not want to be left, as it was frequently put, tête-à-tête with the Germans. This was true of many members of the French Cabinet including Maurice Petsche, the Minister of Finance, as well as the French socialists. The messages, formal and informal, from the Quai d'Orsay confirm a desire for British participation. Schuman, as we have seen, had repeatedly to assure the Foreign Affairs Committee of the National Assembly that the British would be there.[28] Thirdly, if the French government did not want us, there are at least two questions which it would be difficult to answer. Why, after they had obtained agreement from the other five participants to their draft communiqué, were they prepared to go back to them to secure a change which, they thought, would help the British? The change that they made should have helped the British. Why should they have offered the British the benefit of the Netherlands reservation, even if only informally?

Fourthly, Schuman's initiative towards Franco-German reconciliation was prompted by the US Administration, notably by Dean Acheson. The Administration then gave it firm support, despite many worries. Even though some in Washington saw Britain as an obstacle to deeper European integration, British participation in such a limited exercise as the Schuman Plan would have brought benefits. Washington wanted Britain to play a role partly because it was thought the Schuman Plan might otherwise collapse, partly because of the fear of French (and German) neutralism. Both Schuman and Monnet were very concerned to retain American support and, indeed, it was quite crucial during the

---

[27] *DBPO* 103, Message from Harvey to Younger, 16 June 1950.

[28] Schuman continued to assure Harvey that he had wanted the British involved even when Harvey gave him a clear opportunity to say the opposite: *DBPO* 122, record of a conversation between Harvey and Schuman, 29 June 1950.

subsequent negotiations. If for no other reason, and there were many other reasons, Schuman would have done everything he reasonably could to secure British participation. No one outside this country could understand why, if the various memoranda to Paris and the public statements in the House and elsewhere did truly represent the British position, the UK did not accept the French invitation. Britain was not being asked to accept federalism, whatever Monnet's talk about the ramparts of sovereignty. There was nothing about federalism in the draft communiqué. Britain was being asked to accept a functional project which, to recommend it, had the enormous benefit of Franco-German reconciliation.

The argument that 'they did not want us' sometimes appears in another form. It is sometimes argued that 'they' wanted the UK in the ECSC but not in the negotiations which would prepare the treaty establishing the ECSC. If Britain was present at the negotiations, it would just be too difficult for France to get its way. But the UK would be welcome once there was a treaty which if could be invited to sign.[29] In this form, the argument is no more persuasive. For the same or similar reasons as already presented, the probability must be that Britain was wanted. How could the French government take the risk that Britain would tamely join if it had played no part in the negotiations?

Of course it is impossible to tell what was in people's hearts whatever they said or did. Yet the emphasis in so much British comment on the theme that the French did not really want the UK whatever their overt statements and actions, is no more than a further excuse for the major British error of non-participation. Even if an argument could be successfully made that Monnet preferred Britain's absence to its presence, that should not have been enough to deter the British government especially as so many in France were making it clear that they did want British participation and there was an invitation.

Young comments that 'the cost of Monnet's tactics was a limited Europe, of only six nations, based on bureaucratic, functional lines rather than an evolving, living, political organism, covering a wide area of Europe, such as Bevin had always hoped to create.'[30] But that was not the cost of Monnet's tactics. It was the cost of Britain's unnecessary self-exclusion. The best is the enemy of the good. The good was within Bevin's grasp had he only shown imagination and leadership. Instead

[29] See e.g. Ch. 12 above for *The Economist*, 10 June 1950.
[30] Young (1984) 166.

he allowed Britain to be excluded. If all that Monnet created was a Little Europe, he has the defence that his failure to establish a wider Europe required the co-operation of a myopic UK government. Whatever Monnet wanted or did not want, it was the British government that refused its participation and which must therefore take the blame.

MINISTERS, OFFICIALS, AND THE BACK-BENCHES

An enduring impression from the history of this period is of the subordination of ministers to officials.[31] The peremptory tone of the important minute of 2 June from Sir William Strang to Kenneth Younger, quoted in Chapter 8, can perhaps be explained by the special circumstances. Strang was addressing a somewhat rebellious junior minister. The wording is, nevertheless, significant: 'It has been the consistent advice of the Foreign Office and other departments, accepted by Ministers as a basis for policy, that we should not become involved in Europe in the economic sphere, beyond the point of no return.'[32] The policy was the policy of officials and had been accepted by ministers. Officials, not ministers, were the source of policy though constitutional propriety required the endorsement of ministers. This situation is certainly not unusual. Constitutional theory notwithstanding, ministers frequently rely on officials for their policy for lack of any other source from which they can confidently derive it. In the case of the Schuman Plan there was, apart from Cripps's momentary hesitations, no suggestion of any mutiny by senior ministers against the advice they were receiving. Ministers and officials were of one mind. Ministers had, however, been hardened in their opinions by the 'consistent advice' of officials. They had lacked the independence or, latterly, the intellectual vigour to question it adequately.

The leading members of the Attlee government were not merely elderly and sick. They were also unprepared. They had been long in office and some had served in the earlier Labour governments. But neither experience in war nor their brief membership of earlier Labour

---

[31] Cairncross writes of this phenomenon in the economic sphere. He says 'more commonly Ministers were the reluctant pupils of their officials. On one economic issue after another—the American Loan, the coal crisis, the dollar problem, devaluation, the European Payments Union—they were slow to grasp the true options of policy and had great difficulty in reaching sensible conclusions': Cairncross (1985) 20.

[32] *DBPO* 75.

governments had prepared them for the post-war world. It is fair to stay that officials were equally unprepared. But officials had worked for pre-war governments in which Britain's global status was more assured. The belief that what had been true before the war could once more become true after the war is understandable but hardly laudable. It fed Bevin's vanity that he really was one of the big three Foreign Ministers. Unprepared officials led unprepared Ministers. Bevin's powers of leadership, his exceptional position within the government, were wasted. Although he proved incapable of framing a European policy for himself, his intuitive Europeanism would have been a ready recipient for constructive briefing from a Foreign Office that understood the post-war world. Such briefing would have equipped him to fight the opposition to European entanglements issuing from the Treasury and Board of Trade. As it was, he was left bereft.

As we have seen, the illusions that spawned the advice of officials and decided the policies of ministers penetrated the thinking even of such independent back-benchers as Richard Crossman. There was little sign on the back-benches of any serious rebellion against the Attlee government's European policy. Bullock attempts to explain why the Labour Party was so ignorant of the realities of the post-war world. During the war the leaders of the Labour Party had been unable to fulfil their natural function of educating their followers.

Because they were members of a coalition not a party government, and because wartime conditions cut them off behind a screen of secrecy, ministers' responsibilities were not shared in the normal way with other members of the PLP, still less with the rank and file in the constituencies. The leaders, busy with their official duties, found little time to argue the case for the change which had taken place in their own views and were in any case reluctant, in time of war, to raise issues which could only prove divisive.[33]

This may well be so.[34] But even after the war, and when in a one-party government, there was insufficient attention to the process of education partly because ministers were themselves uncertain what they should teach and partly because experience of the wartime coalition had left them insensible to the importance of Europe in the future of Britain. In these circumstances it might have been expected that the Foreign Office

---

[33] Bullock 66.

[34] In considering the applicability of this explanation to the period after 1945, and even more to the period after 1950, it should be remembered that, at the dissolution in 1945, there were only 166 members of the PLP, that many of the wartime back-benchers had left the House, and many others were themselves in the government.

would have been instructing ministers in the realities of the post-war world thereby instilling a message that ministers could pass on to their followers. But Foreign Office officials showed no greater understanding than the ministers they were paid to serve.

HINDSIGHT?

The answer to any accusation of hindsight is that there were people in positions of responsibility, though in less exalted ranks than those at which the damaging decisions were being taken, who did wish to join in the negotiations. One was Kenneth Younger, Minister of State at the Foreign Office, who was rebuked for his pains by a contemptuous bedridden Bevin who, unlike Younger, would not live to see the consequences of his blindness.[35] Younger's main reason as he recalled it many years later was that 'by standing aside we might make ourselves responsible for perpetuating Franco-German enmity'.[36] R. B. Stevens, Assistant Under-Secretary of State in the German Section of the Foreign Office, in a memorandum of 10 May 1950, expressed the hope that 'we could adopt an attitude . . . which was neither hesitant nor hostile' and added that 'if [the Schuman Plan] comes off the political advantages must inevitably outweigh the economic disadvantages to us however great they may be'.[37] Robert Hall, Director of the Economic Section of the Cabinet Office, accurately perceived the significance of the Schuman Plan. He argued in the early official meetings on the Plan that 'if they could carry it through it would change the face of Europe'.[38] Unfortunately he was absent in Washington during the crucial days after 26 May.[39] Butt fought hard and gallantly against the dismissive attitude of the Foreign Office in favour of full membership or, in default of that, of the most substantive form of association negotiable.

Sir Oliver Franks, British Ambassador in Washington, had frequently, during his days as Chairman of the CEEC, expressed sorrow at Britain's

[35] Bevin's reputed response to Younger was: 'Splash about, young man, you'll learn to swim in time': Hunter 13.
[36] Younger 27. But Younger comments that 'Subsequently it took me a good ten years to become convinced that membership of the European Community is the only satisfactory solution for Britain so I am in no position to lecture anyone. Even with hindsight, I find it difficult to blame the Government of which I was a member for reaching the conclusion it did in 1950 . . . '
[37] *DBPO* 7.   [38] Hall, 17 May 1950.
[39] Ibid., 17 May and 25 May 1950.

indifference to its European role.[40] Danchev, his biographer, writes:
'Never to offer gratuitous advice was an article of faith with Oliver
Franks.'[41] Despite this reluctance to interfere from afar in other people's business, he did his best to make the Foreign Office understand
the French enthusiasm for a sovereign High Authority, and to find ways
whereby the UK could 'ally or associate ourselves with the Plan, though
of necessity not members of it'. He was assured by Sir Roger Makins
that this was precisely what the UK government was trying to do but,
in the upshot, the association that was achieved was far less effective
than Franks, probably, would have desired.[42] Later Franks wrote that 10
August 1952 was likely to be regarded by future historians as the most
important date in the post-war decade of Western Europe because 'It
was the day on which the Schuman Plan became a reality'.[43] Franks, in
Washington, was best placed to compare the reality of American power
with the unreality of British global pretensions. One can only speculate
whether, had he been on the spot instead of in Washington, he would
have realized that association was a mirage, that the real choice was
between membership and the sidelines, and would therefore have opted
for membership. Forty years later, he told Peter Hennessy that 'we
ought to have gone in'.[44] It was Franks who wrote: 'the decision [not
to join the Schuman Plan] cost us the leadership of Europe which we
had enjoyed from the end of the war until May 1950.[45]

Cripps's initial reaction at his meeting with Monnet on 15 May gave
hope that the UK would participate in the negotiations.[46] But his
follow-up was half-hearted and rapidly degenerated into an acceptance
of the arguments of the myopic and the discipline of collective responsibility. In one of his moments of lucidity about the Schuman Plan, in
early June, Cripps expressed the view that perhaps Britain had been

[40] While Franks was Chairman of the CEEC he was also Provost of The Queen's
College, Oxford, where I was a don. He expressed to me his criticism of Britain's
inability to see the opportunities it was losing through its refusal to lead Europe.

[41] Danchev 72.

[42] *DBPO* 140 and 142. In his Reith Lectures, Franks said: 'I am aware that I am
advocating a measure of federation. . . . I believe it to be in our long term interest to work
for further instalments of political union, limited perhaps but real, in western Europe.'
However, noting that the British people 'have not got that active sense of belonging to
western Europe' and that 'We are not prepared to let anyone but ourselves settle our
social policies, our policies about employment', Oliver Franks advocated 'neither joining
a political union nor rejecting it but taking out what I call a country membership',
something less than full membership: Franks 43, 46–7.

[43] Franks 37. See also ibid. 41.   [44] Danchev 74.

[45] Ibid. 75.   [46] See Ch. 7 above.

'mesmerized' by words.[47] One gets the impression that if Cripps had been Foreign Secretary, consideration of the Schuman Plan in London might have led to a happier outcome. In fact, he was too sick to fight the Foreign Office and five months later he had been forced to relinquish his responsibilities as Chancellor of the Exchequer and as Member of Parliament. The conclusive answer to an allegation that criticism of the Attlee government and of the Foreign Office is based on hindsight must be the columns of *The Economist*. *The Economist*'s analysis at the time of why Britain should take part, given in Chapter 12, could hardly be bettered even today.

ARGUMENTS IN MITIGATION

Contemporaries of these events insist that, for many reasons, it was impossible for the UK to participate in the Schuman negotiations. Presumably they would also reject the possibility of a British initiative of the kind outlined in Chapter 11. Neither the one nor the other would, apparently, have been possible for any government of either party. Plowden is of this view. He quotes Lord Home. He asked Lord Home in December 1985 whether 'he thought any government under any leader could have taken us into the ECSC in 1950'. Lord Home's answer was that 'the British public was still too near to the glory of Empire to accept the role for Britain of just another country in Europe. A British PM cannot make that sort of deal over the heads of the people.'[48] There is a simple answer to this special pleading. The Schuman Plan would not have made of the UK 'just another country in Europe'. It would still have been at the centre of the Commonwealth and Empire. It would have lost none of the characteristics which, in the view of successive British governments, made it special. If the French could do it, the British could do it. There was no British political problem comparable with the French political problem. If Frenchmen such as Robert Schuman could press for *rapprochement* with Germany based on equality of rights within the ECSC, and carry their countrymen with them, there was no reason why an equivalent political effort could not have succeeded in Britain. The obstacle was neither the Empire nor federalism nor even the supranational and undemocratic High Authority. The obstacle was lack of leadership, of imagination, of analytical and diplomatic skills.

[47] *DBPO* 93.   [48] Plowden 95.

Bullock argues by way of mitigation that Britain *had* provided leadership in Europe in 1947/9, that it was a key member of NATO, that it was taking part in other important forms of European co-operation such as the EPU, and that its failure to participate in the Schuman Plan would in no way have prejudiced its ability to join in the negotiations leading to the establishment of the EEC. It could still have been a signatory of the Treaty of Rome and therefore a founding member of the EEC providing only that the British government of the time had had sufficient foresight.[49]

Leadership is in the eye of the beholder. Britain had played a positive role after the war in ensuring European security. But so far as economic integration and reconciliation with Germany were concerned, the story is very different. Dragged along by the USA, repelled by Europe, the UK could only criticize the ideas of others not elaborate ideas of its own. France could usurp Britain's leadership role in Europe only because the UK was not perceived as playing that role. The Schuman Plan was a political initiative in economic guise. Bullock's plea in mitigation underestimates the political effects of Britain's refusal to join the Schuman Plan negotiations. It thereby deprived itself of the opportunity to shape the ECSC Treaty. It demonstrated to Western Europe what it had previously scarcely believed, that it could integrate, and achieve Franco-German reconciliation, without any assistance from the UK. It taught Europe that the UK was not interested in any form of European unity however designed. It entrenched a Franco-German leadership in Europe into which the UK, even after twenty years' membership of the European Community, has never been able to penetrate.

Britain lost the experience of European co-operation as manifested in the operations of the ECSC, in particular how little of substance there was in the High Authority's independence marked as it always was by the governments of nation states. If the UK had joined the ECSC at its inception, it would have joined the EEC at its inception and both would have been somewhat different as a result. When the UK did not join the ECSC it made it far less likely that it would be participant in the next stage of European economic integration. In 1950 it had spared itself the intellectual effort of actually reappraising Britain's position in the world. Without the stimulus of experience in the ECSC, it was unlikely to do much fresh thinking on Europe by 1955. The objections would be the same and therefore the outcome was likely to be the same.

[49] Bullock 786–90.

Bullock, in discussing this failure, illustrates the misunderstanding of the Schuman Plan which was so destructive of rational thought in London. He says: 'There were few people in Britain in 1950, whether Socialist or not, who really believed that Britain should hand over to a supranational authority control of the two industries on which her industrial power had been built.'[50] But there was no sense in which the High Authority had 'control' of the coal and steel industries of Europe that could, in practice, have been damaging to British interests. Bullock says it was different for the French and the Germans because the French wanted reconciliation with Germany, and influence over its conduct, and the Germans wanted recognition. No German government, or French government, would have been prepared for such reasons to give away anything that they regarded as essential to their economic well-being. Both wanted reconciliation but in ways consistent with their economic well-being.

Finally, Bullock considers Bevin's attitude to the Schuman Plan within a wider context. He discusses the criticism that 'for all his achievement, Bevin failed to recognize the permanence of the change in Britain's international position at the end of the War and, in a vain attempt to maintain a world role, set the country off on the wrong course.' He comments:

That this [the painful scaling down of the country's commitments—and pretensions] had to be done eventually is incontestable but the force of the argument, so far as Bevin is concerned, rests upon a concealed assumption. . . . That assumption is that the sooner this process could have been put in hand after the end of hostilities, the better, and that Bevin is to blame for not having acted accordingly.

Bullock concludes that this concealed assumption is ill-founded. He comes to this conclusion for a variety of reasons but mainly because it was right for the UK to play the fullest part it could in the post-war 'creation' whether that proved to be a peace settlement while hope of Soviet co-operation remained or, as it turned out, the establishment of NATO and of the Marshall Plan. 'Neither Bevin nor Attlee felt so much confidence in the goodwill or wisdom of the Russian and American governments as to be willing to leave them to make the post-war settlement by themselves.'[51]

Bullock's response is based on a misunderstanding of the charge. It

[50] Bullock 789.   [51] Ibid. 843–4.

was, of course, right for the UK to play the fullest part it could in the post-war settlement. That is not in dispute. Human foresight does not have a good reputation but it is stretching arguments in mitigation rather far to suggest that it would not have been better if Bevin had seen what others saw, that is, that there had been a permanent change in Britain's international status. Recognizing such a change would not have excluded Britain from a role in the post-war settlement. Both the USA and the Soviet Union perceived that such a permanent change in the UK's status had occurred, and took account of that fact in their policies and actions. It could not, therefore, have been harmful to Britain's influence on the post-war settlement if Bevin had understood the realities as well.

But none of this is relevant to the Schuman Plan. Participation in the Schuman Plan did not imply any downgrading of Britain's position in international affairs whatever that turned out to be. France continued to fight for its empire long after the establishment of the ECSC and, at the time of its establishment, had no intention of confining itself simply to a European role. The same would have been true of the UK. Participation in the Schuman Plan would have strengthened Britain's international role. It would not have implied any acceptance of its weakening or disappearance. Paradoxically, to believe that participation in the Schuman Plan would undermine Britain's international role demonstrated lack of confidence in the reality of Britain's claimed global status. Whether Britain was still a Great Power, or had descended to the ranks of the middling powers, it should have participated in the Schuman Plan.

It is also argued by way of mitigation that, at the time of the Schuman Plan, Bevin was an old, sick, and even dying, man. This was certainly true but helps to rescue neither his reputation nor that of the Attlee government. It was absurd that such a man, however exceptional his previous services, should have been allowed to continue in office as Foreign Secretary. There were younger and fitter men available capable of doing the job and, if there were not, it says little for the Labour government's claims to continue in office in 1950. A major responsibility falls on Attlee for his complacent acceptance that Britain could be governed by invalids.

But the British policy failure at the time of the Schuman Plan reflected accurately the Foreign Office's neglect of all constructive thought about European unity in the previous years when Bevin was not quite as sick as he had become by May 1950. It had failed to generate ideas for European unity of a kind, more consonant with UK interests, which rejected Monnet's and American federalism, but which could still serve the principal purposes of European economic integration and of a Franco-German reconciliation guaranteed by Britain. Bevin's advisers at the Foreign Office were not sick and yet did no better than their master. Nor is it enough to say that the Foreign Office was diverted from Europe by the UK's global pretensions which were so widely shared in the political Establishment. Even if the Foreign Office lacked sympathy with what was happening in continental Europe, it had a duty to understand what was happening, the movements of opinion, what initiatives might therefore emerge, and how Britain might act and react. The failure in 1950 and before was a failure of the Labour government and of its Foreign Secretary, but also of the Foreign Office in its most elementary duties.

Britain had no greater foreign friend at this time than René Massigli, the French Ambassador. He was prepared to extend to British policy a sympathy that it did not deserve. He was a bitter critic of Monnet, and of Schuman's apparent inability to control Monnet's misguided enthusiasms. Massigli's retrospective judgement is, therefore, worth quoting. 'In the Franco-British divorce our responsibilities were great, but those of the British were not less and this is a judgement that ... history should record.'[52] In this humane judgement, Massigli does British ministers and civil servants too much justice. By a large margin, the principal fault was in them.

Messina gave the UK another chance but that too was missed. By its neglect the UK made of itself a permanent outsider protesting at the visions of others, unable to gain support for its own vision of European unity even when it had discovered one. It has been left to history to demonstrate that for Europe the federal idea was either premature or inappropriate. But Britain was no longer a persuasive advocate of its own case.

[52] Massigli 234.

Published books and articles

Acheson, Dean, *Present at the Creation: My Years in the State Department* (W. W. Norton & Company: New York, 1969).

Adenauer, Konrad, *Memoirs, 1945–53*, trans. Beate Ruhm von Oppen (Weidenfeld & Nicolson: London, 1966).

Attlee, C. R., *As it Happened* (Odhams: London, undated).

Balfour, Corinna, *The Anglo-American Loan Negotiations—The US viewpoint*, Appendix C to John Fforde, *The Bank of England and Public Policy, 1941–58* (Cambridge University Press: Cambridge, 1992).

Blackhurst, Richard, Marian, Nicolas, and Tumlir, Jan, *Trade Liberalization, Protectionism and Interdependence*, GATT Studies in International Trade (GATT: Geneva, 1977).

Boothby, Robert, *Recollections of a Rebel* (Hutchinson: London, 1978).

Brittan, Samuel, *Steering the Economy: The Role of the Treasury* (Penguin Books: London, 1970).

Brivati, Brian, and Jones, Harriet (eds.), *From Reconstruction to Integration: Britain and Europe since 1945* (Leicester University Press: Leicester, 1993).

Brown, George, *In My Way* (Gollancz: London, 1971).

Bullen, R. J., 'An Idea Enters Diplomacy: The Schuman Plan, May 1950', in R. J. Bullen, H. Pogge von Strandmann, and A. B. Polonsky (eds.), *Ideas into Politics: Aspects of European History 1880–1950* (London: Croom Helm; Totowa, NJ: Barnes & Noble Books, 1984).

Bullock, Alan, *Ernest Bevin, Foreign Secretary 1945–51* (Oxford University Press: Oxford, 1983).

Cairncross, Alec, *Years of Recovery: British Economic Policy 1945–51* (Methuen: London, 1985).

—— *The British Economy since 1945: Economic Policy and Performance, 1945–1990* (Blackwell for the Institute of Contemporary British History: Oxford and London, 1992).

Callaghan, James, *Time and Chance* (Collins: London, 1987).

Clarke, Sir Richard, *Anglo-American Economic Collaboration in War and Peace, 1942–49* ed. Alec Cairncross (Clarendon Press: Oxford, 1982).

Cooke, Colin, *The Life of Richard Stafford Cripps* (Hodder and Stoughton: London, 1957).

Crossman, R. H. S. (ed.), *New Fabian Essays* (Turnstile Press: London, 1952).

Dalton, Hugh, *High Tide and After: Memoirs 1945–1960* (Frederick Muller Ltd.: London, 1962).

—— *The Political Diaries of Hugh Dalton, 1918–40; 1945–60*, ed. Ben Pimlott (Jonathan Cape: London, 1986).

Danchev, Alex, *Oliver Franks, Founding Father* (Clarendon Press: Oxford, 1993).

Dell, Edmund, *The Politics of Economic Interdependence* (Macmillan: London, 1987).

Bibliography and References

Manuscripts and Official Papers

Anglo-French Discussions regarding French proposals for the West
pean Coal, Iron and Steel Industries, May–June 1950 (Cmd. 797
C. R. Attlee Papers owned by the Master and Fellows of University
Oxford (Bodleian Library, Oxford).
Bullen, Roger, and Pelly, M. E. (eds.), *Documents on British Policy*
series ii, vol. i, *The Schuman Plan, the Council of Europe and*
European Integration 1950–1952 (HMSO: London, 1986) (cited a:
Hugh Dalton Papers and Diary (British Library of Political and I
Science, London).
Ernest Davies Papers (British Library of Political and Economic
London).
House of Commons Debates
PRO CAB 124/1140
PRO FO 371/87136
PRO FO 371/87141
PRO FO 371/87161
PRO FO 371/87165
PRO T 229/291
PRO T 229/749–51
PRO T 230/180–2
PRO T 232/183–6
PRO T 232/194
Kenneth Younger Diaries (unpublished)

Main Newspapers and Journals quoted

Daily Express
The Economist
Financial Times
Manchester Guardian
The Times

Diebold, William, Jr., *The Schuman Plan: A Study in Economic Cooperation, 1950–1959* (Published for the Council on Foreign Relations by Frederick A. Praeger: New York, 1959).

Dobson, Alan P., *The Politics of the Anglo-American Economic Special Relationship* (Wheatsheaf Books Ltd.: Brighton, 1988).

Donoughue, Bernard, and Jones, G. W., *Herbert Morrison: Portrait of a Politician* (Weidenfeld & Nicolson: London, 1973).

Dow, J. C. R., *The Management of the British Economy, 1945–60* (Cambridge University Press: Cambridge, 1964).

Eden, Anthony, *Full Circle: The Memoirs of Sir Anthony Eden, KG, PC, MC* (Cassell: London, 1960).

Elgey, Georgette, *La République des illusions* (Fayard: Paris, 1965).

Ezra, Derek, *Coal and Energy* (Ernest Benn: London, 1978).

Fieldhouse, D. K., 'The Labour Governments and the Empire-Commonwealth 1945–51', in Ritchie Ovendale (ed.), *The Foreign Policy of the British Labour Governments 1945–51* (Leicester University Press: Leicester, 1984).

Franks, O. S., *Britain and the Tide of World Affairs*, The BBC Reith Lectures 1954 (Oxford University Press: London, 1955).

Gaitskell, Hugh, *The Diary of Hugh Gaitskell, 1945–1956*, ed. Philip Williams (Jonathan Cape: London, 1983).

Gardner, R. N., *Sterling–Dollar Diplomacy* (Oxford University Press: Oxford, 1956).

George, Stephen, *An Awkward Partner: Britain in the European Community* (Oxford University Press: Oxford, 1990).

Gillingham, John, *Coal, Steel and the Rebirth of Europe, 1945–1955: The Germans and French from Ruhr Conflict to Economic Community* (Cambridge University Press: Cambridge, 1991).

Gilpin, Robert, *The Political Economy of International Relations* (Princeton University Press: Princeton, NJ, 1987).

Greenwood, Sean, *Britain and European Cooperation since 1945* (Blackwell: Oxford, 1992).

Haas, Ernst B., *The Uniting of Europe: Political, Social and Economical Forces 1950–1957* (Published under the auspices of The London Institute of World Affairs, Stevens & Sons: London, 1958).

Lord Hailsham of St Marylebone, *A Sparrow's Flight: Memoirs* (Collins: London, 1990).

Hall, Robert, *The Robert Hall Diaries, 1947–53*, ed. Alec Cairncross (Unwin Hyman: London, 1991).

Hanley, D. L., Kerr, A. P., and Waites, N. H. (eds.), *Contemporary France: Politics and Society since 1945* (Routledge & Kegan Paul: London, 1979).

Harrod, Roy, *The Life of John Maynard Keynes* (Macmillan: London, 1951).

Healey, Denis, *Western Europe—The Challenge of Unity* (Canadian Institute of International Affairs: Toronto, 1950).

—— *The Time of My Life* (Michael Joseph: London, 1989).

Healey, Denis, *When Shrimps Learn to Whistle* (Michael Joseph: London, 1990).

Hennessy, Peter, *Never Again: Britain 1945–1951* (Jonathan Cape: London, 1992).

Hogan, Michael J., *The Marshall Plan: America, Britain, and the Reconstruction of Western Europe, 1947–1952* (Cambridge University Press: Cambridge, 1987).

Horne, Alistair, *Macmillan*, vol. i (Macmillan: London, 1990).

Hunter, Leslie, *The Road to Brighton Pier* (Arthur Barker Ltd.: London, 1959).

Jay, Douglas, *Change and Fortune: A Political Record* (Hutchinson: London, 1980).

Kennan, George F., *Memoirs 1925–1950* (Hutchinson: London, 1968).

—— *Around the Cragged Hill* (W. W. Norton & Company: New York, 1993).

Leffler, Melvyn P., *A Preponderance of Power: National Security, The Truman Administration and the Cold War* (Stanford University Press: Stanford, Ca., 1992).

Ludlow, Peter, *The Making of the European Monetary System: A Case Study of the Politics of the European Community* (Butterworth Scientific: London, 1982).

Macmillan, Harold, *Tides of Fortune, 1945–55* (Macmillan: London, 1969).

Marjolin, Robert, *Europe in Search of Its Identity*, The Russell C. Leffingwell Lectures, Sept. 1980 (Council on Foreign Relations: New York, 1981).

—— *Architect of European Unity: Memoirs 1911–1986* (Weidenfeld & Nicolson: London, 1989).

Massigli, René, *Une comédie des erreurs, 1943–1956: Souvenirs et réflexions sur une étape de la construction européenne* (Plon: Paris, 1978).

Mayne, Richard, 'Jean Monnet, Europe and the British: A Witness Account', in Brian Brivati and Harriet Jones (eds.), *From Reconstruction to Integration: Britain and Europe since 1945* (Leicester University Press: Leicester, 1993).

Milward, Alan S., *The Reconstruction of Western Europe, 1945–51* (Methuen & Co. Ltd.: London, 1984).

—— *The European Rescue of the Nation-State* (Routledge: London, 1992).

—— Lynch, Frances M. B., Ranieri, Ruggero, Romero, Federico, and Sorensen, Vibeke, *The Frontier of National Sovereignty: History and Theory 1945–1992* (Routledge: London, 1993). Cited as Milward *et al.*

Monnet, Jean, *Memoirs*, trans. Richard Mayne (Collins: London, 1978).

Morgan, Kenneth O., *Labour in Power 1945–1951* (Clarendon Press: Oxford, 1984).

—— *The People's Peace: British History 1945–1989* (Oxford University Press: Oxford, 1990).

Newton, Scott, 'Britain, the Sterling Area and European Integration, 1945–50', *Journal of Imperial and Commonwealth History*, 13/3 (May 1985).

—— 'The 1949 Sterling Crisis and British Policy towards European Integration', *Review of International Studies*, 11/3 (July 1985).

Ovendale, Ritchie (ed.), *The Foreign Policy of the British Labour Governments 1945–51* (Leicester University Press: Leicester, 1984).

Pimlott, Ben, *Hugh Dalton* (Jonathan Cape: London, 1985).

Pliatzky, Sir Leo, *Getting and Spending: Public Expenditure, Employment and Inflation* (Basil Blackwell: Oxford, 1982).

Plowden, Edwin, *An Industrialist in the Treasury: The Postwar Years* (André Deutsch: London, 1989).

Poidevin, Raymond, *Robert Schuman, homme d'État 1886–1963* (Imprimerie Nationale: Paris, 1986).

—— *Robert Schuman*, introd. Raymond Barre (Beauchesne: Paris, 1988).

—— (ed.), *Origins of the European Integration, March 1948 to May 1950* (Établissement Émile Bruylant: Brussels, 1986).

Ranieri, Ruggero, 'Inside or Outside the Magic Circle? The Italian and British Steel Industries face to face with the Schuman Plan and the European Coal Iron and Steel Community', in Milward *et al.*, *The Frontier of National Sovereignty: History and Theory 1945–1992* (Routledge: London, 1993).

Roberts, Sir Frank K., 'Ernest Bevin as Foreign Secretary', in Ritchie Ovendale (ed.), *The Foreign Policy of the British Labour Governments 1945–51* (Leicester University Press: Leicester, 1984).

Sahm, Ulrich, 'Britain and Europe, 1950', with a comment from Kenneth Younger, *International Affairs*, 43/1 (Jan. 1967).

Schuman, Robert, *French Policy towards Germany since the War*, Fourth Stevenson Memorial Lecture, delivered 29 Oct. 1953 at the Royal Institute of International Affairs (Oxford University Press: London, 1953).

Spierenburg, Dirk, and Poidevin, Raymond, *The History of the High Authority of the European Coal and Steel Community: Supranationality in Operation* (Weidenfeld and Nicolson: London, 1994).

Stirk, Peter M. R., and Willis, David (eds.), *Shaping Postwar Europe: European Unity and Disunity 1945–57* (Pinter Publishers: London, 1991).

Stikker, Dirk U., *Men of Responsibility: A Memoir* (Harper & Row: New York, 1966).

Thomas, Hugh, *John Strachey* (Methuen: London, 1973).

Warner, Geoffrey, 'The Labour Governments and the Unity of Western Eruope 1945–51', in Ritchie Ovendale (ed.), *The Foreign Policy of the British Labour Governments 1945–51* (Leicester University Press: Leicester, 1984).

Williams, Philip, *Hugh Gaitskell* (Jonathan Cape: London, 1979).

Young, John W., *Britain, France and the Unity of Europe 1945–1951* (Leicester University Press: Leicester, 1984).

—— *Cold War Europe 1945–89: A Political History* (Edward Arnold: London, 1991).

Index

316 *Index*

Financial Times 61, Chapter 12 *passim*
Finebel 30, 33, 43, 78, 103 n.
Foreign Office (Diplomatic Service) viii,
1, 6, 10, 11, 13, 19, 31, 33, 38, 69,
106, 109, 111–12, 132, 133, 136,
Chapter 8 *passim*, 193, 201–2, 212,
215–16, 224, 229, 234–6, 238,
241–2, 245, 247, 249, 251, 253,
259, 263, 266, 284–5, 287, 292,
296–9, 302–3
moles 232
uncertain about association 273,
275–8
whether Ministers are prepared in
principle to abrogate certain
sovereign rights 139, 145–6, 154
France 2, 67, 68 n., 272
association idea counter-productive
281
expansion of steel output 42
favoured partner of USA 12, 51
more polite than it feels about the
UK 140
policy on Germany 2, 7–8, 24, 49,
152
Franco-Italian Customs Union 11, 30,
30 n., 85, 87, 148, 148 n.
François-Poncet, André, French High
Commissioner in Germany 24
Franks, Sir Oliver, later Lord Franks,
Chairman of the CEEC, later UK
Ambassador to Washington vii, 35,
64–5, 82, 82 n., 84, 107 n., 297–8,
298 n.
European Unity 207–8
on 10 August 1952 298
freedom of trade 60
and stability 60–1
French Foreign Ministry, *see* Quai d'Orsay
Fritalux, *see* Finebel
full employment 54, 61, 77–8, 120–1,
147, 190–1, 195, 198, 201–2, 213,
254
functionalism 99–103, 236

Gaitskell, Hugh, Minister for Economic
Affairs, later Chancellor of the
Exchequer 57, 61, 73 n., 73–5,
76–7, 128 n., 132, 200, 279, 279 n.
contrasts British economic policy with
deflationary policies of continental
countries 77–8
on Younger 154

Gallup 235 n.
GEN 322, Cabinet Committee 119–20,
125, 127
General Agreement on Tariffs and Trade
(GATT) 257, 260, 266, 276
German competition 85–6, 88
Germany 2
divided 1–2
economic and military prowess 67
Germany, Federal Republic of 9, 149,
152, 198, 210, 254, 272, 281 n., 282
to be committed indefinitely 20
economic recovery 35
expectation of release from controls
17, 285–6
German armaments industry 239
rearmament 18, 28, 49, 197, 211, 284,
286 n.
the Schuman Plan balance 285–6
Gillingham, John, historian 4 n., 50 n.,
92 n., 103–4, 281 n., 288 n.
Gordon Walker, Patrick, Secretary of
State for Commonwealth Affairs
132
Guedalla, Philip, historian 246

Haas, Ernst B., on High Authority
182–3
Hailsham, Lord, *see* Hogg, Quintin
Hall, Robert, later Lord Roberthall,
Director of the Economic Section of
the Cabinet Office 31, 33, 77, 84,
85, 281 n., 297
on dogs in mangers 118–19
on full employment 54
on mystical distinctions 75
'Note on Integration' 57–60, 97–8
supports Butt 273–4
UK not poorer if Europe richer 268–9
wishes British Ministers would refuse
aid 48
Hall-Patch, Sir Edmund, UK
Ambassador to the OEEC 26, 33,
39, 40, 61, 73, 82–4, 93, 96, 174 n.,
216, 224, 259, 264
Harriman, Averell, the ECA's special
representative in Europe 23, 51 n.,
61, 76
Harvey, Sir Oliver, later Lord Harvey,
UK Ambassador to the French
Republic 11 n., 19, 33, 87, 113 n.,
138, 138 n., 160, 163, 203, 215,
229 n., 288 n., 293, 293 n.

Kennan, George (*cont.*):
understanding of French anxieties
about Germany 9
Keynes, John Maynard, Lord Keynes,
economist 47, 52, 54
Keynesian, Keynesianism 78, 191
kinsmen 199
Kissinger, Dr Henry, US Secretary of
State 91
Knowland, William, US Senator 206
Korean War 18, 35 n., 76, 183 n., 201,
208, 253, 264, 266, 266 n.

Labour government, *see* Attlee
government
Labour Party 76, 108, 112, 115 n., 149,
Chapter 10 *passim*, 230
European socialism 209
on international control of basic
industries 195
Laudale, R. T., civil servant 284 n.
Law 27 and Law 75 39, 39 n., 50 n.,
114, 284 n.
Lawther, Sir William, President of the
NUM 169
League of Nations 246
Le Figaro 73
Le Monde 136, 141
Lend-Lease 46–7, 51, 51 n., 67
Le Populaire 135
Lewis, Professor W. Arthur, economist
191
Levy, Benn, former Member of
Parliament (Labour) 115 n.
Liberal Liberty League 234 n.
liberalization 43, 61, 125–6, 200,
254–5, 260
as British alternative to European
integration 72–5, 88, 125–6
Lloyds Bank Review 271
Loan, American, see Anglo-American
Financial Agreement
Lorraine 41
Ludlow, Peter 109 n.
Luxembourg 120, 123 n., 149, 284

Maastricht, Treaty of 90 n.
McCloy, John, American High
Commissioner in Germany 41
McGowan, Lord, Chairman of ICI 86 n.
Mackay, R. W. G. ('Kim'), Member of
Parliament (Labour) 34, 102, 262–3
MacMahon, G. J., civil servant 257 n.

Macmillan, Harold, later Earl of
Stockton, Member of Parliament
(Conservative) 41, 64, 79, 132, 136,
232
on Foreign Office myopia 232, 232 n.
on French ingratitude 28
functionalist 100
ideas for the European coal and steel
industry 174, 176, 229 n., 230–1,
231 n.
on Schuman 65 n.
Maginot line 7
Makins, Sir Roger, later Lord Sherfield,
civil servant 61, 61 n., 68, 107,
149 n., 247 n., 259
alternative British ideas not to be
advanced 222 n., 223
awaits ratification by National
Assembly 265
briefs Younger on Schuman Plan 153
defining the difference 165–6
discussions with Monnet 127, 129–30,
171, 177, 177 n.
on lack of prior consultation, 111–12
Note to Bevin 19 May 1950 133–4
Notes for Schuman Plan debate 46,
63, 90, 215, 284–5
only the French 215, 228
revisits federalism 266
unreality and the common
market 133 n.
Malaya 80
Mallalieu, E. L., Member of Parliament
(Labour) 273
Mallet, I., civil servant 209
Mallet, Sir Victor, UK Ambassador to
Italy 11 n.
Manchester Guardian 17, 25, 41, 99, 136,
140, 156, 178, Chapter 12 *passim*
European Unity 192
Marjolin, Robert, Secretary General of
the OEEC, French and European
public servant, economist, Member
of the 'Committee of Three Wise
Men' vii, 8, 32, 61, 76, 227 n., 229
on Britain's post-war prestige vii, 89
despair in France 261
European Customs Union 87
on European federalism 103–5,
104 n., 261–2
fears American recession 43
on High Authority 182
Monnet's federalism 262